JOSH MUGLIA

Idolatry

Journey out of Egypt

First edition

ISBN: 978-0-578-62681-9

Editing by Janet Muglia
Cover art by Celeo Ramos

This book was professionally typeset on Reedsy.
Find out more at reedsy.com

Contents

IV   The End of the Matter

Preface

Hello dear reader, welcome to my book, I pray it finds you well. This book was written by one who is in Christ, to those who are also in Christ. Anyone is, of course, welcome to read this book, but I think that unless you have a very real and personal relationship with Christ, you will not get as much out of this book. The purpose of this book is the edification of His precious saints. The definition for edification is, "the instruction or improvement of a person morally or intellectually". This is exactly what I aim to accomplish with writing this book. Many of the things we will discuss throughout this book are both morally thought provoking, but also intellectually stimulating. My approach to this information reflects this combination of morality and reason, and I aim to utilize both scripture and basic logic as we move through this book.

Now, all of that being said, understand, dear reader, that this will not be an easy book to read. This book is full of very difficult subject material. I have no doubt that many will give up on this book only a fraction of the way through. I fully expect much of what I say will be rejected by many, and I fully expect to step on some toes. Such is the nature of exploring Scripture. All I can ask of you, is that if you begin to read this book, that you continue to do so until the end. I will reference this scripture multiple times throughout this book as a reminder:

> *Proverbs 18:13 He who answers a matter before he hears it, it is folly and shame to him.*

You see, we are tragically indisposed in this common day to just close off our ears the moment we hear something we dislike or disagree with. If you're watching something on TV, you just flip the channel if it's not to your liking. If we hear someone saying something that we disagree with, we often just walk away. If we hear a preacher say even one thing we disagree with, we often times will disregard everything else they have to say. These are natural responses of course, but they aren't always the wisest of responses. Proverbs admonishes us to hear a matter fully out before we make a decision upon it. You have the option of putting this book down and walking away, but if you do decide to read it, and I pray that you do, read it all the way to the end before making up your mind on the matter. When approaching any matter of faith, we need to be humble enough to listen and consider, patient and wise enough to hear the whole matter out, and then slow to make a decision, as we need to digest the information and make an informed decision for ourselves.

Now, this is a long book, and a big undertaking. Why would one want to read this book? Well, dear reader, I believe the information contained therein to be not only of the utmost importance, but also very timely considering the things going on in the world today, and the amount of time left before the return of our Master. This book, if you take the time to hear it out and study out the information for yourself, will make a tremendous impact on your walk, and on your life. This book explores many of the things I've learned in the past few years, and I have found them to be both challenging, but also extremely rewarding in bringing me closer to my God. It has been a time of tremendous pruning, but also growth, and I aim to bring growth to your life as well. At the end of the day, we all are trying to walk out our faith, and find ourselves in Him, especially as we prepare to meet Him. I pray that this book helps you on your journey and strengthens and helps you reach this goal.

Acknowledgement

There are so many that I would like to thank that to list them off, it would take quite a while. Frankly, this writing process has shown me how weak, inefficient, and lacking I am in so very many areas. I could not have hoped to complete this work through my own power. Without the help of many people, this book would not have been completed. I wish I could thank you all who have helped me in my journey and on my walk by name, but I must sadly only pick a few of the biggest influences who helped me in finishing this book.

First and foremost I would like to praise and lift up on high my God and His Son, who have strengthened me and encouraged me countless times and in countless ways. Without Him, I am nothing, and can do nothing. I am so very thankful that He has chosen the weak and foolish of this world to show forth His glory, because otherwise I would have no chance to accomplish anything. Where I was weak He made me strong, where I was lacking He supplied, where I was blind He gave me sight. He has blessed me so abundantly and in so many ways I cannot begin to list them all. Eternity is a fitting time frame to have for praising Him, as to list all the ways that He is good will take all of eternity. Halleluyah!

Next I would like to thank my wonderful wife, who has been such a support and such a massive help throughout this process. My wife has tirelessly encouraged me, pushed me, helped me, and even did the editing for this book. Twice. I had previously written a whole other book, that she tirelessly edited. When it was getting close to the time to publish it, I decided I had to scrap it entirely and start from scratch. My wife did not hassle me, or give me a hard time for having wasted hours and hours of her time, she instead encouraged me to write anew, and complete the work that was put into my hand to do. Janet, I cannot thank you enough, and I love you. Thank you for the unconditional love and support you show me everyday. I am so thankful and so blessed to have you in my life. I could not have asked for a better wife and friend.

Next I would like to thank my mom, who has been a constant companion, and another source of unconditional love, support, and help. Thank you for all the interesting articles, all the long phone calls and random visits. Thank you for talking things out with me, and helping me to learn and grow. Thank you for always being there for me at the drop of a hat, and always being willing to help me in any way you can. I am so proud to call you my mother, and I could not have asked for a better one. Many people think they have the best mom, but they're wrong, because I have the best mom. No contest.

Next I would like to thank two of my brothers in particular. Justin, I cannot thank you enough for everything you've done for me. You've encouraged me, talked with me, helped to instruct me, admonished and corrected me, and have been there for me consistently. I have learned so much from you and am so thankful to know you. Adam, I have also learned so much from you, and am so thankful for the instruction, and teaching.

Celeo, thank you for the awesome cover art and for being so patient with me with the alterations and changes made in design. You were a massive help, and I couldn't have finished this project without you.

To my daughter Lexi, who is still far too young to read this, thank you for making this writing process so interesting and providing entertaining diversions throughout. I love you more than you can ever understand, and I cannot imagine my life without you. You are so very precious to me, and I thank God for you daily.

Lastly a big thank you to those of you who provided financial support in the publishing of this book, you know who you are, and I am extremely thankful. Thank you for helping to make this book a reality.

To all the rest, friends, family, neighbors, brothers and sisters in Christ, and all the rest who have been a part of my life I thank you for the love, lessons, help, and all the other countless ways you have touched my life. May God bless all of you in countless ways.

I

A Firm Foundation

1

What is Idolatry?

The place we need to begin with this entire study is to understand first and foremost what Idolatry is. The short and sweet of it is this; Idolatry is worshiping or serving anything other than the One True God. This is a basic definition though, and we need to know not only what it is, but what it looks like. Idolatry, like so many other things, has taken on different forms and different names throughout the centuries. Idolatry is just about as old as mankind, and we find traces of it all throughout the scriptures. A few hundred years after Adam and Eve's creation, before the great flood, we find people turning to idolatry and falling into evil. After all of mankind outside of Noah and his family were destroyed, we see idolatry once again rear it's ugly head, and it has perpetuated since. Abraham, Isaac, Jacob, and the children of Israel (Jacob) all served the One True God, while the nations and people around them served other false gods. Even Israel often fell to serving these other gods.

Idolatry goes back even before Adam however. Idolatry was actually birthed in the heavens themselves. Satan was the first idolater, and the god he decided to worship instead of the One True God, was himself. We find this account of Satan in Isaiah.

> *Isaiah 14:12-14 How you are fallen from heaven,*
> *O Lucifer, son of the morning!*

How you are cut down to the ground,
You who weakened the nations!
13 For you have said in your heart:
'I will ascend into heaven,
I will exalt my throne above the stars of God;
I will also sit on the mount of the congregation
On the farthest sides of the north;
14 I will ascend above the heights of the clouds,
I will be like the Most High.'

So Satan decided he would attempt to be like God, and to exalt himself as high as God. He felt he should be equal with God, and worshiped like God. Satan replaced God with a new god, namely himself. Not only that, but he even convinced a third of the angels to join him according to Revelation 12:4. These angels also committed idolatry with him, choosing to serve someone other than the One True God. The result was that they were cast out of heaven, and thrown down, living out the rest of their time until judgement ultimately falls upon them. Interestingly, Satan has not stopped his goal of finding people to worship and serve him. He still pursues his same goal of promoting himself above The Most High, and being praised and worshiped as such. This is essentially the heart of idolatry.

Now, as I said, not all idolatry has to do with actual graven image idols in particular. The popular TV show "American Idol" demonstrates that quite well. An idol is anything that is worshiped and glorified, and takes priority over The Most High. This can be celebrities, this can be sports, this can even be family or children or oneself. Humanism is a whole ideology that can be summed up as self idolatry. The idea of idolatry can manifest in many ways, but the focus of this book, is on what I call true idolatry, which is the worship of other gods. We are going to look at this more in the next chapter, but the idea is that of intentionally worshiping and honoring other false gods instead of the One True God. This sin may seem as if it is far from you, dear reader, and doesn't apply to you, but as you will find out throughout the course of this book, idolatry lurks and hides in places and ways we do not expect it, and though it is not usually intentional in the realm of Christianity, it is still idolatry, and as we will see very shortly, God has some strong words to say regarding this subject.

So how does Idolatry manifest itself? Well, in a myriad of ways really. Mankind sought to honor these false gods they were turning to, and they, whether through the evil imaginations of their own hearts, or from instruction from Satan and his princes of darkness, came up with many ways to worship and serve their gods. We will examine some of these closely later on, and unfortunately due to the nature of these false gods, things will get a bit graphic and at times shocking. This information isn't brought forth for the sake of being graphic or shocking, but so you can fully grasp and understand what idolatry is, and why it is such a serious matter.

Nearly every culture from around the world has forms of idolatry it holds. This is often renamed as "culture" but when you look at things as they truly are and not just as they are presented, you will see them for what they are. The term "legends" or "myths" also often encompasses idolatry. We will look more closely at this later on, but there is an ever increasing amount of entertainment that is derived from "mythology" which is another way to say the stories of false gods. Idolatry also manifests itself in cultural customs and traditions. Many traditions in many cultures around the world are derived straight from idolatry that was practiced long ago, and the practices were handed down through generations until often times, people lose the understanding of the traditions they hold but continue to ignorantly participate in pagan rites and rituals without knowing it.

Recently I was blessed enough to be taken on a vacation to Hawaii to the island of Maui. One of the prominent "cultural experiences" that people often do while on the island is go to a luau. At these events there are people dressed in headdresses and specific ceremonial garb that do traditional tribal dances and chants, and put on a big show. To the patrons watching, and the majority of the performers, these things are just fun traditions handed down through the culture and performed as a way to commemorate a culture, and as a form of entertainment. The truth however, is that these practices originated as forms of worship and rituals performed by their ancestors as ways to honor their false gods. In nearly all of the chants, if you pay close attention, you can hear the names of pagan gods being spoken, such as Pele, Maui (which the island is named after) and Ku. These things may seem rather innocent as a stage show, after all, few really take it serious. I wonder if it would be taken serious however if it was done around a fire complete with an idol in the midst and sacrifices going on.

Again, this may not seem to affect you very much, but as this book unfolds, you will have more and more exposed to you as idolatry, and the question we will ask ourselves throughout this book is this: Should we, as followers of Christ, be participating in these practices? To answer that question, we must look at what the scripture says, and see what God's perspective on the matter is.

2

Divine Perspective

So, after our introduction on idolatry, and an understanding on the nature of the idolatry we will be exploring throughout this book, we need to see what God's perspective is on this subject. Idolatry was something that God actually dealt with extensively in the Old Testament. God chose His people, Israel, to bear His name, and to follow His ways. The nations around however, bore the names and ways of their gods, and practiced some rather abominable things. Human sacrifices, temple prostitutes and grand idols of gold and precious metals were commonplace in the other nations. These were known as the gentiles, and the word gentile itself, actually just means "other nations" denoting nations other than Israel. These gentiles fought against Israel in the name of their own gods, and tried to conquer vast areas of land. When Israel was serving God, and walking in His ways, these other nations had no chance of standing against them and their God. The false gods of the gentiles and their servants sought to overthrow Israel and their God, but their strength was nothing compared to the strength of our God.

Satan, as he often does, instead of fighting against the people of God with force, decided to do so in a more covert and quiet way. If he couldn't beat God's people with force, he would infiltrate them, and weaken them from the inside out. Sadly, this strategy paid off in spades. If you read through the Old Testament, there are hundreds of times that Israel is reprimanded for turning away from God and turning to idolatry. It was so prevalent in fact, that God taught a song to Moses to teach to Israel regarding the cycle he knew they would fall into.

> ***Deuteronomy 31:19-22 Now therefore, write down this song for yourselves, and teach it to the children of Israel; put it in their mouths, that this song may be a witness for Me against the children of Israel. 20 When I have brought them to the land flowing with milk and honey, of which I swore to their fathers, and they have eaten and filled themselves and grown fat, then they will turn to other gods and serve them; and they will provoke Me and break My covenant. 21 Then it shall be, when many evils and troubles have come upon them, that this song will testify against them as a witness; for it will not be forgotten in the mouths of their descendants, for I know the inclination of their behavior today, even before I have brought them to the land of which I swore to give them. 22 Therefore Moses wrote this song the same day, and taught it to the children of Israel.***

God knew before they even did that they would turn against Him, and turn to other gods. He also declared to them that when they turned away from His covenant and to other gods, that they would have many troubles and evils fall on them. God would send judgment upon His people in order to turn them back to Him. If you read the book of Judges in particular, you see this cycle repeat itself over and over again. This cycle continued until ultimately Israel was shattered, and both the House of Israel, and the House of Judah were taken away captive by neighboring nations. So, why did God deal so harshly with idolatry? Well for many reasons, but I want to bring out two in particular.

First and foremost, we need to understand that when God brought Israel out of captivity in Egypt, led by Moses, He entered into a covenant with them. This covenant was actually a marriage. God essentially told them, that He would be their God, and take care of them, and provide for them, and watch over them. Israel's side of the vows were that they would keep His commandments, and His law, and proclaim His name and show forth His glory in the earth. We know this was a marriage because we see that later on, God actually issued the House of Israel (after Israel and Judah separated) a certificate of divorce.

> *Jeremiah 3:8 Then I saw that for all the causes for which backsliding Israel had committed adultery, I had put her away and given her a certificate of divorce; yet her treacherous sister Judah did not fear, but went and played the harlot also.*

> *Isaiah 50:1 Thus says the Lord: "Where is the certificate of your mother's divorce, whom I have put away? Or which of My creditors is it to whom I have sold you? For your iniquities you have sold yourselves, and for your transgressions your mother has been put away."*

In the second verse, God is talking to the Children of Israel, calling Israel their mother. God actually divorced the children of Israel for their idolatry, and He was right to do so. In the law that He gave, He declared, and Jesus echoed, a man could put away his wife for adultery.

> *Deuteronomy 24:1 When a man takes a wife and marries her, and it happens that she finds no favor in his eyes because he has found some uncleanness in her, and he writes her a certificate of divorce, puts it in her hand, and sends her out of his house*

> *Matthew 19:8-9 He said to them, "Moses, because of the hardness of your hearts, permitted you to divorce your wives, but from the beginning it was not so. 9 And I say to you, whoever divorces his wife, except for sexual immorality, and marries another, commits adultery; and whoever marries her who is divorced commits adultery."*

So God had absolutely lawful grounds to divorce His wife in the house of Israel because she continually committed adultery against Him. How did she do this? Idolatry. If Israel was married to God, and then went after other gods, they were essentially breaking their vows of following His commandments and serving Him alone, and entered into relationships with other gods. God saw this as being spiritual adultery, and a myriad of verses echo this fact. Here are a few:

> *Deuteronomy 31:16 And the Lord said to Moses: "Behold, you will rest with your fathers; and this people will rise and play the harlot with the gods of the foreigners of the land, where they go to be among them, and they will forsake Me and break My covenant which I have made with them."*

> *Ezekiel 23:7 Thus she committed her harlotry with them, all of them choice men of Assyria; and with all for whom she lusted, with all their idols, she defiled herself.*

> *Ezekiel 23:30 "I will do these things to you because you have gone as a harlot after the Gentiles, because you have become defiled by their idols."*

Now, if we take this exact scenario and apply it to the world today, this would be the scenario: A man married a woman, and brought her to his home. He provided for her, and loved her, and gave her wealth, and comfort, and safety. In spite of this, the woman decided to go out and cheat on her husband with the neighbors. Not just with one neighbor either, but every man in the neighborhood she could find, she went and slept with. This is what Israel did to God. They continually fell into idolatry, and took on whatever gods the neighboring nations were worshiping at the time. They would adopt the gods, idols, practices, and worship of these pagan gods, and turn away from the One True God entirely. Now a wife committing adultery even once often times destroys a marriage and many marriages end after just one instance of it happening. This particular marriage however, had a husband so merciful and loving, that He forgave her over, and over, and warned her over, and over, until finally, He couldn't take it anymore because she just would not stop whoring herself out to other gods.

So God took idolatry serious enough that He was willing to divorce the people that He entered into a marriage covenant with, because of her idolatry. Now, God actually gave Israel laws on how to deal with idolatry, and if they would've followed the laws He put forth, they would not have fallen to it. He commanded them multiple times not to have any other gods such as in these verses:

> *Exodus 20:2-6 "I am the Lord your God, who brought you out of the land of Egypt, out of the house of bondage. 3 You shall have no other gods before Me. 4 You shall not make for yourself a carved image—any likeness of anything that is in heaven above, or that is in the earth beneath, or that is in the water under the earth; 5 you shall not bow down to them nor serve them. For I, the Lord your God, am a jealous God, visiting the iniquity of the fathers upon the children to the third and fourth generations of those who hate Me, 6 but showing mercy to thousands, to those who love Me and keep My commandments."*

> *Exodus 23:13 "And in all that I have said to you, be circumspect and make no mention of the name of other gods, nor let it be heard from your mouth."*

God commanded them multiple times not to have any other gods. This was the first commandment they broke when they began to turn to idolatry. However, there was even another safe guard in place, because those who were faithful to God had a responsibility to keep other laws as well. The children of Israel were supposed to bring the fiercest judgement down on anyone who began practicing idolatry.

Deuteronomy 13:12-18 If you hear someone in one of your cities, which the Lord your God gives you to dwell in, saying, 13 'Corrupt men have gone out from among you and enticed the inhabitants of their city, saying, "Let us go and serve other gods"'—which you have not known— 14 then you shall inquire, search out, and ask diligently. And if it is indeed true and certain that such an abomination was committed among you, 15 you shall surely strike the inhabitants of that city with the edge of the sword, utterly destroying it, all that is in it and its livestock—with the edge of the sword. 16 And you shall gather all its plunder into the middle of the street, and completely burn with fire the city and all its plunder, for the Lord your God. It shall be a heap forever; it shall not be built again. 17 So none of the accursed things shall remain in your hand, that the Lord may turn from the fierceness of His anger and show you mercy, have compassion on you and multiply you, just as He swore to your fathers, 18 because you have listened to the voice of the Lord your God, to keep all His commandments which I command you today, to do what is right in the eyes of the Lord your God.

I want to make special note of this section of scripture, and I recommend reading it again, because it will help us to keep in mind the importance of this subject as we go. Out of all the sins that an Israelite could be punished for, Idolatry carried the strictest punishment of all, and didn't affect only the one who sinned, but all those around them as well. If a man and a woman were caught in adultery by two or three witnesses, the law stated that both that man and woman had to be put to death. If however, a person was caught teaching others to commit idolatry in a city Israel had captured, if they found it to be true, they had to find who was pulling people into idolatry, kill them, kill the other inhabitants of the city, kill the livestock, gather up all the plunder from that city, burn it all, burn the whole city down, and never rebuild on it. This law would've meant that if you were living in a city in ancient Israel, and you began hearing rumors of idolatry going on in your city, you would've had to grab your stuff, and get out of Dodge, because that city was about to be completely destroyed. Idolatry carried THE most severe punishment of any sin in the entirety of scripture. Not only did God punish Idolatry with this much severity, He absolutely hated any hint of it. Learn these verses, as they will be a common theme throughout this book.

Deuteronomy 12:29-32 When the Lord your God cuts off from before you the nations which you go to dispossess, and you displace them and dwell in their land, 30 take heed to yourself that you are not ensnared to follow them, after they are destroyed from before you, and that you <u>do not inquire after their gods, saying, 'How did these nations serve their gods? I also will do likewise.' 31 You shall not worship the Lord your God in that way;</u> for every abomination to the Lord which He hates they have done to their gods; for they burn even their sons and daughters in the fire to their gods. 32 Whatever I command you, be careful to observe it; you shall not add to it nor take away from it.

Deuteronomy 12:1-4 These are the statutes and judgments which you shall be careful to observe in the land which the Lord God of your fathers is giving you to possess, all the days that you live on the earth. 2 You shall utterly destroy all the places where the nations which you shall dispossess served their gods, on the high mountains and on the hills and under every green tree. 3 And you shall destroy their altars, break their sacred pillars, and burn their wooden images with fire; you shall cut down the carved images of their gods and destroy their names from that place. <u>4 You shall not worship the Lord your God with such things.</u>

God so hated Idolatry, that He commanded Israel not to imitate the gentiles at all in their worship. He said do not worship Him the way the other nations worship their gods, only worship Him in the ways that He commanded them. This meant even if their intentions were to worship God, they could not do it in certain ways. Trying to worship God in ways that were foreign and that He didn't command them to also carried a tremendous penalty.

> **Leviticus 10:1-2 Then Nadab and Abihu, the sons of Aaron, each took his censer and put fire in it, put incense on it, and offered profane fire before the Lord, which He had not commanded them. 2 So fire went out from the Lord and devoured them, and they died before the Lord.**

This word profane here is sometimes translated as strange, but it basically indicates that what they offered was something foreign, or pagan, and something God didn't command. So, God destroyed them for bringing a profane offering before Him. He also brought fierce judgement upon Israel for participating in Idolatry. He commanded them to destroy any hint of idolatry in their camp. I think we can safely conclude that's God's perspective on idolatry is about as severe as it can get. No sin is taken more seriously and judged more harshly than idolatry in the entirety of the scripture. Even in the New Testament, Idolatry was absolutely forbidden. When new converts were being added into the kingdom, the apostles actually chose to give them a very short list of sins they absolutely had to stay away from when starting their walk.

> **Acts 15:28-29 For it seemed good to the Holy Spirit, and to us, to lay upon you no greater burden than these <u>necessary things: 29 that you abstain from things offered to idols</u>, from blood, from things strangled, and from sexual immorality.**

In fact, even in the new heaven and new earth, we are told there will be some who cannot enter into the New Jerusalem because of this sin.

Revelation 22:14-15 Blessed are those who do His command-ments, that they may have the right to the tree of life, and may enter through the gates into the city. 15 But outside are dogs and sorcerers and sexually immoral and murderers and <u>idolaters</u>, and whoever loves and practices a lie.

Old Testament or New, idolatry is absolutely a forbidden thing. This is because of a simple truth; God does not change.

Malachi 3:6 "For I am the Lord, I do not change;..."

Numbers 23:19 (NIV) God is not human, that he should lie, not a human being, that he should change his mind.

James 1:17 (NIV) Every good and perfect gift is from above, coming down from the Father of the heavenly lights, who does not change like shifting shadows.

Hebrews 13:8 Jesus Christ is the same yesterday, today, and forever.

The way God felt about idolatry in the Old Testament is exactly the way He feels about it today because He does not change. It is absolutely one of the most offensive and vile things in His eyes. In His eyes, it is adultery against Him, and He loathes it. Now, what does this mean for us? Well, let's keep moving.

3

Our Role in His World

While this will be a short little chapter, I think it is important we understand what our role in God's world is, because it very much determines how we will react to God's opinions. The first thing to understand is that it is God's world. It is not ours. He is the creator, we are the creation. We serve Him, and follow Christ. We are servants of our Messiah, and we are sons of God. All of these ideas make it very clear, He is in charge, and we are just along for the ride. Miss Underwood has the song "Jesus take the wheel" but the fact is, He shouldn't be in the passenger seat, occasionally taking over for us, He is supposed to be driving the whole time. This scripture gives us a perfect image of how this is supposed to work.

> *Matthew 11:29-30 "Take My yoke upon you and learn from Me, for I am gentle and lowly in heart, and you will find rest for your souls. 30 For My yoke is easy and My burden is light."*

This metaphor more often than not goes over our heads in the modern day because our lives are so different, but back then, these were farming terms, and specifically related to plowing the land. When there was a farm animal, such as an ox, and a younger ox would come into the picture, it would have to learn how to pull a plow. The way they would teach the young ox, is by hooking up the younger ox to a yoke with an older seasoned ox who knew the way and make them work together until the younger one got the pattern down. The older ox would lead, and the younger one would need to follow along side, or else the yoke would strain at the younger one and cause him pain. Now if you apply this idea to our walk it's very plain, we yoke ourselves to Christ, and learn to walk as He walks. He leads us, and we follow. He shows us the way, and we fall in line, or else we are disciplined. He is Lord, and when we begin to try to take charge, problems and difficulties end up arising.

All too often people put themselves on a pedestal without really realizing it. They put their wants and desires over God's. They act as if they are living their life, and Christ is just along for the ride as an occasional crutch to lean on. They act as if they've got God in their pocket as fire insurance for the afterlife or like a get out of jail free card. Instead of weighing our actions against how He feels about it, all too often we simply act based upon how we feel, thus straining against His yoke. We are all guilty of it at times. The idea though is to begin to walk more and more in line with Him, to become like Him, and walk like Him, and do His will instead of our own.

1 John 2:6 He who says he abides in Him ought himself also to walk just as He walked.

We need to realize that we exist for His pleasure, and to bring Him glory. We do not live our lives for ourselves, we live our lives for Him. We lay down our lives for Him just as He laid His life down for us. We do His will of seeking the lost, and building up one another, and showing forth His love, His life, and His light to a dark and dying world. This is our purpose. This pertains directly to what we are going to be learning in this book. We need to understand and keep in mind, that the things we do should be the things that please Him, and not ourselves. We should ask how the things we do make Him feel, and not ask how they make us feel. We should ask if He would want us to do it, not if we want to do it. This is paramount, and cannot be overstated.

17

Remember the beatitudes found in Matthew 5? If we take all the attributes that are blessed, and set aside the promises given, we end up with this list: Blessed are the poor in spirit, those who mourn, the meek, those who hunger and thirst after righteousness, the merciful, the pure in heart, the peacemakers, those who are persecuted for righteousness sake. These are the attributes Christ wants us to have. We should be meek, and merciful, gentle and humble, loving and pure, and we should hunger for righteousness. We should want to be pleasing to Him. We should want to be pure for Him.

> *1 John 3:2-3 Beloved, now we are children of God; and it has not yet been revealed what we shall be, but we know that when He is revealed, we shall be like Him, for we shall see Him as He is. 3 And everyone who has this hope in Him purifies himself, just as He is pure.*

> *James 1:27 Pure and undefiled religion before God and the Father is this: to visit orphans and widows in their trouble, and to keep oneself unspotted from the world.*

> *1 Peter 1:13-16 Therefore gird up the loins of your mind, be sober, and rest your hope fully upon the grace that is to be brought to you at the revelation of Jesus Christ; 14 as obedient children, not conforming yourselves to the former lusts, as in your ignorance; 15 but as He who called you is holy, you also be holy in all your conduct, 16 because it is written, "Be holy, for I am holy."*

We are called to be holy. The word holy simply means "set apart". It's the idea of being separated from a filthy world, and its filthy ways, and being pure, and clean for Him. Like a bride who keeps herself pure for the man she is betrothed to. No bride sees her wedding day approaching and really just lets herself go, not caring if she puts on extra pounds or ends up with some extra pimples, blemishes or scars. No bride gets to her wedding day and decides she's gonna skip the shower, skip the makeup, throw her hair up into a messy bun, and meet her groom in yesterday's sweat pants. No good bride at least. We want to be pure for our Beloved, by His definition of pure, not by ours. We must align our thoughts and opinions and actions with what He wants. As I said, a short little chapter here, but something very important to keep in mind as you read this book. With this foundation firmly under our feet, we can move on to exposing the idolatry hiding in our lives.

II

Usurper

4

The Grand Mythos

I mentioned before that nearly every single culture has it's own unique brand of idolatry. There are Greek myths, Egyptian myths, Mesopotamian myths, Norse myths, and many others. What if I told you that all of these myths are all linked together, because they share a common origin? It sounds crazy, and very unlikely, and yet, I will show you that it's true. This will be a bit of a lengthy chapter, as we will walk through a few thousand years of history. As a disclaimer, this chapter is packed full of pagan myths, and while I don't relish having to delve into all of this idolatry, it is important that we do, as it really builds a solid foundation for more of what's to come. Another quick disclaimer is this; much has been lost to the sands of time, and while some of the information I have to offer is easy to find and consistent in its message, other things will have differences in details and nuances depending upon the source you find it from. Much of the older history not contained in the Bible is a series of clues left over from ancient civilizations that archaeologists and linguists have attempted to connect the dots on, and while the general themes remain intact, some of the smaller details conflict depending on the source. If your findings differ from mine in minor ways, this would be why.

We are going to start all the way back to the time very near after the flood, and move forward from there. Now, when we go back to that time, we find a man named Nimrod. We aren't told a whole lot about this man, but we have this account in Genesis:

> *Genesis 10:8-12 Cush begot Nimrod; he began to be a mighty*
> *one on the earth. 9 He was a mighty hunter before the Lord;*
> *therefore it is said, "Like Nimrod the mighty hunter before the*
> *Lord." 10 And the beginning of his kingdom was Babel, Erech,*
> *Accad, and Calneh, in the land of Shinar. 11 From that land he*
> *went to Assyria and built Nineveh, Rehoboth Ir, Calah, 12 and*
> *Resen between Nineveh and Calah (that is the principal city).*

So, we see that Nimrod was a mighty hunter, and a king, and he took his followers, and established multiple cities. Of the cities he established, none are as infamous as Babel except perhaps for Nineveh. Not only was Babel the site of the infamous tower of Babel, which we are about to look at, but the ruined heap later became Babylon, but we'll get to that more later. Here we have the account of the tower of Babel found in Genesis:

> *Genesis 11:1-9 Now the whole earth had one language and one*
> *speech. 2 And it came to pass, as they journeyed from the east,*
> *that they found a plain in the land of Shinar, and they dwelt*
> *there. 3 Then they said to one another, "Come, let us make bricks*
> *and bake them thoroughly." They had brick for stone, and they*
> *had asphalt for mortar. 4 And they said, "Come, let us build*
> *ourselves a city, and a tower whose top is in the heavens; let us*
> *make a name for ourselves, lest we be scattered abroad over the*
> *face of the whole earth." 5 But the Lord came down to see the city*
> *and the tower which the sons of men had built. 6 And the Lord*
> *said, "Indeed the people are one and they all have one language,*
> *and this is what they begin to do; now nothing that they propose*
> *to do will be withheld from them. 7 Come, let Us go down and*
> *there confuse their language, that they may not understand one*
> *another's speech." 8 So the Lord scattered them abroad from*
> *there over the face of all the earth, and they ceased building the*

city. 9 Therefore its name is called Babel, because there the Lord confused the language of all the earth; and from there the Lord scattered them abroad over the face of all the earth.

Now, this is really a rather short account and leaves us with many questions. Why did God prevent them from building this tower? Does God just really hate towers? Why was it so wrong that they didn't want to be scattered over the whole earth? It says nothing would be withheld from them, but what was it that God didn't want them to do? These questions are never answered for us in the Biblical canon. This is all the account we get. If however, you will suffer me for a moment to go outside the Biblical canon, I can provide you with more potential details. The book of Jasher has much more to say on this subject, and provides us with more insight. Now most have not heard of the book of Jasher, and most people dismiss any work not included in their 66 book canon. I want to point out three verses in the canon though, that you may not be aware of.

Joshua 10:13 So the sun stood still, And the moon stopped, Till the people had revenge Upon their enemies. Is this not written in the Book of Jasher? So the sun stood still in the midst of heaven, and did not hasten to go down for about a whole day.

2 Samuel 1:17-18 Then David lamented with this lamentation over Saul and over Jonathan his son, 18 and he told them to teach the children of Judah the Song of the Bow; indeed it is written in the Book of Jasher:

2 Timothy 3:8 Now as Jannes and Jambres resisted Moses, so do these also resist the truth: men of corrupt minds, disapproved concerning the faith;

The first two verses clearly reference the book of Jasher by name. The third verse at first glance appears to add nothing to my presentation, until you realize that nowhere in the entirety of the canon do we see the names of Jannes and Jambres that Paul is referring to. We do however find an account of these two sorcerers by name in the book of Jasher. Now, whether you want to accept the book of Jasher as authentic or not is not what I am here to debate. I merely wish to expound upon the events that we see in Genesis, and the book of Jasher does this quite nicely. If you are truly adamant against the using of this book, understand that none of the points I am going to make further are dependent upon this account, it merely enriches it and helps to bring out some ideas.

Jasher 9:20-33 And king Nimrod reigned securely, and all the earth was under his control, and all the earth was of one tongue and words of union. 21 And all the princes of Nimrod and his great men took counsel together; Phut, Egypt (Mitsrayim), Cush and Canaan with their families, and they said to each other, "Come let us build ourselves a city and in it a strong tower, and it's top reaching heaven, and we will make ourselves famed, so that we may reign upon the whole world, in order that the evil of our enemies may cease from us, that we may reign mightily over them, and that we may not become scattered over the earth on account of their wars. 22 And they all went before the king, and they told the king these words, and the king agreed with them in this affair, and he did so. 23 And all the families assembled consisting of about six hundred thousand men, and they went to seek an extensive piece of ground to build the city and the tower, and they sought in the whole earth and they found none like one valley at the east of the land of Shinar, about two days' walk, and they journeyed there and they dwelt there. 24 And they began to make bricks and burn fires to build the city and the tower that they had imagined to complete. 25 And the building of the tower was unto them a transgression and a sin, and they began to build it, and while they were building against The Lord God of Heaven, they imagined in their hearts to war against

Him and to ascend into heaven. 26 And all these people and all the families divided themselves in three parts; the first said "We will ascend into heaven and fight against him"; the second said, "We will ascend to heaven and place our own gods there and serve them"; and the third part said, "We will ascend to heaven and smite Him with bows and spears"; and God knew all their works and all their evil thoughts, and he saw the city and the tower which they were building. 27 And when they were building they built themselves a great city and a very high and strong tower; and on account of its height the mortar and bricks did not reach the builders in their ascent to it, until those who went up had completed a full year, and after that, they reached to the builders and gave them the mortar and the bricks; thus was it done daily. 28 And behold these ascended and others descended the whole day; and if a brick should fall from their hands and get broken, they would all weep over it, and if a man fell and died, none of them would look at him. 29 And God knew their thoughts, and it came to pass when they were building they cast the arrows toward the heavens, and all the arrows fell upon them filled with blood, and when they saw them they said to each other, "Surely we have slain all those that are in heaven" 30 For this was from God in order to cause them to err, and in order; to destroy them from off of the face of the ground. 31 And they built the tower and the city, and they did this thing daily until many days and years were elapsed. 32 And God said to the seventy angels who stood foremost before Him, to those who were near to Him, saying, "Come let us descend and confuse their tongues, that one man shall not understand the language of his neighbor" and they did so unto them. 33 And from that day following, they forgot each man his neighbor's tongue, and they could not understand to speak in one tongue, and when the builder took from the hands of his neighbor lime or stone which he did not order, the builder would cast it away and throw it

upon his neighbor, that he would die.

That was a much longer passage than the account found in Genesis and offers us a bit more insight into why God would be upset with the building of this tower. According to this account, they wanted to build a tower up to heaven, and fight against God, and set up their own gods. Now it is important to note, that their kings at that time and thereafter, were quite often to be considered gods. An example is found here:

Acts 12:21-22 So on a set day Herod, arrayed in royal apparel, sat on his throne and gave an oration to them. 22 And the people kept shouting, "The voice of a god and not of a man!"

So, in the case of Nimrod, he was a mighty hunter, likely the most powerful man in the world at that time, and became king over a majority of people on earth. He set about building a tower that would be the seat of his kingdom, and they would build a tower up to heaven and overthrow God, but God intervened, and scattered their languages, thus destroying their ability to work together. Now, this is actually very significant, because you have to remember, all of these men who now spoke with different languages, were scattered all over the earth, but they all came from under the rule of the same king. This king was Nimrod, who was venerated as their god. In fact, Nimrod actually ended up with his own little mythos which was the primary religious system of those days. Again, even if you reject the account in Jasher in it's entirety, we still end in the same place, the people were scattered and spoke with different languages, but they all had over them at one time, the same king, Nimrod. Let's examine the mythos surrounding Nimrod.

Ancient Babel

Nimrod was a mighty hunter who became king over many thousands. He took to himself a wife named Semiramis. Nimrod and Semiramis ruled over the people as king and queen. One day, while out hunting, Nimrod was killed by a great beast. Upon his death, he ascended into the sky and became the god of the sun. Semiramis mourned the loss of her husband, and doubly so, because she had no children and no heir to the throne. Nimrod, now being the god of the sun, decided to intervene, and he impregnated his wife Semiramis, by a ray of sunlight. Months later, Semiramis gave birth to Tammuz, who grew up and became a mighty man like his father.

Tammuz was considered the rebirth of his father Nimrod, and he took his mother Semiramis as his wife when he was of age. Tammuz ruled over the people with Semiramis as his father had done. Years passed however, and eventually Semiramis died, but when she went up to be with Nimrod, her first husband, he sent her back down because it was not yet her time to die. She came back down to earth in an egg (which represented fertility and new birth) and the egg landed in the Euphrates river and burst open. Out of the egg came Semiramis who came out in the form of a rabbit, again symbolizing fertility, who then turned back into a woman. Some years after that, Tammuz, like his father, was killed by a wild boar while hunting. Semiramis mourned his death for 40 days at which point Tammuz was deified as the rising sun. Some time later, Semiramis finally died herself once again, and was deified as well. Tammuz was deified as the sun like his father, and Semiramis was deified as the moon and stars. Tammuz was the sun rising in the east, and Nimrod was the sun setting in the west. Nimrod represented the sun waning and dying over the horizon, and Tammuz represented the sun being reborn and rising out of the ashes of his father in the East. Semiramis represented the moon and stars, the counterpart to the sun, and the female presence to balance the male presence. The gods of the day, and the goddess of the night.

This little mythos of Nimrod, Semiramis, and Tammuz became the basis by which many people were ensnared into idolatry. This was one of the first instances we see of the worship of the sun, moon, and stars. The Bible actually directly mentions this exact form of idolatry, as it would appear even Israel got swept up in it.

> *Ezekiel 8:13-16 And He said to me, "Turn again, and you will see greater abominations that they are doing." 14 So He brought me to the door of the north gate of the Lord's house; and to my dismay, women were sitting there <u>weeping for Tammuz.</u> 15 Then He said to me, "Have you seen this, O son of man? Turn again, you will see greater abominations than these." 16 So He brought me into the inner court of the Lord's house; and there, at the door of the temple of the Lord, between the porch and the altar, were about twenty-five men with their backs toward the temple of the Lord and <u>their faces toward the east, and they were worshiping the sun toward the east.</u>*

What is being described here is a pagan festival where during a certain time of year, people would spend 40 days weeping for Tammuz just as Semiramis did. They would conclude the 40 days of weeping for Tammuz with worshiping him, as it represented him being reborn after death as the sun and rising in the east. Now, remember that this mythos was what the majority likely held during the building of Babel, but when they were scattered, although the general story they had was the same, the names, and some of the details would've changed. Next we will examine the mythos in Egypt. Now as a quick disclaimer, there were actually many stories in the Egyptian pantheon and they also held many gods. This was but one of the myths that was a central one, that dealt with some of the more prominent gods.

Egypt

There were two parents, Geb, the god of vegetation, and harvest, and Nut, the goddess of the stars and sky as well as creation. Geb was depicted as a strong king, with a bird that would rest on his head as a pet of sorts. Nut was often depicted as a nude woman with the sun, moon and stars moving across her body. To break down these two further, Geb in a big way represented the sun, as the harvest and vegetation were directly dependent upon the sun and daylight, and whoever controlled the sun controlled the harvest. Nut on the other hand was the goddess of night, as the goddess of the moon, the stars and the sky.

Geb and Nut gave birth to children, three of which were Osiris, Set, and Isis. Osiris was granted to rule over Egypt as heir as well as taking his sister Isis as his wife. Set meanwhile got basically nothing, and in his jealousy, sought to usurp the throne from his brother. Set devised a devious plan to kill Osiris by trickery, and carried out his plan thus murdering his brother Osiris. Isis, Osiris' sister and wife, mourned the loss of her husband, and decided to resurrect him. First however, she needed to procure his body. Set found out about his sisters' plan, and to stop her from resurrecting Osiris, he dismembered the body into 14 pieces. Isis determined not to let this stop her, and went looking for the body parts of Osiris. In spite of her best efforts, she only found 13 of the 14 pieces. The 14th piece that Isis could not find, was the phallic organ, which Set had thrown into the Euphrates river and was eaten by fish, thus preventing Osiris from ever having an heir.

Isis, after finding all Osiris' body parts except for the one, raised Osiris from the dead, but according to the law of nature, once a soul had been in the underworld, it could no longer live on earth. Osiris thus lost his throne on earth, and became the god of the underworld, remaining there. This however still left an issue, as there was no rightful heir to the throne, and Osiris, missing his phallic organ, could not impregnate Isis with an heir. Isis could not allow the treacherous Set to hold the throne, and thus she needed to bring forth an heir to take it from her brother. The solution she came to was to erect a stone spire called an obelisk, which represented her late husband's phallic organ that was never recovered. Using this obelisk and a bit of magic, Isis impregnated herself by it, and months later gave birth to Osiris' son and heir, Horus.

After Horus grew old enough, he and Isis decided to launch a coup against Set in an effort to take back the throne. Horus and Isis fought against Set, ultimately defeating him. Horus took up his father's throne, and became ruler over Egypt. Interestingly, Horus ended up with Hathor as a consort or concubine. Hathor

31

was the daughter of another sun god, Ra, and was the goddess of the sky, and sexuality. She was commonly depicted as a semi nude woman or a cow, and she had a headdress of the crescent moon holding the sun inside of it representing the male aspect of the sun, sitting inside the female aspect of the moon. Even more interestingly, some texts even suggest Hathor was Horus' real mother, thus she would've been both his mother, and his lover.

Now, Egypt had a bit of a long running culture, and though some details remained the same, there were many other gods added and altered, and details of who married who, and who did what, did change somewhat over time. In this account however, we see many mirrors back to the mythos of Babel. We see a god of the harvest and the sun, married to a goddess of the night, and stars. We see a god who dies, and needs to provide an heir, but cannot do so under normal circumstances due to having been killed. The goddess ends up impregnated by mystical means, and bears an heir to the throne and the child ultimately takes over for his father. We also see a common incestuous relationship, either between a brother and sister, or between mother and son, depending on which version of the myth you look at. We also see a goddess that is associated with fertility and sexuality that ends up as a consort of the heir. These are some themes to look out for as we continue looking at mythologies.

Babylon

Gilgamesh was a mighty king, and ruler. He was not however, a kind king, and he oppressed the people in his kingdom of Uruk. The people prayed to their gods for deliverance. The gods responded by creating a wild man named Enkidu, who was given the task of assassinating Gilgamesh. Enkidu set out to fulfill his task but first he had to find his mark. While pursuing Gilgamesh, Enkidu meets a prostitute. The prostitute seduces him, which caused Enkidu's wild nature to dissipate. This left Enkidu rather more civilized, and far less dangerous than he initially was. Eventually, he finds his way to Uruk, and challenges Gilgamesh to a fight. Due to his weakened state, Gilgamesh is able to defeat Enkidu. During the struggle, Gilgamesh sees in Enkidu a fierce warrior, and a kindred spirit, and ends up befriending him after their battle.

Thereafter, the two of them decide to go on a journey to a legendary cedar forest to slay a mighty guardian of the forest, Humbaba the terrible. During the journey, they end up derailed in purpose when the goddess Ishtar sees Gilgamesh and wants to lay with him. She tries her best to seduce Gilgamesh, but he resists her advances and rejects her. Enraged, Ishtar decides to send the bull of heaven, a great and fierce beast to slay Gilgamesh. Gilgamesh and Enkidu prove too powerful however, and slay the bull of heaven. In doing so, the pair enrage the rest of the gods, who are sorely displeased that Enkidu, whom they sent to stop Gilgamesh, has instead joined with him and together killed the sacred bull of heaven. In retaliation, the gods slay Enkidu leaving Gilgamesh alone. Gilgamesh, sorely grieved by the death of his friend, and coming to realize his own mortality, decides to journey across the world searching for the secret to eternal life.

Now this mythos is rather different from the others, but many of the elements are actually present. We see Gilgamesh being a mighty hunter and king, mirroring the mighty hunter, king Nimrod. We see a sexually charged goddess present who wants to seduce Nimrod and be with him, just as Semiramis was with Nimrod. We see a great struggle between the bull of heaven, and Gilgamesh, just as there was a great struggle between Nimrod and the beast, or Tammuz and the wild boar. Ishtar, it should be noted, is also most often depicted as a nude or partially nude woman, with large breasts and wide hips representing fertility, and wings representing ruling over the sky. In many depictions she is seen holding two circular objects in her right and left hand, which could symbolize the rising and setting sun. While the details differ, many similar elements are present. Let's move on.

Canaan

Next we have the story of Baal. Yes, the same Baal we see the children of Israel falling to in the Old Testament over and over. Now this myth has very little verifiable evidence, but there are enough fragments of writings that we can kind of piece together the story. This mythos was easily the most difficult to find information for, but thanks to a research paper done by Trudy Tannen [1], I was able to find this information.

There was a god named El who was the chief over all other gods. I want to quickly mention that the name El, was actually the Hebrew word that meant deity, or God. It was not a proper noun as a name for God, but merely the impersonal noun that meant God. Anyways, El had a wife named Asherah who was the goddess of war, as well as love and fertility. She is often depicted as a nude woman with large breasts, once again hearkening to fertility. Asherah and El had many children, one of which was Baal. Baal was the god of weather, harvest, and agriculture and was depicted as half man, half bull. Baal was exceptionally strong, and eventually grew strong enough to attack his father, El. Baal overthrew his father, and seized El's throne for himself. Not only did Baal take his father's throne, he also took El's wife Asherah, his mother, as his wife. Beyond Asherah, Baal also took his sister Anath, who was depicted as a young virgin, some sources say as a wife, and others, just as a helper loyal to him.

Anyways, El was not happy about this turn of events, and he joined forces with another of his sons, Yamm, and together they attempted to overthrow Baal and restore El to his throne. Yamm transformed himself into a giant sea dragon, and fought against Baal. Things did not go well however, and Baal defeated them both. With his place on the throne secure, Baal decided he deserved an even grander palace that would befit his new position as chief of the gods. Baal sent Asherah to El to request the building of this new grander palace, and El agreed. The palace was built and Baal took the seat on his new throne.

After construction was completed, Mot, another brother of Baal and god of the underworld, requested that Baal come and visit him in the underworld. Baal agreed and journeyed to meet his brother. On the way, Baal encountered a cow who apparently attracted the part of Baal that was a bull, and he impregnated this cow. Eventually he arrives in the underworld where his brother Mot, had a dastardly trap waiting for him. The exact methods aren't exactly known, but somehow Baal was forced to admit defeat and submit to his brother Mot who it seems executed him. Upon hearing the news of Baals demise, surprisingly, El mourns his loss, and instructs Asherah to find a successor to Baal. Asherah sets out to find a suitable heir to the throne, but Anath, Baal's sister/wife/helper decides instead to seek out the body of Baal. While searching for the body of Baal, she encounters Mot, and in a fit of vengeance, cuts him open and kills him.

Soon after this event, El has a dream in which Baal was brought back to life, presumably because Anath killed Mot, and thus set Baal's soul free from the underworld. Seven years later, Baal returns to take his place on the throne, but not only did Baal come back to life, his foe Mot did as well, and a battle ensues. Without the use of his traps though, Mot is overpowered, and soundly defeated. Baal then retakes his place on the throne, becoming chief of the gods.

So, many of the elements of this story mirror the mythos of Nimrod once again. Fertility goddess gives birth to god of weather and agriculture pertaining again to the sun. The son takes his mother as his wife when his father is struck down. The sun god dies, but ends up ascending and becoming chief of the gods. The imagery of a bare breasted fertility goddess is present, the imagery of a great bull is present, and generally speaking, things look rather similar. Again and again we see some differences between myths, but also striking similarities. I want to briefly mention, Dagon was another god that was held in these same areas at this same time, and it seems that Dagon was basically another name for Baal, as Dagon was the god of grain, and the harvest, and much of the mythos surrounding Dagon is the same as the story of Baal. Dagon was indeed a half man half fish as opposed to half man half bull, but was again associated with the harvest and weather, and fertility.

Miscellaneous

I want to point out a few other religions/myths that have some common themes.

First is Mithra who was the god of light, and the sun, closely associated with the Greek god Helios and the Sol Invictus, a Roman god of the sun. Mithra was alleged to have been born out of the earth itself, and rode around on the cosmic bull. Through some event, Mithra ended up killing the cosmic bull, and it's blood flowed out into the earth, making the earth fertile, and causing plants and agriculture to bloom. A deity representing the sun, and associated with the harvest fights against a mighty beast, killing it. Mithra was married to Anahita, the goddess of fertility, water, and the spring time. Anahita is depicted as a semi nude, beautiful woman with large breasts, wings, and a crown atop her head.

Next we have Zoroaster. Zoroaster doesn't have a full mythos really attributed to him, and he mirrors more of what Buddhism or Islam have in the form of a primary prophet. Essentially Zoroaster received divine visions that enlightened him and led him to become a prophet and teacher. What is interesting to note here, is in the original etymology, Zoro translates as son of, and Aster, well, you can likely guess that one, Aster, or Asherah, or Ashtoreth, or Anath. This prophet's name was literally son of Aster (Asherah).

Next we find Islam, in which we find some striking imagery. Modern Islam tries to bury it, but the origins of Islam actually arise out of an older Arabian religion. Allegedly Allah, the chief god, had three daughters, named Allat, Manat, and Al-Uzza. These sisters were the goddesses of fate, fortune, time, and destiny. Even Muhammad wrote about these goddesses, but these writings are called the "Satanic verses" as they believe that when Muhammad received this revelation in particular, it was infernal inspiration, instead of divine. These three goddesses directly mirror the sisters of fate in Greek mythology, Clotho, Lahkesis, and Atropos. The symbol for these goddesses was once again the crescent moon and stars, as they were associated with the moon and stars, and even in modern times, the Islamic flag still bears this symbology. Interestingly, Wicca has this same symbol of a five pointed star sitting in a crescent moon featured prominently in occultic imagery.

Wiccanism hold that there are three primary deities that govern the earth. There is the wild man Pan, the horned god, often depicted as half beast and half man, Diana, queen of heaven depicted as a beautiful woman with bare breasts, associated with fertility and the moon, bearing the symbol of the crescent moon on her head, and Mercury or Hermes, who is their child, who is depicted as a young male child with wings and a staff. Once again, Nimrod, Semiramis, and Tammuz.

Greek mythology has Zeus, the chief god of the sky and lightning. Zeus has relations with one of his concubines, Leto. Leto is the goddess of fertility, family, and maternal activity, depicted as a bare breasted woman surrounded by children. She gives birth to Apollo who is nurtured with ambrosia and honey until he is strong. When he grows into a man, Apollo fights against the great serpent Python, and becomes the god of light, and justice, and healing, and the sun.

Norse mythology has Odin, the god of death, healing, knowledge, battle, and poetry, basically acting as the chief god. Odin has his wife Freya, or Frigg depending upon the source you find. Freya is the goddess of fertility, and battle, and depicted as a beautiful woman clothed in armor (I guess it was too cold in the frozen north for her to be topless). Freya and Odin give birth to Thor who is the god of lightning, and the sky, storms and trees. Thor is said to fight against a great serpent at the end of the world, and thereafter shares the role of chief of the gods with his father Odin.

We know very little about Remphan, but we do know that the image of

Remphan was a six pointed star. Once again hearkening back to the stars and sky.

It goes on, and on, and on. Again, the myths change over time, gods and goddesses were added as time went on. The stories changed, the names changed, but ultimately, there are so many common themes shared between them that it's hard to deny that they are all connected to the same source. Beyond Nimrod though, what is the original source?

It's rather simple really. Satan thinks himself a king, a god even. He wanted to be like the most high (Isaiah 14:13). He fought against God with his angels, and was cast down to the earth, like lightning fallen from heaven (Luke 10:18). Essentially, he fought against a great being, God, or in his versions of the story, a great beast. He was cast down to the earth and soundly defeated. Satan needed a new heir to take his place, as he had already been defeated, but is unable to produce an heir on his own. He needed mankind and specifically women, to bear him an heir. Satan has spent the last few thousand years setting the stage to bring forth his son, the antichrist, who will sit in the temple of God, declaring himself to be God (2 Thessalonians 2:4). Satan, through his "son" will attempt to rule and reign over the earth. In all the myths, Tammuz, Horus, Gilgamesh, Baal, Mithra, Hermes, Apollo, Thor, are all victorious, but we know that our God will be the one to be victorious. Mythology is nothing more and nothing less than the stories Satan has told about himself and his minions throughout the ages to those foolish enough to follow him and serve him.

Now Christianity also contains a God who has a Son who rules and reigns. How is this any different? Much in every way. There is no other book that has as much historical, archaeological, mathematical, logical, and even scientific evidence going for it, as the Bible does. You can search this out for yourself. We know the scripture is true because no other book has as accurately pinpointed sites of ancient battles, or as accurately foretold the future, or has had more impact in the world than the Bible. No other book has been as attacked, no other book have men attempted to destroy hundreds of times throughout history as the Bible. There is a veritable mountain of evidence that we have to stand on when it comes to believing the scriptures. Most of these "intellectual" people who scoff at the Bible, are throwing rocks from a house made of glass, and are willingly ignorant of the greater evidences that are presentable in favor of the authenticity and divine authorship of the scriptures.

But still, this whole pattern of idolatry seeming to have similarities to Christianity is indeed troubling, so how do we answer this? Well, Satan is a liar and a deceiver, and an exceedingly talented one at that. Both God and Christ existed in eternity past (John 8:58). After he was created, Satan was the anointing Cherub who covered (Ezekiel 28:14), and was with God. Remember that God knew from eternity past all that would transpire throughout the ages. He knew He would create mankind. He knew mankind would fall. He knew He would need to provide a way to redeem us. He knew He would have to send His son to die for us. Satan was right there with them, how could he not know at least some of the plan? After his fall, when Satan caused Adam and Eve to fall, God prophesied that he would bruise the heel of the woman's seed (Christ) but that Christ would bruise his head. (Genesis 3:15). Satan knew the plan all along. That is why Satan tried so hard to have Christ put to death through Herod (Matthew 2:16). That's why Satan tried to tempt Jesus at the outset of His ministry (Matthew 4:1-11), because he knew that if he could cause Christ to sin, the plan would be ruined, and he would win.

Satan knew he was doomed from the beginning, and not only did he do his best to prevent Christ from coming, he also created multiple fake Christs through the ages in an effort to ensnare, deceive, and destroy mankind and try to once again, be like the Most High. Tammuz, Baal, Thor, these and the others are nothing more and nothing less than images of the antichrist, who Satan intends to bring forth as his final attempt to be worshiped as God. We also know the antichrist will gather the nations of the world against Christ at the battle of Armageddon (Revelation 16:16). Satan intends to fight one last time, just as Baal fought Mot, or Horus fought Set, or any of the other myths. As I said though, things won't go his way.

I want to make a quick but important mention of something pertaining to the antichrist. Everyone assumes that somehow the antichrist will be the antithesis of Christ, as if he would be the opposite in nature and purpose, but this isn't necessarily the case. The term antichrist can of course mean opposed to Christ, but it can also mean in place of Christ. The antichrist will very much be opposed to the true Messiah, but he will also come as a deceiver, to try to convince the world that he is the true Christ. This is why Jesus gave us warning in Matthew regarding these things. He strictly warns if someone says look, here is the Christ, or there, don't believe them. He gave this warning because He knew many would be fooled into following this impostor Christ. This false christ will deceive if possible, even the elect.

Now, sadly, Israel actually fell to these antichrist gods over and over. God gave them many warnings such as this one.

> *Deuteronomy 4:15-19 Take careful heed to yourselves, for you saw no form when the Lord spoke to you at Horeb out of the midst of the fire, 16 lest you act corruptly and make for yourselves a carved image in the form of any figure: the likeness of male or female, 17 the likeness of any animal that is on the earth or the likeness of any winged bird that flies in the air, 18 the likeness of anything that creeps on the ground or the likeness of any fish that is in the water beneath the earth. 19 And take heed, lest you lift your eyes to heaven, and when you see the sun, the moon, and the stars, all the host of heaven, you feel driven to worship them and serve them, which the Lord your God has given to all the peoples under the whole heaven as a heritage.*

But they still fell over and over.

> *Judges 2:11-14 Then the children of Israel did evil in the sight of the Lord, and served the Baals; 12 and they forsook the Lord God*

of their fathers, who had brought them out of the land of Egypt; and they followed other gods from among the gods of the people who were all around them, and they bowed down to them; and they provoked the Lord to anger. 13 They forsook the Lord and served Baal and the Ashtoreths. 14 And the anger of the Lord was hot against Israel.

2 Kings 23:4 And the king commanded Hilkiah the high priest, the priests of the second order, and the doorkeepers, to bring out of the temple of the Lord all the articles that were made for Baal, for Asherah, and for all the host of heaven; and he burned them outside Jerusalem in the fields of Kidron, and carried their ashes to Bethel.

Acts 7:42-43 Then God turned and gave them up to worship the host of heaven, as it is written in the book of the Prophets: 'Did you offer Me slaughtered animals and sacrifices during forty years in the wilderness, O house of Israel? 43 You also took up the tabernacle of Moloch, and the star of your god Remphan, images which you made to worship; and I will carry you away beyond Babylon.'

Now this all seems rather far removed from our lives today correct? Well, yes and no. We don't really see Christians turning away from God and worshiping the sun, moon and stars right? Well, that's where you'd be wrong. The sad truth is, this idolatry has actually infiltrated the church today in a major way, and the vast majority of people don't even realize it. I'm afraid this antichrist worship is far more prominent in even the most conservative churches today than people really realize. The next chapters will be dedicated to exposing these pagan practices in the church. To give you fair warning, it will be a rather uncomfortable experience for many, but these things are necessary. Remember that in the previous chapter, we just went over how we need to purify ourselves, and get ourselves ready for the coming of our Beloved. Keep these things in mind as we move forward.

5

R.C.C.

So, what does R.C.C. mean? I wanted this to be an enigma up until this point. See, I want many people to read this book, but many will see one phrase or name, and dismiss everything I present without hearing anything I have to say. I veiled some things in the naming of chapters and sections because I wanted people to have to read the book, in order to learn what it is all about. Yes, it's about idolatry, but what specifically? These are the things I have partially hidden from the average eye. You see, this chapter in particular, could be highly offensive to many, including many relatives of mine, who I care about very much. I do not seek to attack, or to hurt, but only to help and heal. That's what this whole book is about really. I want to help as many people as I can find truths hidden away in the swarm of lies in this world. As I begin to reveal these things dear reader, I ask that you do not be offended, or angry, but that you be lowly of spirit, and humble, hearing the matter out before you make up your mind. (Proverbs 18:13)

Well, to reveal this chapter's enigma, R.C.C. simply stands for Roman Catholic Church. Now, what does everything we've learned up till this point have to do with the Roman Catholic Church? What does the Roman Catholic Church have to do with the modern day Christian Church? Sadly the answer dear reader, is everything. It has everything to do with it. In the next chapters we will begin to see exactly how Roman Catholicism affects modern Christianity, but for this chapter, we will focus solely on some history and quotes from the Roman Catholic Church.

So what is the Roman Catholic Church (which I will return to referring to as RCC for sake of simplicity)? It is one of the single largest religious organizations in the world today. The RCC is a very old institution that has been around for around 1700 - 1800 years now and has been a prominent force in the world since its inception. It officially began around the year 300 A.D. The official birth of the RCC began with a man named Flavius Valerius Aurelius Constantinus Augustus, or as he is commonly referred to, Constantine. Constantine was the emperor of Rome between 306 and 337 A.D.. Now, during that time, the Roman Empire was absolutely filled with idolatry. The Roman pantheon in particular was particularly accepting of other cultures gods, and because of this, they ended up with many. Rome carried Romanized forms of gods from many cultures. Rome took these gods, and gave them new names. Zeus became Jupiter, Hera became Juno, Aphrodite became Venus, Artemis became Diana, Hermes became Mercury, Dionysus became Bacchus, and so on and so forth, although interestingly, Apollo kept his original name. Another note is that at this time, there was a dramatic rise of a cult that followed the god Mithra. Mithraism was becoming mingled with faith in Christ, and the gospel was becoming perverted thanks to the efforts of some wicked men, but we will look at that more in a while.

Well, the story goes that Emperor Constantine was preparing for a large battle for the Milvian bridge against his relative Maxentius. Maxentius proved to be the one real threat to Constantine's rule over Rome, and so he was troubled about the coming battle. Before the battle, Constantine saw a divine vision. Eusebius recorded this vision for us: "He saw with his own eyes the trophy of a cross of light in the heavens, above the sun, and bearing the inscription, CONQUER BY THIS." He then put this symbol on the shields of his army, and though greatly outnumbered, they managed to drive back the armies of Maxentius. Thankful for the divine intervention, Constantine with his authority as emperor, declared the Christian God to be the One True God, and legally instituted the Roman Catholic Church forcing everyone to convert to Christianity.

Now this story is all well and good, but unfortunately, this is the high point of the tale. It all goes rather downhill from here. The Romans, as I stated earlier were completely taken with paganism and their pantheon of gods played its part in nearly every one of their activities. From their days of the week, months of the year, festivals, architecture, sports, you name it, it was associated with their gods. Even the famous red capes and plumed helmets associated with Roman soldiers was to honor Mars, their god of war who's official color was red. Supposedly, when Constantine was faced with the reality that he was trying to enforce Christianity in an entirely pagan culture, he decided it would be better to repaint, rather than replace. He took the pagan Roman pantheon, and adopted it as a part of his new church. In fact, as an interesting side note, Catholic literally means "all embracing". That is just what it did, it embraced all of the pagan gods that Rome was already worshiping, and gave them a new paint job. This is a quote taken from a website called Catholic Straight Answers which is a website that is by Catholics, for Catholics to offer answers for their religion. This quote can be found in a few other places as well, and is easily verifiable information.

> *In 609, the Emperor Phocas gave the Pantheon in Rome to Pope Boniface IV, who rededicated it on May 13 under the title St. Maria ad Martyres (or St. Mary and All Martyrs).* [2]

So Emperor Phocas gave the Roman Pantheon of false gods to Pope Boniface IV in the year 609, and the Pope rededicated it as the Saint Mary and martyrs. What does this mean? It means that the RCC officially accepted all the pagan gods that the Romans held as their own, and renamed the gods according to the names of Mary, and various Martyrs or "Saints". Speaking of these saints, very recently, a man named John Henry Newman was officially canonized as a saint. In 1845 he wrote a paper entitled "Essay on the Development of Christian Doctrine". This is an excerpt from it:

We are told in various ways by Eusebius, that Constantine, in order to recommend the new religion to the heathen, transferred into it the outward ornaments to which they had been accustomed in their own. It is not necessary to go into a subject which the diligence of Protestant writers has made familiar to most of us. The use of temples, and these dedicated to particular saints, and ornamented on occasions with branches of trees; incense, lamps, and candles; votive offerings on recovery from illness; holy water; asylums; holydays and seasons, use of calendars, processions, blessings on the fields; sacerdotal vestments, the tonsure, the ring in marriage, turning to the East, images at a later date, perhaps the ecclesiastical chant, and the Kyrie Eleison, are all of pagan origin, and sanctified by their adoption into the Church. {374}
3

So this Catholic Saint, clearly acknowledges that a large portion of the practices in Catholicism are actually pagan in origin, because Constantine had to get the heathen to accept Christianity. The RCC took these practices, and sanctified them somehow, making them acceptable for followers of God to participate in. This is in direct opposition to what God commanded.

Deuteronomy 12:3-4 And you shall destroy their altars, break their sacred pillars, and burn their wooden images with fire; you shall cut down the carved images of their gods and destroy their names from that place. 4 You shall not worship the Lord your God with such things.

In fact, this portion specifically mentions sacred pillars, this is a direct reference to the obelisk I mentioned in the previous chapter that represented the phallic organ of Osiris. If you go to the Vatican right now, you will find two obelisks. The first one is smack in the middle of the St. Peter's square, and is actually one of the original obelisks from Egypt that actually stood in one of their pagan temples. This is an excerpt from a website called Stpetersbasilica.info

The Obelisk from Egypt was brought to Rome by Emperor Caligula in 37 AD. It originally stood in his circus on a spot to the south of the basilica, close to the present Sacristy. Sixtus V had Domenico Fontana move it in 1586 to the center of St. Peter's Square. It is also a sun dial, its shadows mark noon over the signs of the zodiac in the white marble disks in the paving of the square. The obelisk rests upon four couchant lions, each with two bodies whose tails intertwine.

Obelisk is from obeliscus - "in the shape of a spear". For pagans, the obelisk was a solar symbol that represented a vital flow between heaven and earth, a way of communicating to the divine. As a pagan monument in the greatest Christian square, it is a symbol of humanity reaching out to Christ. Originally inscribed to "Divine Augustus" and "Divine Tiberius" and now dedicated to the Holy Cross - "Christus Vincit, Christus Regnat, Christus Imperat. Christus ab omni malo plebem suam defendat." It is topped by a bronze cross containing a fragment of the true Cross. [4]

So, this particular obelisk, was actually brought over straight from Egypt, and stood in the circus of Emperor Caligula which is also called the circus of Nero. Now, if you don't know who Caligula was, or what his "circus" was like, you should know that Caligula was one of the most vicious and evil emperors to ever live. He severely persecuted followers of Christ in the most twisted and awful ways. His so called circus was one of the places he would torment and execute Christians for the masses. Caligula was known for his cruelty, sadism, sexual perversion, and general insanity. Based upon his tastes, you can imagine what kind of acts went on around this particular obelisk. It's also interesting that this pagan phallic symbol directly from Egypt pleased a man so debased and wicked that he spent a great amount of money to have it transferred to his circus as a decoration. So the RCC decided to take this pagan phallic symbol that sat in the middle of Egyptian temples, and then belonged to one of the most evil and insane men who ever ruled Rome, and stuck it right in the center of their most prominent and grand square, the capital of their church. The other obelisk you will find in Vatican city is the Lateran obelisk which is the largest obelisk in the world today.

Sadly, this is only the beginning of the objects associated with idolatry. In the Vatican Museum alone, they have statues of Aelius, Apollo, Artemis, Athena, Eros, Fortuna, Hera, Ariadne, Mercury, Diana, and many other pagan gods and goddesses.

> **Deuteronomy 12:3 And <u>you shall destroy</u> their altars, <u>break their sacred pillars</u>, and burn their wooden images with fire; <u>you shall cut down the carved images of their gods and destroy their names</u> from that place.**

This is to say nothing of their paintings and works of art that are contained therein. If you look at nearly every single painting that has come from RCC sources, the Martyrs, Apostles, Mary, Joseph, Christ, all of them are displayed with a "halo" behind their heads. This is not something new that the RCC thought up. The halo is actually a term that pertains directly to the sun, and more often than not, these halos, appear as the sun itself. In fact, you can find this imagery of the sun shining behind the heads of gods in art from pagan cultures all over the world. Why would the RCC depict these Biblical persons and saints in the same ways the pagans depicted their pagan gods? Because they adopted their pagan gods and repainted them.

If you look at nearly all the Catholic paintings you will also notice a particular hand sign that has the pointer and middle finger pointed upward, the ring and the pinky fingers pointed downward. This particular hand sign is seen all over pagan statues. and is even seen in nearly every single statue of Baphomet. Baphomet by the way, in nearly every single statue also has either a disc or circle behind its head, or a flame above it, or both. This is an excerpt from the BBC website regarding the hand sign Baphomet makes.

48

Two fingers on the right hand point up and two on the left hand point down, meaning "as above, so below"

These words and the accompanying gesture are familiar to occultists. They are drawn from the ancient works of Hermes Trismegistus, whose writings became popular during the Renaissance and Reformation.

The phrase is also used in relation to science, the universe and God, but Levi wrote that, by making the gesture, his Baphomet "expresses the perfect harmony of mercy with justice" [5]

If you take a moment and search "as above so below handsign" and look at the images, you will find this hand sign all over. After that search "Catholic paintings of Jesus" and look at the hand signs.

The Rosary is a necklace made of a specific number of beads that pertain to certain prayers you are supposed to say in a certain order. The Buddhists, Hindus, and Muslims have this exact practice in each of their religions also. The Pope carries with him a crosier which is an item from the days of Egypt that the Pharaoh used to carry as a symbol of the authority of the god Osiris. Catholics are supposed to eat fish on Fridays. It just so happens Friday was the day Romans worshiped Salacia, the fish goddess, and they would eat fish in honor of her. There are different "patron saints" for different aspects of life, just as their are patron gods in paganism. Mary is often depicted with the moon under her feet and stars behind her head, and is commonly called "Mary Queen of Heaven" matching Diana's title and imagery perfectly. Offering flowers and burning incense to statues of Mary are common occurrences among Catholics. Offering incense to the queen of heaven is nothing new.

Jeremiah 44:16-23 "As for the word that you have spoken to us in the name of the Lord, we will not listen to you! 17 But we will certainly do whatever has gone out of our own mouth, to burn incense to the queen of heaven and pour out drink offerings to her, as we have done, we and our fathers, our kings and our princes, in the cities of Judah and in the streets of Jerusalem. For then we had plenty of food, were well-off, and saw no trouble. 18 But since we stopped burning incense to the queen of heaven and pouring out drink offerings to her, we have lacked everything and have been consumed by the sword and by famine."

19 The women also said, "And when we burned incense to the queen of heaven and poured out drink offerings to her, did we make cakes for her, to worship her, and pour out drink offerings to her without our husbands' permission?"

20 Then Jeremiah spoke to all the people—the men, the women, and all the people who had given him that answer—saying: 21 "The incense that you burned in the cities of Judah and in the streets of Jerusalem, you and your fathers, your kings and your princes, and the people of the land, did not the Lord remember them, and did it not come into His mind? 22 So the Lord could no longer bear it, because of the evil of your doings and because of the abominations which you committed. Therefore your land is a desolation, an astonishment, a curse, and without an inhabitant, as it is this day. 23 Because you have burned incense and because you have sinned against the Lord, and have not obeyed the voice of the Lord or walked in His law, in His statutes or in His testimonies, therefore this calamity has happened to you, as at this day."

Catholics claim that this practice of calling Mary "queen of heaven" and burning incense to her and venerating her are not pagan because Solomon's mother, Bathsheba, was referred to as the "queen mother" and enjoyed a prominent place in Solomon's court. What they fail to remember is that Solomon's heart was turned away to idolatry by his wives, and adopted their pagan practices, and built temples to this queen of heaven, Ashtoreth, and was severely judged for it. Funny that in the very place they claim to have biblical foundation for this practice, you see an example of a "queen mother" having important position in the palace of a man who turned away his heart from God and ran after Ashtoreth. You also never find any examples of people worshiping or offering incense, cakes, and other things to the queen mother. The only "Biblical foundation" you'll find for burning incense to the queen of heaven is in Jeremiah where God destroys a people for it.

The garb the Catholic Priests use are directly pagan in origin.

> "In order to attach to Christianity great attraction in the eyes of the nobility, the priests adopted the outer garments and adornments which were used in pagan cults." (Life of Constantine, Eusabius, cited in Altai-Nimalaya, p. 94)

It goes on, and on, and on. If you just begin to look at statues, paintings, and symbology in the RCC and specifically the Vatican, and compare it to pagan symbology, you will find more similarities than you can shake a stick at.

Now how is this answered by the RCC? Well, it's rather simple really. The Pope is known as the Vicar of Christ, and is venerated as the physical representation of Christ on the earth. According to the RCC, the Pope carries all the same authority on the earth as if he was Christ Himself. In fact, the Pope is actually equal with God Himself according to the RCC.

> "To believe that our Lord God the Pope has not the power to decree as he is decreed, is to be deemed heretical." (the Gloss "Extravagantes" o.f Pope John XXII Cum inter, Tit. XIV, Cap. IV. Ad Callem Sexti Decretalium, Paris, 1685)

> "The Pope and God are the same, so he has all power in Heaven and earth." (Pope Pius V, quoted in Barclay, Chapter XXVII, p. 218, "Cities Petrus Bertanous)

> "Hence the Pope is crowned with a triple crown, as king of heaven and of earth and of the lower regions." (Ferraris, «Prompta Bibliotheca», 1763, Volume VI, 'Papa II', p.26)

Not only that, but the Pope now has the same responsibilities and honors as Christ Himself.

> *"This is our last lesson to you: receive it, engrave it in your minds, all of you: by God's commandment salvation is to be found nowhere but in the Church; the strong and effective instrument of salvation is none other than the Roman Pontificate."* (Pope Leo XIII, Allocution for the 25th anniversary of his election, February 20, 1903; Papal Teachings: The Church, Benedictine Monks of Solesmes, St. Paul Editions, Boston, 1962, par. 653)

> *"The Saviour Himself is the door of the sheepfold: 'I am the door of the sheep.' Into this fold of Jesus Christ, no man may enter unless he be led by the Sovereign Pontiff; and only if they be united to him can men be saved, for the Roman Pontiff is the Vicar of Christ and His personal representative on earth."* (Pope John XXIII in his homily to the Bishops and faithful assisting at his coronation on November 4, 1958)

So the leader of the RCC that encompasses elements of nearly every single religion is the replacement for Christ here on this earth. He can offer salvation, forgive sins, and has absolute unquestionable authority. Under his authority, idolatry is not really such a big deal now. In fact, the RCC rewrote the ten commandments.

1. "I am the Lord thy God, thou shalt not have any strange gods before me."
2. "Thou shalt not take the name of the Lord thy God in vain."
3. "Remember to keep holy the Sabbath day."
4. "Honor thy father and mother."
5. "Thou shalt not kill."
6. "Thou shalt not commit adultery."
7. "Thou shalt not steal."

8. "Thou shalt not bear false witness against thy neighbor."
9. "Thou shalt not covet thy neighbor's wife."
10. "Thou shalt not covet thy neighbor's goods."

Notice something missing here?

> **Exodus 20:4-6 "You shall not make for yourself a carved image—any likeness of anything that is in heaven above, or that is in the earth beneath, or that is in the water under the earth; 5 you shall not bow down to them nor serve them. For I, the Lord your God, am a jealous God, visiting the iniquity of the fathers upon the children to the third and fourth generations of those who hate Me, 6 but showing mercy to thousands, to those who love Me and keep My commandments."**

This was the second commandment given right after "You shall have no other gods before me." but I guess all the idolatry that God absolutely hated and severely judged in the Old Testament is no big deal now, because the replacement (Vicar of) Christ said it's okay to have idols now. Oh, and speaking of idols, it would seem Mary has taken over some interesting responsibilities as well.

> "The foundation of all our confidence is found in the Blessed Virgin Mary. God has committed to her the treasury of all good things, in order that everyone may know that through her are obtained every hope, every grace, and all salvation. For this is His will: That we obtain everything through Mary." (Pope Pius IX)

> "In fact, by being assumed into heaven she has not laid aside the office of salvation but by the manifold intercession she continues to obtain for us the grace of eternal salvation." (John Paul II, Dives in Misericordia, 1980, quoting Lumen Gentium)

But hey, why not? Apparently Mary was every bit as perfect as Christ. I found this quote in the page of an old Catechism that my grandma had from years ago. I cannot seem to find this exact quote, but I have the picture to prove it was in her Catechism.

> *p.28 - "Who was born without original sin?*
>   *The Blessed Virgin Mary, the Mother of God, was conceived and*
> *born, lived and died without any stain of sin.*

So according to the RCC, Mary was also immaculately conceived herself by her mother St. Anne, in spite of not one single prophecy or mention in the entire Bible stating that there would be any immaculate inception except for Christ's. Further, despite the Bible blatantly stating that Jesus had physical brothers multiple times, they claim she was a virgin from birth until death. In other words, Catholicism claims she was every bit as perfect and sinless as Christ. No wonder they claim we can receive salvation from her. So I guess Christ can take a load off. After all, between the Pope and Mary, they've got pretty much everything covered. The pope and his priests can forgive sins whether God likes it or not.

> "And God himself is obliged to abide by the judgment of his priest and either not to pardon or to pardon, according as they refuse to give absolution, provided the penitent is capable of it." (Liguori, «Duties and Dignities of the Priest», p.27)

> "This judicial authority will even include the power to forgive sin." (The Catholic Encyclopaedia Vol xii, article 'Pope' pg 265)

The pope can rewrite the Bible however he sees fit and issue laws.

> "The Pope is of great authority and power that he can modify, explain, or interpret even divine laws... The Pope can modify divine law, since his power is not of man, but of God, and he acts as vicegerent of God

upon earth." (Lucius Ferraris, Prompta Ribliotheca, Papa, art. 2, translated)

"The belief in the Bible as the sole source of faith is unhistorical, illogical, fatal to the virtue of faith, and destructive of unity." (The Catholic Encyclopedia, Volume XIII, Protestantism, Section III A - Sola Scriptura ("Bible Alone"), Nihil Obstat, February 1, 1912 by Remy Lafort, D.D., Censor, Imprimatur. +John Cardinal Farley, Archbishop of New York)

So I guess for salvation, forgiveness of sins, instruction on how to live, and anything else we can really think of, we have the Pope to direct us. In fact, we don't even need the Bible anymore, as we can just throw it out and listen to the Pope. After all, to base your theology off of the Bible is apparently unhistorical, illogical, and destructive to faith and unity. I hope you are seeing what I am seeing dear reader.

The RCC has changed times, with the advent of the Gregorian Calendar which we will look at in a bit, that was instituted by Pope Gregory XIII. They have changed laws. They have replaced Christ completely. They have embraced all things pagan, and in the world today are actively setting up temples or houses of worship, that function for Catholics, Jews, Muslims, Buddhists, and many others. Very recently, the Vatican hosted the "Amazonian Synod" where there are multiple pictures and video footage of natives and guests from the Vatican bowing down to a bare breasted pregnant fertility goddess idol in a big circle. Pope Francis even blessed this idol though the Vatican has tried to deny it in spite of a myriad of physical evidence and eye witnesses.

Another massive and deep study in itself is this: nearly every single government in the world today is controlled by members of a secret society known as the Free Masons. This whole one world kingdom, global agenda is being directly engineered by members of the Free Masons at the highest levels. Free Masonry is actually a branch off of a much older group known as the Jesuits, and the Jesuits, contrary to what is commonly taught, were a hidden arm of the Roman Catholic Church. In fact, Pope Francis who currently sits in the Vatican is a Jesuit himself. This is an excerpt from the "Extreme Oath and Induction of the Society of Jesus (Jesuits)"

> *"I do further promise and declare that I will have no opinion or will of my own but will unhesitatingly obey each and every command that I may receive from my superiors in the militia of the Pope. (...) I will rage a relentless war, secretly and openly against all heretics (...) I will spare neither age nor sex (...) I will rip up the stomachs and wombs of their women, and crush their infants' heads against the walls in order to annihilate their execrable race. I will secretly use the poisonous cup, the strangulation cord (...) either in public or private, as I at any time may be directed to do so by any agents of the Pope or superior of The Brotherhood of the Holy Father of The Society of Jesus."*

Look this stuff up for yourself. I could not make it up even if I wanted to. Search everything I have presented to you on the RCC and see if the quotes, imagery, activities, and assertions are not accurate. All of this ends up leading to a very simple conclusion: the Roman Catholic Church is one of the most blasphemous and idolatrous organizations to ever exist in the world. Now I need to make mention, I do not hate Catholics at all. There are many people who I care about very much, relatives, coworkers, and friends who are still stuck in Catholicism. They have no idea about the true nature of the RCC. They were raised in it, and have been told just what they needed to hear to be fooled into thinking it was somehow good. I know many Catholics with the best of intentions, who genuinely want to walk with God. This is not an attack on Catholics, but an exposé on the Roman Catholic Church that has pulled the wool over the eyes of Catholics. Again, my heart isn't to attack anyone, but merely to warn, to heal, to help. If someone you loved was in a burning building wouldn't you try to pull them out? Ultimately, I cannot pull anyone from this building set on fire by Hell, but I can call out to them to come out of it. If you are a Catholic, the biggest piece of advice I can give you is the same advice I give to anyone: Humble yourself, and seek out the truth. Question, test, reason, research, find the truth at any cost and then walk in it.

Now, we aren't even really half way through this book, and many of you are probably asking what this all has to do with you? My general demographic of people I wanted to get this book to was primarily Christians, and outside of Catholics, most Christians are not part of the RCC. Most Christians or "protestants" I talk to already know a little about the RCC, and understand that it is not wise to be a part of it, so what does all of this talk about the RCC have to do with protestants? Keep reading and find out.

6

All Roads...

Baptist, Lutheran, Methodist, Presbyterian, Pentecostal, Non Denomina-tional, all of these, and thousands more, represent different denominations within Christianity. Each of these, and others, have different doctrines, and different authority structures. They differ on many things. Some believe in the spiritual gifts, some do not. Some hail from specific teachers, some do not. Within Christianity, there is a vast spectrum of beliefs. In spite of these differences, there are actually many similarities when looking between different denominations. This is because the vast majority of modern Christianity sprouted from the same three sources; protestants, separatists, and reformationists. These three groups comprise the foundation for nearly all of the denominations today with a few exceptions.

Now what does this have to do with Catholicism? To understand we need to back up quite a far ways. Constantine established the RCC around 300 B.C. The years ensuing saw the rise of the Roman Catholic Church, and the stamping out of any sort of follower of Christ who was not willing to come under their banner. True Christianity was essentially swallowed up completely within a few hundred years as the RCC grew exponentially thanks to their willingness to adopt paganism, and the military strength of Rome. Eventually however, we know that Rome fell. The period of time thereafter were known as the "dark ages" and generally refer to the period between 500 and 1500 AD. In the midst of this space of time rose the "Holy

Roman Empire" which became a great kingdom in the earth. The official beginning of this empire was in 800 A.D and it lasted all the way until 1806 A.D..

In the early years of the Holy Roman Empire, nearly every nation was beholden to the Roman Catholic Church, and cardinals and popes were given authority often equal to kings. In the years prior to this period as I stated earlier, the RCC had just about stamped out all signs of Christianity besides it's own personal brand of it, and this totalitarian control continued in the Holy Roman Empire. During this time a huge amount of Bibles were confiscated and burned, and anyone caught reading the Bible was killed. The RCC translated the Bible into Latin, which became the official language that was used by the RCC and continues to be so until this day. The reason for this shift in language was because Latin was a dead language by around the year 600 AD. By translating the Bible into the dead language of Latin, and destroying any Bible that wasn't in Latin, Catholicism ended up essentially preventing anyone from reading the Bible for themselves. During this time the people were wholly dependent upon the RCC to teach them scripture. Well, as always, as time went on, they began to lose their grasp on total scriptural control, and Bibles began to resurface in other languages.

In the years leading up to the 1500s, there was a massive return of Bibles as people began to find and translate Bibles for themselves, and people were once again able to read the scriptures for themselves. This spelled trouble for the RCC however, because people began to realize that what the RCC was doing, was not at all what scripture taught. Men began to form together in order to share the truth, and call people out of Catholicism. Between about 1400 and 1650, leaders began to arise and groups began to form and operate with three in particular becoming prominent. The names of each of these reveal at a glance what they were all about. We have the Protestants who protested against the RCC, we have the Separatists, who decided to separate from the RCC, and we have the Reformationists who decided to try and reform the RCC. It was during this general time period when men like John Calvin, Martin Luther, John Wycliffe, William

Tyndale and others began to arise. These men began teaching truth, and God used them in a mighty way to kick start the Church as a separate and independent entity from the RCC. This event known as the Protestant Reformation formed the foundation for modern Christianity.

Now, these men were great men, and God did use them in a mighty way, but I want to remind you that they were merely men. Men are fallible, and make mistakes. Men cannot really understand everything pertinent to the world around them because there is far too much information for even the most intelligent brain to hold. These men had a tremendous influence and effect on the church, and I do not want to diminish anything they did, as I believe they did exactly as they were directed to. I would suggest however, that while they broke free of much of the influence of the RCC, they didn't break free from all of it. There is an old saying that says you can take an animal out of the wild, but you can't take the wild out of the animal. In much the same way, though these men walked out of Roman Catholicism, they still carried with them Catholic elements that they didn't even realize were Catholic. The old saying goes "all roads lead to Rome". This same idea is present within modern Christian denominations.

The rest of this section goes through and examines some of these practices. We already saw in previous chapters that God hates idolatry, and does not want to be worshiped in a manner that is pagan. We also saw that paganism all hails back directly to Satan. We know and understand that paganism is not something that we should have in our lives at all, and yet as you will see, there is an alarming amount of paganism still in Christianity today, hiding in plain sight. Some of these things will be easy to let go of and put out of our lives. Other things, such as the next chapter, I'm still not sure what to do with. Nonetheless, I will begin to expose for you the idolatry likely hiding in your own life in order to help you to purify yourself as the day of Christ's return approaches.

7

Times and Seasons

One of the first things we will look at is the calendar. Now as I mentioned in the previous chapter, this will be a tricky one. The reason for this, is this information is difficult to know what to do with. Some of the other topics we will look through are easy to see the problem, as well as the solution. This chapter however presents a problem, without a foreseeable solution. Nevertheless, this chapter sets up much of what we will examine in the rest of this section so it's necessary to understand this information.

Now regarding the calendar, we need to understand that mankind has used multiple different types of calendars over the centuries. Interestingly, in the vast majority of cultures, this all tied directly into the worship of the sun, moon, and stars. It is nearly impossible to have an accurate layout of many of the calendars that the ancients used, as most of these things were lost. If you were to write down all the important things you wanted the next generation to know, you likely wouldn't write down anything pertaining to the calendar, as it's something we take for granted will just kind of be there. It's not something we really think about even. Most haven't stopped to think about the nature of the calendar we use, where the days of the week came from or how the months were named.

Now, God gave us all the building pieces for a calendar, some of which is accounted in Genesis.

> *Genesis 1:14 Then God said, "Let there be lights in the firmament*
> *of the heavens to divide the day from the night; and let them be*
> *for signs and seasons, and for days and years;"*

As you read through Genesis you also see that God established what we commonly call a week. It is a grouping of 7 days that ends up being a repeating pattern that feeds into all the other repeating patterns such as months and years. Israel had a calendar in place, but there is much debate about whether or not it has survived. The Bible doesn't give us a whole lot of details surrounding the specific calendar that Israel had, but we know that they too had things broken up into months.

> *Haggai 2:1 In the seventh month, on the twenty-first of the*
> *month, the word of the Lord came by Haggai the prophet,*
> *saying:*

So this structure of weeks and months and years is something that God Himself set up for us and pertains to the cycles of the sun, and the moon that He gave for times and seasons. We also know that the idea of four seasons was directly given by God as well.

> *Genesis 8:22 "While the earth remains, seedtime and harvest,*
> *cold and heat, winter and summer, and day and night shall not*
> *cease."*

So we see there is a seedtime season (spring), a harvest season (fall), a cold season (winter), and a heat season (summer). All of these things were given by God, and are good, as they give us a structure to our lives. The trouble comes however, when we look at the cultures who worshiped the sun instead of the Creator of it.

The pagans created something called the solar wheel. The solar wheel was an eight pronged wheel that broke up what they found to be the cycles pertaining to the sun. In particular, there were four prominent spires, and four less prominent spires. The four prominent spires were the two equinoxes, and the two solstices. The equinox pertains to when the day and night are of equal length which occurs twice throughout the year. Remember according to pagan beliefs, the sun pertained to the male aspect, and the moon pertained to the female aspect. The sun and moon being in equilibrium meant it was a time of fertility. These equinoxes took place in the spring and fall, which of course pertained to planting and harvest. They attributed this not only to crops however, but also to sexual planting and harvesting in the form of inception and child birth. Because of this, spring in particular is heavily associated with fertility. Remember that pagans worship nature alongside their false gods. Basically, they worship anything but the One True God. Naturally these equinoxes were a big deal to them.

Beyond the equinoxes, they also had two solstices. The summer solstice was when the longest day and shortest night of the year occurred, and the winter solstice was the inverse, having the shortest day and longest night. These two days they attributed as the days that their sun gods, patterned after Nimrod and Tammuz, the death and rebirth of the sun god, to take place. These of course took place in the summer and the winter. This gave us the four primary spokes of the wheel pertaining to the seasons, and their significance. The other spokes of the wheel were given to break up the periods of time in between the equinoxes and solstices. Each of these spokes on the wheel were marked with a celebration and they were associated with different gods depending upon the culture. These seasons in wicca, satanism, and general neo-paganism are as follows.

1. Ostara - Spring Equinox
2. Beltane
3. Litha - Summer Solstice
4. Luchnassad
5. Mabon - Fall Equinox
6. Samhain
7. Yule - Winter Solstice

8. Imbolc

Then the whole cycle repeats itself. As you may have noticed, some of the names of these time periods are listed in the chapter headings. There is a very good reason for this, and you will learn why shortly. For now however, I merely wanted to introduce you to this pagan calendar to set the stage for things we will learn in a bit.

Moving on, I want to examine the calendar we are currently on, with the days, months, and years. Now most people never even stop to think about the days of the week or the months, or anything regarding it. However, it is an institution that is a foundation to our lives. Many know that the vast majority of the world is under the same calendar commonly called the modern civil calendar. What few realize is that the calendar we have today had it's origin in ancient Rome and has RCC finger prints all over it.

The calendar that set the foundation for our modern calendar came from Greece. This calendar was commonly known simply as the Greek calendar. The Greek calendar, just like their culture, completely revolved around their pantheon of gods. All of their months were named after their gods. They had months for Mars, Juno, Aphrodite, Maia, Janus, Lupus, and more. Each one of these months was dedicated to the deity it was named for, and had a celebration to honor the corresponding god or goddess of the month.

Now, when Rome conquered Greece, they adopted many things from their culture, one of which, was their calendar. This calendar didn't remain as it was for long though. Roman politics were as interesting and unpredictable back then as they are in the modern day. During the transitionary period of the calendar, an amusing trend began to happen. The Roman rulers would alter the calendar and shift the days for personal advantage, to lengthen their rule, or cut short the rule of someone who opposed them. I guess politics haven't changed much, and bending the rules for personal advantage was just as prevalent then as it is now. Anyways, Julius Caesar decided he needed to put an end to the ever changing calendar, and put in place the Julian Calendar on January 1st, 45 BC. This calendar became the most prominent calendar in use for most of Europe, the territories of Rome, and most of the civilized world.

This calendar stayed in place for a very long time, all the way up until 1582 in fact. Remember that in around 800 A.D. the Holy Roman Empire sprouted up and by 962 A.D. it was completely solidified. For many years the Holy Roman Empire was happy to use the calendar they had taken with them from Rome. Eventually however, Pope Gregory XIII decided that they needed to make adjustments to the calendar, and in 1852 he put forth the Gregorian calendar named after himself. This calendar, due to the absolute authority of the RCC at that time quickly became the worldwide standard and is still in use until this day.

Now, remember that the pagan Roman calendar revolved around pagan gods and paid homage to them by naming the months after them. Now that the Pope put forth a new calendar, he was able to get rid of all the idolatry and change the months to reflect Christianity right? Nope. The all embracing (Catholic) church, decided to adopt even more pagan gods into the calendar and continued to honor pagan gods, and long dead Roman emperors. Each of our months has a name that means something. I will walk you through them now.

We have January, being derived from Janus the god of beginnings. We have February derived from Dies Februatus associated with the wolf god Lupus. We have March derived from Mars the god of war. We have April derived from the word Aprilis which means "to open" and was associated with Aphrodite, the fertility goddess, and signified not only the opening of the flowers but also of the womb. We have May derived from Maia, the goddess of growth. We have June derived from Juno, the goddess referred to as the wife of Jupiter, who was also called the "queen of heaven". Thereafter we break away from the pagan gods and have July, which was named after Julius Caesar, and August, named after Augustine. Following these two we have months named after numbers. The numbers indicate what month they traditionally were in the original 10 month Roman calendar. September derived from Septem, meaning 7, October, derived from Octo, meaning 8, November, derived from Novem, meaning

9th, and December derived from Decem, meaning 10.

So, Pope Gregory instituted a calendar that honors a combination of pagan Roman gods, as well as Emperors of Rome. He didn't stop there though, no, he also instituted new names for the days of the week as well. Surely these must reflect Christianity right? Nope. Allow me to explain the days of the week for you.

We begin our week with the day given the most prominent position at the beginning of the week, Sunday. Sunday comes from the Greek heméra helíou which was a day that honors Sol Invictus, the official sun god of Rome who was another form of the god Jupiter. Jupiter was the Roman name for Zeus. Sol Invictus was known as the "Unconquered sun". This name was translated into Latin as Dies Solis, which means, "day of the sun". Also in Latin, this day has a secondary name for it, which is Dies Dominica, which means "day of the Lord". We will look at this more thoroughly soon, but yes, the RCC took the day that belonged to the sun god Sol Invictus (Zeus), renamed it either "The Lord's Day (Dies Dominica)" or Day of the Sun (Dies Solis) which when brought into the English is Sunday. Here is a lovely little quote for you taken directly from the official Vatican website, vatican.va entry #1166.

> *The Lord's day, the day of Resurrection, the day of Christians, is our day. It is called the Lord's day because on it the Lord rose victorious to the Father. If pagans call it the "day of the sun," we willingly agree, for today the light of the world is raised, today is revealed the sun of justice with healing in his rays.* [6]

Remember Apollo, the god of light, the sun, justice, and healing? Yeah… Again, we will look at this more in depth later on, but for the moment, suffice it to say there are some things about Sunday that are concerning.

Moving on we have Monday. Monday comes directly after Sunday and enjoys the second most prominent position in the week, as well as being squeezed in right next to Sunday. Monday came from the Anglo Saxon word mōnandæg, which was put into Latin as Dies Lunae, which means "day of the moon". Moon day was later shortened in modern English to Monday. Moon day was a day to honor and celebrate the moon.

Next is Tuesday. Tuesday comes from the Latin, Dies Martis. This one at first glance seems totally different right? Allow me to explain. Dies Martis means "day of Mars". Mars was the Roman god of war and law. Mars was later adopted by the vikings and renamed Tyr, or Tiw. When dies Martis was brought into the European territories (where the vikings were) it was translated into Old English as Tiwesdæg. This later became Tuesday when brought to modern English.

Wednesday is derived from the Old English Wōdnesdæg. Wōdnesdæg as English evolved became Wednesdei, and finally Wednesday. Wōdnesdæg translates into "day of Woden". Woden was the Old English spelling for the Norse God Odin. We already covered who Odin was, but it is worth mentioning that just as the vikings adopted Mars and renamed him Tyr, it is very likely that Odin was derived from the Greek god Zeus.

Thursday is taken from the Old English þūnresdæg, which later become Thuresday and finally becoming Thursday. Thursday meant "Thor's Day". Thor as we already covered was the son of Odin, and the god of thunder and the sky.

Friday came from the Old English Frīgedæġ, which eventually evolved into Friday. Frīgedæġ is translated as "day of Frige (frigg)". The day of Frigg was of course a day to honor the goddess Frigg. Frigg is the wife of Odin, and the goddess of wisdom and foresight and the sky.

Lastly we have Saturday. Saturday is from the Latin, Dies Saturni, or "day of Saturn". Saturn was the god of agriculture, wealth, and liberation. Saturn was derived from the Greek god Cronus.

So, the Roman Catholic Pope Gregory XIII, put forth days of a week that honor

- Sol Invictus, god of the sun (Sunday) (The Lord's Day)
- The moon (Monday)
- Mars, the god of war (Tuesday)
- Odin, the god of death, magic and wisdom (Wednesday)

- Thor, the god of thunder (Thursday)
- Frigg, the goddess of wisdom and the sky (Friday)
- Saturn, the god of agriculture and wealth (Saturday)

So my question is, how is this even remotely Christian in any way, shape, or form? Meanwhile, in Exodus…

> **Exodus 23:13** *"And in all that I have said to you, be circumspect and make no mention of the name of other gods, nor let it be heard from your mouth."*

Thanks to the RCC, we now have the whole world daily speaking the names of pagan gods and unknowingly dedicating days and months to them. Now, as I said earlier in this chapter, what do we do with this? Some of the things in this book aim to inspire action and help us rid ourselves of idolatry lurking in our lives. It's kind of the whole point of this book, to call the body of Christ away from idolatry, and get us ready for the coming of our Messiah. This subject however just kind of ends on a frustrating note. It is important because it helps to set up the rest of of this section, but outside of that, what do we do with this information? Well, keep it in mind I suppose. We really are not in a position to be able to just stop using the calendar we are on, at least as long as we a part of society. Our jobs, our schools, our friends, our families, and pretty much everything in our lives runs on this system, and so to try to just stop using it would be pretty much impossible. I suppose it makes a good case against Catholicism if you have the opportunity to share it with a Catholic, but that's really about it.

We are going to move into more applicable territory as we go into the next chapter, but I pray that this information is relevant to you, dear reader, and helps you to have a clearer picture of the world around you.

8

Ostara

So, now we get into more applicable territory. Ostara, if you recall is one of the nodes on the pagan sun wheel, pertaining to the spring equinox. As I have already explained briefly, the spring equinox in paganism represents equilibrium and balance between the male aspect of the sun, and the female aspect of the moon. This is a time where flowers and vegetation are coming out of the winter time, and the animals begin to reappear. This is a time of planting and new life and as I mentioned, is heavily associated with fertility. So what does this have to do with Christianity? Well, everything I'm afraid. You see, Christians celebrate a holiday in this portion of the time wheel each year that directly worships the various fertility goddesses without even knowing it. This holiday I'm afraid, is Easter.

Now, for many of you, I know very well this is going to be a difficult study, and hard for many to hear, but Easter truly has nothing to do with the resurrection of Christ, and I can prove it. Everything about this holiday, from the time it takes place, to the customs kept on the day, to the themes, and even the name of the holiday itself, are all pagan, and directly bring glory to the pagan fertility goddess we see running throughout every pagan culture. I guess to start with the easiest part of this, you may notice the name of the holiday, Easter. This name is not a random combination of letters that mean "Jesus rose from the grave". It is actually a name, just spelled ever so slightly different. This name is Eastre, also known as Eostre, or Ostara. Yep, this portion of the solar wheel is specifically named after this goddess. Ostara is a Germanic goddess and is the goddess of spring, resurrection, and fertility. Here are a few excerpts from a website called journeyingtothegoddess about this goddess.

"Ostara's themes are fertility and rebirth. Her symbols are eggs. The Teutonic Goddess Ostara presides over personal renewal, fertility and fruitfulness. Now that spring is here, it's a good time to think about renewal in your own life. Ostara represents spring's life force and earth's renewal. Depicted as lovely as the season itself, in earlier writings She was also the Goddess of dawn, a time of new beginnings (spring being the figurative dawn of the year). One of Ostara's name variations, Esotara, slowly evolved into the modern name for this holiday, Easter.

The Goddess Ostara, or Eostre, is the Anglo-Saxon Goddess of Spring, the East, Resurrection, and Rebirth, is also the Maiden aspect of the Three-fold Goddess. She gave Her name to the Christian festival of Easter (which is an older Pagan festival appropriated by the Church), whose timing is still dictated by the Moon. Modern Pagans celebrate Her festival on the Vernal Equinox, usually around March 21, the first day of Spring.

As Ostara is Goddess of the Dawn, we can understand why sunrise services have always been an important aspect of the spring resurrection/rebirth observances of other cultures.

Eggs and rabbits are sacred to Her as is the full moon [though there is no historical record of this], since the ancients saw in its markings the image of a rabbit or the hare. Pagan Anglo-Saxons made offerings of colored eggs to Her at the Vernal Equinox. They placed them at graves especially, probably as a charm of rebirth. (Egyptians and Greeks were also known to place eggs at gravesites). The Goddess of Fertility was also the Goddess of Grain, so offerings of bread and cakes were also made to Her. Rabbits are sacred to Ostara, especially white rabbits, and She was said to be able to take the form of a rabbit.

Ostara, the Goddess of Dawn (Saxon), who was responsible for bringing spring each year, was feeling guilty about arriving so late. To make matters worse, She arrived to find a pitiful little bird who lay dying, his wings frozen by the snow. Lovingly, Ostara cradled the shivering creature and saved his life. Legend has it that She then made him Her pet or, in the X-rated versions, Her lover. Filled with compassion for him since he could no longer fly because of his frost-damaged wings, the Goddess Ostara turned him into a rabbit, a snow hare, and gave him the name Lepus. She also gave him the gift of being able to run with astonishing speed so he could easily evade all the hunters. To honor his earlier form as a bird, She also gave him the ability to lay eggs (in all the colors of the rainbow, no less), but he was only allowed to lay eggs on one day out of each year. [7]

Now this is only one website, but there are dozens and dozens of others just like it. The name of the holiday, the imagery of the Easter bunny bringing eggs, the dying of the eggs, the sunrise service, all of it pertains directly to Ostara, the fertility goddess. Even the theme of resurrection from the dead has to do with this goddess. If you look even deeper, you may recall a few chapters back when I talked about the myth surrounding Semiramis, that she came down from the heavens in an egg, and came out as a rabbit. This too directly pertains to the Easter bunny and the egg hunts.

Ostara, Ishtar, Semiramis, Asherah, all of these goddess are the same goddess, just recycled and altered over the ages. In fact, some pagans even admit that these goddesses are all the same. This is a quote from a website that is rather disturbing, and though I hate to have to reference sites like these, they do an excellent job of stating what I am trying to show you. This quote is from joyofsatan.org

"Easter" was stolen from Astaroth. Originally known as "Ashtar." This holiday coincides with the Vernal Equinox of spring when day and night are of equal length. Known as "Eastre" to the Anglo-Saxons. As the Goddess of fertility, she was associated with rabbits and eggs. The Christians stole this holiday and twisted its meaning. Other names include: Easter, Eastre, Eos, Eostre, Ester, Estrus, (Estrus is when an animal goes into heat; mating season) Oestrus, Oistros, and Ostara. [8]

Here are a couple more quotes from a different website called learnreligions.com

In many cultures and society, the egg is considered the perfect magical symbol. It is, after all, representative of new life. In fact, it is the life cycle personified. While many of us take note of eggs around springtime, because the Ostara season is chock full of them, it's important to consider that eggs feature prominently in folklore and legend all year long.

In some legends, eggs, as a fertility symbol, are associated with that other symbol of fertility, the rabbit. [9]

The Festival of Isis was held in ancient Egypt as a celebration of spring and rebirth. Isis features prominently in the story of the resurrection of her lover, Osiris. Although Isis' major festival was held in the fall, folklorist Sir James Frazer says in The Golden Bough that "We are told that the Egyptians held a festival of Isis at the time when the Nile began to rise... the goddess was then mourning for the lost Osiris, and the tears which dropped from her eyes swelled the impetuous tide of the river." [10]

One last quote on Ostara from huffpost.com

Ostara, or Eostra, is an Anglo-Saxon goddess who represents dawn. As a spring goddess she oversees the budding plants and burgeoning

fertility of the earth. The Horned God, sometimes envisioned as the god Pan, symbolizes the festive enjoyment of nature through hunting and dancing.

Similar to those observed at Easter, symbols for Ostara include eggs, rabbits, flowers and seeds. Many neopagans believe these symbols to represent the fecundity of spring and incorporate them into rituals, altars and celebratory feasts. [11]

Isis, Ostara, Semiramis, Ashteroth, these are all the same goddess. Let's see how God felt about His people worshiping this goddess.

Judges 2:11-15 Then the children of Israel did evil in the sight of the Lord, and served the Baals; 12 and they forsook the Lord God of their fathers, who had brought them out of the land of Egypt; and they followed other gods from among the gods of the people who were all around them, and they bowed down to them; and they provoked the Lord to anger. 13 They forsook the Lord and served Baal and the Ashtoreths. 14 And the anger of the Lord was hot against Israel. So He delivered them into the hands of plunderers who despoiled them; and He sold them into the hands of their enemies all around, so that they could no longer stand before their enemies. 15 Wherever they went out, the hand of the Lord was against them for calamity, as the Lord had said, and as the Lord had sworn to them. And they were greatly distressed.

Judges 10:6-7 Then the children of Israel again did evil in the sight of the Lord, and served the Baals and the Ashtoreths, the gods of Syria, the gods of Sidon, the gods of Moab, the gods of the people of Ammon, and the gods of the Philistines; and they forsook the Lord and did not serve Him. 7 So the anger of the Lord was hot against Israel; and He sold them into the hands of the Philistines and into the hands of the people of Ammon.

2 Kings 23:13 Then the king defiled the high places that were east of Jerusalem, which were on the south of the Mount of Corruption, which <u>Solomon king of Israel had built for Ashtoreth the abomination</u> of the Sidonians, for Chemosh the abomination of the Moabites, and for Milcom the abomination of the people of Ammon.

1 Kings 11:33-35 because <u>they have forsaken Me, and worshiped Ashtoreth the goddess</u> of the Sidonians, Chemosh the god of the Moabites, and Milcom the god of the people of Ammon, <u>and have not walked in My ways</u> to do what is right in My eyes and keep My statutes and My judgments, <u>as did his father David</u>. 34 However I will not take the whole kingdom out of his hand, because I have made him ruler all the days of his life for the sake of My servant David, whom I chose because he kept My commandments and My statutes. 35 <u>But I will take the kingdom out of his son's hand</u> and give it to you—ten tribes.

So God harshly judged His people for worshiping Ashtoreth, He called her an abomination, and took 10/12 of the kingdom of Israel out of Solomon's hand for building a temple to her. Do you really think it's an okay thing for Christians today to do? Remember, our God does not change. The way He felt about it then is the way He feels about it today, regardless of what the Pope claims.

Now you may be asking, didn't Jesus die on Good Friday, and rise from the grave on Easter Sunday? Doesn't it still pertain to Christ? Well, yes and no. First of all, can you please explain to me, how Friday afternoon to Sunday morning is three days and three nights?

Matthew 12:40 For as Jonah was three days and three nights in the belly of the great fish, so will the Son of Man be three days and three nights in the heart of the earth.

We know that it was about the 3:00 P.M. when Christ died so we can't really count that as a day, because most of the day was over, so this would've put Sunday at 2 days later. Even if we want to claim that Friday counted, and it was three days, we are still left with the problem of 3 nights. Friday night would've been 1, Saturday night would've been 2, and then Sunday morning is when He allegedly rose from the grave, so what happened to the third night? The Good Friday, Resurrection Sunday bit, doesn't even add up. Furthermore, as I will prove to you later on, Christ didn't even rise again on Sunday. In other words, Easter is a sad attempt at a Christian paint job, over a pagan fertility goddess festival that celebrated the rebirth of spring.

A few more things I wanted to mention to you, first of all, Lent, the 40 days leading up to Easter, is nothing more than imitating Semiramis mourning for Tammuz. This was something I had written earlier in the book that I want to bring to your remembrance.

> *Some years after that, Tammuz, like his father, was killed by a wild boar while hunting. Semiramis mourned his death for 40 days at which point Tammuz was deified as the rising sun.*

So for 40 days, leading up to Tammuz being resurrected and deified as the god of the rising sun, Semiramis mourned for the death of Tammuz at the hands of a wild boar. Notice that the official Easter Dinner meal is an Easter Ham. I guess that boar had it coming for killing poor Tammuz so why not commemorate the whole event by eating it every year? I also showed this Bible verse earlier, but it bears repeating again.

> **Ezekiel 8:13-16 And He said to me, "Turn again, and you will see greater abominations that they are doing." 14 So He brought me to the door of the north gate of the Lord's house; and to my dismay, women were sitting there weeping for Tammuz. 15 Then He said to me, "Have you seen this, O son of man? Turn again, you will see greater abominations than these." 16 So He**

brought me into the inner court of the Lord's house; and there, at the door of the temple of the Lord, between the porch and the altar, were about twenty-five men with their backs toward the temple of the Lord and their faces toward the east, <u>and they were worshiping the sun toward the east.</u>

God was absolutely appalled at what He saw Israel doing, in that they were weeping for Tammuz, and worshiping the rising sun toward the east in a sunrise service, and yet that is exactly what we are doing today with Lent and our sunrise services and Easter. There is nothing new under the sun, and just as the people of God fell into idolatry back then, they have once more fallen into it again. Keep in mind, in the book of Judges, each time God's people fell into idolatry, judgement came from God in order to turn them back to Him. Now, in the final hours of this age, as the end rapidly approaches, God's people have once again fallen into idolatry on the eve of the greatest judgement that will ever come upon the earth. This should very much scare you. What then can we do? Well, take a line from God's people.

1 Samuel 12:10 Then they cried out to the Lord, and said, 'We have sinned, because we have forsaken the Lord and served the Baals and Ashtoreths; but now deliver us from the hand of our enemies, and we will serve You.'

Thankfully, our God is forgiving, and gracious.

1 John 1:9 If we confess our sins, He is faithful and just to forgive us our sins and to cleanse us from all unrighteousness.

And once again, our God does not change, and He sent His servant Samuel to give His people this message.

1 Samuel 7:3 Then Samuel spoke to all the house of Israel, saying, "If you return to the Lord with all your hearts, then put away the foreign gods and the Ashtoreths from among you, and prepare your hearts for the Lord, and serve Him only; and He will deliver you from the hand of the Philistines."

Now, Easter is just the beginning I'm afraid. The chapter after this one shouldn't be quite as bad for most, but the chapter after that is probably one of the most shocking in this entire book. Nobody said this walk was easy, but, walk it we must. Let's move on.

9

Samhain

Given the previous chapter we looked into was named after a part of the pagan solar wheel and dealt with a modern holiday, you may have surmised that this chapter will follow the same pattern. This chapter will deal with another prominent holiday, Halloween. Now, many Christians have already separated from Halloween... kind of. When looking at Easter, it would be a bit difficult to tell from the surface that it was so pagan, Halloween on the other hand, is rather obvious. The general themes of darkness, death, and fear are not hard to spot. Further, we know that darkness, death, and fear are complete opposites of our God who is light, and life, and peace. What you may not know though, is the RCC is directly responsible for bringing this holiday to the modern times.

To start at the beginning, Halloween has it's origin as Samhain, pronounced sah-win. Samhain was a Celtic practice, but like so many other things, the all embracing church embraced these things as well. Samhain was the time of the year the pagans believed the "veil" separating the physical world from the spiritual world was at it's weakest. It also marked the year transitioning into the darkest parts of the year, as winter rapidly approached. Further, after the long summer and harvesting of the crops, the cattle and other animals would be brought in from their pastures, and many would be slaughtered to provide meat for the long winter. All of these things in combination, the closeness to the spirit world, the darkness looming, and slaughtering of animals was the perfect recipe for pagan sacrifices and rituals to their gods. Here is an excerpt from the Wikipedia page for Samhain.

Like Bealtaine, Samhain was seen as a liminal time, when the boundary between this world and the Otherworld could more easily be crossed. This meant the Aos Si, the 'spirits' or 'fairies', could more easily come into our world. Most scholars see the Aos Sí as remnants of the pagan gods and nature spirits. At Samhain, it was believed that the Aos Sí needed to be propitiated to ensure that the people and their livestock survived the winter. Offerings of food and drink were left outside for them. The souls of the dead were also thought to revisit their homes seeking hospitality. Feasts were had, at which the souls of dead kin were beckoned to attend and a place set at the table for them. Mumming and guising were part of the festival, and involved people going door-to-door in costume (or in disguise), often reciting verses in exchange for food. The costumes may have been a way of imitating, and disguising oneself from, the Aos Sí. Divination rituals and games were also a big part of the festival and often involved nuts and apples.
12

So, just off the top, we see the origins of dressing up, going door to door trick-or-treating, and even bobbing for apples and the like wrapped up nicely in Samhain. I have 2 more quotes about Halloween before I go into explaining how it came from Catholicism, but before I do, due to the nature of the source of the quotes, I need to explain something regarding Satanists. There are two primary veins of Satanism, theistic Satanism, and atheistic Satanism. Atheistic satanism is also known as LeVeyan Satanism, as this sect of Satanism was founded and popularized by Anton LeVey through the church of Satan. Theistic Satanism is much older, and much darker, as well as more difficult to find information on. Knowing this will make the quotes here, and some quotes later on, make more sense. The first quote is taken from churchofsatan.com regarding Halloween.

Question: Is Halloween important to Satanists?

Answer: We see this holiday as the night when the mundane folk try to reach down inside and touch the "darkness" which for Satanists is a daily mode of existence. Particularly in the United States, Halloween is a time for celebrating monster films, wearing costumes of a macabre nature, and evoking the thrill of "fun fear." Children (of all ages) can indulge their fantasies by donning costumes that allow for intense role-playing and the release of their "demonic cores" the parts of their personalities often hidden from their friends, co-workers and families.

Though there are traditions making this an occasion for recalling the dead, it has been popularized as a time to play with what historically were fears directed towards what were thought to be unquiet spirits of the departed. And the grand traditional question "Trick or treat?" has become a means for fulfilling an indulgence in sweets, without the need to resort to the optional coercion.

Satanists embrace what this holiday has become, and do not feel the need to be tied to ancient practices. This night, we smile at the amateur explorers of their own inner darkness, for we know that they enjoy their brief dip into the pool of the "shadow world." We encourage their tenebrous fantasies, the candied indulgence, and the wide-ranging evocation of our aesthetics (while tolerating some of the chintzy versions), even if it is but once a year. For the rest of the time, when those not of our meta-tribe shake their heads in wonder at us, we can point out that they may find some understanding by examining their own All Hallows Eve doings, but we generally find it simpler to just say: "Think of the Addams Family and you'll begin to see what we're about." [13]

So the church of Satan very much enjoys Halloween, and enjoys watching "mundane" people dabble in darkness and magic, and the children get in touch with their "demonic cores" If this all wasn't disturbing enough, let me share with you another excerpt from a website called thesun.co.uk

On Samhain, it was believed that the veil lifted between the worlds of the living and the dead, allowing spirits, demons and other mythical creatures such as faeries a chance to walk amongst us.

But the reality of Halloween through the eyes of the Celts and Druids is scarier than any horror film.

According to old documents, in its most primitive guise, Samhain would have featured many sacrifices to the Celtic gods of death, with both animals and humans thrown in to huge firepits as offerings.

People claimed the ancient Druids ate their first born children on Samhain, or collected the blood of their sacrificial humans in cauldrons and drank it.

The stories get gorier, claiming that hollowed out pumpkins and turnips would be filled with fat from previous sacrifices and lit.

It was the arrival of the Romans in 55 BC that signalled the start the end of Druid culture in the UK.

Julius Caesar even commented about the ancient Brits that in times of danger, "unless the life of a man be offered, the mind of immortal gods will not favour them." [14]

So, human sacrifices, the eating of children, and the drinking of blood, were fun Samhain activities for those who established it. Oh, and lest you think this is just some crazy article, here are a few more quotes for you from a website called av1611.org. Pay special attention to the places these quotes come from, as some are relatively reputable sources.

First-born sacrifices are mentioned in a poem in the Dindshenchas, which records that children were sacrificed each Samhain . . . (Rogers, Nicholas. Halloween: From Pagan Ritual to Party Night, p. 17)

Halloween. That was the eve of Samhain . . . firstborn children were sacrificed. . . Samhain eve was a night of dread and danger. (National Geographic. May 1977, pp. 625-626)

They [Druids] sacrificed victims by shooting them with arrows, impaling them on stakes, stabbing them, slitting their throats over cauldrons (and then drinking the blood). . . (Guiley, Rosemary Ellen. Harper's Encyclopedia of Mystical & Paranormal Experience, p. 167)

. . . since they are man-eaters as well as heavy eaters, and since, further, they count it an honourable thing, when their fathers die, to devour them, and openly to have intercourse, not only with the other women, but also with their mothers and sisters;. . . (Strabo, Geography) [15]

Sorry to get graphic on you dear reader, but yes, cannibalizing the dead, bleeding out victims to drink their blood, child sacrifice, and public incestuous orgies were common practices among the druids who invented this holiday. You may not see these things going on today, but believe it or not, they still do. There are many who have been saved out of witch covens, and occultic groups and secret societies who can personally attest to having witnessed and experienced these things. They are hidden from the public eye, but I assure you, they still go on. While Christians are getting their children ready in their costumes to go to their local churches to celebrate trunk or treat, there are pagans performing ritual orgies in preparation to brutally sacrifice children and eat their flesh and drink their blood.

This is some dark stuff to research, and I'm sorry to have to get that graphic, but it is absolutely disgusting to me that we have made this holiday into a fun little festival for children to enjoy when this holiday revolves around these absolutely monstrous pagan practices. If you do decide to research these things, I would advise you to do so with caution, but as I said, multiple people can attest to these exact practices, and worse, still happening today each Halloween. Meanwhile, while God sees these abominations going on, He also sees His own people joining in on the fun and acting as if it's just good innocent fun.

The people who went to the Coliseum in ancient Rome, and watched

Christians get slaughtered and torn apart by lions weren't technically doing these things themselves but wasn't showing up bad enough? If your children dressed up and had a fun little game of pretending to be Nero making human candles out of Christians, would you just laugh along at their innocent fun? It's only a game after all, and look, the kids are enjoying themselves, it's all in good fun. Ultimately, it is your decision on whether or not you will allow your children and yourself to participate in this monstrous holiday, but I pray that every single time you begin to dress your child in a costume, or head to that trunk or treat event, that you would remember all that you have read here.

Now, one last question to answer is this, what does the RCC have to do with this holiday? Well, you may have noticed that Halloween and Samhain have next to no similarity between them as far as name goes. This is because the name Halloween is actually derived from All Hallows Eve, which was the evening before All Hallows Day, or All Saints Day. Remember that November 1st, the day after October 31st, (Samhain) was considered to be the Pagan New Year, and during this time they would throw a "dumb supper" which was a feast to honor the dead, in which they would leave a spot open at the table with food for the dead to come and dine with them.

When the RCC began spreading it's message, it came across this pagan celebration of Samhain. Now as is seen over and over and over again from even Catholic sources, when missionaries went out into the world to spread their message, they were instructed to "Christianize" their traditions and practices. This involved, as we have seen, taking their gods, and practices, and slapping new labels over them. The missionaries encountered this day that the pagans celebrated honoring the dead, and the feasts they would throw for them, and decided to Christianize this holiday as well. This became All Saints Day, which was of course a day to honor all the Saints who had passed on. This became a major Catholic holiday. This is an excerpt from britannica.com

All Saints' Day, also called All Hallows' Day, Hallowmas, or Feast

of All Saints, in the Christian church, a day commemorating all the saints of the church, both known and unknown, who have attained heaven. It is celebrated on November 1 in the Western churches and on the first Sunday after Pentecost in the Eastern churches. In Roman Catholicism, the feast is usually a holy day of obligation. [16]

So the Catholics have a day with feasting for the dead, exactly like the pagans did and do. This day, and the evening before it, All Hallows Eve, are now practiced by Catholics around the world. In fact, there is a website you can check out called elizabethclareblog.com [17] that gives you 16 ways to celebrate All Saints day. It takes you through throwing an All Saints party, doing trunk-or-treat at your local perish, dressing up your children in costumes, carving pumpkins, trick or treating, eating special saint themed snacks, decorating the house, having a feast to honor the saints, and praying to the saints. These are an exact mirror of what the pagans would do, minus the orgies, cannibalism, and sacrifices. So yeah, the RCC also gave us Halloween, or at least popularized it.

This isn't the only Holiday that Catholicism allowed though, take Mexico for instance. More than 80% of Mexicans are professing Catholics, and Catholicism is deeply rooted in their culture. Instead of celebrating Halloween, the Catholic Mexicans celebrate Dia de los Muertos, or the Day of the Dead. Here are some excerpts from the Day of the Dead wikipedia page.

The Day of the Dead (Spanish: Día de Muertos) is a Mexican holiday celebrated throughout Mexico, in particular the Central and South regions, and by people of Mexican heritage elsewhere. The multi-day holiday focuses on gatherings of family and friends to pray for and remember friends and family members who have died, and help support their spiritual journey.

The holiday is sometimes called Día de los Muertos in Anglophone countries, a back-translation of its original name, Día de Muertos. It is particularly celebrated in Mexico where the day is a public holiday. Prior to Spanish colonization in the 16th century, the celebration took place at the beginning of summer. Gradually, it was associated with October 31, November 1, and November 2 to coincide with the Western Christianity triduum of Allhallowtide: All Saints' Eve, All Saints' Day, and All Souls' Day. Traditions connected with the holiday include building private altars called ofrendas, honoring the deceased using calaveras, aztec marigolds, and the favorite foods and beverages of the departed, and visiting graves with these as gifts. Visitors also leave possessions of the deceased at the graves.

Scholars trace the origins of the modern Mexican holiday to indigenous observances dating back hundreds of years and to an Aztec festival dedicated to the goddess Mictecacihuatl. The holiday has spread throughout the world, being absorbed into other deep traditions in honor of the dead. It has become a national symbol and as such is taught (for educational purposes) in the nation's schools. Many families celebrate a traditional "All Saints' Day" associated with the Catholic Church. [18]

So once again, the Catholic Church adopted the Mexican culture's pagan practices going back to the Aztecs worshiping their pagan goddess, and communing with their dead. So the RCC traveled to the Celtic pagans, and the Aztecan pagans, and decided instead of doing away with these practices, we will Christianize them. Meanwhile in Deuteronomy...

Deuteronomy 18:9-14 "When you come into the land which the Lord your God is giving you, you shall not learn to follow the abominations of those nations. 10 There shall not be found among you anyone who makes his son or his daughter pass through the fire, or one who practices witchcraft, or a sooth-sayer, or one who interprets omens, or a sorcerer, 11 or one who conjures spells, or a medium, or a spiritist, or one who calls up the dead. 12 For all who do these things are an abomination to the Lord, and because of these abominations the Lord your God drives them out from before you. 13 You shall be blameless before the Lord your God. 14 For these nations which you will dispossess listened to soothsayers and diviners; but as for you, the Lord your God has not appointed such for you.

Now, regarding all of these things, I know the intention of Christian parents are generally good. They want to do something fun for their children. Costumes and candy are fun for kids. They don't want them to feel left out. Many Christians use this time to witness to kids, as they hand out gospel tracts with the candy they give to the children. The thing is, good intentions do not mean good actions. Participating in evil pagan holidays as a way to witness is not the right way to witness. Does a man go get drunk at the bar to fit in with the other guys and begin preaching the gospel? Does a woman go strip at the club while preaching to the men there? When your actions contradict your message, you end up not only being an ineffective witness, you actually damage the name of God, and make Him look bad. We are supposed to be Holy, and set apart.

1 Peter 1:15-16 but as He who called you is holy, you also be holy in all your conduct, 16 because it is written, "Be holy, for I am holy."

Leviticus 20:6-7 'And the person who turns to mediums and familiar spirits, to prostitute himself with them, I will set My face against that person and cut him off from his people. 7 Consecrate yourselves therefore, and be holy, for I am the Lord your God.

How are we being Holy, and set apart, if we are doing the same stuff as the unbelieving, and even worse, following the traditions of pagans? What did Jesus and His disciples preach?

Matthew 3:1-2 In those days John the Baptist came preaching in the wilderness of Judea, 2 and saying, "Repent, for the kingdom of heaven is at hand!"

Matthew 4:17 From that time Jesus began to preach and to say, "Repent, for the kingdom of heaven is at hand."

Luke 5:32 "I have not come to call the righteous, but sinners, to repentance."

Proverbs 1:23 Turn at my rebuke; surely I will pour out my spirit on you; I will make my words known to you.

How can we call people to repent, which means to turn away from their sin, when we are openly and proudly doing the same things they do? The answer is, we can't, else we're hypocrites, saying one thing and doing another. As I have demonstrated through a myriad of verses, God does not want us participating in the ways of the world, and especially not the ways of pagans. Churches having trunk or treats are doing the exact thing Catholicism did. Taking the pagan traditions and slapping a Christian image on it. It is an abomination to mix the holy and profane. How can we call people to be set apart and holy, while doing the exact opposite by participating in paganism? This is blatant hypocrisy. Again, I know many churches and friends who have done these things with the best of intentions, and the purpose of all of this isn't to attack, but to help and to heal. The idea is to help one another become more sanctified as the end approaches. Think of how God views these practices. Ask yourself if your conduct is pleasing to God, and double check with the scriptures as you do. Now, we must move on, to the next holiday we need to examine.

10

Yule

This chapter, for many, will likely be the one of the most difficult ones in this entire book. Out of all the holidays that people love and enjoy, by far, the biggest holiday of the year is Yuletide, or as we commonly know it, Christmas. This past Christmas I saw posts all over my Facebook page saying things like "Remember who Christmas is really about." or "Put Christ back in Christmas!" The vast majority of us have grown up singing Christmas songs, opening gifts, gathering together with family, caroling, eating Christmas cookies, going to parades, going to special Christmas services at our churches, and many more traditions. Nearly everyone, be they Christian or not, love Christmas. The stores set up decorations months early, the radio stations begin playing Christmas music months early, channels like Hallmark begin playing their heartwarming Christmas movies the whole month long. People love Christmas. Tragically, Christmas is every bit as bad, if not worse, than the other holidays we've looked at up until now, and I will prove it.

An interesting thing to look at before we really get into it, is a quiet historical footprint that few know about. This is a quote from History.com, which is the website associated with the History Channel. While I wouldn't trust everything they say, this factoid is verifiable from multiple records and sources.

After the Puritans in England overthrew King Charles I in 1647, among their first items of business after chopping off the monarch's head was to ban Christmas. Parliament decreed that December 25 should instead be a day of "fasting and humiliation" for Englishmen to account for their sins. The Puritans of New England eventually followed the lead of those in old England, and in 1659 the General Court of the Massachusetts Bay Colony made it a criminal offense to publicly celebrate the holiday and declared that "whosoever shall be found observing any such day as Christmas or the like, either by forbearing of labor, feasting, or any other way" was subject to a 5-shilling fine. [19]

The Puritans, and the early Colonial Americans were so against Christmas, they made it illegal, and anyone caught celebrating it at all, was fined 5 shillings. Why would the puritans make a holiday about Christ's birth illegal? Because they knew something that most don't know.

In my other sections on holidays, I began with the origin and meaning of the holiday, and then went into the customs and the practices associated with it, but in this section, I really wanted to do it in reverse. You see the largest impact comes from realizing what this holiday is all about, and the practices associated with it are secondary. However, due to the nature of the information, without beginning with the conclusion, and moving from there, much of the information will be less relevant for you.

To begin, this section is entitled Yule, which corresponds to the pagan calendar season of Yule and more specifically, a very special time known as Yuletide. The link between Christmas and Yule is less hidden than you may think.

Christmas Time is Here
"Sleigh bells in the air, beauty everywhere, Yuletide by the fireside, and joyful memories there."

Have Yourself a Merry Little Christmas

"Have yourself a merry little Christmas, make the yuletide gay.
From now on, our troubles will be miles away."

Mistletoe and Holly
  "Then comes that big night
  Giving the tree the trim
  You'll hear voices by starlight
  Singing a yuletide hymn"

Deck the Halls
  "Troll the ancient Yuletide carol
Fa la la la la, la la la la"
  (Later on)
  "See the blazing yule before us
Fa la la la la, la la la la"

So what is this yuletide anyways, and what does it have to do with Christmas? Here is a quote from the Wikipedia page on Yule.

Yule or Yuletide ("Yule time" or "Yule season") is a festival historically
observed by the Germanic Peoples. Scholars have connected the
original celebrations of Yule to the Wild Hunt, the god Odin, and
the pagan Anglo-Saxon Mōdraniht.
    Later departing from its pagan roots, Yule underwent Christianized
reformation resulting in the term Christmastide. Many present-
day Christmas customs and traditions such as the Yule log, Yule
goat, Yule boar, Yule singing, and others stem from pagan Yule
traditions. Terms with an etymological equivalent to Yule are still
used in Nordic countries and Estonia to describe Christmas and other
festivals occurring during the winter holiday season. Today, Yule is
celebrated in Heathenry and other forms of Neopaganism, as well as
in LaVeyan Satanism. [20]

We are going to break this down much further, but right off the bat, we see that Christmas was a direct "Christianization" of Yule and is tied directly to another pagan festival as well. This quote is taken from churchofsatan.org

> *Question: What about the Christmas holiday?*
>
> *Answer: The Christians stole this holiday from the pagans—Santa Claus has come to signify indulgence, and he is a combination of Dionysos and Silenus from Roman and Greek myths (the Romans celebrated the orgiastic Saturnalia at this time).*
>
> *The Nazarene has little place in the general public's celebrations of this season, which were meant by pagans to be celebrations of abundance during a season of cold and emptiness.*
>
> *So for the Yule holiday season we enjoy the richness of life and the company of people whom we cherish, as we will often be the only ones who know where the traditions really came from!* [21]

So Christmas hearkens back to Yule, but also Saturnalia. There is actually a very good reason for this, but that will be revealed later. Now, if you look at Yule, Yule was Norse, which as we know, the vikings came after the Romans, and ended up adopting some of their gods. Now as the quote above said, Yule was all about an event known as the Wild Hunt, which was a time when Odin, astride his eight legged horse Sleipnir, would fly through the sky with a group of ghostly hunters in tow. Now if you haven't already figured it out, there are some striking similarities between Santa Claus, and Odin. This is an article from a website called The Norwegian American, and amusingly is called "Don't take Odin out of Yule"

> *Santa Claus owes his very existence to the old Norse myths. He's changed a lot over the centuries, but his origins in Scandinavia and Northern Europe cannot be denied.*
>
> *Here's a look at how Santa Claus emerged from the lands of the Vikings, exchanging the Norse god Odin's more terrifying traits for those of a plump, chuckling man of eternally good nature.*

Odin was chief among the Norse pagan deities. (We still remember him in the day of the week named for him, Wednesday, Woden's Day.) He was spiritual, wise, and capricious. In centuries past, when the midwinter Yule celebration was in full swing, Odin was both a terrifying specter and an anxiously awaited gift-bringer, soaring through the skies on his flying eight-legged white horse, Sleipnir.

Back in the day of the Vikings, Yule was the time around the Winter Solstice on Dec. 21. Gods and ghosts went soaring above the rooftops on the Wild Ride, the dreaded Oskoreia. One of Odin's many names was Jólnir (master of Yule). Astride Sleipnir, he led the flying Wild Hunt, accompanied by his sword-maiden Valkyries and a few other gods and assorted ghosts.

The motley gang would fly over the villages and countryside, terrifying any who happened to be out and about at night. But Odin would also deliver toys and candy. Children would fill their boots with straw for Sleipnir, and set them by the hearth. Odin would slip down chimneys and fire holes, leaving his gifts behind.

Centuries passed, and the world was changing. About the time paganism was being replaced by Christianity—which happened centuries later in the north than the rest of Europe—honoring Odin became forbidden. Yule was rescheduled to coincide with the Christian celebrations, and Odin was pushed out of the picture.

First the chief god was replaced by the goodly Christian Saint Nicholas, a fourth-century Greek bishop. Always depicted wearing a red cloak, he became known as the patron saint of giving in most parts of Europe—but not Scandinavia. He had helpers who would report on which children were good. He'd deliver gifts to the good kids. Beware the punishments dealt out to those who were bad!

After the Reformation, Nick and the other saints became forgotten in all the Protestant countries of Europe except Holland. There he morphed into Sinter Klaas, a kind and wise old man with a white beard, white dress, and red cloak. He'd ride the skies and roofs of the houses on his eight-legged white horse, delivering gifts through the chimney to the well-behaved children on his birthday, Dec. 6, St. Nicholas Day. Reminds you of Odin, right?

17th-century Dutch immigrants brought their tradition of Sinter Klaas to America, and his name changed into Santa Claus.

Later on we have this portion.

As for the elves in Santa's North Pole workshop who work all year long making Christmas toys, it was Odin who was the lord of Alfheim, home of the elves. And all magical weapons and jewelry of the gods and goddesses were fashioned by highly skilled dwarves, who dwelled deep within the earth.

And lastly, this portion.

Folklore experts can't deny the legacy of Odin, and his transformation into new versions of Yule gift-bringers. Margaret Baker, author of "Discovering Christmas Customs and Folklore" comments that "The appearance of Santa Claus or Father Christmas, whose day is the 25th of December, owes much to Odin, the old blue-hooded, cloaked, white-bearded Giftbringer of the north, who rode the midwinter sky on his eight-footed steed Sleipnir, visiting his people with gifts." [22]

Sorry for the wall of text, but whoever wrote this article did a wonderful job at presenting the information. Just to verify much of this information, I have two more sources to echo this idea, just so you know this isn't a fluke. The next quote is taken once again from history.com regarding the practice of leaving out milk and cookies for Santa.

The original roots of this holiday food tradition go back even further—all the way to ancient Norse mythology. Odin, the most important Norse god, was said to have an eight-legged horse named Sleipner, which he rode with a raven perched on each shoulder. During the Yule season, children would leave food out for Sleipner, in the hopes that Odin would stop by on his travels and leave gifts in return. Such a tradition continues today in countries such as Denmark, Belgium and the Netherlands, where children still believe that horses carry Santa's sleigh instead of reindeer. On Christmas Eve, they leave carrots and hay—sometimes stuffed into shoes—to feed the exhausted animals. In return, they might hope to receive such holiday treats as chocolate coins, cocoa, mandarin oranges and marzipan. [23]

And now a quote from Catholic.com

The stories commonly told today about Santa Claus are based on legends surrounding the life of a real person. St. Nicholas of Myra was a fourth-century Catholic bishop in Turkey. He participated in the First Council of Nicaea—where he was famously purported to have slugged the heretic Arius for denying Christ's divinity—and has been considered a patron of children for his generosity to them during his lifetime. For example, he is said to have provided dowries for three girls who would have been sold into slavery if they could not make good marriages. Over the centuries, the legends of St. Nicholas's life have been supplemented with Northern European myths, eventually culminating in the children's story A Visit from St. Nicholas by Clement C. Moore, which imagined St. Nicholas as a "right jolly old elf," traveling the world on Christmas Eve in a sleigh pulled by reindeer, distributing gifts to children. [24]

Leave it to the RCC to suggest that tales of Saint Nicholas were merely "supplemented" by "Northern European myths". In case you missed it, Northern Europe was where the vikings are from. So what's the more likely scenario, that the story of St. Nicholas was supplemented with pagan elements, or that they took the pagan Wild Hunt, and Odin, and slapped a big Saint Nicholas sticker on it and called it Christian?

Anyways, we have a ton of things to break down here from the above wall of quotes but before I do, one more quote. This is a quote from a website called syracuse.com regarding the names of the reindeer.

> *"Dunder and Blixem" is a Dutch expression that means "thunder and lightning." While Livingston spoke Dutch, Moore spoke German. The 1844 reprint changes "Blixem" to "Blitzen." The latter is the German word for lightning, while the former is Dutch.*
>
> *The change of "Dunder" to "Donder" was likely an error that Moore failed to notice when he reprinted the poem (since he didn't speak Dutch). Eventually, "Donder" became "Donner," which is the German word for thunder.* [25]

So yeah, Santa rides through the sky pulled by eight reindeer, two of which are thunder, and lightning. Odin rides through the sky on an eight legged horse and his son was the god of thunder and lightning. Odin is depicted as a large semi-elderly man with a large white beard. Santa is depicted as a large semi-elderly man with a large white beard. Santa climbs down chimneys and gives gifts. Odin would climb down chimneys and give gifts. Santa goes out one night a year, on Christmas Eve, which happens to be December 24th. Odin goes on the wild hunt one night a year, during Yule, specifically December 23rd. Odin makes a differentiation between those who are well behaved, and those who are not. Santa has a naughty and nice list. Odin would punish those who were on his bad side. Santa would punish those on his bad side with either a lump of coal (in American Christmas) or with his blackjacks (European Christmas) which we will look more at in a moment. Children would leave shoes stuffed with hay and carrots out for Odin's horse. Children leave milk and cookies out for Santa and his reindeer, as well as hanging their socks on the mantle place in hopes of them being filled up. Santa is immortal and known for being old and wise. Odin was the immortal god of wisdom. Santa has a workshop where he lives with elves and makes toys as an overseer of the workshop. Odin is lord over Alfheim, where the elves reside, and the dwarfs who make weapons. Need I go on? The similarities are endless.

The bad news doesn't stop there for Santa either. Remember that Santa Claus has a nickname. Old Saint Nick right? Ah, good old Nick. Here are some entries for the name "Old Nick"

> *Wikipedia page for Old Nick - Old Nick: 1: A nickname for the Devil. 2: A nickname for Santa.*

> *Mirriam Webster dictionary definition for Old Nick: Used as a name of the Devil.*

> *The free dictionary by Arlex: Old Nick: a name for the Devil or Satan.*

> *Cambridge English Dictionary: Old Nick: The Devil.*

I think it's pretty obvious that something about Old Saint Nick isn't quite right. And hey, remember that trademark laugh of his? "Ho! Ho! Ho!"? This is a quote taken from oldwierdalbion.wordpress.com

> *Once the central figure of holiday festivities – not just midwinter, but May Day and harvest and other season-cycle touch points – the Wild Man was banished to a peripheral role over the centuries by Christianity's increasing hold on England. What remained, however, at midwinter, was a general idea of the "world turned upside down": A carnivalesque atmosphere that made peasant into priest and left the gentry to fear wassailers as they threatened their curses in exchange for firkins of ale. And the chief troublemaker of this atmosphere was to become Robin Goodfellow – known to Shakespeare readers as Puck.*
>
> *In The Mad Pranks and Merry Jests of Robin Goodfellow, a book existent from 1628 that probably predates that by quite some time, in a section entitled "How Robin Good-Fellow Was Wont To Walke In The Night," Robin is described as a chimney-sweep whose practical jokes would be followed by his traditional cry of, "Ho, Ho, Ho."*
>
> *As one can guess from the, umm, less than modest portrayal in this*

portrait, Robin hangs onto many of the Wild Man's jobs as fertility symbol and cloven-hoofed central figure of the circular merriment of May Day. But as Siefker might point out, that beard and mustache look familiar – slap a red hat over those horns and put the feet on a reindeer before him, and we're starting to see something... [26]

Here's another quote from a website called schoolofdragons.com

But the devil connection leads to another theory on the origin of Robin Goodfellow's name. Some think, being an old puki, Puck or Robin Goodfellow is actually an old god (possibly the Green Man, who we will discuss later). Some say that this god's name was, in fact, Robin and may have been connected to the orange-breasted bird of the same name. With the Christianization of the British Isles, pagan gods and spirits were often relabeled demons to try to keep converted Christians who still believed in them from worshiping them. If the beliefs were particularly powerful, these old gods may even be said to be the devil himself in disguise. The fact that he is also called Puck, an alternate name for a nature spirit, god, or ghost across most of northern Europe, adds credence to this theory. Even today, there are witch covens and neo-pagan groups who refer to their god as "Robin," a traditional name for such a god in many parts of the British Isles. So Robin, made a demon or devil by Christian followers seeking to kill pagan idols, may in fact have been the name of a powerful god, made into a small and inconsequential trickster as he became less relevant. Robin is said to haunt and live in areas of standing stones, which is where ancient gods of the British Isles were worshiped. It is believed this green god may have been the god of vegetation and the forest and the spring and summer seasons. [27]

So, Old Saint Nick is a perfect mirror for Odin, but beyond that, he also has heavy similarities with a character associated with the Devil, and a name associated with the devil. On top of that, he also has links to the horned, cloven hoofed "wild man" which the pagans associated with fertility and sex. The wild man came directly from Greek mythology from the god Pan, the bisexual half man, half goat god, who looks an awful lot like the bisexual, transsexual depiction of Baphomet, who is commonly known to be Satan. Oh and did you know about the krampus? Well, remember how Odin was both terrifying and benevolent based upon whether you were good or not? Santa in modern America just gives you a piece of coal if you're bad. Elsewhere in the world, such as Austria and Germany, if you're bad, Santa sends out Krampus after you. Please take a moment to check out this link, and watch the video. [28] If you are reading this book in good old book form, please take a moment and search "National Geographic Who is Krampus". You really need to see this for yourself. For those of you either unable, or unwilling to go to this website and see for yourself, here is an excerpt from the text.

> When listening to the radio in December, it's unlikely to hear holiday songs singing the praises of Krampus: a half-goat, half-demon, horrific beast who literally beats people into being nice and not naughty. Krampus isn't exactly the stuff of dreams: Bearing horns, dark hair, fangs, and a long tongue, the anti-St. Nicholas comes with a chain and bells that he lashes about, along with a bundle of birch sticks meant to swat naughty children. He then hauls the bad kids down to the underworld.

> Krampus's name is derived from the German word krampen, meaning claw, and is said to be the son of Hel in Norse mythology. The legendary beast also shares characteristics with other scary, demonic creatures in Greek mythology, including satyrs and fauns.

> Krampus was created as a counterpart to kindly St. Nicholas, who rewarded children with sweets. Krampus, in contrast, would swat "wicked" children, stuff them in a sack, and take them away to his lair.

So, just to recap this little part, the counterpart to Saint Nicholas is the horrific, terrifying Krampus, who is depicted as a demonic half man half goat with long black horns. Krampus is known as the son of Hel who rules the underworld. Guys, take the name Santa and just move the n in the middle to the end of the name. Oh yeah, Santa and his counterpart Krampus is a perfect match for Odin and Satan himself. Here is one last quote from the website joyofsatan.org to drive it all home.

YULE/WINTER SOLSTICE
December 22nd-23rd

Although the Solstice begins on the 21st-22nd of December, the 23rd is a very special Personal Day for Father. The Sun enters the sign of the Goat which represents Satan. The Night of December 22nd-the eve of December 23rd is the Highest Satanic Holy Night of the year. (This was dictated from him personally). It is the day after the longest night of the year. Again we look forward to beginnings, as the days will begin to get longer as the year goes on. This is a time for intense celebration and devotion to Lord Satan. Indulgence, decorating the home, family celebrations and get-togethers. The Night of Dec. 22nd should be spent in dedication to Satan. This is an excellent time to focus on planning for the year. If one wishes to make personal resolutions this is a good time to do so.

At the high point of a ritual, personal resolutions can be written on paper and burned. Father Satan is always there to help us in having the strength to carry through with our intentions. After the rite, intense celebrating should take place.

The Yule holidays for Satanists are times of indulgence and taking pleasure in the physical and material aspects of life. Actually, Xmas trees and wreaths are Pagan in origin, so there is no reason not to celebrate this holiday with our families with gift giving, baking, and decorating. This is what the TRUE Yule season is about, not that filthy worthless Nazarene. [29]

As bad as this already is, it gets so much worse. Now we have to look at Saturnalia, which is the other basis for Christmas. Saturnalia was a pagan celebration in ancient Rome that revolved around the pagan god Saturn. Before we learn all about what this holiday was about, I want to briefly show you how it was celebrated so you can see how deeply it runs through Christmas. There is a 10 step "How to celebrate Saturnalia" on wikihow.com. I will list the steps for you here with minor paraphrasing:

1. Wear green and gold, the colors pertaining to Saturnalia.
2. Decorate your windows and stair cases with green garlands.
3. Decorate trees on your property with sun and star symbols.
4. Make specially shaped cookies either like suns or herd animals.
5. Drink special cold weather drinks like mulsum (wine & honey).
6. Greet people with the holiday cry of "Io! Saturnalia!"
7. Invite friends and family over for a dinner feast.
8. Give small gifts to one another.
9. Light candles in honor of Saturn.
10. Let yourself be free, setting aside any social inequalities.

Literally everything listed here is commonly found in Christmas celebrations with slight alterations. Here is a list of things commonly done, which in times past, I have personally done to celebrate Christmas:

1. Wear red, green, and gold, the Christmas colors.
2. Decorate your windows and stair cases with green garlands.
3. Decorate your Christmas tree with shining ornaments and a star on top.
4. Make specially shaped cookies like stars or snowmen.
5. Drink special cold weather drinks like hot chocolate or wine.
6. Greet people with the holiday cry of "Merry Christmas!"
7. Gather with family and friends for a dinner feast.
8. Exchange presents with one another.
9. Light candles, because they're just so Christmas-y.

10. Set aside any social inequalities in the "spirit of Christmas"

Pretty much every tradition, every fun thing we do for Christmas, every snack, every decoration, every activity, all of it, either directly pertains to Yuletide, or Saturnalia. I feel the need to remind you at this time, that this festival wasn't just a fun time for people to celebrate, this was worship. These were many of the ways that the Romans worshiped their pagan gods. Further, this tied directly back to the worship of the sun. This is an excerpt from a website called Carnaval.com/Saturnalia.

> *The Saturnalia festival has an astronomical character, referring to the completion of the sun's yearly course, and the commencement of a new cycle. Saturn, from whom we get the word for the day of the week, Saturday, represented by the sun at its lowest aspect at the winter solstice. The earth is cold, most plants are dead, and it was believed that the sun might also be approaching death. Today winter solstice is around December 21, but because of calendar changes, it was originally December 25th. Saturnalia celebrated the sun overcoming the power of winter, with hope of spring when life would be renewed. In Roman times, Bacchus, the god of wine, became the lord of these festivals.* [30]

So Saturnalia, as did most pagan celebrations, revolved around the sun. Saturnalia was tied directly to the winter solstice which as I explained prior, and this author mentioned, was when the shortest day of the year occurred. As stated, this was seen as the sun dying off, and then being born anew. This is where it really begins to hit home. For the grand reveal, we will next look at one more tradition we hold. The centerpiece, the ever important and needful grand decoration of the holiday, the Christmas tree. The Christmas tree, decorated with the most beautiful of decorations: colored lights, beautiful metallic orbs, and strings of popcorn. The Christmas tree that we set all of our presents under, and give the central place in the house to. The Christmas tree that we gather round and and sing, "O Christmas

Tree" to. First, a passage of scripture:

> ***Jeremiah 10:2-5 Thus says the Lord: "Do not learn the way of the Gentiles; do not be dismayed at the signs of heaven, for the Gentiles are dismayed at them. 3 For the customs of the peoples are futile; for one cuts a tree from the forest, the work of the hands of the workman, with the axe. 4 They decorate it with silver and gold; they fasten it with nails and hammers so that it will not topple. 5 They are upright, like a palm tree, and they cannot speak; they must be carried, because they cannot go by themselves. Do not be afraid of them, for they cannot do evil, nor can they do any good."***

Many people will try to say that this passage is not talking about Christmas trees, but about making idols. I absolutely disagree with this assertion. This is dead on the money talking about Christmas trees. Allow me to explain.

First of all, It says that *"one cuts a tree from the forest, the work of the hands of the workman, with the ax"*. People claim this is the carving of the idol. Does one carve an intricate statue with an ax? No, it is saying that it did not cut itself down, but had a workman cut it down with his own hands. This idea is reinforced in verse 5 where it says they cannot speak, and they have to be carried because they cannot walk on their own. Essentially, it can't cut itself down, so a workman has to cut it down with an ax. It cannot walk on it's own, so it has to be carried. It cannot hold itself up so it has to be fastened with hammers and nails. Again though, one would not choose a woodman's ax to carve an intricate statue.

Then it says *"they decorate it with silver and gold"*. People will claim this is them overlaying it with gold and silver as one does with an idol after it's done being carved. The only problem is, the word used here isn't overlay. The word used here is Strong's #3302 yaphah, which specifically means to make beautiful or decorate. The word overlay used many other times in the Old Testament is Strong's #6823 tsaphah which literally means to lay out or lay over, or overlay. It's a totally different word and meaning. The word used here very much means to decorate it, to make it beautiful, just as one decorates and makes beautiful a Christmas tree.

It then says *"they fasten it with nails and hammers so that it will not topple"*. If one is carving a statue, one of the first things you do is cut the wood blank in question down to size and make sure it has a flat steady base so it can be carved. Nobody carves a statue while it's unstable and toppling all over, so the first thing you do is stabilize it with a base. Further, you will be hard pressed to find a statue or idol that needs nails to hold it up. Again, this is because a statue is designed to hold itself up, otherwise it's a terrible statue. If the object in question needs to be held up, it's because it's top heavy, tall, and awkwardly proportioned. In other words, it's a tree with a narrow base and all the branches still attached making it top heavy and unstable. In the next verse it solidifies this assertion even further when it compares this object to a palm tree standing upright. This is a dead ringer for a Christmas tree, and as you will see in a moment, the palm tree was used in the same manner as the fir tree used so prominently today.

The reasons Christians try to say this is not a Christmas tree is two fold. First, they want to defend their tradition of men from the scriptures, and knowing they as Christians cannot openly defy the scriptures, they instead just decide to reinterpret it according to their fancy, and claim this was something else being talked about altogether. The second reason, is they will claim that Christmas trees were not around until much later after those days. There was no Christmas tree until after Christ's birth after all right? Wrong. They had Christmas trees all the way back in ancient Egypt and I will prove it in a moment.

This passage in Jeremiah describes perfectly the Christmas tree, and God commands His people not to do this thing that the pagans do. Meanwhile year after year I see Christians putting up and decorating their trees, and taking photos in front of it to post on social media or slap on Christmas cards. It's all in good fun though right? God doesn't seem to think so. Let me show you why. This is another quote from Carnaval.com/Saturnalia

The tradition of the Christmas tree symbolically portrayed the death and reincarnation of Osiris in his son, Horus:

The Christmas tree, now so common among us, was equally common in Pagan Rome and Pagan Egypt. In Egypt it was the palm tree; in Rome it was the fir; the palm-tree denoting the Pagan Messiah, as Baal-Tamar, the fir referring to him as Baal-Berith. The mother of Adonis, the Sun-God and great mediatorial divinity, was mystically said to have been changed into a tree, and when in that state to have brought forth her divine son. If the mother was a tree, the son must have been recognized as 'Man the Branch.' And this entirely accounts for putting the Yule Log into the fire on Christmas Eve and the appearance of the Christmas tree the next morning. As Zero-Ashta, 'The seed of the woman,' ...he has to enter the fire on 'Mother night,' that he may be born the next day out of it, as the 'Branch of God,' or the Tree that brings divine gifts to men.

Another, from joyofsatan.org

Baal-Bereth is the Father of the Yule season and the Yule (xmas) Tree. "The Christmas tree, now so common among us, was equally common in Pagan Rome and Pagan Egypt. In Egypt that tree was the palm-tree; in Rome it was the fir; the palm-tree denoting the Pagan Messiah, as Baal-Tamar, the fir referring to him as Baal-Berith." "The Christmas-tree, as has been stated, was generally at Rome a different tree, even the fir; but the very same idea as was implied in the palm-tree was implied in the Christmas-fir; for that covertly symbolised the new-born God as Baal-Berith, "Lord of the Covenant," and thus shadowed forth the perpetuity and everlasting nature of his power, not that after having fallen before his enemies, he had risen triumphant over them all."

In Egypt they worshipped Nimrod as a palm tree, referring to him as the Messiah "Baal-Tamar." Among the most ancient of Baals, he was known as Baal-Bereth, "Lord of the fir-tree." He evolved into Baal-Berith, "Lord of the Covenant." In Ancient Rome, where they also worshiped the fir tree, they called him "Baal-Berith."

The 25th of December, was observed in Rome as the day when the victorious God reappeared on earth, and was held at the Natalis invicti solis, "The birth-day of the unconquered Sun." Now the Yule Log represents the dead stock of Nimrod, known as the Sun-God, but cut down by his enemies; the xmas-tree represents Nimrod- the slain God reborn. The ancient practice of kissing under the mistletoe bough, most common to the Druids, was derived from Babylon, and was a representation of the Messiah, "The man the branch." The mistletoe was regarded as a divine branch —a branch that came from heaven, and grew upon a tree that sprung out of the earth. Nimrod, the God of nature, was symbolized by a great tree. But having been cut down and killed in his prime, he was now symbolized as a branchless tree stump, called the Yule Log. Then the great serpent came and wrapped itself around Nimrod (the stump). Miraculously, a new tree appeared at the side of the stump, which symbolized Nimrod's resurrection and victory over death. [31]

Yes, dear reader, there it is, the abominable truth. Christmas does indeed celebrate the birth of a christ, but it is not God's Christ. Christ merely means "chosen" or "annointed". Christmas is the combination of the word Christ, and "mass" referring to the "holy" gathering of the Roman Catholic Church. Christmas, is the celebration of the birth of the antichrist. Remember near the beginning of this book when I made mention that Satan was the original idolater? Satan wanted to be worshiped as god, and tried to overthrow god. Satan was soundly defeated and cast out of heaven, and down to the earth. Satan was defeated, and knew he needed an heir to take his place. Satan will bring forth his chosen one, his christ, to once again fight against the True Christ at the battle of Armageddon.

Santa Claus, works all Yule long, getting ready for the big day. He busies himself overseeing his elves, checking his naughty and nice list, and separating out humanity accordingly to who he will bless, and who he will punish. His work culminates on the night of the 24th, Christmas eve when he goes into overtime, delivering his gifts to the entire world, in just one night. The following morning, everyone who Santa deemed good receives their gifts, while the naughty get punished. During this time everyone celebrates the birth of christ while those who were not good are left out of the festivities.

Satan has worked for thousands of years getting ready for the big day. He has busied himself overseeing his demons, and drawing people away from God, unto himself. He has carefully set the stage to bring forth his mark, in which he will separate humanity into two groups; those are "nice" and take his mark, and will be rewarded, while those who are "naughty" will reject it, and be punished by death. He goes into overtime at the end, to make sure his mark is brought to everyone. As soon as he finishes setting the stage, his work will conclude, and he will take the throne of this world in the form of his heir, the antichrist, whom everyone will worship, except those who have not accepted him, who will be unable to buy, sell, or trade, and will be hunted down and slaughtered.

Christmas, in it's entirety, from the time of the year, to the customs and themes, to the characters, to the patterns, and every single aspect of it, is the celebration of the future event of the establishment of the mark of the beast, the solidification of the kingdom of the beast, and the rise of the antichrist to sit upon the throne of this world. That, dear reader, is what millions of Christians all around the world celebrate every single year, and think they are glorifying the One True God. This is the holiday that I myself once celebrated and loved. This is the holiday that I have to watch my family and my friends and everyone in the world around me celebrate every year. This is the holiday that grieves me more deeply than any other.

Many Christians realize that December 25th is not the birthday of Christ, but they shrug it off, because that's just a minor detail right? The truth is, December 25th is the birthday of the solis invictus, the unconquerable sun. The Birthday of Tammuz, the first image of the antichrist. All the decorations, customs, and practices are all tied directly to worshiping the antichrist and Satan himself. This holiday has nothing whatsoever to do with the true Messiah at all, thus any assertion to "put Christ back in

Christmas" are completely backwards. He was never in this holiday to begin with, and to try to slap Christ as the message over this holiday is to put the image of our King on the form of antichrist. I know this is a hard pill to swallow, but this holiday only celebrates Satan, the "father" in the form of Old Nick and Odin, and his "son" the antichrist. Can you imagine how this makes Christ feel? Can you imagine what He must see as His people get swept up in the "spirit of Christmas"? He sees all the Christmas parties, and Santa hats, and feasts, and presents, and all He sees are His people being led away to worship Satan and the antichrist.

Many Christians I have talked to have, as they walked with God, felt something wasn't right about Christmas. They have begun to lose any desire of it. It begins to grieve them. This dear reader, is why. Have you ever stopped to wonder why the world who hates Christ would allow a celebration all about Him to become the single biggest celebration of the year? Why would they throw parades, and make thousands of Christmas movies and thousands of songs about Christmas if it had anything to do with the Christ they hate and cannot stand. This is why. We need to repent, and flee from this holiday as quickly as we can. Me and my family will never celebrate another Christmas from now until the day I die. I walk through the department stores and see Christmas trees, the image of Baal Berith everywhere. I see people wearing Santa (Satan) themed clothing. I see Christians getting all excited for this holiday as the season gears up and proclaiming Christ is the reason for the season. I see special church services in honor of Christmas. All of it makes me want to vomit. It is not "the most wonderful time of the year" it is the saddest, as I watch the world, and even those who belong to Christ, worshiping and honoring Satan and the antichrist. After all of this, there are still a few things I need to address. Let's move on from this chapter, dear reader.

11

Dominus

In this chapter, we will look at several different things, which are very difficult to accept. As if the last three chapters were not difficult enough, this one will not be any easier to get through. We are going to look at several subjects, and so it will be a lengthier chapter. I maybe should have broken it up more, but I didn't think having 4 chapters with just a few pages a piece was really necessary, plus all of this information interlocks rather well.

So, the RCC established and disguised the celebration of the antichrist and has nearly the whole world worshiping him at least once a year, including Christians. This is bad. What if I told you that they are not only celebrating the antichrist once a year, but consistently every single week? As you may have surmised already, we need to look at our weekly gathering together on Sun-day. Now most people who have looked into this matter at all, believe they have scriptural basis for gathering on the first day of the week. They cite verses like these:

> *Acts 20:7 Now on the first day of the week, when the disciples came together to break bread, Paul, ready to depart the next day, spoke to them and continued his message until midnight.*

> *1 Corinthians 16:2 On the first day of the week let each one*

of you lay something aside, storing up as he may prosper, that there be no collections when I come.

So this conclusively tells us that the disciples broke bread, gathered together, preached, and collected offerings on the first day of the week right? We also have several verses that claim that Jesus rose on the first day of the week right?

Mark 16:9 Now when He rose early on the first day of the week, He appeared first to Mary Magdalene, out of whom He had cast seven demons.

John 20:1 Now the first day of the week Mary Magdalene went to the tomb early, while it was still dark, and saw that the stone had been taken away from the tomb.

So clearly we have abundant scriptural evidence to support us gathering together on the first day of the week right? Well, the RCC would disagree with you there.

Cardinal James Gibbons, The Faith of Our Fathers (Ayers Publishing, 1978): 108:
But you may read the Bible from Genesis to Revelation, and you will not find a single line authorizing the sanctification of Sunday. The Scriptures enforce the religious observance of Saturday, a day which we never sanctify.

Chancellor Albert Smith for Cardinal of Baltimore Archdiocese, letter dated February 10, 1920:
If Protestants would follow the Bible, they should worship God on the Sabbath day by God is Saturday. In keeping the Sunday, they are following a law of the Catholic Church.

Stephen Keenan, Catholic—Doctrinal Catechism 3rd Edition: 174:

Question: Have you any other way of proving the Church has power to institute festivals of precept?

Answer: Had she not such power, she could not have done that in which all modern religionists agree with her, she could not have substituted the observance of Sunday the 1st day of the week, for the observance of Saturday the 7th day, a change for which there is no Scriptural authority.

Our Sunday Visitor (February 5, 1950):

Practically everything Protestants regard as essential or important they have received from the Catholic Church... The Protestant mind does not seem to realize that in accepting the Bible and observing the Sunday, in keeping Christmas and Easter, they are accepting the authority of the spokesman for the church, the Pope.

Catholic Priest T. Enright, CSSR, lecture at Hartford, KS, Feb 18, 1884:

I have repeatedly offered $1000 to any one who can furnish any proof from the Bible that Sunday is the day we are bound to keep...The Bible says, "Remember the Sabbath day to keep it holy," but the Catholic Church says, "No, keep the first day of the week," and the whole world bows in obedience.

Catholic Record (September 1, 1923):

The [catholic] Church is above the Bible, and this transference of the Sabbath observance is proof of that fact.

Letter from C.F. Thomas, Chancellor of Cardinal Gibbons on October 28, 1895:

Of course the Catholic Church claims that the change was her act...And the act is a mark of her ecclesiastical power and authority in religious matters.

American Catholic Quarterly Review (January 1883):
Sunday...is purely a creation of the Catholic Church.

Catholic American Sentinel (June 1893):
Sunday...It is a law of the Catholic Church alone...

John A. O'Brien, The Faith of Millions: the Credentials of the Catholic Religion Revised Edition (Our Sunday Visitor Publishing, 1974): 400-401:
But since Saturday, not Sunday, is specified in the Bible, isn't it curious that non-Catholics, who claim to take their religion directly from the Bible and not from the Church, observe Sunday instead of Saturday? Yes, of course, it is inconsistent; but this change was made about fifteen centuries before Protestantism was born, and by that time the custom was universally observed. They have continued the custom even though it rests upon the authority of the Catholic Church and not upon an explicit text in the Bible. That observance remains as a reminder of the Mother Church from which the non-Catholic sects broke away—like a boy running away from home but still carrying in his pocket a picture of his mother or a lock of her hair. [32]

Catholics openly mock non Catholics for observing Sunday for which many claim there is no scriptural basis for. So how then do we have all of these verses, and yet not have scriptural basis? It's very simple.

Jeremiah 8:8 "How can you say, 'We are wise,
And the law of the Lord is with us'?
Look, the false pen of the scribe certainly works falsehood.

Nearly every modern translation of scripture we have ultimately comes back to the Vatican. This is going to be rather upsetting to the KJV only people, but the fact is, the Catholic church purposely made little changes to scripture, in order to deceive the masses. There are some translations from earlier, but by far the most prominent version of the Bible is in fact the King James Version (KJV). Now the KJV was first released in 1611 by King James VI, who was the king of Scotland. Now remember, at this time, the Holy Roman Empire was in full swing, and every European monarchy structure had included in it officials from the Catholic Church in the form of Cardinals and Priests. These Catholic officials enjoyed a position of authority akin to that of a king as there were many kings, but only one Pope, and these were the direct servants of the pope.

Around this time if you recall as well, is when the protestant reformation began to get traction. People were waking up out of the haze of the Catholic Church, and beginning to realize that their customs, teachings, and theologies were not found in scripture at all. This was a time of great unrest. The Catholic Church began to watch as it's self enforced ekklesiastical authority crumbled in the light of scripture. In order to attempt to once again consolidate power, together with King James VI, they set to put forth a new and "official" translation and canon of the Bible.

It had to be mostly accurate as large differences would certainly be noticed and rejected, so they had to make subtle changes instead. We will look at this more later, but the biggest and most obvious change came in the form of removing the name of God completely out of the Bible and replacing it with the phrase "The Lord your God". Other very subtle changes were made, but given that the majority of people had no access really to original manuscripts at this time, they had to get their translations somewhere. Their choices were either from the random translators such as Matthew Tyndale who weren't really Hebrew and Greek scholars, or from the "highly qualified and trustworthy, professional" Catholic scribes.

One of these changes, was to purposefully mistranslate passages related to the resurrection of Christ, and the gathering together of the church as being on the first day of the week. The fact is, the Greek word for week, εβδομάδα (evdomada), is not found a single time in any of the passages that talk about them meeting on the first day of the week. Further, the Greek word for day, ημέρα (iméra), was never in these passages either. So passages like this one below add words and mistranslate words. First, we know the word day isn't even in the text, so that is crossed out, second, the word evdomada isn't in the text, and instead has the Greek word sabbaton, so we will replace that, and this is what we come up with:

> **1 Corinthians 16:2 On the first ~~day~~ of the ~~week~~ sabbaton let each one of you lay something aside, storing up as he may prosper, that there be no collections when I come.**

So "on the first of the sabbaton" is how it should read. Now, what is the word sabbaton? If you jump on google and go the the Greek to English translator and type in the word sabbaton, the result you will get is sabaton. Same word. This signifies that there is no English translation of this word. It should not be translated as week. If you type in the word evdomada, it immediately comes up with week. So where did this mysterious word sabbaton come from? When something is being translated between languages, often there are words in a language for which there is no equivalent word in the translated language. In these cases, the word is then transliterated, which means to take the phonetic structure of the word, make the closest phonetic equivalent with the new languages alphabet, and then assign that meaning to that word.

An example of this is the word baptize, or baptism. When the Bible was being translated to English they ran into the Greek word vaptizo, which there really wasn't an English equivalent word for the idea of what the word meant. Because of this the translators were forced to transliterate the word into English, and suddenly we had the word baptize. Now sabbaton is also a transliteration from the Hebrew language, to the Greek. The original Hebrew word where they got sabbaton from was the Hebrew word, Shin Bet Het, which is pronounced shabbat. This word shabbat did not have a Greek equivalent word, and so they needed to transliterate the word into Greek, where they made the closest equivalent word, sabbaton. This word is the word from which we get sabbath. Shabbat became sabbaton, and sabbaton became sabbath.

So, this word has no business whatsoever being translated as week. In fact, as I mentioned earlier, there was a word already in the Greek that meant week, which was evdomada. Beyond that, even if they wanted to use a different word for week, they would've used the term evdomas imera, which means seventh day, as this was a phrase used in the Septuagint. Essentially, there is no logical explanation for why the scribes would translate the word sabbaton as week, except that they were trying to validate their position of changing the sabbath which was the last day of the week, to Sunday, The Lord's Day, which was the first day of the week. They have deceived millions by mistranslating the scripture. The lying pen of the scribes indeed. So now every single verse they have to try to validate the early church meeting on the first day of the week, or Christ rising on the first day of the week, are debunked as are any verses that suggest the early church gathered especially on the first day of the week. Look into it yourself, find each one of these verses in the interlinear, and see for yourself.

> *Mark 16:2 Very early in the morning, on the first day of the Sabbath (sabbaton), they came to the tomb when the sun had risen.*

> *Mark 16:9 Now when He rose early on the first day of the Sabbath (sabbaton), He appeared first to Mary Magdalene, out of whom He had cast seven demons.*

> *Luke 24:1 Now on the first day of the Sabbath (sabbaton), very early in the morning, they, and certain other women with them, came to the tomb bringing the spices which they had prepared.*

> *John 20:1 Now the first day of the Sabbath (sabbaton) Mary Magdalene went to the tomb early, while it was still dark, and saw that the stone had been taken away from the tomb.*

Acts 20:7 Now on the first ~~day~~ of the Sabbath (sabbaton), when the disciples came together to break bread, Paul, ready to depart the next day, spoke to them and continued his message until midnight.

1 Corinthians 16:2 On the first ~~day~~ of the Sabbath (sabbaton) let each one of you lay something aside, storing up as he may prosper, that there be no collections when I come.

There are only two verses that talk about this that I didn't list above, because they need just a bit more explanation to understand. The word Sabbath didn't ONLY refer to the last day of the week. The term Sabbath merely meant a Holy day that was an observance to God. Outside of the weekly Sabbath, the feasts were also known as Sabbaths. The day of atonement, Passover, and others were also known as Sabbaths. With this in mind, we can understand these two slightly more confusing verses.

Matthew 28:1 Now after the Sabbath (sabbaton), as the first ~~day~~ of the Sabbath (sabbaton) began to dawn, Mary Magdalene and the other Mary came to see the tomb.

John 20:19 Then, the same day at evening, being the first ~~day~~ of the Sabbath (sabbaton), when the doors were shut where the disciples were assembled, for fear of the Jews, Jesus came and stood in the midst, and said to them, "Peace be with you."

So how could it be after the Sabbath, but also on the first of the Sabbath in Matthew 28:1? Because it was after Passover, which was a Sabbath, but also on the first of another Sabbath, the feast of unleavened bread which follows immediately after Passover. Therefore on a Sabbath but also after a Sabbath. This also completely explains John 20:19. Because many feasts took place over the course of multiple days, it would've been accurate to call the first day of unleavened bread the first of the Sabbath. So the whole foundation of gathering together on the first day of the week, or Jesus rising from the dead on the first day of the week, are all debunked. The Catholics were right, there really is no scriptural basis whatsoever for the observance of Sunday as the day to gather together. So why then did the RCC change the observance from the last day of the week to the first day of the week? The answer, as so many answers pertaining to the RCC are, is disturbing. Remember this quote from Vatican.va?

> *The Lord's day, the day of Resurrection, the day of Christians, is our day. It is called the Lord's day because on it the Lord rose victorious to the Father. If pagans call it the "day of the sun," we willingly agree, for today the light of the world is raised, today is revealed the sun of justice with healing in his rays.* [33]

As we already learned in the previous chapters, the RCC's holidays are all about pagan antichrist worship and this transference of observance is no different at all. Now one thing of very important note is this, Sunday observance is known as "The Lord's Day". The RCC took out the name of God and replaced it with the term "The Lord your God" in their translation of the Bible. The prayer Christ prayed when the disciples asked Him how to pray is called by the RCC "The Lord's Prayer". Communion is referred to by the RCC as either the Eucharist, or "The Lord's Supper".

Speaking of the Lord's Supper, the Eucharist is about as full of sun god worship as it can be. The dish from which people take is decorated with a large golden sun. Oh, and transubstantiation, the belief that by eating the bread and drinking the wine they are literally partaking of the actual flesh and blood of Christ that is magically transformed as they eat it, does not originate with them at all. Groups like the Mayans and the Incas practiced this exact thing, ritualistically eating foods they claimed to be the physical flesh and blood of their gods. Funny that we follow their pattern instead of the one that Christ partook of, but we will examine that more later.

Why replace and label everything with the term "The Lord"? We will discuss this more in a chapter later on, but the reason they instituted this term as the catch all term for everything, is because the name Baal, the pagan god the Israelites fell to over and over, means "The Lord". Let me say that again, the name Baal translates as "The Lord" and in a chapter coming later on we will study this further. Go look it up for yourself. Baal (the lord) your God, Baal's (the lord's) day, this change in names, as hard as it is to believe, goes back to Baal, the pagan god and another shadow of the antichrist. Don't take my word for it, this is taken from Strong's Greek #896.

Baal = "lord"
the supreme male divinity of the Phoenician and Canaanitish nations, as Ashtoreth was their supreme female divinity

Now from Strong's Hebrew #1168

Baal = "lord"
supreme male divinity of the Phoenicians or Canaanites

One more from biblestudytools.com

The name appropriated to the principal male god of the Phoenicians. It is found in several places in the plural BAALIM (Judges 2:11; 10:10; 1 Kings 18:18; Jeremiah 2:23; Hosea 2:17). Baal is identified with Molech (Jeremiah 19:5). It was known to the Israelites as Baal-peor (Numbers 25:3; Deuteronomy 4:3), was worshipped till the time of Samuel (1 Samuel 7:4), and was afterwards the religion of the ten tribes in the time of Ahab (1 Kings 16:31-33; 1 Kings 18:19 1 Kings 18:22). It prevailed also for a time in the kingdom of Judah (2 Kings 8:27; comp 11:18; 16:3; 2 Chr 28:2), till finally put an end to by the severe discipline of the Captivity (Zephaniah 1:4-6). The priests of Baal were in great numbers (1 Kings 18:19), and of various classes (2 Kings 10:19). Their mode of offering sacrifices is described in 1 Kings 18:25-29. The sun-god, under the general title of Baal, or "lord," was the chief object of worship of the Canaanites. [34]

So, the sun god, under the generic title of "lord" was the chief object of worship by the Canaanites. How is this any different from today? I have talked to dozens of Christians who have no idea whatsoever what the name of God really is, they just call Him "Lord". I want you to notice something interesting as well.

Matthew 7:21 "Not everyone who says to Me, 'Lord, Lord,' shall enter the kingdom of heaven, but he who does the will of My Father in heaven."

Notice that the phrase "Lord, Lord" is in additional quotation marks within this quote, signifying that this was a quote of something people would be literally saying. Let me ask you a question, do you know where the term "Church" came from? This is an excerpt from etymonline.com for the word church:

Old English cirice, circe "place of assemblage set aside for Christian worship; the body of Christian believers, Christians collectively; ecclesiastical authority or power," from Proto-Germanic *kirika (source also of Old Saxon kirika, Old Norse kirkja, Old Frisian zerke, Middle Dutch kerke, Dutch kerk, Old High German kirihha, German Kirche).

This is probably borrowed via an unrecorded Gothic word from Greek kyriake (oikia), kyriakon doma "the Lord's (house)," from kyrios "ruler, lord," from PIE root keue "to swell" ("swollen," hence "strong, powerful"). [35]

So according to this website, the word church is derived from kryios, which translates into "The Lord's House" which is still a name referenced by the RCC to this day. But, this is only one opinion. There is another more disturbing answer found in multiple other places. These are a series of quotes taken from a website called grahamhancock.com, which had quotes from other sites. [36]

1. The etymology of this word is generally assumed to be from the Greek, kurios oikos (house of the Lord); but this is most improbable, as the word existed in all the Celtic dialects long before the introduction of the Greek. No doubt the word means 'a circle.'

The places of worship among the German and Celtic nations were always circular (witness circular Stonehenge, the most ancient stone megaliths on earth).

Compare Anglo-Saxon 'circe', a small church, with 'circol', a circle. In Scotland it is called "Kirk" and in Gemany it is "Kirche," in England it is the word "Circe" (the "c" having a "k" sound).

"Kirke/Circe" was also the name of a Goddess. Kirke or Circe was the daughter of the Sun god, who was famous for taming wild animals for her circus.

2. Circe was an evil, or perhaps just cruelly quirky, sorceress. She was very powerful and turned all of Odysseus' men into swine (they bearly escaped). She also had the power to purify and cleanse the Argonauts of the murder of Apsyrtus. Her name means "Falcon" and that seems pretty appropriate for her character. Circe was the daughter of Helios (the Sun) and Perse, and was the aunt of Medea. She was wayyyyy dangerous because she was so powerful and so bored.

3. This is the word used in most English versions as a rendering of the New Testament's Greek word ekklesia. Ekklesia really means "a calling out" a meeting or a gathering. Ekklesia is the Greek equivalent of the Hebrew qahal, which means an assembly or a congregation. Neither ekklesia nor qahal means a building. Tyndale, in his translation, uniformly translated ekklesia as "congregation" and only used the word "churches" to translate Acts 19:37 for heathen temples! Whence the word "church" then? Ecclesiastical sources give the origin as kuriakon or kyriakon in Greek. However, to accept this. one has to stretch your imagination in an attempt to see any resemblance. Also, because kuriakon means a building (the house of Kurios=Lord), and not a gathering or meeting of people, as the words ekklesia and qahal imply, therefore this explanation can only be regarded as distorted, even if it is true. Our common dictionaries, however, are honest in revealing to us the true origin. They all trace the word back to its Old English or Anglo-Saxon root, namely circe. And the origin of circe? Any encyclopaedia, or dictionary of mythology, will reveal who Circe was. She was the goddess-daughter of Helios, the Sun-deity!

So we replaced the word ekklesia, or congregation, for the word church, which either hearkens back to the Greek kyurios meaning "the lord's house" or derives from the Anglo-Saxon word Circe, who was a pagan goddess, the daughter of the sun god. Every time we refer to ourselves as "the church" we are effectively referring to ourselves as either the house of Baal, or the daughter of the sun god who turns men into swine. You can't make this stuff up people. The roots of pagan sun god worship are strewn all throughout Christianity. In fact, if you place a spire that narrows as it comes up and ends in a point on the ground, it's called an obelisk. If you stick it on top of a church, it's suddenly called a "steeple". Why would the builders of churches include this steeple on the top of so many churches? Because it was an architectural tradition of the RCC and associated with the "church". What function does this steeple perform? Does it add to the structural integrity of the building, or provide some sort of service for the rest of the building? Nope, it is purely cosmetic, and the origin of this decoration comes from the pagan sun god worship of the RCC.

Sadly, in spite of Sunday being dedicated to the pagan sun gods, the name of the day being associated with Baal in the term "The Lord's Day", the RCC openly agreeing with pagans that the day of the sun is associated with their christ, the Catholic Church mocking protestants for keeping their replacement sabbath, there being no scriptural basis for keeping Sunday as sabbath, and about a dozen other issues, many Christians who truly love God and want to honor him are still keeping this false sabbath and choosing this day to be the day to gather together. We gather together in "the house of the Lord" to worship "the Lord". There we observe "The Lord's Table" and follow the pattern of the pagan Eucharist. We adorn our places of worship with obelisks and images of the sun, and all the while thinking we are doing everything just fine. We have the mark of the Catholic Church all over us. Catholics claim that the evidence, or proof, of their authority on the earth, is that they changed the sabbath.

Stephen Keenan, Catholic—Doctrinal Catechism 3rd Edition: 174:

Question: Have you any other way of proving the Church has power to institute festivals of precept?

Answer: Had she not such power, she could not have done that in which all modern religionists agree with her, she could not have substituted the observance of Sunday the 1st day of the week, for the observance of Saturday the 7th day, a change for which there is no Scriptural authority.

They claim that the proof that the Catholic church has absolute authority as the true church on earth, is that they changed the Sabbath, and thus they call it the mark of their authority.

Letter from C.F. Thomas, Chancellor of Cardinal Gibbons on October 28, 1895:

*Of course the Catholic Church claims that the change was her act...And the act is a **mark** of her ecclesiastical power and authority in religious matters.*

They claim that by keeping Sunday, Easter, and Christmas, we are submitting to the authority of the pope.

121

Our Sunday Visitor (February 5, 1950):

Practically everything Protestants regard as essential or important they have received from the Catholic Church... The Protestant mind does not seem to realize that in accepting the Bible and observing the Sunday, in keeping Christmas and Easter, they are accepting the authority of the spokesman for the church, the Pope. [37]

You know what? They're right. Christianity has unknowingly submitted to the rules of the Pope and taken upon itself the mark of his ekklesiastical authority. We have taken on the pagan name of church, we have decorated our churches with obelisks and imagery hearkening back to the sun, many churches have even made sure their churches face to the East as to catch the rays of the rising sun coming in the window. We have unquestioningly accepted a host of idolatrous traditions and doctrines and have been completely blind to it for a very long time. This is the end of the age, we are at the door, and at this time, God has chosen to begin to wake up His people out of their idolatry.

12

Revelations

This chapter is called Revelations. The reason for this is two fold, we are going to have a very important truth revealed to us, as well as look through the book of Revelation. Before we go forward, the things we are about to discuss are some of the most hotly contested in the entirety of Christianity. There are dozens of debates on this matter, I simply desire to offer you a perspective that I believe has a large amount of weight to it. If you disagree with my findings, you are free to do so, as much of what we are going into are interpretive, however, I ask that you at least consider the things I have to say, and to hear the whole matter, before you make up your mind.

The subject I want to examine in this chapter, is the beast of the end times. In this section, I have shown that all of the idolatry from all the nations are all linked together, and that they go all the way back to the tower of Babel and Nimrod, Semiramis, and Tammuz. I have shown that the RCC has instituted worship of Satan and the antichrist, and is responsible for most of the world falling into idolatry. Now I want to show that the identity of the Roman Catholic Church, is none other than the beast spoken of in Revelation.

To begin this study, we will go all the way back to the book of Daniel. In the book of Daniel, there are two dreams that Daniel ends up interpreting. The first one is found in chapter 2.

Daniel 2:31-35 "You, O king, were watching; and behold, a great image! This great image, whose splendor was excellent, stood before you; and its form was awesome. 32 This image's head was of fine gold, its chest and arms of silver, its belly and thighs of bronze, 33 its legs of iron, its feet partly of iron and partly of clay. 34 You watched while a stone was cut out without hands, which struck the image on its feet of iron and clay, and broke them in pieces. 35 Then the iron, the clay, the bronze, the silver, and the gold were crushed together, and became like chaff from the summer threshing floors; the wind carried them away so that no trace of them was found. And the stone that struck the image became a great mountain and filled the whole earth.

So we see this statue, or image. The first thing to realize is that an image, or statue made up of metal, in the likeness of a man, perfectly constitutes what an idol would be. In fact, in the very next chapter, Nebuchadnezzar sets up a giant "image of gold" for all the people to worship and bow down to. This giant idol would have no doubt been made in the image of one of the pagan sun gods they worshiped or in the image of the king himself. In fact, he may have gotten the inspiration for this great image from the dream he had. Now this image that Nebuchadnezzar saw was made up of multiple kingdoms as revealed later, but each kingdom still fit inside, and enforced the same image. It was not four or five separate images that all looked different, no, it was one consistent image with multiple kingdoms represented within it. It was one idol carried along by multiple kingdoms.

Daniel actually gives us the meaning of this dream, and explains it to us so let's look at that before we make any other notes.

Daniel 2:37-44 You, O king, are a king of kings. For the God of heaven has given you a kingdom, power, strength, and glory; 38 and wherever the children of men dwell, or the beasts of the field and the birds of the heaven, He has given them into your hand, and has made you ruler over them all—you are this head of gold. 39 But after you shall arise another kingdom inferior to yours; then another, a third kingdom of bronze, which shall rule over all the earth. 40 And the fourth kingdom shall be as strong as iron, inasmuch as iron breaks in pieces and shatters everything; and like iron that crushes, that kingdom will break in pieces and crush all the others. 41 Whereas you saw the feet and toes, partly of potter's clay and partly of iron, the kingdom shall be divided; yet the strength of the iron shall be in it, just as you saw the iron mixed with ceramic clay. 42 And as the toes of the feet were partly of iron and partly of clay, so the kingdom shall be partly strong and partly fragile. 43 As you saw iron mixed with ceramic clay, they will mingle with the seed of men; but they will not adhere to one another, just as iron does not mix with clay. 44 And in the days of these kings the God of heaven will set up a kingdom which shall never be destroyed; and the kingdom shall not be left to other people; it shall break in pieces and consume all these kingdoms, and it shall stand forever.

So, Daniel clearly explains for us that this singular image, is made up of multiple materials that were meant to represent multiple kingdoms. He even gives us the identity of the first kingdom. Now before we go into depth in this, we also need to understand that there was another dream or vision in Daniel 7 that speaks of the same things that Daniel himself had.

Daniel 7:2-8 Daniel spoke, saying, "I saw in my vision by night, and behold, the four winds of heaven were stirring up the Great Sea. 3 And four great beasts came up from the sea, each different from the other. 4 The first was like a lion, and had eagle's wings. I watched till its wings were plucked off; and it was lifted up from the earth and made to stand on two feet like a man, and a man's heart was given to it.

5 "And suddenly another beast, a second, like a bear. It was raised up on one side, and had three ribs in its mouth between its teeth. And they said thus to it: 'Arise, devour much flesh!'

6 "After this I looked, and there was another, like a leopard, which had on its back four wings of a bird. The beast also had four heads, and dominion was given to it.

7 "After this I saw in the night visions, and behold, a fourth beast, dreadful and terrible, exceedingly strong. It had huge iron teeth; it was devouring, breaking in pieces, and trampling the residue with its feet. It was different from all the beasts that were before it, and it had ten horns. 8 I was considering the horns, and there was another horn, a little one, coming up among them, before whom three of the first horns were plucked out by the roots. And there, in this horn, were eyes like the eyes of a man, and a mouth speaking pompous words.

These we know were also about kingdoms, because we are told so when Daniel receives the interpretation.

Daniel 7:15-22 "I, Daniel, was grieved in my spirit within my body, and the visions of my head troubled me. 16 I came near to one of those who stood by, and asked him the truth of all this. So he told me and made known to me the interpretation of these things: 17 Those great beasts, which are four, are four kings which arise out of the earth. 18 But the saints of the Most High shall receive the kingdom, and possess the kingdom forever, even forever and ever.'

19 "Then I wished to know the truth about the fourth beast, which was different from all the others, exceedingly dreadful, with its teeth of iron and its nails of bronze, which devoured, broke in pieces, and trampled the residue with its feet; 20 and the ten horns that were on its head, and the other horn which came up, before which three fell, namely, that horn which had eyes and a mouth which spoke pompous words, whose appearance was greater than his fellows.

21 "I was watching; and the same horn was making war against the saints, and prevailing against them, 22 until the Ancient of Days came, and a judgment was made in favor of the saints of the Most High, and the time came for the saints to possess the kingdom.

There is much more relevant text in the rest of the chapter to explore, but we'll set that aside for a moment. Interestingly we see that there are five materials in the image, gold, silver, bronze, iron, and iron mingled with clay, but, we only see 4 beasts. The fourth beast is different from all the beasts before it, but we know that it had 10 horns. One more scripture section to compare, and then we'll go into the interpretations.

Revelation 13:1-3 Then I stood on the sand of the sea. And I saw a beast rising up out of the sea, having seven heads and ten horns, and on his horns ten crowns, and on his heads a blasphemous name. 2 Now the beast which I saw was like a leopard, his feet were like the feet of a bear, and his mouth like the mouth of a lion. The dragon gave him his power, his throne, and great authority. 3 And I saw one of his heads as if it had been mortally wounded, and his deadly wound was healed. And all the world marveled and followed the beast.

So, let's put this all together. Daniel 7 tells us there will be 4 (beasts) kingdoms that will arise in the earth. Daniel 2 tells us that there is one image made up of 5 different materials, and explains in the interpretation that there are 4 kingdoms that will arise, but the last one will have two phases to it, one of just iron, and one of iron and clay. We also know that this will take place chronologically because we are told that Nebuchadnezzar's kingdom (the head) is the first, and then the other kingdoms will arise after it. This would indicate that this final kingdom would undergo some kind of drastic change partway through it's reign, thus being 5 materials, but only 4 kingdoms. More interesting still is with the 4 beasts. The first

3 are their own separate entities, but the fourth kingdom according to Revelation is a bit of a frankenstein. The first beast was a lion, the second beast was a bear, the third beast was a leopard. The fourth beast however was like a leopard, but had the head of a lion, and the feet of a bear, in other words, it was a beast made up of parts of the other beasts, or a kingdom made up of parts of all the other kingdoms.

Now we are given the identity of the head of the statue, as well as the first beast. The golden head was the kingdom of Babylon which reigned until 539 B.C.. The lion also represented Babylon. In fact, the official symbol representing Babylon was the golden lion of Babylon. Further, we know that the king of Babylon, Nebuchadnezzar himself actually underwent a point of time where he became like a wild beast, but after 7 years, he came to his senses, and it changed his heart completely toward God. This signified the wings being plucked off, and being made to stand on two feet, having the heart of a man given to it. Further, Babylon was one of the most richly abundant kingdoms to ever exist and they had an abundance of gold, part of which was taken from Israel, when they went into captivity. The spoils were so abundant, that when the king who conquered Babylon came in, he had no problem giving Israel back their gold because there was plenty to go around.

> *Ezra 1:7-11 King Cyrus also brought out the articles of the house of the Lord, which Nebuchadnezzar had taken from Jerusalem and put in the temple of his gods; 8 and Cyrus king of Persia brought them out by the hand of Mithredath the treasurer, and counted them out to Sheshbazzar the prince of Judah. 9 This is the number of them: thirty gold platters, one thousand silver platters, twenty-nine knives, 10 thirty gold basins, four hundred and ten silver basins of a similar kind, and one thousand other articles. 11 All the articles of gold and silver were five thousand four hundred. All these Sheshbazzar took with the captives who were brought from Babylon to Jerusalem.*

This would be why gold was the metal representing Babylon. This passage also lets us know who the next kingdom was who came after Babylon. This was the kingdom of the Medes and Persians, and if you noticed, king Cyrus of Persia, was the one dividing up the spoils of Babylon. The kingdom of Media and Persia were two separate kingdoms that decided to join together, thus the chest, and arms joined together. The Medes and Persians ruled from 539 B.C. until 311 B.C.. This kingdom of the Medes and Persians was a massive kingdom, consisting of an estimated 2.5 million troops. This kingdom definitely had the strength of a bear. Further, the beast was raised up on one side, this was because in 553 B.C. Persia actually conquered the Medes, but treated them as equals so it was more of a partnership. This is an excerpt from a website called michaeltsarion.com

> *Thus were the Medes subjected to their close kin, the Persians. In the new empire they retained a prominent position; in honor and war, they stood next to the Persians; their court ceremony was adopted by the new sovereigns, who in the summer months resided in Ecbatana; and many noble Medes were employed as officials, satraps and generals.*
> 38

So we see why the bear was raised up on one side, it was because technically one side was higher than the other, but both were working together. Further, we see that the bear had three ribs in it's mouth. The Medes and Persians ended up conquering three main kingdoms on it's rise to power, Libya, Babylon, and Egypt. Thus it had three ribs in it's mouth, and devoured much flesh. Lastly, the Persians were famous the world over for their craftsmanship and silver work, as they made beautiful weapons, armors, decorations and furniture from silver. You can see that to this day as Persian silver work is some of the highest quality. Thus silver was the metal symbolizing this kingdom.

The next kingdom, the waist of bronze, the leopard with four heads, and four wings, was the kingdom that conquered the Medes and Persians, namely the Greeks under Alexander the Great which reigned from 311 B.C. to 168 B.C.. Alexander the great had only about 35,000 troops, but conquered the other nations and rose to power in an astoundingly short time being small, but fast. A leopard was the perfect representation of the kingdom of Greece. Further, the Greek army had four generals who divided and conquered, thus four wings to carry the beast to where it needed to go. Alexander the Great also divided his kingdom up into 4 when he died, giving each of his 4 sons a portion of the kingdom, thus 4 heads of the kingdom. Lastly, the breastplates of the Grecian army were made of bronze as well as many other things, thus that period of time is known commonly as the bronze age matching the waist of bronze.

Greece was conquered thereafter by the fourth kingdom, the kingdom of Rome. Rome was astoundingly powerful, and with their weapons and breastplates of iron, crushed all armies that were in their paths thus that time was known as the Roman iron age. They were a bit of a hodgepodge, as they had a unique method of growth. This is a quote taken from khanacademy.org

> The Romans did not set out any deliberate plan to build an empire. Instead, Rome expanded as it came into conflict with surrounding city-states, kingdoms, and empires and had to create ways to incorporate these new territories and populations. The Romans did not try to turn everyone they conquered into a Roman. For the most part, cities and regions that came under Roman control were allowed to maintain their existing cultural and political institutions. The only major requirement that Rome imposed on its defeated enemies was that they provide soldiers for military campaigns. In the ancient world, military victory usually meant a share of the loot taken from the conquered, so participating on the winning side of a conflict offered incentives to Rome's new allies. [39]

So Rome truly was a hodgepodge of all the other nations put into one, thus it trampled the residue (residual kingdoms and territories), while also being made up of multiple parts of other beasts. I also want to mention quickly that the method of Roman Catholicism's conversions mirror that of Rome's military practices. Rome would come upon a people, and take them over. They would allow them to keep their culture, but take on the name of Rome. They would then supply Rome with soldiers for their campaign. The RCC comes upon a culture, and takes it over, allowing the culture to retain it's pagan practices, just rebranded, and coming under the title Catholic. These cultures then supply money in tithes and offerings to the Vatican. It's a dead ringer.

Now, one important thing I decided to wait until now to mention is this: we are told explicitly that this particular beast, the fourth beast, will persist until the end, and the beast in Revelation is clearly seen at the end times. That means that whatever kingdom the fourth beast was, would continue, and be a ruling power in the world until the eternal kingdom is established (the Kingdom of Christ) and the stone (that the builders rejected) would shatter the image as the final act of the age. This means that fourth beast has been present with us for the past 2000 years and is present today and will be until the end.

This idea is mirrored in the image of the statue. If you look at the basic proportions of the human body, the head (or according to Hebrew tradition the head and neck) would account for a relatively small amount of the human body, perhaps 1/6 or 1/7 depending upon the person. The reign of Babylon was a respectable length of time as we know Israel's captivity happened around 600 B.C. which means Babylon was around for at least 61 years, although we can surmise that Babylon was around quite a while before that, as Babylon was powerful enough to conquer Israel by the time they did, and evidence suggests they were around before. We can comfortably assume that the reign of Babylon was probably around 100-150 or so years. Thereafter was the kingdom of the Medes and the Persians, which reigned 228 years between 539-311 B.C.. This is consistent with human anatomy as the chest and arms would make up a larger portion of the body. Thereafter came the Grecian empire, which lasted a relatively short amount of time from 311-168 B.C. which is consistent with the relatively small portion of the human body that is the waist.

Lastly though, we have the legs and feet. Anatomically speaking, the legs account for about half of the overall height of a body. If length of time is comparable to anatomy, then the legs would easily be the longest portion of time. This too is consistent with this kingdom being the last kingdom before Christ takes His world back from Satan and destroys the image. All of these things all point unequivocally to the fact that the final kingdom, the franken-beast made up of multiple other beasts, would be the final kingdom ruling until the end times. This of course, is Rome.

You may argue that Rome only ruled until 476 A.D. when it fell, which was a very long time anyways (168 B.C-476 A.D.= 644 years though some sources claim it was much longer and over 1000 years) compared to the other kingdoms but Rome never really disappeared did it? Yes, Rome fell, but it just reformed itself into the Holy Roman Empire which officially lasted from 800 A.D., all the way until 1806, which was another 1000 years, and the Roman Catholic Church persists even to this day. You may not think they are ruling, but the truth is, the RCC is the origin and overseer of groups such as the Jesuits, the Free Masons, the Knights Templar, and many more. They rule the vast majority of the world from the shadows, and most have no idea. Look into these things for yourself. Check out the mysterious entity known as "The City" consisting of the Vatican, Washington D.C., and the City of London. Notice also that the Pope is honored and venerated by pretty much every world ruler, and even at the UN the Pope is given special honor. The Roman Empire has undergone a dramatic change, being broken up from a solid iron rule, to being broken and mingled with clay, but has continued throughout the last 2000 years, and is alive and well today. They are partially weak, in the religious face they put forward, but also partially still of iron, in that they rule the nations from the shadows.

What about the 7 heads of the beast? At the time John had received the vision, where it was revealed the beast had 7 heads, he says this:

Revelation 17:9-11 "Here is the mind which has wisdom: The

seven heads are seven mountains on which the woman sits. 10 There are also seven kings. Five have fallen, one is, and the other has not yet come. And when he comes, he must continue a short time. 11 The beast that was, and is not, is himself also the eighth, and is of the seven, and is going to perdition.

First of all, Rome was famous for having 7 hills, this is common knowledge. We also see the woman riding on this beast, but we will talk about her later on. Secondly, when this was penned, Rome had undergone 5 types of ruling government:

1. Kings
2. Republic
3. Decemvri
4. Triumvirate
5. Dictators

Dictators such as Julius Caesar were merely that, they dictated what everyone was to do, and they did it. Five heads of government had been. One type was active at the time of John's vision which was Emperors. Emperors differed from Dictators as Rome had gotten so big, that it needed multiple kings to keep it afloat. King Herod was an example of one of these kings, however, they all had one king over them which was the emperor. All the kings were subservient to the emperor. Thus, was the 6th head of government or kingship were the emperors. The final head, the seventh, came in the form of the Popes who came up after the fall of Rome, and reigned all throughout the reign of the Holy Roman Empire. Seven heads of government have ruled this beast.

In 1806 Napoleon came onto the scene, and conquered the majority of Europe, Napoleon personally saw to it that the Popes were deposed and in fact kidnapped some of them. This was described in this passage.

Revelation 13:3 And I saw one of his heads as if it had been

mortally wounded, and his deadly wound was healed. And all the world marveled and followed the beast.

The head or rulership of the Pope was indeed mortally wounded by Napoleon, but in 1929, Benito Mussolini signed the Lateran Treaty, which gave the Vatican back it's sovereignty, re-establishing the rule of the Roman Catholic Church. The deadly wound that was healed. This also accounts for this passage:

Revelation 17:11 The beast that was, and is not, is himself also the eighth (head), and is of the seven (heads), and is going to perdition.

The Papacy being re-established separated itself from the previous Papacy, being one of the seven forms of rulership, but also the eighth. The head wound was miraculously healed.

Now we also know that the beast had 10 horns, but a little horn came up among them, and uprooted three of them. At the outset of the Holy Roman Empire, during the rise of the Papacy, there were 10 kingdoms (or kings) at that time who were able to either become a part of the Holy Roman Empire, or to resist it and be decimated. They were:

1. Alemani (Germany)
2. The Franks (France)
3. The Burgundians (Switzerland)
4. The Suevi (Portugal)
5. The Heruli (Destroyed by the Holy Roman Empire in 493 A.D.)
6. The Visigoths (Spain)
7. The Anglo-Saxons (England)
8. The Ostrogoths (Destroyed by the Holy Roman Empire in 538 A.D.)
9. The Lombards (Italy)
10. The Vandals (Destroyed by the Holy Roman Empire in 534 A.D.)

So during the rise of the Papacy, ten kingdoms were ruling, but three of them were uprooted and destroyed when they decided to go against the Papacy. Ten horns of the Roman Empire, three of which, were uprooted and destroyed when the little horn (the Pope) came up among them. We are also given these descriptions of the little horn:

Daniel 7:25 He shall speak pompous words against the Most High,
Shall persecute the saints of the Most High, and shall intend to change times and law.

We know Rome was the primary persecutors of the followers of Christ, and we know this trend was continued by the papacy, through things like the crusades and inquisitions thus they have throughout history persecuted the saints of the Most High. The Papacy also changed times in the form of causing the vast majority of the world to come under the pagan Gregorian Calendar that worships the false gods and Roman emperors. Rome has also changed many of the laws. Take for example the altering of the 10 commandments, changing the Sabbath, and instituting pagan holidays. Lastly, the Pope has assuredly spoken pompous words against God.

Pope, Ferraris' ecclesiastic Dictionary:
The Pope is of so great dignity and so exalted that he is not a mere man, but as it were God, and the vicar of God.

Catholic Record (September 1, 1923):
The [catholic] Church is above the Bible, and this transference of the Sabbath observance is proof of that fact.

Pope Leo XIII, Praeclara Gratulationis Publicae (The Reunion of Christendom), June 20, 1894:
We hold upon this earth the place of God Almighty.

If those aren't pompous words against The Most High, I don't know what are. We also have these descriptions:

> *Daniel 11:36-39 "Then the king shall do according to his own will: he shall exalt and magnify himself above every god, shall speak blasphemies against the God of gods, and shall prosper till the wrath has been accomplished; for what has been determined shall be done. 37 He shall regard neither the God of his fathers nor the desire of women, nor regard any god; for he shall exalt himself above them all. 38 But in their place he shall honor a god of fortresses; and a god which his fathers did not know he shall honor with gold and silver, with precious stones and pleasant things. 39 Thus he shall act against the strongest fortresses with a foreign god, which he shall acknowledge, and advance its glory; and he shall cause them to rule over many, and divide the land for gain.*

The Papacy has assuredly exalted and magnified himself above every god in claiming he is god, thus speaking blasphemes against the Most High. The Papacy also enjoys a position of enormous wealth and prosperity and all signs point to that trend continuing until Christ interrupts this imposter. The Papacy does not regard the God of his fathers, as he has replaced God with the sun god. He honors these false pagan gods with gold, and silver, and precious stones and pleasant things. He can act impudently against the strongest fortresses, because he does so behind the scenes in the name of a pagan god. He has advanced the worship and recognition of this pagan god and he helps to set up rulers, and divide land. The Pope is also forbidden from marrying, or having any relations with women, thus he has no regard for any women that desire him.

Remember at the beginning of this chapter when I mentioned that while all the kingdoms had different metals, they all were in unison forming the same idol? The Roman Catholic Church now carries the torch of the pagan sun god worship that has transferred from culture to culture from the time of Babylon, to Persia, to Greece, to Rome, and even long before, and in fact brings together all of these pagan gods into unison in the form of Catholicism. Further, we know the antichrist will seek to unite the world and unite religions. The Papacy has actively spoken in the UN and from many other platforms calling for unity in world government and has called for a one world government. Pope Francis in particular has called for a single ruler to oversee the nations and help end world hunger, and strife. He has also been actively setting up "Chrislam" which is a hybrid religion of Christianity and Islam, as well as claiming all roads lead to God.

Beyond that, the Ostrogoths were destroyed in 538 A.D. as stated before which was when the Papacy truly rose to full power. Napoleon officially imprisoned Pope Pius VI in 1798 and the mortal wound was dealt. The amount of years in between these events, the solidification of the papacy in 538 till the fall of the papacy in 1798, were exactly 1260 years. I still believe the 1260 days, or 42 months, or 3 1/2 years, (which are all the same EXACT amount of time according to the Hebrew calendar) are going to be a literal period of days, but you cannot deny that these events being exactly 1260 years apart is more than a mere coincidence. The antichrist will reign for 1260 days, and the papacy originally reigned for 1260 years? One last thing to consider is this, I already explained the 7 heads as governmental heads, however, one more interesting factoid is that there have been officially eight popes since the re-establishment of the papacy. They are:

1. Pius XI
2. Pius XII
3. John XXIII
4. Paul VI
5. John Paul I
6. John Paul II
7. Benedict XV
8. Francis

What's truly interesting about all of this, is that technically, according to multiple sources, Pope Benedict XV never "officially" passed the Papacy to Francis, and many within Catholicism claim that he is not actually a real Pope. If this is the case, the next Pope we see may be the final one, being an eight of the seven. All of these facts paint a rather unanswerable conclusion that the Roman Catholic Church, is in fact, the beast of the book of Revelation, and the seat, at least at first, of the imposter vicar of christ, the antichrist.

Every prophecy nails down this beast perfectly. There isn't a single prophecy that doesn't fit like a glove. The question then becomes how will a Pope get Islam, or Hinduism, or Judaism, or Christians to follow him? Well, that part is already beginning now. The Pope is doing those things right now as we speak. This mission represents the full time mission of the Vatican, and they're doing it all in the name of "peace"

> *1 Thessalonians 5:3 For when they say, "Peace and safety!" then sudden destruction comes upon them, as labor pains upon a pregnant woman. And they shall not escape.*

The Pope is actively uniting all religions in the name of peace. Naturally though, there will be some who resist this movement. How will they be convinced?

> *2 Thessalonians 2:9-10 The coming of the lawless one is according to the working of Satan, with all power, signs, and lying wonders, 10 and with all unrighteous deception among those who perish, because they did not receive the love of the truth, that they might be saved.*

Lying signs and wonders. Some apocryphal texts even suggest that the antichrist will descend from the sky and be able to command the sun. This sounds impossible, but so do most of the events in Revelation and we choose to believe those. What if the antichrist is a giant, akin to king Og, who was like a cedar tree? Have you seen the giant golden throne sitting in the middle of the Vatican? Who could make war with a man like that? We don't really know what the antichrist will appear as or do. If the antichrist can perform enough signs and wonders, will there be anyone who doubts him? Only those who truly know and love the truth, and these will be the ones he hates. The Muslims will say, "the Imam" the Jews will say "The Messiah" the Buddhists will say "the enlightened one" many Christians will say "the Christ" and anyone who does not buy into the deception will be universally hated. Men will believe that by killing those who oppose the antichrist, they will be doing a service to God. This has all been foretold. The Vatican is the last empire, the beast made up of pieces of the other beast, the iron mingled with clay, and will be destroyed when the Stone that the Builders rejected comes and smashes the image of idolatry. The beast is revealed.

13

Applications

What do we do? This ought to be the question we are asking ourselves. We, the church, are drenched in idolatry. We have taken on the name "the church" as either the daughter of Helios, or the house of Baal. We have kept Christmas and Easter which represent the birth, death, and resurrection of the antichrist. We have had the true name of God taken out of our Bibles and replaced it with Baal (the lord), and many don't even know the name of the God we serve. We have taken on the pattern of the pagan Eucharist. We have unknowingly taken on ourselves the mark of the Popes "ecclesiastical authority" by gathering on and keeping their Sunday sabbath, and pagan holidays.

Now, I want to make a quick disclaimer regarding this mark of their authority, I do not believe necessarily that this is the mark of the beast as some assert, or at least not in full. We know that unless one has the mark, they cannot buy, sell, or trade, and are hunted down. There are no laws or practices in effect that prevent anyone from buying, selling, or trading unless they keep Sunday sabbath and the pagan holidays, therefore from where I'm sitting, it doesn't seem to fit. That being said, I do think it is extremely important to get this mark of authority off of us sooner than later, as it very well may become the full mark of the beast somehow later on. One other interesting note is that countries all over the world honor Sunday, and in many places, government buildings such as secretary of state, court buildings, and banks are all closed on Sunday. There is even legislature in the United States commonly referred to as the "blue laws" that are government mandated observances of this false Sabbath. With the legislation already in place, all it would take is the government to enforce these laws more harshly and we could see the birth of a militaristic enforcement of this mark of the beasts authority. Just food for thought.

But back to the question at hand; what do we do with all of this information regarding idolatry in our lives? The answer dear reader, is get it out. Turn from it and repent. Have you wondered why the world keeps getting darker and the light and salt that is supposed to illuminate and preserve the world has been failing abysmally? Have you wondered why the church continues to slide deeper and deeper into sin with reckless abandon? Have you wondered why things like Christian witches, and LGBTQ activist Christian churches are popping up all over? Have you wondered why thousands upon thousands are leaving Christianity behind because they see no power in it as well as seeing inconsistencies and hypocrisy? The truth is, we have been unknowingly lying in the bed of another man, and our Husband is not happy about it. What's the answer?

> *James 4:7-10 Therefore submit to God. Resist the devil and he will flee from you. 8 Draw near to God and He will draw near to you. Cleanse your hands, you sinners; and purify your hearts, you double-minded. 9 Lament and mourn and weep! Let your laughter be turned to mourning and your joy to gloom. 10 Humble yourselves in the sight of the Lord, and He will lift you up.*

> *Joel 2:12-13 "Now, therefore," says the Lord, "Turn to Me with all your heart, with fasting, with weeping, and with mourning." 13 So rend your heart, and not your garments; return to the Lord your God, for He is gracious and merciful, slow to anger, and of great kindness; and He relents from doing harm.*

Zechariah 1:2-4 "The Lord has been very angry with your fathers. 3 Therefore say to them, Thus says the Lord of hosts: "Return to Me," says the Lord of hosts, "and I will return to you," says the Lord of hosts. 4 'Do not be like your fathers, to whom the former prophets preached, saying, Thus says the Lord of hosts: "Turn now from your evil ways and your evil deeds." ' But they did not hear nor heed Me," says the Lord.

Matthew 3:2 (...) "Repent, for the kingdom of heaven is at hand!"

Matthew 4:17 From that time Jesus began to preach and to say, "Repent, for the kingdom of heaven is at hand."

We need to repent, and turn from the wicked way. We need to mourn, fast, humble ourselves, and seek His face. We need to return to God in truth, not just in the words of our lips. We need to accept what we've done, instead of trying to pretend that it's okay, and ask for forgiveness and change.

That is, by the way, one of the most common things I see when people begin to be presented with this information. They brush it off and say it's not a big deal. They say things like "That's not what it means now." or "That's not what I mean when I celebrate it." or "God knows my heart." Yes, God does know your heart. He knows if you've been sinning on accident by participating in idolatry, that you did so ignorantly, but He also knows if you continue to sin now that you have this knowledge, that your heart is truly hardened, and not soft enough to be molded and changed by Him.

James 4:17 Therefore, to him who knows to do good and does not do it, to him it is sin.

God equates idolatry to committing adultery against Him. Do you really think He doesn't care?

James 4:5 Or do you think that the Scripture says in vain, "The Spirit who dwells in us yearns jealously"?

God has shown consistently from the beginning of scripture and time until now that He hates idolatry and will punish His people for it. Do you really think you can push the worship of Satan and his antichrist off as "no big deal"? Can you find a single example in the Bible where His people worshiped God with pagan rites and He was pleased with it? No. But I have shown several examples of Him being angered when people have done this.

Let me provide one more example for you. Remember the golden calf? Moses went up the mountain to meet with God and while he was away the people made a golden calf and began worshiping it. People might think that they were worshiping some god they brought with them from Egypt but this isn't actually the case. Let's look at this passage together.

> *Exodus 32:2-6 And Aaron said to them, "Break off the golden earrings which are in the ears of your wives, your sons, and your daughters, and bring them to me." 3 So all the people broke off the golden earrings which were in their ears, and brought them to Aaron. 4 And he received the gold from their hand, and he fashioned it with an engraving tool, and made a molded calf.*
>
> *Then they said, "This is your god, O Israel, that brought you out of the land of Egypt!"*
>
> *5 So when Aaron saw it, he built an altar before it. And Aaron made a proclamation and said, "Tomorrow is a feast to the Lord." 6 Then they rose early on the next day, offered burnt offerings, and brought peace offerings; and the people sat down to eat and drink, and rose up to play.*

So just to quickly point out a few things, they decided to set up this golden calf, but who did they say this calf was? Did they say it was Baal? Did they say it was one of the fertility goddesses associated with cows? No, they said this is the god of Israel, who brought them out of Egypt. Then in the next verse Aaron says the next day will be a feast to "the Lord". Remember that this phrase is a placeholder for the name of God that was removed. If you check the interlinear for verse 5, you'll see they did indeed call this golden calf by the proper name given for God (which we will get into a bit later).

So the people were worshiping God, right? I mean look at it, they wanted to worship God, that's what was in their heart right? So they went through all the trouble of making a statue for Him, to honor Him. Not only did they make a statue, they gave up all their jewelry and all their gold to do it, and made a very costly and grand statue. That was so generous right? They gave up all that money to worship Him, He would be pleased right? Then they set aside a whole day, and held a feast in honor of God, and offered peace offerings, and burnt offerings. Surely God saw their hearts were in the right place right? He saw that all they wanted to do was worship Him, and though they did it in a different way than what He wanted, their heart was in the right place right? Yeah, maybe some of these practices had pagan origins, but it didn't matter because they were doing it for Him right? Man looks at the outward appearance but God looks at the heart so God just overlooked the way they did things and looked at their hearts right? And hey, if nothing else the name of God was being glorified right? So everything was cool, and God was pleased, and He sent Moses down the mountain to thank the people for the lovely statue and offerings right? Not quite.

> *Exodus 32:7-10 And the Lord said to Moses, "Go, get down! For your people whom you brought out of the land of Egypt have corrupted themselves. 8 They have turned aside quickly out of the way which I commanded them. They have made themselves a molded calf, and worshiped it and sacrificed to it, and said, This is your god, O Israel, that brought you out of the land of Egypt!' " 9 And the Lord said to Moses, 'I have seen this people, and indeed it is a stiff-necked people! 10 Now therefore, let Me*

alone, that My wrath may burn hot against them and I may consume them. And I will make of you a great nation."

Even though they had given their money and valuables, and even though they had set aside a special day just for Him, and even though they had called the statue by His name, and had offered sacrifices and offerings, and had good intentions, He seemed to be less than pleased. So displeased in fact, He basically said to Moses, let me wipe them all out, and I'll start again with just you and your offspring. That was God's response toward the people worshiping Him in whatever way they saw fit. This was His response to His people taking pagan practices and slapping His name on it, He wanted to destroy them.

In modern times Christians take the pagan practices of other nations, Yule, Saturnalia, Eostre, and others, and they slap the name of Christ on it. They set aside the day to honor Him and they give money and food to have special feasts in His honor. They make sure that they focus on Him, and give the glory to Him, proclaiming His name and saying it's all about Him and what He did. "It's all about Jesus' birth, so let's remember the ultimate gift that God gave to mankind and proclaim it to the nations!" and "Today is all about Christ, about His triumphant rise from the grave, let's take the day to proclaim His resurrection!" God is pleased right? The Israelites said, tomorrow we'll hold a feast to God, and worship Him for bringing us out of Egypt, and we'll offer Him our money and food and praise. None of these things pleased Him then, and rest assured, they do not please Him now. Many of His people are once again gathered around the golden calves of Christmas and Easter, worshiping Him, and proclaiming Him, but He is not pleased.

When you stand before the Great White Throne of Judgement and stand before the Judge over all, do you think "I didn't think you'd mind too much, after all, it didn't mean all that to me." is going to be a good response? Do you think you'll be able to say, "Yeah, I know you warned your people repeatedly against worshiping the way the pagans do, but personally I didn't see any harm in it."? Christ suffered, bled, and died for us, can we not change our lifestyle for Him? This really is the least we can do for our King.

There was a woman named Alice who married a man named Steve. Steve loved Alice and treated her well, but she decided to leave Steve for a man named Carl. She stayed with Carl for a while, but he was a beast of a man. He would beat her, and abuse her. Eventually, she couldn't take anymore and went back to Steve. Steve forgave her for her adultery and they renewed their vows in an attempt to start their marriage fresh. In spite of this, each year, Alice would skip over Steve's birthday, ignoring it completely, and instead would celebrate Carl's birthday. She would make all of Carl's favorite foods on Carl's birthday, and bring it to Steve, wishing him a happy birthday. This however was not Steve's birthday, and Steve didn't like Carl's favorite foods, in fact he hated them, and he hated Carl. He asked Alice if she would please stop celebrating Carl's birthday and making Carl's favorite foods, and instead celebrate his birthday, making his favorite foods. Alice told Steve, "I know it's not really your birthday, but, this is just how I've gotten used to doing things. I don't care about Carl anymore, but I enjoy making Carl's favorite foods, and it's a tradition. It may be Carl's birthday technically, but that's not what it means to me." Is Alice being a good wife? Of course not! But that is exactly what it is like when we celebrate Christmas and say "That's not what it means to me"

Here's another example: When I was a kid, me and my older sister were hanging out in the living room one day. Our younger sister walked in with a big bowl of ice cream. It was three or four big scoops of ice cream, covered in chocolate chips, and whipped cream, and sprinkles, and that chocolate magic shell stuff. It looked delicious. We asked her what it was for, and she told us she made it for us to all share. We were both really touched that she would think to bring us ice cream as she was still pretty young at this time. We were also impressed that she had gone through all the work of gathering the ingredients and putting them on in spite of being so young. We were also, of course, excited to eat the frozen treat she had made for us.

We all started eating it, and were enjoying it, when suddenly my older sister got a piece of something hard in her mouth. She pulled it out and inspected it, and we discovered that it was a hardened piece of food. To our horror we discovered it was a remnant from breakfast which had been hours earlier, and that underneath the ice cream was other chunks of old food. It turns out that my little sister without realizing how gross it would be, had pulled a dirty bowl out of the sink that hadn't been washed yet to use for making her treat. As good as the ice cream was, we were so grossed out by the old food in it, that we ended up throwing the rest away. My little sister had the absolute best of intentions, and her heart was in the right place. It was a sweet gesture, and we appreciated it. Even the ice cream sundae itself was a pleasing thing, but because she had brought it to us in a filthy disgusting container, it became no longer good to eat. The pagan holidays, dear reader, are a filthy and disgusting container. We can bring sincere and honest praise to God, and that's a good thing, but if it's in a filthy disgusting container, it isn't an acceptable offering.

God wants things done His way, not whatever way we decide we want to do them. Remember this passage?

> *Leviticus 10:1-3 Then Nadab and Abihu, the sons of Aaron, each took his censer and put fire in it, put incense on it, and offered profane fire before the Lord, which He had not commanded them. 2 So fire went out from the Lord and devoured them, and they died before the Lord. 3 And Moses said to Aaron, "This is what the Lord spoke, saying:*
>
> *'By those who come near Me*
> *I must be regarded as holy;*
> *And before all the people*
> *I must be glorified.' "*

We cannot bring profane offerings before God, and expect Him to be pleased. He must be regarded as Holy, and if our offerings are not Holy, we cannot bring them to Him, or else we provoke His anger. The truth is, God hates these pagan holidays, and trying to continue to celebrate them all the while claiming your heart is pleasing to Him, is just a lie one tells themselves to continue in rebellion. God is not pleased with a heart that is unwilling to change their ways for Him, and obey Him.

Oh and by the way, I only went over three of the holidays. Many more are pagan in origin. Valentines day came from Lupercalia, the feast of the wolf god Lupus. The Romans would strip naked, sacrifice animals on the alter to Lupus, take the hides and fashion whips with them. They would have the naked women line up and the men would whip them with these whips to increase fertility. They would then take all the names of the women and put them into a raffle, and men would randomly choose the name of the woman they would then spend the evening with in the temple having sex with in public. This would naturally devolve into a massive orgy. They slapped the name of a saint over it, gave it a new name and took out some of the more extreme traditions, and now Christians the world over celebrate it by spicing up their romance. May Day celebrated by many Catholics is the pagan celebration of Beltane, the fire festival. To this day pagans paint their bodies red, and go out into the forest naked and have drunken, sexual parties celebrating the "May queen" which is another pagan fertility goddess. Many holidays are nothing but repainted pagan worship and are filled with references and subtle ways to worship pagan gods.

The question becomes, what do we turn to? Where do we go? You cannot create a vacuum. You cannot take away all the holidays, and the day we gather ourselves to assemble together without a replacement. We cannot take away the name "church" without giving us something to call ourselves. We cannot take away the way we celebrate communion without replacing it with something else. If we take away all of these things without replacing them, we'll have nothing left. Well, Section III deals with this problem. Keep reading, and you'll find more truth.

Before that though, I want to remind you of one last thing in this chapter.

The love of God. When God disciplines us or corrects us, it is Him showing us love.

Proverbs 3:11-12 My son, do not despise the chastening of the Lord, nor detest His correction; 12 for whom the Lord loves He corrects, Just as a father the son in whom he delights.

God loves you, deeply. He wants to draw close to you and heal our lives, but how can He if we are choosing to continue to walk in idolatry?

When I was 4 or so, I was at my grandma's house. She had these monkey bars, but I couldn't quite reach them. I found a little plastic chair, and climbed up onto the monkey bars. Me being a bit of a daredevil, naturally I went for the highest one. Well, I slipped, and fell, right onto the plastic chair. The chair snapped as it was flimsy plastic, and as broken plastic is often times sharp, it gave me a large cut across my stomach. I was bleeding, and crying, and my mom was so concerned about me, she wanted to come over and comfort me. I however, was enraged by the pain I was experiencing, and instead of going to hug my mom and be comforted, and get bandaged up, I decided I was going to rip that chair the rest of the way apart, after all, in my young mind, the chair itself had hurt me. I picked up that chair and began bashing it against the metal pole leading up to the monkey bars with all my might, and flailing wildly with sharp pieces of plastic. My mom couldn't even get close. I ended up fracturing that chair into many small pieces, and to add insult to injury, my dad found out and punished me for destroying the chair and throwing a temper tantrum.

The body of Christ is wounded. It is failing at it's job to be a light, as evidenced by the world growing ever darker and ever more debased. Many of us are sick, and struggling, and even though Christ promised us we would go through trials, I cannot help but think that many of these trials and struggles that Christians are experiencing are being brought on ourselves. God wants to draw close to us, and heal us, but we have two choices. We can either run away from our idolatry and into His open arms to be bandaged and healed, or we can become angry and stubborn, throwing a spiritual temper tantrum, and continue on in our filth. Make no mistake, that path ends in discipline on top of pain, just as it did for my four year old self.

This book is entitled Idolatry: Journey out of Egypt. Now you know why. We have been living in Egypt. In the Bible, Egypt was a physical place, but spiritually speaking, it pertains to the world and the idolatry and wickedness of the world. The body of Christ has been spiritually living in Egypt for far too long. We've taken on the customs and traditions of the world, the worship of their false gods, and doing the very things that God destroyed Israel for in the Old Testament. We cannot serve two masters. We cannot slap the Holy on the profane and pretend it's acceptable to God. We cannot live like Egypt any longer. We need to journey out of Egypt by forsaking the ways of the world, and turning away from them and becoming Holy and set apart. We need to repent and leave Egypt behind.

The choice is up to you dear reader, but remember that the end is rapidly approaching, and the antichrist will rise. If you can't even separate yourself from him when all there is to lose is a bit of fun and family tradition, how do you hope to resist his mark when your food and shelter are in question? I am not here to debate whether or not you will be here for the tribulation period, as frankly, I hope you are not, dear reader, but regardless, we are called to prepare ourselves for the return of our Beloved, and we had better have prepared ourselves and made ourselves ready when He returns. There were wise virgins, and foolish virgins. The wise virgins went into the wedding feast. The foolish ones were left out in the darkness. They were all virgins, but only the wise entered in. Please, dear reader, be a wise virgin, and enter in. Turn from the darkness to the light. Fill your lamp with the oil of truth.

Proverbs 6:23 For the commandment is a lamp, and the law a light; reproofs of instruction are the way of life,

III

The Road Less Traveled

14

Out of the Frying Pan

Many people are waking up to the reality that the Roman origin that the ekklesia has been attached to, is in fact quite dangerous. The RCC has infected pretty much all of modern Christianity with their pagan and idolatrous ways. When people begin to realize this, they do what I admonished you to do in the previous chapter, they repent and flee from it. However, another danger awaits those who follow that path. You see, the narrow path is just that, it's narrow. There is indeed a ditch on one side of the road we need to flee from, but on the other side there is another ditch waiting to ensnare. On one side, we see the RCC, and their idolatry and paganism. But what lies on the other side, creating the other ditch? Well, simply put, Judaism, or to be more specific, Messianic Judaism.

Now before we get any further, I need to make a disclaimer. Regarding Messianic Judaism, not everyone who claims this title is participating in the things I am going to put forth. That being said, I believe the overall movement of Messianic Judaism to reflect the things I will say. This is not meant to be accusatory, but merely informational. When I say Messianic Judaism, I do not mean physical Jews who believe in Messiah, I am referring to the mixture of traditional orthodox Judaism and faith in Christ. The reason for this distinction will become clearer in the following chapters.

Many people when fleeing from the influence of the RCC flee into the influence of Messianic Judaism. Messianic Judaism is exactly what it sounds like, it is Judaism, but it accepts the Messiah. The issue with this is that Judaism is actually just as dangerous as the RCC, and in fact, most people don't even understand Judaism at all. The most prominent explanation of Judaism is that they keep the law of the Old Testament, but that's not actually true at all. Judaism, just like Catholicism, is steeped in mysticism and tradition. In fact, In Jesus' time, He constantly taught against these traditions.

> *Matthew 15:2-6 "Why do Your disciples transgress the tradition of the elders? For they do not wash their hands when they eat bread." 3 He answered and said to them, "Why do you also transgress the commandment of God because of your tradition? 4 For God commanded, saying, 'Honor your father and your mother'; and, 'He who curses father or mother, let him be put to death.' 5 But you say, 'Whoever says to his father or mother, "Whatever profit you might have received from me is a gift to God"— 6 then he need not honor his father or mother.' Thus you have made the commandment of God of no effect by your tradition.*

This next passage is a mirror of the one above.

> *Mark 7:9-13 He said to them, "All too well you reject the commandment of God, that you may keep your tradition. 10 For Moses said, 'Honor your father and your mother'; and, 'He who curses father or mother, let him be put to death.' 11 But you say, 'If a man says to his father or mother, "Whatever profit you might have received from me is Corban"—'(that is, a gift to God), 12 then you no longer let him do anything for his father or his mother, 13 making the word of God of no effect through your tradition which you have handed down. And many such things you do."*

Jesus taught against these traditions of the pharisees many other times throughout the gospels. After Christ ascended, many of these traditions were still hotly debated topics. What were these traditions though? Where did they come from? Well, as I said, the Rabbinical Jews and many prominent teachers in Christianity would have you believe they keep the law of God, but the truth is, they keep the law of their so called sages. Judaism is completely consumed by four main texts or practices; the Zohar, the Talmud, the Kaballah and the Mishneh Torah. We will look briefly at each one. First, here is an excerpt from the Wikipedia page on Talmud:

> *The Talmud (/tlmd, -md, tæl-/; Hebrew: , romanized: talmūd) is the central text of Rabbinic Judaism and the primary source of Jewish religious law (halakha) and Jewish theology. Until the advent of modernity, in nearly all Jewish communities, the Talmud was the centerpiece of Jewish cultural life and was foundational to "all Jewish thought and aspirations" serving also as "the guide for the daily life" of Jews. The term "Talmud" normally refers to the collection of writings named specifically the Babylonian Talmud (Talmud Bavli), although there is also an earlier collection known as the Jerusalem Talmud (Talmud Yerushalmi). It may also traditionally be called Shas (), a Hebrew abbreviation of shisha sedarim, or the "six orders" of the Mishnah.* [40]

The Talmud is, as stated, the primary source of all Rabbinic Judaism law, and theology. The Talmud that is the most prominent version by far, is the Babylonian Talmud, much of which was written while the house of Judah was in captivity in Babylon during the time of Daniel. The Talmud also includes a collection of teachings from the "sages" or wisemen among the Jews throughout the ages, even up to the modern day. This is what Rabbinical Judaism is founded upon. The Talmud is an absolutely monstrous book. If you thought the RCC was bad, this stuff is worse. The Talmud teaches in Gittin 57a, that Jesus (whom they call Yeshu which is an insult roughly meaning "may his name be blotted out") is boiling in his own feces for all eternity. It also teaches a disturbing practice known as "oral circumcision" that involves a rabbi taking the penis of a circumcised child into his mouth and sucking on it to purify it. It teaches that Jews have a soul derived from divininity, while any non Jew has a soul derived from a demonic origin, thus Jews are a more valuable life force, and gentiles are little more than human cattle to try to herd. The Talmud even goes as far as to teach that God Himself is responsible to obey the writings in the Talmud and that what the Rabbi's say is more impactful than what God says. The Talmud is chalk full of blasphemy and filth.

The next book, the Zohar, is a compilation of writings about general spirituality written again by the sages of the ages. It speaks primarily about the nature of God, and the nature of the human spirit, but touches on many subjects. Some things the Zohar teaches are that every action we perform creates either angels or demons. It teaches we should empty ourselves to become one with the universe, and many other things. In fact, here are two quotes you may find a bit familiar. These are taken from a website called carm.org

"From noon until midnight, the sun appears to be declining, which means that the power of loving kindness is waning. When the sun reaches its lowest ebb, the time in which the energy of darkness is strongest, accusing angels have their greatest power. The Kabbalist says that this point is the darkest of the night, the moment when restriction and judgment are at their full power. If we were abandoned in the mystical midnight of creation, we would disappear."

"Cabalists teach that the moon is the mystical vessel in which souls are gathered before they are released to the world. The moon in Kabbalah represents receptivity... the mystical implication is that souls are influenced by the phase of the moon when they become associated with bodies, each having different levels of expansiveness or contracted this... we would say that this describes why some of us are more extroverted while others are more introverted..." [41]

Oh look, it's the sun and the moon given additional power and authority over different aspects of life. AGAIN. The moon is a mother that holds within herself the souls of men almost like a symbol of fertility? The sun directly oversees the power of angelic and demonic forces kind of like a god? Where have we seen this before?

Then there's the Zohar that is directly related to the Kabbalah. Here is an excerpt from the wikipedia page for Kabbalah:

Kabbalah (Hebrew: , literally "reception, tradition" or "correspondence") is an esoteric method, discipline, and school of thought in Jewish mysticism. A traditional Kabbalist in Judaism is called a Mequbbāl (). The definition of Kabbalah varies according to the tradition and aims of those following it, from its religious origin as an integral part of Judaism, to its later adaptations in Western esotericism (Christian Kabbalah and Hermetic Qabalah). Jewish Kabbalah is a set of esoteric teachings meant to explain the relationship between God, the unchanging, eternal, and mysterious Ein Sof (, "The Infinite"), and the mortal and finite universe (God's creation). It forms the foundation of mystical religious interpretations within Judaism.

Jewish Kabbalists originally developed their own transmission of sacred texts within the realm of Jewish tradition, and often use classical Jewish scriptures to explain and demonstrate its mystical teachings. These teachings are held by followers in Judaism to define the inner meaning of both the Hebrew Bible and traditional rabbinic literature and their formerly concealed transmitted dimension, as well as to explain the significance of Jewish religious observances. One of the fundamental kabbalistic texts, the Zohar, was first published in the 13th century, and the almost universal form adhered to in modern Judaism is Lurianic Kabbalah. [42]

Kabbalah is nothing more and nothing less than Eastern Mysticism also derived from the worship of the sun god, and attaining enlightenment, and has much in common with Buddhism, Taoism, and other Eastern mysticism. In fact, much of Kabbalah deals with astrology. This is a quote taken from kabbalah.com

> *We do not study astrology so we can learn how to draw up people's horoscopes. On the contrary, the purpose of kabbalistic astrology is to rise above the influences of the cosmos and take control over our own lives.*
>
> *The Zodiac sign in which we are born transmits to us all the negative and positive traits that we will need to effect our own transformation. However, the signs of the Zodiac are not the cause of our personality traits; they are the effect. Our karma from previous lives determines which sign we need to be born under in order to acquire the necessary traits and attributes that will allow us to correct and transform previous negative activity.* [43]

Sadly, these traditions of men, in the form of Kabbalah, the Zohar, and the Talmud, are nothing but the same idolatry and filth that we see in Catholicism. In fact, imagery replete with suns, moons, and stars embedded in solar wheels and Zodiac signs are found everywhere in Judaism. True Messianic Judaism is a trap that Satan has set forth to ensnare those Jews who find Messiah, or those who are fleeing the influence of the RCC. Out of the frying pan and into the fire as it were. Again, this doesn't refer to those of Jewish decent who have come to Messiah, but those who hold these extra Biblical writings from the Jewish sages that are filled with idolatry.

One last thing of note with all of this is that you will notice that the Jews do heavily keep the law of the Old Testament, but unfortunately what they present, is warped. Another word for the Old Testament law is Torah. Torah merely means instructions. What they keep is a specific method of interpreting the Torah known as the Mishneh Torah, which is essentially the Torah according to the interpretations of the sages. Many of these interpretations are the heavy burdens that Christ spoke of.

Matthew 23:4 For they bind heavy burdens, hard to bear, and lay them on men's shoulders; but they themselves will not move them with one of their fingers.

To give some examples, the Torah says to rest on the Sabbath, and not to work or make anyone else work. The Mishneh Torah says you cannot lift even the slightest object. You cannot even carry objects in your pocket on the Sabbath because they consider this to be bearing a burden. If someone comes to you to deliver a package on the Sabbath, you cannot even carry it inside, as that would be bearing a burden over your threshold. These Rabbinical Jews do the same thing with nearly all of the law, making extreme interpretations of the Torah in order to appear self righteous. Many of these traditions, as Jesus mentioned got in the way of other laws such as their laws regarding "Corban" getting in the way of children honoring their fathers and mothers. This Mishneh Torah is the final foundation for Judaism, and is the only semblance to anything regarding keeping the law. Thus true orthodox Judaism is a combination of Kabbalah and Zohar, Talmud, and Mishneh Torah. Each of these are primarily founded on the traditions of men, many of which are pagan.

This again has nothing to do with the actual bloodline Jews, but with the beliefs of Judaism as a religion. In the chapters to come we will begin to dissect some things some would decry as antisemitic. I want to remind you, dear reader, racism is discrimination against a person based upon the DNA they were born with. I can disagree with a belief system of theology without being against the actual people believing it. You can hate Catholicism, but love Catholics enough to warn them. In today's political climate we are taught to very quickly label things as antisemitic and throw out what's being said without hearing the matter out. This is foolishness once again according to Ecclesiastes. I ask you once again hear out the matter of this section before you reject what I have to say. With this in mind, we can move forward.

15

Pagan Paramour

This chapter is called Pagan Paramour. In case you were not aware, the word Paramour means a lover, especially of an illicit nature, such as a woman that is having an affair. Thus another way of saying this would be a pagan adulteress. Also, I'm afraid I've come once again to mess with your end times theology. Once again, I am making this disclaimer, I do not wish to tell you I am definitively right, but I will suggest I have quite an enormous case from scripture on the information I am about to present. You are free to disagree with me, but I ask that you please hear the entire matter before you make a decision. We saw in Chapter 12 the identity of the Beast in the prophecies of Daniel and Revelation is actually the Roman Catholic Church. This was the first pit believers fall into that I warned against. The second pit I warned against was Judaism. Could it be that Judaism also has some kind of identity in the book of Revelation? Absolutely. I believe that Mystery Babylon: Mother of Harlots is in fact the city of Jerusalem the center of Judaism and in a broader sense, the Zionist movement, and I will prove it to you with a myriad of scripture, a touch of logic, and just a dash of history.

Before we really get into this, I want to say this again. Many will decry everything I am about to say as being anti-Semitic. This is not true at all. I don't make a distinction between people based upon lineage. I don't care if you're white, black, Jewish, Indian, or any other nationality. You are made in the image of God, and are a part of His creation. No ethnicity is any greater or lesser than any other. That being said, I do have a beef with the lies that are present in much of the culture and belief systems surrounding Israel and I will show from scripture why. I love Jews, but I cannot pretend to love Judaism or the things they do. As I said, before you cry "antisemite!" hear all of what I have to say first, then make your judgement.

> *Proverbs 18:13 He who answers a matter before he hears it, it is folly and shame to him.*

The first thing I want to show you is found in Revelation. I am going to throw a few verses at you real quick.

> *Revelation 14:8 And another angel followed, saying, "Babylon is fallen, is fallen, that great city, because she has made all nations drink of the wine of the wrath of her fornication."*

> *Revelation 18:10 standing at a distance for fear of her torment, saying, 'Alas, alas, that great city Babylon, that mighty city! For in one hour your judgment has come.'*

> *Revelation 18:21 Then a mighty angel took up a stone like a great millstone and threw it into the sea, saying, "Thus with violence the great city Babylon shall be thrown down, and shall not be found anymore.*

The first thing we need to see is that in the book of Revelation, the term "that great city" or "the great city" and Babylon, the harlot, are synonymous. You can see this over, and over, and over again. The second thing we need to see, is that Babylon is very clearly a city. She is not an ethnicity or a people, she is a city. A physical city. In fact, it clearly says that there will be a great earthquake, and the great city will be split in three.

Revelation 16:18-19 And there were noises and thunderings and lightnings; and <u>there was a great earthquake</u>, such a mighty and great earthquake as had not occurred since men were on the earth. 19 Now <u>the great city was divided into three parts</u>, and the cities of the nations fell. And great <u>Babylon</u> was remembered before God, to give her the cup of the wine of the fierceness of His wrath.

I do believe that there are belief systems that stem from this city, and that one of the reasons this city will come under judgement is because of it's history of belief systems, but Mystery Babylon is, in fact, a city. The third thing you need to realize, is that we are given the exact identity of this city in plain text.

Revelation 11:8 And their dead bodies will lie in the street of <u>the great city</u> which spiritually is called Sodom and Egypt, where also our Lord was crucified.

So we've established what "the great city" is, it's Babylon. Multiple verses confirm this plainly. There is no other city mentioned in the entirety of Revelation by that title except once, and we will get to that in a moment. So we can logically assume that this city where the bodies of the two witnesses will lie, is Babylon, the great city. Now, it tells us clearly that this city is also the location where our Lord was crucified. Where was Christ crucified? In Jerusalem. Many people argue that though He was crucified in Jerusalem, it was within the bounds of the Roman rule, therefore this verse points to Rome, but we've already seen the Vatican and it's globalist control mechanism is the beast system. Further, if you keep reading, you will see that there are far too many parallels with Jerusalem and too many things that don't fit the Vatican. This verse tells us plainly that Babylon, the great city, is Jerusalem. Remember that verse I mentioned that calls a city other than Babylon "the great city" yeah, that's found here:

Revelation 21:10 And he carried me away in the Spirit to a great and high mountain, and showed me the great city, the holy Jerusalem, descending out of heaven from God,

So, there are ten times through the book of Revelation that the term "the great city" is used. The first nine of them are referring to Babylon (Jerusalem), and the only other time is referring to the NEW Jerusalem. So this term in Revelation, really only ever refers to Jerusalem as the great city, and the final instance shows a shift or completion to the story of "the great city" transitioning from a place of evil and corruption, into the Holy place where Christ rules from. Interestingly though, in that verse that identifies that great city as the place where our Lord was crucified, it also calls that city spiritually Sodom, and Egypt. Was Jerusalem ever spoken of in this manner?

Isaiah 1:1 The vision of Isaiah the son of Amoz, which he saw concerning Judah and <u>Jerusalem</u> in the days of Uzziah, Jotham, Ahaz, and Hezekiah, kings of Judah.

Isaiah 1:8-11 So the daughter of Zion is left as a booth in a vineyard, as a hut in a garden of cucumbers, as a besieged city. 9 Unless the Lord of hosts had left to us a very small remnant, we would have become like Sodom, we would have been made like Gomorrah. 10 <u>Hear the word of the Lord, you rulers of Sodom;</u> Give ear to the law of our God, you people of Gomorrah: 11 "To what purpose is the multitude of your sacrifices to Me?" says the Lord. "I have had enough of burnt offerings of rams and the fat of fed cattle. I do not delight in the blood of bulls, or of lambs or goats.

So Isaiah says this word is concerning Judah (Jews) and Jerusalem, and then 10 verses later calls them Sodom. I included the verse afterward as well to prove that he is referring to Israel with this, as the actual physical city of Sodom never offered burnt offerings to God and these were only done in the temple in Jerusalem. Isaiah clearly calls Jerusalem a spiritual form of Sodom. Ezekiel also affirms this.

Ezekiel 16:3 and say, Thus says the Lord God to Jerusalem: (...)

Ezekiel 16:46 "Your elder sister is Samaria, who dwells with her daughters to the north of you; and your younger sister, who dwells to the south of you, is Sodom and her daughters.

Now we're going to look at this more in a moment, but the kingdom of Israel was split into two parts, the northern house of Israel, and the southern house of Judah. This verse clearly identifies the southern house of Judah as being a spiritual Sodom. The southern house of Judah of course contained Jerusalem. Twice we have evidence of Jerusalem being spiritually called Sodom.

One other blatant witness to this fact is found here:

1 Peter 5:13 She who is in Babylon, elect together with you, greets you; and so does Mark my son.

Obviously Peter knows the physical kingdom of Babylon had already fallen over a thousand years ago by this time, but he is still referring to a city and calling it Babylon. Which city was this? It had to be a city that was around during his time, as well as one that is around today right? The greetings in the letter also give us a strong hint. We don't know exactly who this woman was who greets the recipients of the letter, but we can fairly comfortably assume this is likely his wife. We know Peter was married, and had a son, Mark. It would make sense that Peter was writing the letter, and then his wife and son both wanted to say hello as well to those he was writing to. Thus, she who is in Babylon and Mark my son greet you. Even if this is not the case, we know exactly where Peter lived with his son Mark, with the other disciples, in Jerusalem. We know Peter and John are persecuted in

Jerusalem and remained there from accounts in the book of Acts. Further, we know Herod imprisoned Peter in Jerusalem and then was released. This verse adds another witness that the apostles already recognized Jerusalem as being Babylon. This also fits as a city that was around during the time of Peter, but is also around once again in modern times.

There is still so much evidence to go over though so let's keep moving. Now we need to examine some other descriptions of this woman, Babylon.

> *Revelation 17:4-6 The woman was arrayed in purple and scarlet, and adorned with gold and precious stones and pearls, having in her hand a golden cup full of abominations and the filthiness of her fornication. 5 And on her forehead a name was written:*
>
> > *MYSTERY, BABYLON THE GREAT,*
> > *THE MOTHER OF HARLOTS*
> > *AND OF THE ABOMINATIONS*
> > *OF THE EARTH.*
>
> *6 I saw the woman, drunk with the blood of the saints and with the blood of the martyrs of Jesus. And when I saw her, I marveled with great amazement.*

So there are several things to notice here. The first of which, is that Babylon was arrayed in purple and scarlet, and gold and precious stones and pearls. She possessed these things as she wore them, but she also had much more. She also sold many wares as well. This is after the fall of Babylon in Chapter 18, when it is speaking of the merchants of the earth mourning over her.

> *Revelation 18:11-13 And the merchants of the earth will weep and mourn over her, for no one buys their merchandise anymore: 12 merchandise of gold and silver, precious stones and pearls, fine linen and purple, silk and scarlet, every kind of citron wood, every kind of object of ivory, every kind of object of most precious wood, bronze, iron, and marble; 13 and cinnamon*

and incense, fragrant oil and frankincense, wine and oil, fine flour and wheat, cattle and sheep, horses and chariots, and bodies and souls of men.

So we find a large list of wares that Babylon sold including the things she wore such as purple and scarlet and gold, precious stones, and pearls. I will compile them here for ease of viewing.

1. Gold
2. Silver
3. Precious Stones
4. Pearls
5. Fine Linen
6. Purple
7. Silk
8. Scarlet
9. Wood
10. Ivory
11. Bronze
12. Iron
13. Marble
14. Cinnamon
15. Incense
16. Fragrant Oil
17. Frankincense
18. Wine
19. Oil
20. Fine Flour
21. Wheat
22. Cattle
23. Sheep
24. Horses
25. Chariots

26. Slaves (bodies and souls of men)

So, let's see if we can find these wares in Jerusalem. In the books of 1st & 2nd Chronicles, we are given the story of different events surrounding the temple that Solomon built in Jerusalem to God, which was the second temple that was destroyed after the ministry of Jesus.

> *1 Chronicles 9:29-30 Some of them were appointed over the furnishings and over all the implements of the sanctuary, and over the fine flour(20,21) and the wine(18) and the oil(19) and the incense(15) and the spices. 30 And some of the sons of the priests made the ointment of the spices(16).*

Fine flour is both #20 fine flour, as well as #21, wheat, because where there is fine flour, there is wheat.

> *1 Chronicles 28:18 and refined gold(1) by weight for the altar of incense(14,15,17), and for the construction of the chariot, that is, the gold cherubim that spread their wings and overshadowed the ark of the covenant of the Lord.*

You may have noticed I included #14, #15 and #17 here, which are cinnamon, incense and frankincense. This is because the incense used in the temple had frankincense and cinnamon in it as two of the primary oils used to create it, as detailed in Exodus 30:34-35.

> *1 Chronicles 29:2 Now for the house of my God I have prepared with all my might: gold(1) for things to be made of gold, silver(2) for things of silver, bronze(11) for things of bronze, iron(12) for things of iron, wood(9) for things of wood, onyx stones, stones to be set, glistening stones of various colors(4), all kinds of precious stones(3), and marble(13) slabs in abundance.*

2 Chronicles 1:16-17 And Solomon had horses(24) imported from Egypt and Keveh; the king's merchants bought them in Keveh at the current price. 17 They also acquired and imported from Egypt a chariot(25) for six hundred shekels of silver, and a horse for one hundred and fifty; thus, through their agents, they exported them to all the kings of the Hittites and the kings of Syria.

2 Chronicles 2:13-14 And now I have sent a skillful man, endowed with understanding, Huram my master craftsman 14 (the son of a woman of the daughters of Dan, and his father was a man of Tyre), skilled to work in gold(1) and silver(2), bronze(11) and iron(12), stone and wood(9), purple(6) and blue, fine linen(5,7) and crimson(8), and to make any engraving and to accomplish any plan which may be given to him, with your skillful men and with the skillful men of my lord David your father.

2 Chronicles 2:17-18 Then Solomon numbered all the aliens who were in the land of Israel, after the census in which David his father had numbered them; and there were found to be one hundred and fifty-three thousand six hundred. 18 And he made seventy thousand of them bearers of burdens, eighty thousand stonecutters in the mountain, and three thousand six hundred overseers to make the people work.(26)

2 Chronicles 5:6 Also King Solomon, and all the congregation of Israel who were assembled with him before the ark, were sacrificing sheep(23) and oxen(22) that could not be counted or numbered for multitude.

2 Chronicles 8:6 also Baalath and all the storage cities that Solomon had, and all the chariot cities(25) and the cities of the cavalry(24), and all that Solomon desired to build in Jerusalem, in Lebanon, and in all the land of his dominion.

2 Chronicles 9:17 Moreover the king made a great throne of ivory(10), and overlaid it with pure gold(1).

So with these verses, we have covered every single one of these wares that Babylon had to sell. All of these were contained in the temple which was in Jerusalem. Further, this isn't the first time we see Jerusalem all dressed up in fine apparel. Compare what Babylon is wearing to these verses:

Ezekiel 16:3, 9-13 and say, Thus says the Lord God to Jerusalem: (...) 9 "Then I washed you in water; yes, I thoroughly washed off your blood, and I anointed you with oil. 10 I clothed you in embroidered cloth and gave you sandals of badger skin; I clothed you with fine linen and covered you with silk. 11 I adorned you with ornaments, put bracelets on your wrists, and a chain on your neck. 12 And I put a jewel in your nose, earrings in your ears, and a beautiful crown on your head. 13 Thus you were adorned with gold and silver, and your clothing was of fine linen, silk, and embroidered cloth. You ate pastry of fine flour, honey, and oil. You were exceedingly beautiful, and succeeded to royalty.

This image rings pretty true to Babylon, and given that every single one of her wares could be found in the temple, and given that God called idolatry and giving herself to the other nations her harlotry, it would make sense that she was selling her wares to the nations. Further, we also see Jerusalem called a harlot. A lot.

Isaiah 1:21 How the faithful city has become a harlot! It was full of justice; righteousness lodged in it, but now murderers.

Ezekiel 16:3, 15-17 and say, Thus says the Lord God <u>to</u>
<u>Jerusalem</u>: (...) 15 "But you trusted in your own beauty, played
the harlot because of your fame, and poured out your harlotry
on everyone passing by who would have it. 16 You took some
of your garments and adorned multicolored high places for
yourself, and played the harlot on them. Such things should not
happen, nor be. 17 You have also taken your beautiful jewelry
from My gold and My silver, which I had given you, and made
for yourself male images and played the harlot with them.

Ezekiel 16:22 And in all your abominations and acts of harlotry
you did not remember the days of your youth, when you were
naked and bare, struggling in your blood.

Ezekiel 16:25-26 You built your high places at the head of
every road, and made your beauty to be abhorred. You offered
yourself to everyone who passed by, and multiplied your acts of
harlotry. 26 You also committed harlotry with the Egyptians,
your very fleshly neighbors, and increased your acts of harlotry
to provoke Me to anger.

Ezekiel 16:28-29 You also played the harlot with the Assyrians,
because you were insatiable; indeed you played the harlot with
them and still were not satisfied. 29 Moreover you multiplied
your acts of harlotry as far as the land of the trader, Chaldea;
and even then you were not satisfied.

I apologize for all of the references from the same chapter, but frankly, there are just so very many. The whole chapter of Ezekiel 16 is basically calling Jerusalem a harlot over, and over, and over in increasingly strong terms. This, by the way, comes right after that portion from earlier when Jerusalem is spoken of as a beautiful woman adorned in every finery. When you really stop and think about it, Jerusalem really does fit the description of a whore as well, as Jerusalem has at different times fallen to just about every pagan religion there has been. Baal, Asherah, Dagon, Remphan, Eastern Mysticism (Buddhism, Taoism, Hinduism), Islam, Catholicism, and more. Now, we also know that Mystery Babylon is full of abominations. Is Jerusalem ever spoken of as being filled with abominations? We already saw a few, but here are a few more.

> *Jeremiah 13:27 I have seen your adulteries and your lustful neighings, the lewdness of your harlotry, your abominations on the hills in the fields. Woe to you, O Jerusalem! Will you still not be made clean?*

> *Ezekiel 16:2 Son of man, cause Jerusalem to know her abominations*

> *Jeremiah 7:30 "For the children of Judah have done evil in My sight," says the Lord. "They have set their abominations in the house which is called by My name, to pollute it."*

So Jerusalem is a perfect match for every description of Babylon that we have seen thus far. The next description is her holding a cup full of the filthiness of her fornication. Another thing to note about this cup she is holding is that it gets filled double.

> *Revelation 18:6 Render to her just as she rendered to you, and repay her double according to her works; in the cup which she has mixed, mix double for her.*

So can we find Jerusalem bearing a cup that contains filthiness and fornications, that is filled with a double portion? This portion deals with a prophecy regarding two sisters:

> *Ezekiel 23:4 Their names: Oholah the elder and Oholibah her*

sister; they were Mine, and they bore sons and daughters. As for their names, Samaria is Oholah, and Jerusalem is Oholibah.

This chapter goes over how Oholah (the land of Israel that became part of Samaria after her divorce), and Oholibah, which is Jerusalem, acted toward God. Now the best thing for you to do is just read the chapter so you get the full understanding. Basically God is telling Jerusalem that she watched her sister Israel get divorced for her harlotry (idolatry), and yet she didn't learn from her sister's mistakes, but in fact became twice as much of a harlot as her sister. Then this statement is made:

Ezekiel 23:31-35 You have walked in the way of your sister; therefore I will put her cup in your hand. 32 "Thus says the Lord God: 'You shall drink of your sister's cup, the deep and wide one; you shall be laughed to scorn and held in derision; it contains much. 33 You will be filled with drunkenness and sorrow, the cup of horror and desolation, the cup of your sister Samaria. 34 You shall drink and drain it, you shall break its shards, And tear at your own breasts; for I have spoken,' says the Lord God. 35 "Therefore thus says the Lord God: 'Because you have forgotten Me and cast Me behind your back, therefore you shall bear the penalty of your lewdness and your harlotry.' "

So we see that Jerusalem had to bear not only her own penalty, but also the penalty of her sister. In other words, her sister's cup. If she had her own cup that she filled via her own filthiness and fornication, and her sister's cup full of the same, wouldn't that make a double portion? That is why Babylon's cup is mixed double, because she has to atone for her sins, as well as her sisters. To enforce this more, we have this verse that states it plainly.

Isaiah 40:1-2 "Comfort, yes, comfort My people!" says your God 2 "Speak comfort to Jerusalem, and cry out to her, that *her warfare is ended, that her iniquity is pardoned; for <u>she has</u>* *<u>received from the Lord's hand double for all her sins.</u>"*

So Jerusalem receives double for all of her sins, as does Mystery Babylon. Again, it's a perfect scriptural fit. The next description we see is that she is drunk off of the blood of the saints and martyrs. We already saw that the language of drunkenness was used when talking about Jerusalem drinking from the cup of wrath, but this verse specifically says she is drunk off of blood. Can we find that anywhere?

Matthew 23:34-38 Therefore, indeed, I send you prophets, wise *men, and scribes: some of them you will kill and crucify, and* *some of them you will scourge in your synagogues and persecute* *from city to city, 35 <u>that on you may come all the righteous blood</u>* *<u>shed on the earth, from the blood of righteous Abel to the blood of</u>* *<u>Zechariah</u>, son of Berechiah, whom you murdered between the* *temple and the altar. 36 Assuredly, I say to you, all these things* *will come upon this generation. 37 "O Jerusalem, Jerusalem, the* *one who kills the prophets and stones those who are sent to her!* *How often I wanted to gather your children together, as a hen* *gathers her chicks under her wings, but you were not willing!* *38 See! Your house is left to you desolate;*

So Jesus Himself pronounces judgements on Jerusalem, and says that all the blood of all the prophets and martyrs will be upon her head. Further, there are a few places where Jerusalem is called "the bloody city" for the same reason, killing the prophets and martyrs.

Ezekiel 24:6 Therefore thus says the Lord God: "Woe to the *bloody city, to the pot whose scum is in it, and whose scum is* *not gone from it! Bring it out piece by piece, on which no lot has* *fallen.*

Ezekiel 24:9 Therefore thus says the Lord God: "Woe to the bloody city! I too will make the pyre great.

Ezekiel 22:2 "Now, son of man, will you judge, will you judge the bloody city? Yes, show her all her abominations!

Now many argue that this was fulfilled in 70 A.D. when Jerusalem was besieged by Rome and the temple was destroyed, and it was, but sadly, this story repeats itself. By the way, this was the first instance of the beast (Rome) who had previously supported the woman, turning and devouring the woman, which is the same thing we will see at the end.

Ecclesiastes 3:15 That which is, has already been, and what is to be, has already been; and God requires an account of what is past.

These things repeat themselves. Further, we have certainly seen that Jerusalem has not turned from it's idolatry AT ALL, but in fact, has only gotten worse since it was destroyed in 70 A.D. In fact, not only is Jerusalem the center for Orthodox Judaism which is chalk full of all kinds of pagan mysticism and wickedness such as the Talmud, and Kabbalah, we also know there are multiple other religious centers in Jerusalem such as multiple Roman Catholic Churches and even the Dome of the Rock, which is one of the most prominent and important Muslim sites in the world. Jerusalem is filled with her abominations more than she has even been in the past, and truly what is to be has already been.

It says that the sins of Babylon will be called to remembrance. Is there anywhere that says Jerusalem's sins will be called to remembrance?

Ezekiel 21:23-24 And it will be to them like a false divination in the eyes of those who have sworn oaths with them; but he will bring their iniquity to remembrance, that they may be taken. 24 "Therefore thus says the Lord God: 'Because you have made your iniquity to be remembered, in that your transgressions are uncovered, so that in all your doings your sins appear—because you have come to remembrance, you shall be taken in hand.

Once again, the descriptions and prophecies match one another. Babylon's sins are come to remembrance before God, and when this happens, He pours out his wrath on her, punishing her. Another phrase that means to punish is to be taken in hand. This verse states it plainly.

The next description we see with Babylon is that she is riding on the Beast. We learned in the last section that the Vatican and the RCC is the beast. How does Jerusalem ride on the Vatican or Roman Catholicism? Well, it's very simple really. As I stated earlier, the Vatican is essentially one of the three pillars that currently rule the world alongside Washington D.C. and the City of London. The City of London is actually where the Rothschild family holds their fortune and has their base of operations. If you didn't know, the Rothschilds are one of the main players in the globalist agenda, as well as one of the richest families in the elite. The Vatican has always had links to these elite families, as most of these families are involved with the Jesuits, Free Masons, or Templars. The Vatican and the Rothschilds are so tied together in fact, that although there is no official paper trail (there wouldn't be), it is believed that the Rothschilds personally help to oversee the finances of the Vatican. What do the Rothschilds have to do with Israel? This is a quote from the Wikipedia page for the Balfour Declaration:

> *The Balfour Declaration was a public statement issued by the British government in 1917 during the First World War announcing support for the establishment of a "national home for the Jewish people" in Palestine, then an Ottoman region with a small minority Jewish population.* [44]

So the Balfour Declaration began the process of giving Israel back their land. Who was the Balfour Declaration addressed to? Why not just read it for yourself?

Foreign Office
November 2nd, 1917
    Dear Lord Rothschild,
    I have much pleasure in conveying to you, on behalf of His Majesty's Government, the following declaration of sympathy with Jewish Zionist aspirations which has been submitted to, and approved by, the Cabinet
    His Majesty's Government view with favour the establishment in Palestine of a national home for the Jewish people, and will use their best endeavors to facilitate the achievement of this object, it being clearly understood that nothing shall be done which may prejudice the civil and religious rights of existing non-Jewish communities in Palestine or the rights and political status enjoyed by Jews in any other country.
    I should be grateful if you would bring this declaration to the knowledge of the Zionist Federation.
    Yours,
    Arthur James Balfour

Yup, the Balfour Declaration that led to the establishment of the nation state of Israel was brought about directly through the efforts of the Rothschild families and the beast system of global domination. The Rothschilds helped to start and established the Zionist agenda behind the scenes, and they still financially support it today. In fact, the Rothschilds are honored in Tel Aviv by having a road named after them, namely Rothschild Boulevard. Remember that the woman also sits on 7 hills though. This could be in a spiritual sense that she is sitting on the 7 heads of the beast, but it is also interesting to note that there are 7 mountains around Jerusalem that this woman sits on.

    Another note is that the Pope is currently all about Jerusalem, and is working with the Rabbinic Jews to set up multi faith areas and activities as mentioned earlier. The Pope is also concerning himself with the peace talks trying to help strike a deal for peace in Jerusalem. Israel is also being massively funded by Washington D.C. and families such as the Rockefellers and others that are tied to the elite and the Vatican. The woman is assuredly riding the beast, and the beast assuredly hates the woman, and will eventually turn and devour her once again, as it has done in the past. Remember that in Jesus' time, this event took place:

> *John 19:14-15 Now it was the Preparation Day of the Passover, and about the sixth hour. And he said to the Jews, "Behold your King!" 15 But they cried out, "Away with Him, away with Him! Crucify Him!" Pilate said to them, "Shall I crucify your King?" The chief priests answered, "We have no king but Caesar!"*

The woman was riding the beast back in that time as well, being supported and helped by Rome. What has been, will be again.

Beyond this though, the woman is spoken of as being ruler over the kings of the earth. How does this fit Jerusalem? Very easily, at the time of the end, Jerusalem will be the final seat of power for the antichrist. Thus, Jerusalem will be ruler over the kings of the earth while riding upon the beast.

> *2 Thessalonians 2:3-4 Let no one deceive you by any means; for that Day will not come unless the falling away comes first, and the man of sin is revealed, the son of perdition, 4 who opposes and exalts himself above all that is called God or that is worshiped, so that he sits as God in the temple of God, showing himself that he is God.*

Many argue that there will be no temple rebuilt in Jerusalem but what many don't know is the temple is already largely rebuilt underground and most don't even realize it.

Further, one could make the argument that with the Rothschilds and other elite families having such a personal relationship with Israel, it would not be a stretch to suggest she is helping to rule the world even now.

Regarding the beast devouring the woman, are there any prophecies about Jerusalem being destroyed or having wrath poured out on them?

> *Ezekiel 21:1-3 And the word of the Lord came to me, saying, 2 "Son of man, set your face toward Jerusalem, preach against the holy places, and prophesy against the land of Israel; 3 and say to the land of Israel, Thus says the Lord: "Behold, I am against you, and I will draw My sword out of its sheath and cut off both righteous and wicked from you.*

> *Ezekiel 22:19-22 Therefore thus says the Lord God: 'Because you have all become dross, therefore behold, I will gather you into the midst of Jerusalem. 20 As men gather silver, bronze, iron, lead, and tin into the midst of a furnace, to blow fire on it, to melt it; so I will gather you in My anger and in My fury, and I will leave you there and melt you. 21 Yes, I will gather you and blow on you with the fire of My wrath, and you shall be melted in its midst. 22 As silver is melted in the midst of a furnace, so shall you be melted in its midst; then you shall know that I, the Lord, have poured out My fury on you.' "*

What about this statement?

> *Revelation 18:23 The light of a lamp shall not shine in you anymore, and the voice of bridegroom and bride shall not be heard in you anymore. For your merchants were the great men of the earth, for by your sorcery all the nations were deceived.*

> *Jeremiah 7:34 Then I will cause to cease from the cities of Judah and from the streets of Jerusalem the voice of mirth and the voice of gladness, the voice of the bridegroom and the voice of the bride. For the land shall be desolate.*

Every single description we have of Babylon; everything she wears, everything she sells, everything she does, every title, every comparison, and every picture of her and her punishment, directly reflects prophecies given about Jerusalem in the Old Testament. Beyond that, Revelation tells us plainly who this harlot is. There can be little doubt that Jerusalem is Mystery Babylon, Mother of Harlots and the abominations of the earth.

So what does this mean? Well, it means that on one side of the narrow road, we have the danger of falling into the camp of the beast, the RCC, which is, at it's heart, pure idolatry. The christ they present is not the one who died for our sins. The saints they portray are pagan gods with a paint job slapped on. Just out of Catholicism, but still under it's influence and possibly it's authority, we have modern Christianity that has taken the pagan practices and traditions from Rome, and unknowingly polluted itself with idolatry being still under the influence of the beast. On the other side of the road in the ditch we find Judaism and the harlot Jerusalem, which has rejected Christ altogether, and has also become pretty much purely idolatrous. They treat their sages as their god, ignoring the scriptures in favor their so called wisdom, which is also derived from mysticism, occultic practices, and idolatry. Out of that camp, but still within the reach of it's influence, is Messianic Judaism, which accepts the Messiah, but also accepts the idolatrous ways of Judaism and has unknowingly been polluted as well.

Somewhere in between these four paths is the narrow path. The pagan traditions of men are the real danger to us, and these traditions in idolatry have absolutely infested both of these camps on each side of the road, as well as the roads that run alongside these pits. So what does the middle of the road look like? Well, we will look into that in the coming chapters.

16

Nation State

So, if Jerusalem is Mystery Babylon, and Judaism is packed full of paganism, how are the Jews God's chosen people? How is Israel the holy land? What's the deal with the land of Israel? If Jerusalem is to be destroyed, what of all the verses that talk about Israel dwelling safely? These are the kinds of questions we need to begin to ask, and find answers for. Spiritually speaking, Jerusalem is indeed Sodom, and sadly the rest of Israel around it is much the same. Sodom was particularly infamous for it's sexual immorality. Many don't know that Israel is particularly liberal in this area as well. Tel Aviv is known as one of the most LGBTQ friendly cities in the world and holds a massive pride parade every year. Prostitution is also incredibly prominent in Tel Aviv, with 50% of prostitution in the country going on in that city alone, and an estimated 14,000 prostitutes working legally in Israel. The majority of Israeli voters are very liberal, with the view of things like abortion being overwhelmingly positive. Does this sound like God's holy people? The answer, dear reader, is we have allowed yet more lies to slip into the ekklesia.

This lie is that the physical Jews and the nation called Israel are actually God's chosen people, as has been popularized by a myriad of prominent teachers. We will explore many of these things in the next two chapters, but for now, I want to focus specifically on the land of Israel. Many preachers today teach that it is the Christian responsibility to support Israel without question. They tell us to do anything less is to invite judgement upon yourself. They use verses like these to back up their claims:

Zechariah 12:2-3 "Behold, I will make Jerusalem a cup of drunkenness to all the surrounding peoples, when they lay siege against Judah and Jerusalem. 3 And it shall happen in that day that I will make Jerusalem a very heavy stone for all peoples; all who would heave it away will surely be cut in pieces, though all nations of the earth are gathered against it.

Zechariah 2:8 For thus says the Lord of hosts: "He sent Me after glory, to the nations which plunder you; for he who touches you touches the apple of His eye.

Genesis 12:2-3 I will make you a great nation; I will bless you and make your name great; and you shall be a blessing. 3 I will bless those who bless you, and I will curse him who curses you; and in you all the families of the earth shall be blessed."

These verses are often quoted to claim that if we allow America to pull support from the land of Israel, our own nation will collapse under judgement. They teach Israel will never fall, no matter how many nations rise against it, because it is God's holy land. Is this consistent with prophecy though? They will recite verses such as these to say that Israel will never fall:

Jeremiah 32:37-41 Behold, I will gather them out of all countries where I have driven them in My anger, in My fury, and in great wrath; I will bring them back to this place, and I will cause them to dwell safely. 38 They shall be My people, and I will be their God; 39 then I will give them one heart and one way, that they may fear Me forever, for the good of them and their children after them. 40 And I will make an everlasting covenant with them, that I will not turn away from doing them good; but I will put My fear in their hearts so that they will not depart from Me. 41 Yes, I will rejoice over them to do them good, and I will assuredly plant them in this land, with all My heart and with all My soul.'

Has this passage been fulfilled? Is the regathering of the Jews into Israel what is spoken of? No, and I will prove it very clearly from scripture. There is a very common couple verses that are repeated over and over for the sake of trying to make this argument, but they are all easily dismantled. For example, these verses:

Jeremiah 16:14-15 "Therefore behold, the days are coming," says the Lord, "that it shall no more be said, 'The Lord lives who brought up the children of Israel from the land of Egypt,' 15 but, 'The Lord lives who brought up the children of Israel from the land of the north and from all the lands where He had driven them.' For I will bring them back into their land which I gave to their fathers.

The funny part however, is that if you read just a little further, we find this portion:

Jeremiah 16:17-18 For My eyes are on all their ways; they are not hidden from My face, <u>nor is their iniquity hidden from My eyes. 18 And first I will repay double for their iniquity and their sin, because they have defiled My land;</u> they have filled My inheritance with the carcasses of their detestable and abominable idols."

So this portion so often quoted, in context, clearly claims that they will receive double for their sins before this prophecy is fulfilled. This is consistent with the last chapter where Jerusalem receives double for her sins as mystery Babylon. How about this portion?

> *Isaiah 66:7-8 "Before she was in labor, she gave birth; before her pain came, she delivered a male child. 8 Who has heard such a thing? Who has seen such things? Shall the earth be made to give birth in one day? Or shall a nation be born at once? For as soon as Zion was in labor, She gave birth to her children.*

They quote "Can a nation be born at once?" and then say, "Yup! It was on May 14th 1948! The day Israel became a nation!" Interestingly, this picture of a woman giving birth to a male child is seen in Revelation.

> *Revelation 12:4-6 His tail drew a third of the stars of heaven and threw them to the earth. And the dragon stood before the woman who was ready to give birth, to devour her Child as soon as it was born. 5 She bore a male Child who was to rule all nations with a rod of iron. And her Child was caught up to God and His throne. 6 Then the woman fled into the wilderness, where she has a place prepared by God, that they should feed her there one thousand two hundred and sixty days.*

This event too happens during the great tribulation, and has not happened yet which is consistent with the timeline we see elsewhere. How about this one? This is a prophecy speaking of the same event.

> *Ezekiel 37:11-14 Then He said to me, "Son of man, these bones are the whole house of Israel. They indeed say, 'Our bones are dry, our hope is lost, and we ourselves are cut off!' 12 Therefore prophesy and say to them, 'Thus says the Lord God: "Behold, O My people, <u>I will open your graves and cause you to come up from your graves</u>, and bring you into the land of Israel. 13 Then you shall know that I am the Lord, when I have opened your graves, O My people, and brought you up from your graves. 14*

I will put My Spirit in you, and you shall live, and I will place you in your own land. Then you shall know that I, the Lord, have spoken it and performed it," says the Lord.' "

Have we seen graves opened and people resurrected from the dead? I certainly haven't. We know when Christ returns, He brings with him those who have died in Him (1 Corinthians 15:52), so again, this is clearly at the end of the age. Again, how can this be fulfilled?

I want to draw your attention to one more prophecy regarding the land of Israel. I will break this portion up with some commentary in between, as this is a slightly longer section:

Ezekiel 36:1-8 "And you, son of man, prophesy to the mountains of Israel, and say, 'O mountains of Israel, hear the word of the Lord! 2 Thus says the Lord God: "Because the enemy has said of you, 'Aha! The ancient heights have become our possession,' "

Where are the ancient heights? Could that be the Golan heights that are so hotly contested by the nations and fought over?

3 therefore prophesy, and say, Thus says the Lord God: "Because they made you desolate and swallowed you up on every side, so that you became the possession of the rest of the nations, and you are taken up by the lips of talkers and slandered by the people"—

This is completely consistent with the prophecies regarding Israel being trampled underfoot by gentiles for 42 months, which hasn't happened yet.

4 therefore, O mountains of Israel, hear the word of the Lord God! Thus says the Lord God to the mountains, the hills, the rivers, the valleys, the desolate wastes, and the cities that have been forsaken, which became plunder and mockery to the rest of the nations all around— 5 therefore thus says the Lord God: "Surely I have spoken in My burning jealousy against the rest of the nations and against all Edom, who gave My land to themselves as a possession, with wholehearted joy and spiteful minds, in order to plunder its open country." '

Again, consistent with the beast turning and devouring the woman, Jerusalem, and the land of Israel. Also, these nations gave the land of Israel to the Talmudic Jews and the wealthy elite with joy and spiteful minds.

6 "Therefore prophesy concerning the land of Israel, and say to the mountains, the hills, the rivers, and the valleys, 'Thus says the Lord God: "Behold, I have spoken in My jealousy and My fury, because you have borne the shame of the nations."

This is consistent with Babylon bearing the cup of her harlotries committed with the other nations and God punishing her for it in jealousy and fury as her nakedness is uncovered.

7 Therefore thus says the Lord God: "I have raised My hand in an oath that surely the nations that are around you shall bear their own shame.

This is consistent with the nations of the world gathering together and being defeated and destroyed by Christ when He returns to Israel.

8 But you, O mountains of Israel, you shall shoot forth your branches and yield your fruit to My people Israel, for they are about to come.

So at this point, after the punishment of Israel, and of the surrounding nations, at this point, the people of Israel are **about** to come. They have not already been there for a while, no, these are gathered at the very end back into the land.

These prophecies have not at all been fulfilled, and those who keep claiming they are, sadly are teaching error. Some teach these things in ignorance, not knowing what they are teaching. The thing is, there is a purpose and reason behind all of these teachings, and it is being pushed forward by the wealthy elite. Most of Christianity has a love affair with Israel, but they do not know what goes on behind the scenes. They do not know the prophecies well enough to see the issues. They are all too eager to support these agendas because they do not know what they will lead to. Unfortunately, you will have to wait for later chapters to see the consummation of where these teachings lead because there are many other things to cover first. Most would agree that men like the Rothschild family, George Soros, the Rockefeller family and others are working hard to bring forth the one world system that the beast sits upon, but they do not understand that Israel is one of their prime tools that they are employing to move forward their agendas.

In fact, what if I told you that the symbol for Israel, the Star of David, had nothing to do with David whatsoever? Interestingly, you can search the scriptures over and over, and you will never find anything even remotely similar to any star associated with David. The only references you will find to Israel having a star as an image over them are these ones:

> *Amos 5:25-27 "Did you offer Me sacrifices and offerings in the wilderness forty years, O house of Israel? 26 You also carried Sikkuth your king and Chiun, your idols, the <u>star of your gods</u>, which you made for yourselves. 27 Therefore I will send you into captivity beyond Damascus," says the Lord, whose name is the God of hosts.*

Acts 7:42-43 Then God turned and gave them up to worship the host of heaven, as it is written in the book of the Prophets: 'Did you offer Me slaughtered animals and sacrifices during forty years in the wilderness, O house of Israel? 43 You also took up the tabernacle of <u>Moloch</u>, and <u>the star of your god Remphan</u>, images which you made to worship; and I will carry you away beyond Babylon.'

This "Star of David" is not of David at all, it is the star of Remphan as is also found in much older pagan religions all around the world, including temples and idols in Egypt, Mexico, Russia, Rome, Ireland, and Turkey, not to mention modern Wicca. In fact, the Vatican just allowed a statue of Moloch, which is another name for Remphan as seen above, to be displayed in Rome. [45] Proudly displayed in the center of the image is the "Star of David". It's not even subtle anymore. We have been sold a lie, set up by the rich elite, and made popular by televangelists and preachers who are either duped as well, or working in tandem with these wealthy benefactors. Have you ever wondered how some preachers have so much money they own multiple private jets, a fleet of expensive cars, houses all over the world, and many of these men rose from nothing? Once you begin looking at the money trails, things begin to become more clear.

All of these prophecies and bits of information leave us with one important question, who is going to be gathered? It says all of Israel, or the people of Israel. If this does not mean all of the people in the nation state called Israel, who is this group? This is the golden question, and one of great importance. We will answer this question in the next chapter.

Before we end this chapter, understand that there are thousands of people who live in Israel that are of Jewish lineage who are merely stuck there, or deceived. There are those in Judaism, who just like in Catholicism, genuinely think they are following God. In the same way there are abominations taking place in countries all over the world at the hands of these countries militaristic forces and the people are often left with little power to change it, there are those in Israel who are in this same predicament. Just as there is a very deep and deceptive corruption in American politicians, and most don't know the first thing about what really goes on, many in Israel are unaware of the truth as well. Not everyone in Jerusalem is evil just like not everyone in Russia, or China, or Iran, or the U.S. is evil. In fact, Jesus gave a warning specifically for those in Jerusalem who He knew would be living there in the end times.

> **Luke 21:20-22 *"But when you see Jerusalem surrounded by armies, then know that its desolation is near. 21 Then let those who are in Judea flee to the mountains, let those who are in the midst of her depart, and let not those who are in the country enter her. 22 For these are the days of vengeance, that all things which are written may be fulfilled.***

Lot was living in Sodom but was grieved by the sin going on around him. The scriptures say the city vexed his righteous soul. There are those who are vexed by the things going on around them in Jerusalem right now, just like there are all over the world. Even in the days of Elijah when Elijah thought all of Israel had turned against God, there were those who God reserved for Himself who had not bent the knee to Baal. A remnant will be saved out of Jerusalem.

I also want to say one more thing. Satan seeks division, hatred, and discord. Nobody enjoys discord among the brethren quite like Satan. One of his favorite tactics is to take evil, and pit it against evil and pull people into it. A prime example is our American government. Whether you realize it or not, both major parties are completely corrupt. Many republicans are convinced democrats are completely evil and should be hated. Many democrats are convinced the republicans are completely evil and should be hated. The truth is, there are people with good intentions, and people who are completely corrupt to the core in both camps. You cannot weigh a politician based solely upon the party they are associated with, you need to weigh them based upon their fruit. Even then, you can judge between their actions without totally supporting them in all they do. There are things Trump has done that I agree with. There are also things he has done that I disagree with. To say everything he has done is good, or everything he has done is evil, is foolishness.

Likewise, particularly with Israel, there are those who believe the Palestinians and other nations are justified in hating Israel. On the other side there are those who believe Israel is justified in all that they do, and hate the Palestinians and surrounding nations. The truth is, both sides have tremendous amounts of evil behind the scenes, and Satan has engineered a social situation with the purpose of distracting and dividing the people. There are far too many lies and deceptions being presented to us to fully understand all that goes on, and to choose to stick to one camp or the other, is to accept both the good and the evil in the camp. Israel does some good things, they also do some horrendous things. Palestinians do some good things, they also do some horrendous things. Both sides are guilty, and to paint one like a hero and the other like a villain is to fall into the trap laid by Satan. Neither are innocent, and both need prayer. We need to guard ourselves to not become embroiled in choosing sides in every social situation that blows our way. We have to be only ever on the side of Christ and His truth.

The people living in Israel, are no more God's people than the people living elsewhere, and we will look at why in the next chapter. Suffice it for now to say this:

Romans 9:6-8 But it is not that the word of God has taken no effect. For they are not all Israel who are of Israel, 7 nor are they all children because they are the seed of Abraham; but, "In Isaac your seed shall be called." 8 That is, those who are the children of the flesh, these are not the children of God; but the children of the promise are counted as the seed.

17

Root of David

So, who are the people of Israel in the last times if they are not necessarily those living in the land of Israel? Well, to answer that question, we need to go back into the Old Testament and work forward from there. Israel got it's name from Jacob, who had his name changed to Israel by God. Israel bore 12 sons, and each of these sons became one of the tribes of Israel and they were collectively known as either Israel, or the Children of Israel. Even very early, these sons did not get along. The story of Joseph is included in this early history of Israel, where his brothers sold him into slavery in Egypt. God used this situation to save his brothers when he became a ruler, and there was a famine. The children of Israel ended up moving into Egypt, and building their lives there. Later on, a later pharaoh who did not care for these non Egyptians living in Egypt, enslaved the children of Israel and thus began their days of slavery in Egypt. Eventually, God sent Moses and Aaron to lead the people out of bondage, and into the wilderness, which eventually landed them in the promised land, and this promised land became known as the land of Israel.

This was the land that they dwelt in, and entered into the marriage covenant with God in, and served Him. They built a temple for Him according to His specifications, and were given laws on how they were to conduct themselves. For a while, things went well, and Israel defeated many of her enemies, and became extremely wealthy. The height of this prosperity was under king David, and his son Solomon. Solomon was fabulously wealthy, and all the kings of the earth recognized the greatness and splendor of Israel, however, in this splendor and attention from the other nations, Israel began to become polluted by their idolatry. Solomon took many of the surrounding gentile women as wives, which was against the laws God set forth, and these pagan wives turned Solomon's heart to idols. Solomon did indeed build the first temple to God according to his specifications, but unfortunately, he also built temples to Asherah and Baal, and other pagan deities of the surrounding nations.

In judgement of this turn to idols, God allowed Rehoboam, one of Solomon's sons, to turn the majority of the tribes against Solomon's rule, and it split the kingdom into two parts. The Northern and Southern kingdoms, that were The House of Israel, and the House of Judah. Under different kings, these two did not get along well, and there were many fights against one another. The house of Israel, ended up turning itself completely over to idolatry to the point that God issued her a certificate of divorce, and allowed her to be taken away captive by the Assyrians. This is why Oholah from the verses earlier was called Samaria, because she was taken by the Assyrians, and scattered throughout Assyria and Samaria. This left the House of Judah as the only ones still in covenant with God, after all, she had not been divorced like her sister. Sadly though, as we saw in the verses pertaining to Oholibah, or Jerusalem, which was the capital of the House of Judah, she did not learn from her sister's mistakes. She herself also began to pollute herself ever more with idolatry, and she was punished over and over again for it. She would not turn though, and eventually, God allowed her to be taken into captivity as well, and the first temple was destroyed. This was the time of Daniel when the House of Judah was captive in Babylon.

As we know though, eventually Babylon was overthrown by the Medes and the Persians, and the House of Judah was set free from her captivity. They journeyed back to their land that they had been driven from, and were reestablished in the land that was still called Israel. However, the House of Israel, was nowhere to be found. These were scattered all throughout the world and became known as the dispersion, as it was a dispersion of the House of Israel. They never came back into the land, and have become completely mixed in with every part of the world. There is evidence to suggest peoples in Ireland, The Samoan islands, Japan, native Americans, and many others were originally a part of the house of Israel, but as the bloodlines all mixed, and the culture was lost, most evidence that they were ever even a part of Israel was swallowed up.

So when Christ came on the scene, it was at this time when the Jews (House of Judah consisting of the tribes of Judah and Benjamin) were in Israel, and the second temple built by Herod the Great, was sitting in Jerusalem. Now, we know and understand that Jesus is Immanuel which means God with us.

> *Isaiah 7:14 Therefore the Lord Himself will give you a sign: Behold, the virgin shall conceive and bear a Son, and shall call His name Immanuel.*

So God sent His Son, or His Word, basically being begotten from Him, but also a part of Him, to come and redeem His people. We also know that Christ is referred to as a groomsman, which is marriage language once again. So Christ came to redeem unto Himself a bride. Christ declared quite plainly who He came for.

> *Matthew 15:24 But He answered and said, "I was not sent except to the lost sheep of the house of Israel."*

So Christ declared plainly that He came for the House of Israel which were scattered throughout the nations. There was just one major issue. The House of Israel had been divorced by God, but now God came in the flesh, to redeem her unto Himself. This was a problem because God Himself gave this commandment:

> *Deuteronomy 24:1-4 "When a man takes a wife and marries her,*

and it happens that she finds no favor in his eyes because he has found some uncleanness in her, and he writes her a certificate of divorce, puts it in her hand, and sends her out of his house, 2 when she has departed from his house, and goes and becomes another man's wife, 3 if the latter husband detests her and writes her a certificate of divorce, puts it in her hand, and sends her out of his house, or if the latter husband dies who took her as his wife, 4 then her former husband who divorced her must not take her back to be his wife after she has been defiled; for that is an abomination before the Lord, and you shall not bring sin on the land which the Lord your God is giving you as an inheritance.

When a man takes a woman and divorces her, if she goes to another man that divorces her, for the original husband to take her back again, God calls it a sin, and an abomination. How could God do something that He Himself called an abomination? This provided an impossibility for Christ to take back the House of Israel. Beyond this, it also directly broke this (rather lengthy) prophecy.

Ezekiel 37:15-25 Again the word of the Lord came to me, saying, 16 "As for you, son of man, take a stick for yourself and write on it: 'For Judah and for the children of Israel, his companions.' Then take another stick and write on it, 'For Joseph, the stick of Ephraim, and for all the house of Israel, his companions.' 17 Then join them one to another for yourself into one stick, and they will become one in your hand.

18 "And when the children of your people speak to you, saying, 'Will you not show us what you mean by these?' — 19 say to them, Thus says the Lord God: "Surely I will take the stick of Joseph, which is in the hand of Ephraim, and the tribes of Israel, his companions; and I will join them with it, with the stick of Judah, and make them one stick, and they will be one in My hand." ' 20

And the sticks on which you write will be in your hand before their eyes.

21 "Then say to them, Thus says the Lord God: "Surely I will take the children of Israel from among the nations, wherever they have gone, and will gather them from every side and bring them into their own land; 22 and I will make them one nation in the land, on the mountains of Israel; and one king shall be king over them all; they shall no longer be two nations, nor shall they ever be divided into two kingdoms again. 23 They shall not defile themselves anymore with their idols, nor with their detestable things, nor with any of their transgressions; but I will deliver them from all their dwelling places in which they have sinned, and will cleanse them. Then they shall be My people, and I will be their God.

24 "David My servant shall be king over them, and they shall all have one shepherd; they shall also walk in My judgments and observe My statutes, and do them. 25 Then they shall dwell in the land that I have given to Jacob My servant, where your fathers dwelt; and they shall dwell there, they, their children, and their children's children, forever; and My servant David shall be their prince forever.

So we see that God spoke very clearly that He would regather both the House of Israel, and House of Judah back together, and that David would be prince over them all forever. We also know and understand that king David was a picture of Christ, and so this David who will be prince over them forever, is in fact Christ. So how could God both keep His word of what He said He would do, but also not break His own law? Well, there was only one way that the laws pertaining to a marriage could be severed. It's the same now as it was then, "till death do us part"

1 Corinthians 7:39 A wife is bound by law as long as her husband lives; but if her husband dies, she is at liberty to be

married to whom she wishes, only in the Lord.

The only way a woman could be released from the laws regarding her previous marriage, was for her husband to die. We know Christ came to die for our sins, as the perfect sacrifice to pay for the sins of the world, but He also came to die so that the House of Israel could be remarried to Him after He rose again, without Him breaking the law of God. God sent His Son, a part of Himself, to die, to bring His bride back to Him, in spite of all her harlotry, all her idolatry, all her sin, and all her stubbornness. He has such a great love for His people, His bride, that He would die for her, in spite of all she has done. This is such a deep and incredible love, that we can hardly understand it.

So, now that Christ came to redeem the House of Israel so they could be remarried to Him, who is this House of Israel? As I said earlier, it's all the nations. Everyone. And by the way, this isn't based upon bloodline, though some try to claim it is. Whether you were born of a lineage that was once part of the House of Israel or not, everyone has a chance to become a part of the bride of Christ. It has always been this way. See, being a part of Israel has never really been about bloodline. It has been about covenant.

Ruth and Rahab were both of the other nations, Gentiles as it were, but they were grafted into the tribe of Judah, who brought forth Messiah. When Israel went out from Egypt, there was a mixed multitude who went out with them. Many of this mixed multitude were Egyptians who had seen the mighty power of our God wipe out their gods and Pharoah, and decided they wanted to follow Him. They left their lands and their gods, to follow the True God, and so they were grafted in. The way to become a part of Israel, has always been to enter into covenant with God, and take the marriage vows, take the vows to walk in His ways, and keep His commandments, and in return, He will be your God, and you will be one of His people. Abraham, Isaac, and Jacob were not Jews. They were just men, who God chose to call to Himself, and enter into communion with, and made promises to them.

So what does this mean? It means that if you have entered into covenant with God, you are a part of Israel. If you are born again, you are among the children of Israel. In the Old Testament, God had made His first covenant, or His old covenant, to have His people married to Him, but they broke covenant with Him, and half ended up divorced, and the other half became so reprobated that when He came to them, they put Him to death. So God made a New covenant, or marriage vow for his new (renewed) marriage to His people.

> *Jeremiah 31:31-34 "Behold, the days are coming, says the Lord, when I will make a <u>new covenant</u> with the <u>house of Israel and with the house of Judah</u>— 32 not according to the covenant that I made with their fathers in the day that I took them by the hand to lead them out of the land of Egypt, <u>My covenant which they broke, though I was a husband to them</u>, says the Lord. 33 But this is the covenant that I will make with the <u>house of Israel</u> after those days, says the Lord: <u>I will put My law in their minds, and write it on their hearts; and I will be their God, and they shall be My people.</u> 34 No more shall every man teach his neighbor, and every man his brother, saying, 'Know the Lord,' for they all shall know Me, from the least of them to the greatest of them, says the Lord. For <u>I will forgive their iniquity, and their sin I will remember no more.</u>"*

This is the New Covenant. It is the old marriage Covenant given anew with Christ at the head. The Old marriage covenant was broken, and made null through divorce, and death. The New Covenant is the new marriage between us and God via Christ, who in one fell swoop paid for our sins, and nullified our divorce giving the House of Israel access to become a part of Israel once again. An important note as well is that Christ taught ONLY through Him could men come to God.

> *John 14:6 Jesus said to him, "I am the way, the truth, and the life. No one comes to the Father except through Me.*

John 10:1-3 "Most assuredly, I say to you, he who does not enter the sheepfold by the door, but climbs up some other way, the same is a thief and a robber. 2 But he who enters by the door is the shepherd of the sheep. 3 To him the doorkeeper opens, and the sheep hear his voice; and he calls his own sheep by name and leads them out.

John 10:7-9 Then Jesus said to them again, "Most assuredly, I say to you, I am the door of the sheep. 8 All who ever came before Me are thieves and robbers, but the sheep did not hear them. 9 I am the door. If anyone enters by Me, he will be saved, and will go in and out and find pasture.

So Christ is the ONLY way to the Father, but what then happened to the Old Covenant between Him and the House of Judah? Many prominent teachers claim that the Jews don't need Christ, because they are still in covenant with God, this contradicts what Christ proclaimed, and fails to explain why the Jewish apostles told the Jewish Pharisees that only through Christ is their salvation (Acts 4:12). Keep in mind this was before Cornelius, and before the gospel was even being spread to the gentiles, so why would the Jewish apostles be in trouble from the Jewish pharisees for preaching the gospel to the Jews in Israel, if there was no need for them to hear it? When Christ died, it dissolved the previous marriage, allowing Christ to remarry the House of Israel. With the marriage having been dissolved, Judah's marriage was also dissolved. Many big name teachers teach that the Jews have salvation some other way, but that is a lie. The Jewish apostles knew they needed salvation and it was only found in Christ. They need Christ just as much as anyone, and it is only through Christ, by which men will be saved. The idea that the Jews still have a separate covenant is false. Paul tells us so plainly.

Romans 9:6-8 But it is not that the word of God has taken no effect. For they are not all Israel who are of Israel, 7 nor are they

all children because they are the seed of Abraham; but, "In Isaac your seed shall be called." 8 That is, those who are the children of the flesh, these are not the children of God; but the children of the promise are counted as the seed.

Not everyone who is a physical member of Israel or a physical Jew, is Israel. Those who are born as Jews or Israel in the flesh, are not the children of God, but those who are children of the promise, the new covenant in Christ, they are counted as Abraham's seed.

Galatians 3:29 And if you are Christ's, then you are Abraham's seed, and heirs according to the promise.

So if we are Abraham's seed, what does that mean?

Isaiah 41:8 "But you, Israel, are My servant, Jacob whom I have chosen, The descendants (seed) *of Abraham My friend.*

It means we who are in Christ are now Israel. We are not born into Israel as in the flesh, but born again in the spirit into Israel. Is there anywhere else that echoes this idea?

Ephesians 2:11-13 Therefore remember that you, once Gentiles in the flesh—who are called Uncircumcision by what is called the Circumcision made in the flesh by hands— 12 that at that time you were without Christ, being aliens from the common-wealth of Israel and strangers from the covenants of promise, having no hope and without God in the world. 13 But now in Christ Jesus you who once were far off have been brought near by the blood of Christ.

So let me break this down. The word gentile, as I mentioned earlier, simply means, "of the other nations" besides Israel. Who is Israel? All those who have entered into covenant with God. Remember too, that Paul is writing this to the Romans, who were comprised of a mix of gentiles and Jews. The Jews (also called the circumcision) still believed themselves to be in covenant with God via the flesh, because they were the physical seed of Abraham. But because they rejected the identity of Christ as being God in the flesh, they rejected Him. When Christ died, the previous marriage was dissolved, and the new marriage came only through new birth in Christ, not through the flesh, as one born as the physical seed of Abraham, but as one born of the spirit through Christ, becoming the true seed of Abraham. So Paul basically declares, you who appear to be gentiles (uncircumcision) though you aren't any longer, are called gentiles by those who were previously a part of the covenant (the circumcision). These gentiles according to their flesh, who have now entered into covenant with God through Christ, were once gentiles, and strangers from the covenant, but now in Christ, we have become partakers in the commonwealth of Israel. Another way of saying that would be that now that we are in Covenant, we are no longer strangers from Israel, but are a part of it. Because we have been born of the spirit, we have become the seed of Abraham.

Paul echoes this again when he speaks of wild branches (gentiles) being grafted onto the cultivated olive tree (Israel) and the natural branches (Jews) being broken off in Romans 11. There is no gentile tree to be grafted onto, there is one tree, Israel, with one Root, Christ, and being a part of Israel, in Christ, is the only way to have life, and bear fruit. There's no "church tree". One tree, Israel, one stick, the House of Judah and the House of Israel being brought together as one with Christ as King over all.

Beyond Paul's writings there is one more image that is a far more majestic picture that identifies us as Israel, but we need to look at a few different scriptures to see it.

Isaiah 28:16 Therefore thus says the Lord God: "Behold, I lay in Zion a stone for a foundation, a tried stone, a precious cornerstone, a sure foundation; whoever believes will not act

hastily.

So who is this chief cornerstone?

> *1 Peter 2:1-8 Therefore, laying aside all malice, all deceit,*
> *hypocrisy, envy, and all evil speaking, 2 as newborn babes,*
> *desire the pure milk of the word, that you may grow thereby, 3*
> *if indeed you have tasted that the Lord is gracious. 4 Coming to*
> *Him as to a living stone, rejected indeed by men, but chosen by*
> *God and precious,*

It's Christ. There is something more to see here though that is very important.

> *5 you also, as living stones, are being built up a spiritual house,*
> *a holy priesthood, to offer up spiritual sacrifices acceptable to*
> *God through Jesus Christ. 6 Therefore it is also contained in*
> *the Scripture, "Behold, I lay in Zion a chief cornerstone, elect,*
> *precious, and he who believes on Him will by no means be put*
> *to shame." 7 Therefore, to you who believe, He is precious; but*
> *to those who are disobedient, "The stone which the builders*
> *rejected has become the chief cornerstone," 8 and "A stone of*
> *stumbling and a rock of offense." They stumble, being disobe-*
> *dient to the word, to which they also were appointed.*

So there are a few things to see here, but the first answers our previous question. Who is this precious cornerstone? It is Christ. Now, the question is, what IS a cornerstone? A cornerstone is the single most important part in a building. A cornerstone is just that, a stone that sets the corner. From this cornerstone, the entire rest of the foundation for a building is aligned and makes the foundation to build upon straight. So Christ is the chief cornerstone. This verse also tells us rather plainly that we, as followers of Christ are living stones, being built up as a spiritual house. So, we see that

Christ is the cornerstone, and we are the stones building up the building, or another way to say this would be living bricks. We are the bricks that build up the structure. Who then is the foundation outside of the cornerstone? Christ is the cornerstone, we are the stones, what is the building?

Revelation 21:9-22 Then one of the seven angels who had the seven bowls filled with the seven last plagues came to me and talked with me, saying, "Come, I will show you the bride, the Lamb's wife." 10 And he carried me away in the Spirit to a great and high mountain, and showed me the great city, the holy Jerusalem, descending out of heaven from God, 11 having the glory of God. Her light was like a most precious stone, like a jasper stone, clear as crystal. 12 Also she had a great and high wall with twelve gates, and twelve angels at the gates, and names written on them, which are the names of the twelve tribes of the children of Israel: 13 three gates on the east, three gates on the north, three gates on the south, and three gates on the west. 14 Now the wall of the city had twelve foundations, and on them were the names of the twelve apostles of the Lamb. 15 And he who talked with me had a gold reed to measure the city, its gates, and its wall. 16 The city is laid out as a square; its length is as great as its breadth. And he measured the city with the reed: twelve thousand furlongs. Its length, breadth, and height are equal. 17 Then he measured its wall: one hundred and forty-four cubits, according to the measure of a man, that is, of an angel. 18 The construction of its wall was of jasper; and the city was pure gold, like clear glass. 19 The foundations of the wall of the city were adorned with all kinds of precious stones: the first foundation was jasper, the second sapphire, the third chalcedony, the fourth emerald, 20 the fifth sardonyx, the sixth sardius, the seventh chrysolite, the eighth beryl, the ninth topaz, the tenth chrysoprase, the eleventh jacinth, and the twelfth amethyst. 21 The twelve gates were twelve pearls: each individual gate was of one pearl. And the street of the city was pure gold, like transparent glass. 22 But I saw no temple in it, for the Lord God Almighty and the Lamb are its temple.

Dear reader, Christ is the cornerstone. He set the direction, location, and shape of the rest of the foundation. The rest of the foundation were the twelve apostles, whom Christ Himself taught and trained. These twelve became the foundation of the ekklesia, who went out and made disciples of all nations. Each of us who have come to Christ and have decided to follow Him and serve Him have become living stones, precious and beautiful to Him, building up the spiritual city of the New Jerusalem, where we will dwell with Christ and with God. The twelve gates have on them the names of the twelve tribes of Israel, as nobody can come into the city to become a part of it, unless he first passes through one of the twelve gates signifying becoming part of one of the twelve tribes via entering into covenant with Him. In the center of this city, is the dwelling place of The Most High, and Christ, who are in their temple, built up of us, but also They are the temple, as we are in Them. The entire New Jerusalem is a beautiful picture of us all being part of the bride of Christ and His dwelling place, as well as in Him being our dwelling place.

John 17:20-21 "I do not pray for these alone, but also for those who will believe in Me through their word; 21 that they all may be one, as You, Father, are in Me, and I in You; that they also may be one in Us, that the world may believe that You sent Me.

What could be a more perfect picture of marriage than us and Christ becoming one, He in us, and us in Him, the two becoming one?

Matthew 19:6 "So then, they are no longer two but one flesh. Therefore what God has joined together, let not man separate."

We are His bride, the New Jerusalem! We have been grafted into His people,

Israel, that are called by His name. We are the Bride of Christ.

The entire picture is a beautiful love story of God marrying a bride, Israel, and giving her a Covenant that she would be His, and follow His laws and His ways. She rebelled and betrayed God, becoming a whore who went after other gods and so God divorced her for her unfaithfulness. After she fell into trouble and began to cry out, God took pity on her, and decided to take her back. He couldn't though, unless He first died. Christ came as being the son of God, but also God in the flesh, and died, and rose from the dead, redeeming Israel unto Him, and establishing a New Covenant. This New marriage Covenant was like the Old one, but the differences were that we would have His spirit to write His laws on our hearts so that we would want to obey Him in Spirit and in Truth, out of a heart that loves Him and that we would no longer have to pay the wages of sin with our deaths, because that debt was paid by His perfect sacrifice, thus delivering us from the law of sin and death. In that the law said when we sin, we need to die, or put to death an animal, the New Covenant says Christ already paid the sacrifice, and died in our stead, so we are free to live for Him.

When we entered into this covenant with Him, we became betrothed to Christ, having been born into Israel via the new birth of the Spirit, and are anxiously awaiting His return where He will take us to Himself. Now is the time when the bride watches for the groomsman, and purifies herself in anticipation of being joined to Him. He will come for His bride very soon, and thereafter will be the marriage supper of the Lamb, where we celebrate this union, finally ending in ruling and reigning with Christ as His bride, and as Sons of God. How awesome is our God! Dearly beloved, you are Israel. You have been grafted on to the tree of Israel, and are being supplied with life from the root of David! You are betrothed to the King of Kings and Lord of Lords! You are Israel. The promises, the inheritance, they are yours. Halleluyah!

18

Identity Theft

If we are Israel, how did we lose that identity? How has this knowledge been buried and twisted and distorted into the current image, where some are just born into covenant and have no need of Christ? We have not merely lost our identity, it was stolen from us, and replaced with a false identity. This was engineered by many, and we will now look at how.

"Rightly dividing the word of truth". This single phrase has become (whether you know it or not), the mantra for the vast majority of theology in Christianity today. This phrase is directly attached to the doctrine of Dispensationalism. This doctrine is the preeminent pervading doctrine taught and repeated today among Christians. How old is this doctrine though? What does it teach? What is it's purpose? Where did it come from? I want to answer these questions for you.

The first question of what does it teach, is very simple. Dispensationalism teaches that in order to understand the Bible, you have to "rightly divide the word of truth" as mentioned in 2 Timothy 2:15. This single verse is taken by itself, with no other supporting verses, out of context, and has been extrapolated to mean that God has had completely different expectations of what He wants from His people, based upon the time they were born in, or the DNA they were born with. Basically the idea is this; the history of the world has been broken up into 7 dispensations. In each dispensation, God gives a specific directive for mankind to keep, and judges them based upon whether or not they keep this directive. These 7 dispensations are as follows.

1. First is the age of innocence, where mankind was expected to remain innocent. This dispensation began with Adam and Eve, and ended when they sinned and lost their innocence.
2. The second age is the age of conscience, in which mankind was expected to walk according to their conscience. This began after Adam and Eve sinned, and ended when God destroyed the earth with the flood.
3. The third age is the age of government, which began after the flood. This age mankind were supposed to learn to govern themselves and walk in His ways. It ended at the tower of Babel when God dispersed people into all the languages and nations of the world.
4. The fourth age is the age of promise, where God promised to Abraham to bring forth a people from Abraham, and the expectation was for people to believe the promises of God. This dispensation ended with the deliverance of the children of Israel out of Egypt.
5. The fifth age was the age of law, where God gave His laws to His people and expected them to walk in them. This age began with the Mount Sinai covenant, and ended with the death of Christ.
6. The sixth age is the church age, or the age of grace. This dispensation began with the death and resurrection of Christ and ends in the rapture of the church, and with His return. In this dispensation men are expected to walk in grace, the law having supposedly been abolished, and is marked by trust in His grace.
7. The seventh and final age is the age of the kingdom, which is after the church is raptured, Christ returns and sets up His kingdom and reigns forever. The expectation in this age is to submit to the rule of Christ and serve Him.

So, this all sounds rather good right? Unfortunately, there are some glaring issues with this theology and we will see more and more as we move forward. In spite of the scriptures being clear that those in Christ are now Israel, and those not in covenant through Christ are not, many cling to this theology in an effort to explain why there is a distinction between the "Jew" and the "gentile" as the gentiles have passed into the "church" age, while the "Jews" are stuck in the age of law. Let's learn about where this theology came from, and how it was popularized.

The first whispers of modern dispensationalism is a bit hard to nail down. There were whispers of it in the 1700s, but these are isolated, inconsistent, and inconclusive. Before the 1700s however, there are no writings that really speak of dispensationalism at all. The big "birth" of dispensationalism came at the hands of a man named John Nelson Darby, commonly just referred to as Darby, some time around 1830. Darby was a member of the Plymouth Brethren group, and first put together the foundation of modern dispensationalism. Many people know very little about Darby, and are unfamiliar with some of his other teachings. They take his popularized teachings and accept them eagerly, without questioning the source at all. Darby is venerated among many, and held in high regard, but I will show you from multiple sources that not only was the character of John Nelson Darby questionable as well as his sect of followers, the Plymouth Brethren, but there is strong evidence to suggest he was actually involved in theosophy, and general occultism. Now, I do not wish to attack or slander Darby, but we need to see the quality of man this was, and what his fruit was. The reason for this is we are told that we will know a false prophet by their fruit.

> *Matthew 7:15-16 "Beware of false prophets, who come to you in sheep's clothing, but inwardly they are ravenous wolves. 16 You will know them by their fruits.*

To begin with, we must understand the general consensus surrounding Darby and the Plymouth Brethren, not just in the modern day, but how they acted when they were alive, as well as the perception of these entities by others in the ekklesia in their day. The first witness I will call against Darby is a man named Charles Haddon Spurgeon, one of the most influential preachers of the 1800s. Few know that Spurgeon was adamantly against Darby, and his doctrine, and warned his readers against the teachings of Darby. He addressed Darby and his followers in multiple issues of his publication Sword and Trowel. I will start us off with an account recorded by Spurgeon in the February 1867 edition of Sword and Trowel:

We have been requested to reply to a small tract which has been given away at the door of the Tabernacle, by one of the "Plymouth Brethren," but it is so devoid of all sense, Scripture and reason, that it needs no reply. We have not learned the art of beating the air, or replying to nonsense. The only meaning we could gather from the rambling writer's remarks was a confirmation of our accusation, and a wonderful discovery that a long controverted point is now settled; the unpardonable sin is declared to be speaking against the Darbyites. Our portion must be something terrible if this be correct, but we have so little faith in the spirit which inspires the Brethren, that we endure their thunderbolts as calmly as we would those of the other infallible gentleman who occupies the Vatican. Another of this amiable community, having detected an error in one of our printed sermons, has most industriously spread the tidings that Mr. Spurgeon is a blasphemer. At the doors of their meetings and by enclosures in letters this sweet specimen of Christian charity is abundantly distributed; more to their shame than to our injury. We are persuaded that neither the writer of that cowardly anonymous fly-sheet, nor any other Plymouthist, believes in his heart that Mr. Spurgeon would knowingly blaspheme the glorious name of Jesus, and therefore the issue of the pamphlet is, we fear, a wickedly malicious act, dictated by revenge on account of our remarks upon their party. Our name and character are in too good a keeping to be injured by these dastardly anonymous attacks. Neither Mr. Newton nor Mr. Meuller would sanction such action; it is only from one clique that we receive this treatment. It is worthy of note that even the printer was ashamed or afraid to put his name to the printed paper. Our error was rectified as soon as ever we knew of it, and being fallible we could do no more; but these men, who pretend to be so marvellously led of the Spirit, have in this case deliberately, and in the most unmanly manner, sought to injure the character of one who has committed the great sin of mortifying their pride, and openly exposing their false doctrine.

The story is that Spurgeon warned people that Darby was presenting false doctrine and was leading people into error. Spurgeon was, as I stated earlier, one who had tremendous influence in the church at that time, and so Spurgeon announcing Darby's doctrine as error was a major threat to the dispersion of his doctrine. So, Darby himself, or one of his followers, sent out a mass flier accusing Spurgeon of blasphemy in the form of a sermon typo, as well as blaspheming the Holy Spirit, which he apparently committed by disagreeing with their "spirit led" doctrine. This group slandered Spurgeon openly, painting him as a reprobated heretic. Apparently, this kind of brash and unloving behavior was not an isolated incident either. According to this article on lloydthomas.org there were a few instances of note of Darby's behavior.

He never married. His personality could sometimes be abrasive and intolerant. He was extremely zealous for the principle of separation from what he considered evil, which led to numerous clashes with Christians whom he felt to be in error.

Darby's doctrine of the church required that only one church or congregation could be recognized in each city. (The Chinese Christian teacher Watchman Nee followed Darby on this point).

Darby has been seen as a hard doctrine-driven man regarding differences of opinion within the church. He demanded conformity to what he regarded as the meaning of Holy Scripture. From among Darby's fellow 'brethren', saintly pastor Muller, when approached by Darby to join him in the excommunication of those who held doctrinal

differences, accused Darby of acting –
"so wickedly in this matter" (July 1849). [46]

John Nelson Darby essentially pushed forward his doctrine with reckless abandon, attacking anyone who disagreed with him, citing them as heretics. Darby also taught some rather disturbing doctrines as was noted by Spurgeon once again. These are excerpts from the June 1869 edition of Sword and Trowel.

In association with the doctrine that much of the sufferings of Christ on the cross were without any atoning object or effect, Mr. Darby, advancing a step farther, denies that the atonement for our sins consisted even in Christ's death. But as it is probable some persons will find it difficult to believe that any man, professing to hold evangelical principles, and especially the leader of an important religious sect, also professing to be sound in the faith, could entertain such notions, and that I must have misunderstood Mr. Darby's meaning—it is due to him, and may be desirable for the reader, that I should quote his own words.

"'There was, too, to him,' says Mr. Darby, 'in addition to the pain of the death, the legal curse appended, by God's righteous judgment as King of Israel, to the form of the death; as it is written, 'Cursed is every one that hangeth upon a tree.' But this curse of the law was not the same thing as the wrath, when he cried out, 'My God, my God, why has thou forsaken me?' The thieves bore it as he did; that thief, too, who went with him to paradise the same day, and who could go there to be with his Lord, because he, the Prince of Life, had borne the wrath due to sin in his own body on the tree. But the cross had been endured by many an unrepentant rebel against man and God; and the cross in itself would not take away sin. Yea, more, while the time in which he endured the cross was the period in part of which the wrath came on him (when he endured the wrath of God's judgment against sin),

he only of the three that were crucified together, could or did bear the wrath; and the agony of that wrath, if his alone of the three then and there crucified, was distinct from, though present to him at the same time as the agonies (infinitely lesser) of the cross of wood!'

"The same sentiments are expressed in various other portions of Mr. Darby's writings; and even in some respects in language more objectionable still. That part of his theory, that Christ suffered much and long on the cross before there was anything of an atoning nature in his agonies, and simply as lying under the wrath of God in his character as King of Israel, is brought out more fully and more plainly than in the extract I have given. This is, in effect, to say that Christ actually had sins of his own in virtue of the relation which he sustained to the Jewish nation, as their king or head. There is something inexpressibly painful in the idea that our Lord suffered on the cross in any other capacity than as the Substitute or Sin-bearer for us. There is not a sentence in the word of God which gives the slightest sanction to it, but the contrary:—'While we were yet sinners Christ died for us;' 'He was made sin for us who knew no sin.' Mr. Darby says he did know sin as the King of Israel. 'He died for our sins and rose again for our justification; he died for our sins according to the Scriptures;' 'Who gave himself for our sins;' 'He is the propitiation for our sins;' 'Who bore our sins in his own body on the tree;' 'Who washed us from our sins in his own blood,' etc.

The idea that Christ had any sin of His own, or any atoning to do for Himself is completely heretical. Elsewhere in Darby's writings he firmly stands behind this doctrine and makes comments that those attacking him on this matter do not understand the depth of scripture, and that his teaching is not out of line with any Scripture.

Speaking of scripture, Darby decided to take a whack at his own translation, and while this in and of itself is not an issue as there are many translations, Darby's in particular has many alterations made. Whole lines were removed that are found in the interlinear such as this example:

Luke 11:4 (KJV) And forgive us our sins; for we also forgive every one that is indebted to us. And lead us not into temptation; but deliver us from evil.

Luke 11:4 (WBT) And forgive us our sins; for we also forgive every one that is indebted to us. And lead us not into temptation; but deliver us from evil.

Luke 11:4 (Darby Bible Translation, DBT) and remit us our sins, for we also remit to every one indebted to us; and lead us not into temptation.

Notice something missing? Now many prominent versions are also missing this line, but if you check the interlinear, the line "deliver us from evil" is very much there. Many of these later versions were based on the works of either Darby and Scofield, or Wescott and Hort, who were rather heretical themselves and removed and altered many portions of scripture. How about this portion?

1 Corinthians 10:28 (KJV) But if any man say unto you, This is offered in sacrifice unto idols, eat not for his sake that shewed it, and for conscience sake: for the earth is the Lord's, and the fulness thereof:

1 Corinthians 10:28 (NASB) But if anyone says to you, "This is meat sacrificed to idols," do not eat it, for the sake of the one who informed you, and for conscience' sake;

1 Corinthians 10:28 (BSB) But if someone tells you, "This food was offered to idols," then do not eat it, for the sake of the one who told you and for the sake of conscience—

1 Corinthians 10:28 (DBT) But if any one say to you, This is offered to holy purposes, do not eat, for his sake that pointed it out, and conscience sake;

In this example the KJV is the only version with the last sentence there, while the others remove it. If you check the interlinear, this section is indeed there. Even this aside, if you look at Darby's translation vs the others, since when is "sacrifice to idols" also known as "holy purposes"? There is not one shred of Greek in these sentences to justify this translation. Even if he wanted to butcher the Greek, don't you think one would put "unholy purposes"? There are many questionable changes that Darby made to the Bible and most of it helped to push forward his dispensational doctrine, as well as his views on the end times.

Beyond the questionable teachings and questionable translations that Darby was involved in, Spurgeon also outlines the mode of proselytizing the Plymouth Brethren employed to move forward their movement in the same letter I cited earlier.

But before I proceed farther, I ought to remark that, with very few exceptions, the women are the great propagandists of Plymouth Brethrenism. And, as a natural consequence, women are almost invariably the parties whom they seek to 'convert.' They are wise enough in their generation to know that if a man's wife is got over, she will give her husband no rest until she has made a resolute effort to prevail on him to join the 'gathering' along with her. Of course, it will be understood that I do not mean it to be inferred that there are no exceptions to this, but I do say—and I speak with no small knowledge of the philosophy and history of Plymouth Brethrenism—that the exceptions are rare indeed. In fact, I will go so far as to affirm that it would be almost incompatible with Plymouth 'Sisterdom' not to be a zealous and unwearied laborer in the field of proselytism.

Spurgeon goes on to reference this portion of scripture:

2 Timothy 3:1-7 But know this, that in the last days perilous times will come: 2 For men will be lovers of themselves, lovers of money, boasters, proud, blasphemers, disobedient to parents, unthankful, unholy, 3 unloving, unforgiving, slanderers, without self-control, brutal, despisers of good, 4 traitors, headstrong, haughty, lovers of pleasure rather than lovers of God, 5 having a form of godliness but denying its power. And from such people turn away! 6 For of this sort are those who creep into households and make captives of gullible women loaded down with sins, led away by various lusts, 7 always learning and never able to come to the knowledge of the truth.

I cannot help but feel Spurgeon hit the nail on the head in referencing this portion of scripture. These attributes that I underlined exemplify the tactics and general attitude and character of Darby and his proselytes, and even outlined the methods of their operation. Another quote, same source:

Plymouth Brethren have no feeling wherever their principles are concerned. I know indeed of no sect or denomination so utterly devoid of kindness of heart. It is the most selfish religious system with which I am acquainted. It is entirely wrapped up in itself.

This is attested by multiple writings of that time, and not solely by Spurgeon. There was one particular instance where the Darbyites, and the Bethesdaites, (another sect at that time) came together and ended up embroiled in a three day shouting match where all semblance of brotherly love and order went out the window. It was such a scene, it attracted the attention of many sources both Christian and secular and all these "spirit led" brothers did nothing but bring harm to the image of the body of Christ. This is an excerpt from the publication "A Retrospect of Events That Have Taken Place Amongst The Brethren":

Then began all the evils of religious quarrel, and to the previous love and toleration now succeeded a merciless intollerance and incurable antipathy.

...

If this anecdote is correct, it is a specimen of the spirit that prevailed on both sides; it was by no means confined to only one party. Bitter accusations, personal animosities, domestic feuds, and the disruption of old friendships, were the inevitable consequences where a body lately one was separating, and where the members of that body were arranging themselves under opposite banners. The worst motives were imputed, the most unfriendly interpretations put upon words and actions, religious sentiment was criticized with unsparing severity, every whisper of infamy industriously circulated, every hint of suspicion eagerly improved, and every failure of conduct joyfully published.

Sadly, this kind of activity was not isolated surrounding the Plymouth Brethren and Darbyites. Darby and his followers essentially claimed they were the only church being led by the spirit, and anyone who disagreed with them were to be separated from, and denounced as heretics. You can find account after account of similar reports from multiple sources. Darby was a man that seemed to have no love for his brothers in Christ, but only for himself, his followers, and his doctrine that he so desperately wanted to distribute. His writings claim he has no issue with people who disagreed with him, but his actions and conduct loudly say otherwise.

Matthew 7:15-20 "Beware of false prophets, who come to you in sheep's clothing, but inwardly they are ravenous wolves. 16 You will know them by their fruits. Do men gather grapes from thornbushes or figs from thistles? 17 Even so, every good tree bears good fruit, but a bad tree bears bad fruit. 18 A good tree cannot bear bad fruit, nor can a bad tree bear good fruit. 19 Every tree that does not bear good fruit is cut down and thrown into the fire. 20 Therefore by their fruits you will know them.

John 13:35 By this all will know that you are My disciples, if you have love for one another.

1 John 2:9-11 He who says he is in the light, and hates his brother, is in darkness until now. 10 He who loves his brother abides in the light, and there is no cause for stumbling in him. 11 But he who hates his brother is in darkness and walks in darkness, and does not know where he is going, because the darkness has blinded his eyes.

So Darby's character was widely known and understood as being a zealot who was intolerant of any other opinion or doctrine other than his own. Any who disagreed with him were chopped off and discarded by him, and labeled as heretical.

Beyond all of this, as I mentioned, there is evidence to suggest that Darby was familiar with occultic terms from freemasonry and others, particularly theosophy. Now regarding theosophy, it was not officially brought forward as a belief system until 1882, at the hands of a woman named Helena Blavatsky. Now her magnum opus, The Key to Theosophy, was not published until 1889, which was a few years after Darby had finished his Study Bible. His original work was put forth in 1867, but he revised the work twice more, with one in 1872 and the final revision in 1884. This would suggest that Darby could not have known about a belief system before it was birthed right? Theosophy however, was around long before Blavatsky, and much of the doctrine and symbology was present long before. An example is that the official symbol for theosophy is a hexagram, surrounded by the ouro boros serpent, with a swastika (stylized sun cross) above it, and an Egyptian Ankh in the middle. Each of these symbols predate theosophy, as does the doctrine contained therein. Many teachings in theosophy mirror those found in other works by prominent freemasons such as Albert Pike.

The evidence that John Nelson Darby was likely involved in this occultic activity is reflected in his writings. To begin, Helena Blavatsky defined Theosophy as "the study of the divine mind in nature". Compare this with Darby's writings:

> *J.N Darby: The Distinct Character of the Several Writings of the New Testament:*
>
> *In spiritual subjects, it is the object of much distinct converse in them to be able to present them primarily and vividly, so as to lead the way to fuller <u>investigation of the divine mind.</u>*

Theosophy as well as Free Masonry both use the term "the Architect" or "The heavenly Architect" (the word Architect always capitalized to indicate a proper name) as a name for their god. Darby used these same terms at times.

> *J.N. Darby: Christ the Faithful Witness, 221:*
>
> *But we need a "Faithful Witness." We see God in nature that is true, but all this knowledge does not lead man to God. Man has spoilt all. <u>The traces of God, of the Architect,</u> are there; but it is a ruin. All is defiled from His mind; all is in degradation.*

> *J.N Darby: The House of God; the Body of Christ; and the Baptism of the Holy Ghost:*
>
> *All this is foreign to the view here taken. It is life; that is, Christ, as having, as Son, life in and from the life of the living God, life divine, life in Himself (proved in resurrection), which is the foundation and security of the assembly built by the <u>heavenly Architect,</u> against which he who has the power of death, Satan, cannot prevail.*

Another term Blavatsky used to speak of her god was "the Absolute". Her definition of this being is found in Secret Doctrine I pg. 14:

The Absolute: "*An Omnipresent, Eternal, Boundless, and Immutable PRINCIPLE on which all speculation is impossible, since it transcends the power of human conception and could only be dwarfed by any human expression or similitude. It is beyond the range and reach of thought — in the words of Mandukya, 'unthinkable and unspeakable.'*"

Darby also used this term to refer to God.

J.N. Darby: The Humiliation of Christ:
"*The essential being of Godhead cannot change, as is evident - the Absolute, as men speak - and whatever His humiliation, all the fullness of the Godhead (theotetos) dwelt in Him bodily.*"

There are dozens of examples strewn throughout Darby's writings that use proper occult terminology to describe God, Christ, the Spirit, and many other things. I've only listed a short few, but there are many more that are less pronounced, but still present. This could all be merely coincidence I suppose, but given the infamous character of Darby, the heretical teachings regarding Christ's atonement, his subtle changes to the Bible to push forward his doctrines, the way he treated others, and the way he was seen by other sources such as Spurgeon, I think it would be wise to think twice before taking this man's doctrine and running with it.

Now as I said, my desire is not to stand here as accuser of Mr. Darby, but to make you aware that nearly the entirety of the modern church hold this man in high regard, and base their theology off of his teachings. This is problematic for many reasons, but two prominent ones were the character of the man and the character of his followers, and his other lesser known teachings and beliefs, such as Christ having to atone for His own sin, before He could atone for the sin of others, not to mention the occasional use of prominent occultic terminology.

Darby didn't spread this theology alone though, he had help. Darby continued to push forward his doctrine until he came into contact with a man named Cyrus Ingerson Scofield, commonly known as C.I. Scofield.

Now once again, I do not wish to slander Mr. Scofield, but this man too had a rather controversial life both before and after his conversion. Before his conversion, Scofield was a lawyer, and in fact, got into trouble a few times for breaking laws such as forgery. He was known as a crooked politician, and a liar. He skipped town after his debauchery caught up with him, thus abandoning his wife Leontine, and his two daughters Abigail and Helene. A news publication known as the Atchison Globe printed a news article in 1881 regarding Scofield:

> C. I. Schofield, who was appointed United States District Attorney for Kansas in 1873, and who turned out worse than any other Kansas official, is now a Campbellite preacher in Missouri. His wife and two children live in Atchison. He contributes nothing to their support except good advice.

Another publication picked up this story and expounded upon it a bit. This is an excerpt from the Topeka Daily Capital:

> Cyrus I. Schofield, formerly of Kansas, late lawyer, politician and shyster generally, has come to the surface again, and promises once more to gather around himself that halo of notoriety that has made him so prominent in the past. The last personal knowledge that Kansans have had of this peer among scalawags, was when about four years ago, after a series of forgeries and confidence games he left the state and a destitute family and took refuge in Canada. For a time he kept undercover, nothing being heard of him until within the past two years when he turned up in St. Louis, where he had a wealthy widowed sister living who has generally come to the front and squared up Cyrus' little follies and foibles by paying good round sums of money. Within the past year, however, Cyrus committed a series of St. Louis forgeries that could not be settled so easily, and the erratic young gentleman was compelled to linger in the St. Louis jail for a period of six months.

Essentially, Scofield was a man on the run from the law, having participated in quite a few unlawful activities. In fact, even after fleeing to Canada, when he popped back up in Saint Louis, he got himself in trouble yet again. Enough trouble that he was in jail for his crimes for a bit. Interestingly, after six months, his charges were suddenly dropped, and he was free to go, but we will look at that more in a moment. It is important to note at this time, that even after his conversion, he never returned to his wife, he never reconciled with his daughters, and until the day he died he was estranged from them. His first wife divorced him on grounds of abandonment. The court system ruled in her favor and approved the divorce, as well as denying Scofield any custody of the children, deeming him to be unfit for custody. This didn't stop him though, because within six months of his divorce being finalized, he remarried a woman named Hettie Hall Von Wartz. Who he had been already pursuing before his divorce was finalized as evidenced by the short turn around. In fact, many writings suggest when he began to come up in ministry, he hid his marriage from the congregations he helped to oversee, and presented himself as a bachelor. This was all after his conversion. Call me old fashioned, but I really don't think a man who abandoned his family to escape legal trouble, and kept it a secret, and remarried another woman as soon as he was legally able ought to have been in ministry as fast as Scofield was. Christ does offer forgiveness of sins, and we all have things in our past we aren't proud of, but Scofield never went back to make things right with the family he had abandoned.

> *1 Timothy 5:8 But if anyone does not provide for his own, and especially for those of his household, he has denied the faith and is worse than an unbeliever.*

Anyways, a while after being released from jail, he ended up finding his way into the ministry where he eventually picked up Darby's teachings. Scofield then set about compiling this doctrine of dispensationalism and published it in his first major publication "Rightly Dividing the Word of Truth". This pamphlet began to circulate and caught the attention of some very wealthy people. Remember around this time the Rothschild family were hard at work trying to establish the nation state of Israel. In order to do this however, they knew they would need political support. Who could they find that would blindly support the establishment of a nation state of Israel without question? They approached a few parties, but it came up blank. In order to push forward their Zionist agenda, they had to create a group that would support them and fight for them, without questioning the motives. It was around this time that Scofield attracted some rather interesting allies.

In 1901 after having success with his Pamphlet and some other areas of ministry, he was approached by the Lotos Club, a prestigious art club for the elite. Some noteworthy members were Mark Twain, Andrew Carnegie, Dwight D Eisenhower, Harvey Weinstein, Margaret Mead, and Orson Wells. The man overseeing the admission and acceptance into this prestigious group was a man named Samuel Untermyer, who personally accepted Scofield into this group. Samuel Untermyer had been for a time the president of Keren Hayesod, which was a financial body that lent tremendous support to the Zionist agenda that was being pushed forward by the wealthy elite. Untermyer also played a major role in drafting the Federal Reserve act that has destroyed the American economy by signing it over to be overseen by a private bank that cannot be audited or investigated. He did many things within the political realm, most of which were related to funding or advancing Zionism.

Shortly after being accepted, these generous backers and friends paid for Scofield to travel to Europe where he met with a man named Robert Scott. He told Robert Scott that he was interested in writing a reference Bible, but was unsure who would publish such a thing. Scott was able to introduce him to the head of Oxford University Press, Henry Frowde. Frowde was immediately interested in publishing this work, and struck a deal to publish his reference Bible, before it was ever written. Agreeing to publish a book before the book having been written by the way never happens, as it can turn out a disastrous financial move if the book is bad. What a tremendous stroke of "luck" on Scofield's part eh? It is also worth mentioning Oxford has been, nearly since it's inception, a university dedicated to the degradation of morality, and the spread of the New World Order. It was also owned at this time by a group of Fabian Socialists.

With the help of his friends in Oxford, and their connections, he traveled to Switzerland, a particularly prominent hotbed for elitist bankers. In fact, everyone knows the little symbol for Switzerland right? The little red shield with a white cross in it? Would it shock you to learn that the name Rothschild is actually translated from German in the form of Roth (an old Germanic word for red) and Schild (The Germanic word for Shield) thus the name actually means Red Shields? Anyways, it was in Switzerland that Scofield did much of the work of compiling his reference Bible, and in 1909, he released it. This is an excerpt from the Wikipedia page for C.I. Scofield.

> *As the author of the pamphlet "Rightly Dividing the Word of Truth" (1888), Scofield soon became a leader in dispensational premillenni- alism, a forerunner of twentieth-century Christian fundamentalism. Although, in theory, Scofield returned to his Dallas pastorate in 1903, his projected reference Bible consumed much of his energy, and for much of the time before its publication, he was either unwell or in Europe. When the Scofield Reference Bible was published in 1909, it quickly became the most influential statement of dispensational premillennialism, and Scofield's popularity as Bible conference speaker increased as his health continued to decline. Royalties from the work were substantial, and Scofield held real estate in Dallas, Ashuelot, New Hampshire, and Douglaston, Long Island.* [47]

This reference Bible, being distributed by Oxford and the wealthy elite quickly became one of the most prominent works in the 19th century, which ended up making Scofield filthy rich. I'm going to stop there for just a moment and ask a simple question. Does the world react to truth in a way that causes men to get rich enough to buy at least four houses and get access into a prestigious secular art club?

John 15:18-20 "If the world hates you, you know that it hated Me before it hated you. 19 If you were of the world, the world would love its own. Yet because you are not of the world, but I chose you out of the world, therefore the world hates you. 20 Remember the word that I said to you, 'A servant is not greater than his master.' If they persecuted Me, they will also persecute you.

Anyways, with the popularization of his work exploding in the decade following 1909, he offered a revised version in the year 1917. This version actually became even more prominent than his previous version. Isn't it curious that the Balfour Declaration was put forth in this very same year, really pushing the Zionist agenda into action to establish Israel as a nation? Isn't it curious that about 20 years later in 1939 the world went to war against Germany to combat it's sudden rise to power and conquering of Europe along with the holocost? Isn't it interesting that three years after the fall of Nazi Germany Israel was established as a nation? You really need to search and read Albert Pike's Letter to Manzini written 1871. I promise it's worth the read.

This is an excerpt from wrmea.org regarding Scofield's contributions to Zionism.

Others have been even more explicit about the nature of Scofield's service to the Zionist agenda. In "Unjust War Theory: Christian Zionism and the Road to Jerusalem," Prof. David W. Lutz writes, "Untermeyer used Scofield, a Kansas City lawyer with no formal training in theology, to inject Zionist ideas into American Protestantism. Untermeyer and other wealthy and influential Zionists whom he introduced to Scofield promoted and funded the latter's career, including travel in Europe."

On one of these European trips, Oxford University Press publisher Henry Frowde "expressed immediate interest" in Scofield's project. According to a biography of Frowde, although the OUP publisher was "not demonstrative in his religious views, all his Christian life he was associated with brethren known as 'Exclusive.'" The "Exclusive Brethren" refers to the group of Christian evangelicals that, in an 1848 split in the Plymouth Brethren, followed John Nelson Darby, the Anglo-Irish missionary generally considered to have been the most influential figure in the development of Christian Zionism, and a major influence on Scofield. [48]

Suddenly through Scofield's work, the Rothschilds had a large party who would politically and financially support all their endeavors regarding establishing and supporting a nation state of Israel without question. This was the Christian Church now thoroughly indoctrinated with Zionism.

Now this explosively popular theological book contained many other interesting ideas within it. First and foremost is dual covenant theology. This doctrine teaches that the old covenant between God and His people was not actually dissolved at the cross. It teaches that while the ekklesia is under the new covenant, the physical Jews are all by virtue of their bloodline, a part of God's chosen people, and under the Old covenant still. This means that the Jews have no need of Christ, as they need no new covenant. This directly contradicts Christ teaching throughout Jerusalem to the Jewish people that He was the only way to the Father, as well as fails to offer an explanation for why the Jewish apostles themselves accepted Christ as the only way, and taught other Jews the same. It claims that while the ekklesia is the bride of Christ, the "Jews" are the bride of the Father.

Lastly, it taught that due to the perceived dichotomy between the Jews and Gentiles, portions of the Bible only pertain to the Jews, while others only pertain to the Gentiles. Basically, if a portion of the Bible was written to a "Jewish" audience, it had no bearing on the "Gentile" church. Which we will examine more as we go on, but an important note is that technically everything Jesus taught was technically to a "Jewish" audience, which means that according to this theology, we don't need to obey what He taught. Meanwhile Paul is cited as being the only source of writings truly for the gentiles, thus we only need to listen to Paul. We will look at why this is such a major issue in a few chapters.

So John Nelson Darby and Cyrus Ingerson Scofield are among the two most venerated theologians in the world today, with hundreds of colleges and seminaries dedicated to their theology. Neither of these men showed forth much character, and there are glaring issues with both of these men, as well as the doctrines they taught. They were aided by the Illuminati in spreading their doctrine, and the body of Christ, not knowing their scripture, swallowed the lie. Half the time if you suggest that the ekklesia is Israel, and the Jews need Christ just as much as anyone, they will argue and fight with you. This was foretold:

> *2 Timothy 4:3-4 For the time will come when they will not endure sound doctrine, but according to their own desires, because they have itching ears, they will heap up for themselves teachers; 4 and they will turn their ears away from the truth, and be turned aside to fables.*

So how did this theology become so prevalent in the modern church today and how did it spread so quickly? Well, it's very simple. Outside of the mass distribution the wealthy friends of these men enabled them to accomplish, they also managed to influence just about every major Bible college. In the days of the early ekklesia, teachers were decided upon via their fruit, such as their relationships with others, the state of their children and household, and their character. Also their general reputation among believers, the amount of years they had walked with God, their wisdom in the scriptures, and the spirit bearing witness to them. Basically, just as Christ commanded, they looked for the fruit.

> *Matthew 7:16-20 You will know them by their fruits. Do men gather grapes from thornbushes or figs from thistles? 17 Even so, every good tree bears good fruit, but a bad tree bears bad fruit. 18 A good tree cannot bear bad fruit, nor can a bad tree bear good fruit. 19 Every tree that does not bear good fruit is*

cut down and thrown into the fire. 20 Therefore by their fruits you will know them.

This was the right way to go about things. Men among the ekklesia who lived and learned near other believers would over time build up a good reputation, and having commendations from others of good reputation for love and service, they would be put in a position of an elder, or assistant to the elders, and would be tested until a time they were sure this teacher was trustworthy.

However, in this time period of the late 1800s to the early 1900s, the worship of intellect began to swell, as the technologies and sciences did. The world began to push the idea that wisdom could only be attained via education, and colleges began popping up all over. Prior to this time period, colleges were reserved for the wealthy and studious, and those who attended college were seen as the cream of the crop of society, being the most intelligent and successful people around. The Christian community, as it became more and more like the culture around it, began adopting the practices and thought processes of the world. One of these was to select it's preachers not based upon their character, merit, and trustworthy character, but instead upon academic prowess. The church began choosing it's leadership the same way businesses did, by taking resumes and looking at their academic credentials. This shift spread like wildfire, and Christian Colleges became ever more prevalent to the point that today you basically cannot get a position as a pastor unless you have a Bible degree from a university.

The issue with these Bible colleges are much the same with other universities however, and that is, though while they do teach some things that are good, much of what you learn is based upon the personal whims of those who own and control the college. In other words, you are being indoctrinated according to the curriculum you receive, which is built by men who have vested interest in the college both in reputation and income, and have personal agendas and motives. I have had friends who were very conservative and stayed out of trouble for the most part, who when they went to secular colleges, their morals and ideals were rapidly degraded and replaced with complete liberalism and the dismissal of most morality. This is because in modern colleges, the college owners with the money, the professors and teachers, the curriculum writers, and even most of the staff are all very liberal and the liberal agendas are pushed down your throat constantly while any other opinions are ridiculed and attacked.

This atmosphere of academic pressure to conform is not limited to secular colleges however, and Christian colleges are much the same. The only difference is, instead of it being a question of morality and political agenda, it's a question of theology. If your theological views do not align with that of the college, you can't really excel in their curriculum because it is built upon specific doctrines and theologies. Graduation, more often than not, requires a dissertation where you write about your theological views and beliefs. If your views differ from the views of the college, it affects your grade accordingly, even though they often claim it doesn't. They believe that they have truth, and any deviation from the truth they teach is error. Therefore if they pass someone with a dissertation they deem as being filled with error, they are hurting their reputation and giving a person the credentials to teach others what they deem as error. This cannot happen, and therefore a person must show themselves utterly indoctrinated with the proposed theologies if they hope to graduate. In fact, quite often you can tell exactly what Bible college a person went to based upon their theology because the graduates basically come out cookie cutter, cut to the specifications of the curriculum taught.

This was the other main way dispensationalism spread so rapidly. A man by the name of Lewis Sperry Chafer began to rise in popularity in the early 1900s. This man latched onto the teachings of Darby and Scofield, and ultimately opened a college. This college was one of the most influential Bible colleges of it's time. This was the Dallas Theological Seminary. This college is known as the mecca of modern dispensationalism, and therefore, the graduates of this seminary had to learn and conform to these theologies as well. Some prominent names that attended this seminary are; Chuck Swindoll, Andy Stanley, Hal Lindsay (the self professed Christian Zionist),

Tony Evans, David Jeremiah, Erwin Lutzer, Jim Rayburn, Ernest Pickering, Paul Nyquist, and many others. If you have been around Christianity for much time at all, you probably know some of these names. Other big names, although they themselves weren't directly from the DTS, still picked up on this dispensational theology that was rapidly spreading. Oral Roberts, Kenneth Copeland, Pat Robertson, Benny Hinn, Joel Osteen, Billy Graham and many other equally prominent names, have all bought into this theology in one way or another and taught it to the masses.

This isn't to say that every preacher who teaches dispensationalism is somehow evil, though I would suggest there are some bad apples in the names I mentioned, it simply means that they bear some deception as well. Tony Evans in particular I have heard many of his sermons, and have liked many of them, but I also don't completely agree with everything he says. I believe many are doing the best they can with what they've been given, but there are things these men simply don't understand. I have no doubt there are areas I very likely don't understand either, which is why I admonish you to look into what I say for yourself instead of taking my word for it.

Anyways, what this all means is, successful men who had the money to go to, and often open other Bible colleges began supplying churches everywhere with teachers teaching their own brand of theology, and thus churches began overwhelmingly being taught many of the same doctrines. In this way, certain doctrines such as dispensationalism began spreading like wildfire.

Churches took the idea of spreading the gospel, and altered it into growing their own churches. Meanwhile, these colleges not only taught specific doctrines, but also taught classes on how to engage your audience, how to put together a sermon in a way that was interesting and engaging and entertaining for the people. These teachers, trained in the art of pleasing presentation and palatable teaching styles naturally attracted bigger crowds, thus growing churches at faster rates and to bigger sizes. From a spiritual side this appeared to be something great, as bringing in new people means new converts and souls saved, and from a financial standpoint, this was extremely beneficial as well, as more members directly affected income. Mega churches and billionaire preachers began to rise. Other churches wanting to be as "impactful" as these mega churches, began to adopt their methodology and teachings. The problem was, nobody ever really stopped to examine the teachings that were going out from these churches or the characters of the men they were getting these teachings from. They were far more focused on "reaching more people".

Many of these mega churches today hold weekly rock concerts, complete with professional musicians, laser light shows, smoke machines, and the occasional celebrity presence to boost attendance when people get bored. You can find videos of pastors driving $100,000 cars across the stage all in the name of "reaching more people". There are seminaries, youth camps, outreach programs, TV channels, radio shows, and hundreds of other modes of outreach. You will rarely ever hear words like "Hell" "repentance" or "judgement" spoken in these mega churches, and their primary focus is to spread "the gospel" and reach more people.

The only thing is, this gospel all too often says all you have to do is believe in Jesus and you'll live forever. This gospel claims no obedience or submission necessary, because there's grace. This gospel claims it doesn't matter if you have sin in your life or not, you can live however you see fit and when you die you're as good as in heaven because you had the get out of Hell free card in your back pocket. This gospel says that the church and Israel are completely separate entities, and thus our identity as Israel has been completely stolen from the modern church. This mega Christianity built upon the teachings of Darby and Scofield have begun to implement things like Christian Wicca, Christian LGBTQ, Christian Alchemy, and pretty much anything else you can think of. With the removal of our identity, and the undermining of our foundations of scripture, it becomes easy to get led into error. Essentially, although this form of Christianity does indeed reach many people, the message has become completely distorted and lost. It's a false identity, a false gospel, and a completely lawless and lukewarm message going forth from many churches that is deceiving people by the millions every day.

People have the best of intentions once again, but good intentions don't always make good results. There are many who really do want to do what's right, both preachers and listeners alike, but they've been duped by a false, or at least incomplete gospel. I had gone to churches my whole life and all I ever heard was that all you had to do was believe in Jesus. One day well into my teenage years I finally heard a message that explained that not only do you have to believe in Him, you also have to confess Him as Master in order to be born again. They say just believe, but the steps are repentance and belief. Repentance requires change of life, and submission to Christ. It's not just head knowledge, it's a new life. It wasn't until that message that my life began to drastically change. That change was definitely pronounced and significant, as it was the moment I received new birth. The next biggest change in my walk came when I realized that I was a part of Israel. We will begin to look at what that means from here on out.

19

Branches

So far in this book, we've gone over many things. We went over that our Faith should not look like the RCC, but it also should not be involved in Judaism. We've established that the modern day nation of Israel and Jerusalem are not as innocent as they would like you to believe, and that those of us who are in Christ are the true people of Israel. These things are important, and informative, but they don't really tell us what we are supposed to do. We need to separate from the pagan holidays, and pagan Roman Sabbath, and some of the other pagan based traditions, but what are we supposed to do instead? We are finally going to begin looking at these things. I had to lay some ground work to get to this point, but now we will begin to look at things that are more applicable.

This chapter will not only set the groundwork for the next couple chapters, but it will also give us another interesting perspective on who we are and what we should be doing. This chapter, in particular, is about what we call ourselves.

Now, we use the name Christian, and this makes sense for a few reasons. First of all, we know the early ekklesia were called Christians from these verses:

> **Acts 11:26 And when he had found him, he brought him to Antioch. So it was that for a whole year they assembled with**

the church and taught a great many people. And the disciples were first called Christians in Antioch.

1 Peter 4:16 Yet if anyone suffers as a Christian, let him not be ashamed, but let him glorify God in this matter.

So we do have conclusive evidence that the early ekklesia were referred to as Christians, but the question is, even though they were called this name, is this the name they called themselves? I will show you both scripturally, and historically, they did not adopt this name for themselves, and instead had a different name. First though, we must understand how this term Christian, came about, and what it means. Now, there is a bit of debate as to exactly how the name came about, but there are two primary theories. The first is that Ignacious of Antioch, an early "church" leader coined the phrase in Antioch where he spent some time and began to use the term before Rome picked it up. Ignatius is a bit of a controversial character as supposedly he was a disciple of the apostle John, which earns him some points in his favor. However, there is also evidence to suggest he craved position and power and through his having been associated with John, maneuvered himself to assume ever greater authority over the church eventually taking on the title of Bishop, and putting out anyone who dared question him. In fact, he spoke a whole lot like a pope.

Ignatius to the Ephesians Chapter 6: For we ought to receive every one whom the Master of the house sends to be over His household, as we would do Him that sent him. It is manifest, therefore, that we should look upon the bishop even as we would upon the Lord Himself.

Ignatius to the Magnesians Chapter 6: I exhort you to study to do all things with a divine harmony, while your bishop presides in the place of God,

Ignatius to the Smyrnians Chapter 9: It is well to reverence both God

231

and the bishop. He who honours the bishop has been honoured by God; he who does anything without the knowledge of the bishop, does [in reality] serve the devil.

Ignatius, it would seem, was probably the true founder of the so called Christianity that Constantine made the official religion of Rome. This Christianity involved the Bishop needing to preside over everything, knowing everything, and being put in the place of God. There are many more heretical quotes from this man, and the RCC is fond of him as a foundation to their church. This man may very well be one of the ones John spoke about when he said this:

> *1 John 2:18-19 Little children, it is the last hour; and as you have heard that the Antichrist is coming, even now <u>many antichrists have come</u>, by which we know that it is the last hour. 19 <u>They went out from us, but they were not of us; for if they had been of us, they would have continued with us;</u> but they went out that they might be made manifest, that none of them were of us.*

Ignatius sure seemed to want to be the replacement for Christ, and he also helped to set up many of the pagan observances before Constantine made it the official religion of Rome by mixing the faith with Mithraism.

The second theory as to where the term Christian got it's start, is that the Roman armies invented the term as a derogatory term for those who followed the Christ. Essentially denoting that these "little Christs" would die at their hands just like the Christ did. In either case, it does not seem as if this title was a very good one.

There was however, a name that isn't of questionable origins that the early followers called themselves and it is found here:

> *Acts 24:5 For we have found this man (Paul) a plague, a creator of dissension among all the Jews throughout the world, and a ringleader of the sect of the Nazarenes.*

Acts 28:22 But we desire to hear from you what you think; for concerning this sect, we know that it is spoken against everywhere.

So Paul was cited as being an infamous ring leader among a sect that referred to themselves as Nazarenes. Could this be the name the early followers called themselves? Well, it is worth noting that Christ was in fact, from Nazareth, and thus was called a Nazarene. It is also very interesting to note that the word is actually very prophetic. You see, the the word Nazareth, means branch, thus Nazarenes means branches. With that knowledge, notice this verse:

John 15:5 "I am the vine, you are the <u>branches</u>. He who abides in Me, and I in him, bears much fruit; for without Me you can do nothing.

In the original Hebrew that Messiah spoke, He would've said, I am the vine, and you are the natsarim, or the English transliteration, nazarenes. This is also in line with Romans 11 when Paul refers to believers as branches being grafted into the cultivated olive tree.

Beyond that, in Hebrew when a word has the same root letters as another word, these words become related to one another although the vowel sounds may be different or additional letters added on. The base letters of this word Natsarim, are N-TS-R or in Hebrew Nun-Tsade-Resh. Other words with these same letters in the same order, are related to one another. This is primarily because of the original written Hebrew language being pictographic. Words with the same consonants but different vowels in between have the same basic images in the same order even if the words sound a bit different. One word that is related in this matter to our word Natsarim is the Hebrew word Natsir, which is Strong's Hebrew #5336 and means "preserved". One example is found in this verse:

Isaiah 49:6 Indeed He says, 'It is too small a thing that You should be My Servant To raise up the tribes of Jacob, and to restore the preserved ones of Israel; I will also give You as a light to the Gentiles, that You should be My salvation to the ends of the earth.'

This verse, not only is a prophecy about Christ, but also about Him restoring "preserved" (natsir) ones of Israel, and being a light to the gentiles (other nations) to the ends of the earth. Could it be this prophecy is directly about the followers, the natsarim, carrying the gospel of Christ to the ends of the earth? Maybe. The name Natsarim is one of rich heritage, and meaning. There are many verses that talk about these preserved ones, and often are linked to the end times. Many are waking up out of the stupor of the Catholic Church system and separating themselves from her, could these who throw off her customs, and her pagan rituals be the preserved ones of the end times? Maybe.

There was one more term they used that differentiated their beliefs. See, they didn't follow Christianity, these early converts followed what they called "The Way"

Acts 24:14 But this I confess to you, that according to the Way which they call a sect, so I worship the God of my fathers, believing all things which are written in the Law and in the Prophets.

Paul was giving his defense in Jerusalem and gave this answer when confronted on different matters. He said that they called the group he was a part of "The Way" which was called a sect or cult. This is mentioned again here:

Acts 19:9 But when some were hardened and did not believe, but spoke evil of the Way before the multitude, he departed from them and withdrew the disciples, reasoning daily in the school of Tyrannus.

These Natsarim were followers of The Way.

John 14:6 Jesus said to him, "I am the way, the truth, and the life. No one comes to the Father except through Me.

The early ekklesia were calling themselves Nazarenes, or Natsarim, which is what Christ called them and was Himself called due to being from Nazareth, and they were calling themselves followers of The Way, which is what Jesus said He was. These were beautiful names they kept during the time of the early ekklesia. These names differentiated them from the orthodox Jews who kept the pagan Jewish traditions, as well as the "Christians" who were mostly ruled by Ignatius of Antioch, who was busy setting himself up as an authority akin to God.

The difference between the Natsarim and the Ignatius led Christians were not only in name or structure though, they were also much different in practice. Here are some quotes from other early "church" fathers who followed after Ignatius:

> "But these sectarians... did not call themselves Christians - but "Nazarenes". However they are simply complete Jews. They use not only the New Testament but the Old Testament as well, as the Jews do... They have no different ideas, but confess everything exactly as the Law proclaims it and in the Jewish fashion - except for their belief in Messiah, if you please! For they acknowledge both the resurrection of the dead and the divine creation of all things, and declare that God is one, and that his son is Yeshua the Messiah. They are trained to a nicety in Hebrew. For among them the entire Law, the Prophets, and the... writings... are read in Hebrew, as they surely are by the Jews. They are different from the Jews, and different from Christians, only in the following. They disagree with the Jews because they have come to faith in Messiah; but since they are still fettered by the law- circumcision, the Sabbath, and the rest - they are not in accord with Christians... they are nothing but Jews... They have the good news

according to Matthew in its entirety in Hebrew. For it is clear that they still preserve this, in the Hebrew alphabet, as it was originally written."

   -Epiphanius; Panarion 29 [49]

"The Nazarenes do not differ in any essential thing from them (the Jews), since they practice the customs and doctrines prescribed by Jewish Law; Except that they believe in Christ. They believe in the resurrection of the dead, and that the universe was created by God. They preach that God is one, and that Jesus Christ is His Son. They are very learned in the Hebrew language. They read the Law... Therefore they differ... from the true Christians because they fulfill until now (such) Jewish rites as the circumcision, Sabbath and others."

   -Epiphanius; "Against Heresies," pp. 41,402

"They, (the Nazarenes) are characterized essentially by their tenacious attachment to Jewish observances. If they became heretics in the eyes of the (Catholic) Mother Church, it is simply because they remained fixed on outmoded positions. They well represent, though Epiphanius (the guy with the quotes above) *is energetically refusing to admit it, the very direct descendants of that primitive community, of which our author (Epiphanius) knows that it was designated by the Jews, by the same name, of 'Nazarenes'"*

   -First Century expert Marcel Simon, Judeo-christianisme, [pp 47-48.] [50]

Remember that issue where we lost our holidays and Sabbath because they are of pagan origin? The early followers of The Way didn't have this issue. Whereas many of the followers of The Way were coming out of pagan Rome, they abandoned those idolatrous customs and instead kept God's Sabbath and His feasts. In the modern church, there are many pastors who adamantly teach against the feasts and the Sabbath because they believe them to be "Jewish". They claim that to keep these things is somehow wrong, dangerous, or "acting Jewish" but this couldn't be farther from the truth. Not only did these Nazarenes keep the feasts, Christ, our example, kept all the feasts, and even after His ascension, they still kept the feasts. Paul kept the feasts too, which is ironic because people most of the time try to quote Paul's writings to prove we shouldn't be keeping them.

> *Acts 20:6 But we sailed away from Philippi after the Days of Unleavened Bread, and in five days joined them at Troas, where we stayed seven days.*

> *Acts 18:20-21 When they asked him to stay a longer time with them, he did not consent, 21 but took leave of them, saying, "I must by all means keep this coming feast in Jerusalem; but I will return again to you, God willing." And he sailed from Ephesus.*

> *1 Corinthians 5:7-8 Therefore purge out the old leaven, that you may be a new lump, since you truly are unleavened. For indeed Christ, our Passover, was sacrificed for us. 8 Therefore let us keep the feast, not with old leaven, nor with the leaven of malice and wickedness, but with the unleavened bread of sincerity and truth.*

So Paul kept the feasts himself, and taught others to keep them as well. Now people may argue it was because Paul was Jewish, but as we established, having Jewish blood really doesn't mean anything in the Kingdom of Heaven since Christ died, and even before that "gentiles" such as Rahab and Ruth became a part of Israel and Judah and of the lineage of Messiah. What matters is whether or not you are in covenant with God through His Son. But what about these feasts? Are they Jewish feasts?

> *Leviticus 26:2 You shall keep My Sabbaths and reverence My sanctuary: I am the Lord.*

Leviticus 23:1-2 And the Lord spoke to Moses, saying, 2 "Speak to the children of Israel, and say to them: <u>The feasts of the Lord,</u> which you shall proclaim to be holy convocations, <u>these are My feasts</u>."'

So while mainstream Christianity is claiming these are "Jewish" feasts, in reality the scripture says these are God's feasts. They're also called "His feasts" because they are ALL about Him, but we will look at that more in a future chapter. We will also look more at the Sabbath, but for now I want to show you one thing regarding it. While the Catholic Church is claiming their "Lord's Day" is the mark of their authority, there is another mark in the scriptures.

Ezekiel 20:12 Moreover <u>I also gave them My Sabbaths, to be a sign between them and Me,</u> that they might know that I am the Lord who sanctifies them.

Exodus 31:16-17 Therefore the <u>children of Israel shall keep the Sabbath,</u> to observe the Sabbath <u>throughout their generations as a perpetual covenant. 17 It is a sign between Me and the children of Israel forever;</u> for in six days the Lord made the heavens and the earth, and on the seventh day He rested and was refreshed.

So Christianity says things like "It doesn't matter if we keep the Sabbath" or "The feasts are Jewish! We shouldn't keep those!" or "That stuff is done away with!" the Bible says these Sabbaths are a sign between God and His people, Israel, us, and that the length of this sign is perpetual, or throughout all their generations, or FOREVER. So where did Christianity learn not to keep these feasts and that it was wrong to?

Ignatius to the Magnations Chapter 8: Be not deceived with strange doctrines, nor with old fables, which are unprofitable. For if we still live according to the Jewish law, we acknowledge that we have not received grace. For the divinest prophets lived according to Christ Jesus.

Ignatius to the Magnations Chapter 9: If, therefore, those who were brought up in the ancient order of things have come to the possession of a new hope, no longer observing the Sabbath, but living in the observance of the Lord's Day,

Ignatius to the Philadelphians Chapter 4: Take heed, then, to have but one Eucharist. For there is one flesh of our Lord Jesus Christ, and one cup to [show forth] the unity of His blood; one altar; as there is one bishop, along with the presbytery and deacons, my fellow-servants: that so, whatsoever you do, you may do it according to [the will of] God. But if any one preach the Jewish law unto you, listen not to him. For it is better to hearken to Christian doctrine from a man who has been circumcised, than to Judaism from one uncircumcised.

Ignations to the Smyrnaens Chapter 7: They abstain from the Eucharist and from prayer, because they confess not the Eucharist to be the flesh of our Saviour Jesus Christ, which suffered for our sins, and which the Father, of His goodness, raised up again.

Ignatius, the self inflating bishop avidly taught against keeping the Feasts, the Sabbath, Circumcision, and many other things. He taught that doing any of these things was called being a "Judiazer" and anyone caught keeping these feasts, or the Saturday Sabbath, was excommunicated from his church. He also taught observance to these pagan replacements such as "The Lord's Day" and "The Eucharist". Remember, these things actually predated Catholicism, and were primarily found in Mithraism, which was a cult prominent at that time and in those general regions. Later on during the reign of Constantine, Rome picked up this same form of "Christianity" and with it the opinion of banning anything they deemed "Jewish". These quotes are from jewishvirtuallibrary.com regarding the Justinian law that was signed into effect to be enforced in Rome.

> *NOVELLA 37 (535 C.E.), forbidding Jews and heretics in the newly conquered province of North Africa to practice their religious rites. Synagogues and the meeting places of heretics were to be confiscated and, suitably consecrated, put to ecclesiastical use. Contrary to the prevailing Christian attitude, this novella attempted to view Judaism as a heresy and may have been motivated by suspicion of Jewish support for the Vandal regime overthrown by Justinian and the belief, prevalent in North Africa, in the alleged Jewish role in spreading heresy.*

> *Justinian I, emperor of the Eastern Roman Empire, 527–565, a virulent and consistent persecutor of all non-Orthodox Christians, heretics, pagans, and also of Jews and Judaism.*

> *NOVELLA 131 (545 C.E.), prohibiting sales of ecclesiastical property to Jews, Samaritans, pagans, and heretics, and declaring synagogues built on land subsequently shown to be ecclesiastical property subject to confiscation.* [51]

So essentially, this church based on Mithraism and paganism started by Ignatius under the name "Christianity" grew until it reached Constantine. Constantine then signed laws officially converting Rome to Catholicism. Catholicism took over, and developed an allergy to anything it claimed to be "Jewish". A short time later, Rome militarily enforced obedience to this church, and being Jewish, keeping "Jewish" feasts, or "Jewish" Sabbaths or keeping anything other than the pagan Catholic observances was a crime, many of which were punishable by death. Even just walking according to the Old Testament law became a crime. Keep in mind that the all embracing Catholic church eagerly adopted every pagan practice from a myriad of cultures that they could find, but the one culture they apparently could not stand, was anything according to the law, such as the feasts, the Sabbath, and circumcision. This is quite telling.

This allergy to anything "Jewish" would've posed an issue for those early followers of the way:

> **Acts 3:1 Now Peter and John went up together <u>to the temple</u> at the hour of prayer, the ninth hour.**

> **Acts 2:46 So continuing daily with one accord <u>in the temple</u>, and breaking bread from house to house, they ate their food with gladness and simplicity of heart,**

So the apostles often met in the Jewish temple, I wonder how Ignacious or Justinian would've treated them? How about this portion?

> **Acts 15:19-21 Therefore I judge that we should not trouble those from among the Gentiles who are turning to God, 20 but that we write to them to abstain from things polluted by idols, from sexual immorality, from things strangled, and from blood. 21 <u>For Moses has had throughout many generations those who preach him in every city, being read in the synagogues every Sabbath.</u>"**

So the newly converted gentiles (who had just been grafted into Israel) needed a starting point, so Peter makes this judgement, that these new converts only had to abstain from these specific things (found in the Old Testament law) to be allowed fellowship with the rest of the ekklesia, and accepted into the fold. However, he goes on to say that they will hear Moses (ie the law and the prophets) each Sabbath (not the Lord's Day) in the synagogue (not the "church"). These verses suggest that gentiles were expected to attend the synagogues on the Sabbath and learn the books of Moses. Gentiles going to a synagogue, reading the Old Testament, and keeping the Sabbath all became outlawed by Rome. Essentially, all of this points to a simple truth. The followers of The Way, the early ekklesia, they kept the Feasts, they kept the Sabbath, they learned the Old Testament, and they maintained their Hebraic roots. Meanwhile, the beast sought to completely destroy all hints of anything Hebraic and replaced it with Roman paganism. Have you wondered why our faith is commonly referred to as Judeo-Christian, but anything even remotely pertaining to the Judeo is cast out? Oh it's cool for the Jewish people to follow God's commandments, but DON'T DARE suggest the "church" should! That's heresy! This attitude came directly from the beast itself.

Ironically the people who argue against keeping the feasts and Sabbath most often use Paul's writings to argue against them, but Paul himself kept these things. If Paul was keeping them but then teaching against them wouldn't that be straight hypocrisy? God commanded His people to keep these things forever, throughout all their generations, Christ perfectly kept them, and Paul kept them, but we aren't supposed to? People try to argue that Paul only kept them because he was Jewish but again, didn't Paul himself say this?

> *Galatians 3:28-29 There is __neither Jew nor Greek__, there is neither slave nor free, there is neither male nor female; for you are all one in Christ Jesus. 29 And __if you are Christ's, then you are Abraham's seed__, and heirs according to the promise.*

> *Isaiah 41:8 "But you, __Israel__, are My servant, Jacob whom I have chosen, __the descendants (seed) of Abraham__ My friend.*

So did Paul teach we are all one in Christ and all grafted into Israel, and that there is no Jew or Greek, but then act differently because of his Jewish blood and teach others to do other things because of their Greek blood? Did Paul observe the feasts, and keep the Sabbath, but then teach others they didn't have to because of their DNA? Did Paul teach about one new man referencing the house of Israel and Judah becoming one, and then give one part of the new man different rules to follow? Every time people use

Paul's writings to claim they shouldn't keep the Sabbath or feasts, they are making Paul look like a hypocrite. We are going to talk about this much more in another chapter, so rest assured, we will talk about Paul's thoughts on this subject and go through some of the verses that people use to claim we shouldn't keep the law, but not yet.

Beyond this, not only did Christ keep the feasts, and not only did Paul keep the feasts, and not only did the early ekklesia, the Natsarim, keep the feasts, but when Christ returns, the nations will be required to keep the feasts as well.

Zechariah 14:16-19 And it shall come to pass that everyone who is left of all the nations which came against Jerusalem shall go up from year to year to worship the King, the Lord of hosts, and to keep the Feast of Tabernacles. 17 And it shall be that whichever of the families of the earth do not come up to Jerusalem to worship the King, the Lord of hosts, on them there will be no rain. 18 If the family of Egypt will not come up and enter in, they shall have no rain; they shall receive the plague with which the Lord strikes the nations who do not come up to keep the Feast of Tabernacles. 19 This shall be the punishment of Egypt and the punishment of all the nations that do not come up to keep the Feast of Tabernacles.

Ezekiel 46:9-11 But when the people of the land come before the Lord on the appointed feast days, whoever enters by way of the north gate to worship shall go out by way of the south gate; and whoever enters by way of the south gate shall go out by way of the north gate. He shall not return by way of the gate through which he came, but shall go out through the opposite gate. 10 The prince shall then be in their midst. When they go in, he shall go in; and when they go out, he shall go out. 11 At the festivals and the appointed feast days the grain offering shall be an ephah for a bull, an ephah for a ram, as much as he wants to give for the lambs, and a hin of oil with every ephah.

With Ezekiel 46, the context is not immediately apparent from the passage, but if you read through Ezekiel, chapter 35 and 36 deal with the end times, 37 deals with the resurrection and return of Christ, 38 and 39 deal with the battle of armageddon and Christ destroying the armies of the beast, 40 to 43 describe the New Jerusalem in detail, 44 lays out the duties of the priests, and 45 and 46 begin talking about land outside the Holy city, and the nations surrounding and their responsibilities. Within context, this passage does indeed talk about the millennial reign.

So just to put this together, God commanded the feasts and Sabbaths to be kept throughout all our generations, as a perpetual sign, forever. Christ, our example, kept the feasts and Sabbath. Paul, who also said he was our example, kept the feasts and Sabbath. The followers of The Way, the Natsarim, kept the feasts and Sabbath. When Christ returns at the end of the age, the nations will be required to keep the feasts and Sabbaths, but right now, it's somehow wrong for us to observe them? This doctrine comes from nowhere but Rome.

The truth of the matter is this: if you read the entirety of the Old Testament, you will notice two common occurrences. God commanded His people to walk in His ways, and Satan tempted them to turn away from these ways. God said love one another, Satan said war against one another. God said have no other gods, Satan said follow all the other gods you can find. God said remember His Sabbaths and feasts, Satan said replace them with pagan rites. God said be Holy and set apart, Satan said, act just like the surrounding nations. Satan spent the entire Old Testament tempting the children of Israel to break God's laws and trample on His ways, and practice paganism.

When Christ died, Satan's kingdom was severely shaken. He had just been stripped of power and dominion. This meant the only tool he really had left at his disposal was deception. He had to stamp out the gospel as fast as possible. After all, the gospel undid everything he had accomplished. He accomplished causing ten of the twelve tribes of Israel getting divorced and cut off from God. He had also accomplished deceiving nearly the entirety of the Jewish population through the tradition laden pharisees. Satan had all but stamped out any remnant of a people who truly loved God and walked in His ways.

Then Christ came, and ruined all his plans. Christ offered the New covenant, this new covenant demolished the divorce Satan had worked so hard to bring about. It shook Satan's system of orthodox Judaism that had been infected with mysticism and occultism. It was even bringing in all the other nations to be a part of God's people. So he had to act fast. He had to stamp this out however he could. He chose one of his most effective tactics, which is to infiltrate, and pollute. He infiltrated the early followers of The Way, and began building himself a counterfeit ekklesia. Through men who were greedy for power and position, he began to establish his authority in the newly formed ekklesia, subtly mixing the Holy with the profane. He spread all sorts of lies, through Ignatius, and through many of the "early (Catholic) church fathers" and ultimately through the Catholic Church itself. Rome with it's military might stamped out anything that even resembled keeping God's ways, and replaced them with pagan ways. It put to death anyone who stood against it, and ultimately eclipsed the original Way entirely.

See, the gospel that most often goes out today is basically the gospel of fire insurance. It's the good news that you don't have to pay the penalty for your sins in Hell, and you can have eternal life. This is indeed good news, but this isn't the full gospel. The full gospel is the gospel of the Kingdom.

Matthew 4:23 And Jesus went about all Galilee, teaching in their synagogues, preaching the gospel of the kingdom, and healing all kinds of sickness and all kinds of disease among the people.

Matthew 9:35 Then Jesus went about all the cities and villages, teaching in their synagogues, preaching the gospel of the kingdom, and healing every sickness and every disease among the people.

*Matthew 24:14 And **this gospel of the kingdom** will be preached in all the world as a witness to all the nations, and then the end will come.*

*Mark 1:14 Now after John was put in prison, Jesus came to Galilee, preaching **the gospel of the kingdom of God,***

What is the kingdom of God? It is Israel. Not an Israel through the flesh, but an Israel through the spirit. Not being the physical seed of Abraham, but being the Body of Christ, and through Him being the spiritual seed of Abraham, not through the flesh, but through the Spirit. Not merely through circumcision of the flesh, but also through circumcision of the heart. It is the building of the Temple in Jerusalem, not by fleshly efforts or with fleshly hands, but the building of a spiritual city, the New Jerusalem made by the Hands of God. The gospel of the kingdom is that we are free now to live as if we are part of His kingdom, and that we have been grafted into His heavenly kingdom and some day soon it will come to earth. It is that we can be a part of this New Jerusalem, and this spiritual Israel. I have sat in pews and heard pastors teach from the pulpit that God just gave up on project Israel, and started a new project called the "church". Essentially that God tried a little project and failed. These are lies. God's people, who are called by His name, always have been, and always will be, Israel. God married His people through His covenant that was broken, but now we are betrothed to Christ as being a part of His bride, the New Jerusalem.

We have lost this gospel of the kingdom and have been left with the gospel that forgives our sin. Speaking of sin, people act as if sin is just something we need forgiveness from, and that's where Christ comes in. He just comes along and forgives us for all the bad things we do, and as long as we have Christ, we can just go along our merry way sinning. This is a false gospel. The truth is that He sent His spirit to write His laws on our hearts so that we will walk in His ways, as His people in His kingdom.

Sin isn't just some afterthought that we need to have forgiveness for, sin is a disease eating us alive. Sin is the reason that there are murders, and thefts, and hatred, and fear, and oppression, and disease, and lies and every wicked thing. Sin is like leprosy that eats our flesh devouring us alive, and it spreads to the people around us. Sin isn't something we just need forgiveness for, it is something we need regeneration from. It is something we need taken out of us, and the Spirit does this a little at a time.

> *Isaiah 28:10 For precept must be upon precept, precept upon precept, line upon line, line upon line, here a little, there a little.*

Do you know what a precept is? The dictionary can help us here.

> *precept*
>> *noun*
>> *a commandment or direction given as a rule of action or conduct.*
>> *an injunction as to moral conduct; maxim.*
>> *a procedural directive or rule, as for the performance of some technical operation.*
>> *Law.*

This line upon line, precept upon precept is the New Covenant.

> *Jeremiah 31:33 But this is the covenant that I will make with the house of Israel after those days, says the Lord: I will put My law in their minds, and write it on their hearts; and I will be their God, and they shall be My people.*

This is the gospel of the Kingdom, that we would begin to live as a part of His kingdom, having His laws written on our hearts, and walking in His ways, as His people, with Him as our God. This is the regeneration and cure from sin.

1 John 3:4 (KJV) Whosoever committeth sin transgresseth also the law: for sin is the transgression of the law.

How do we combat lawlessness? By having His laws written on our hearts. Satan spent the first 4000 years of human history trying to keep God's kingdom from functioning, and turn Israel against God's commandments and precepts, and now he is doing the same thing today. In teaching that anything pertaining to Israel is strictly "Jewish" and somehow wrong for us to walk in, he has laid down a massive deception that has destroyed the gospel of the kingdom, and merely left the gospel of fire insurance. It's true that all who call on the name of God and trust in His son will be saved, but getting saved isn't the only goal here. Being born again is only just the first step. Being a light to the nations, and showing forth the light of Christ to the nations as a functioning kingdom of God walking in His ways, is what the gospel of the kingdom is all about. Another goal is to show God love, and be pleasing to Him. Most don't even know what the love of God is.

1 John 5:3 For this is the love of God, that we keep His commandments. And His commandments are not burdensome.

I also want to mention, I am not saying you have to keep all of His commandments to be saved from hellfire. The apostles fought against this very doctrine and we'll talk about this more in a later chapter. No, it's not about salvation, it's about sanctification. There will be many people who are just saved in His kingdom, but there is a hierarchy. There is the bride of Christ, and there are the wedding guests. There are those living in the New Jerusalem, and there are the surrounding nations. There will be those who are part of the first resurrection, and there will be those who are part of the second. There are greatest and least in the Kingdom of Heaven.

Matthew 5:17-20 "Do not think that I came to destroy the Law or the Prophets. I did not come to destroy but to fulfill. 18 For assuredly, I say to you, till heaven and earth pass away, one jot or one tittle will by no means pass from the law till all is fulfilled. 19 Whoever therefore breaks one of the least of these commandments, and teaches men so, shall be called least in the kingdom of heaven; but whoever does and teaches them, *he shall be called great in the kingdom of heaven. 20 For I say to you, that unless your righteousness exceeds the righteousness of the scribes and Pharisees, you will by no means enter the kingdom of heaven.*

All of this is a much larger study than what we have time for here, and there is much on this subject that must be addressed, but that is not for this chapter. I will address many of the arguments against this doctrine in a short while. For now, I just wanted to introduce you to this simple thought: We are Israel, so we should act as such and this is exactly what the early followers of The Way did. This includes keeping His feasts and Sabbaths. These feasts and Sabbaths are beautiful and full of meaning and beauty and I am excited to present them to you, dear reader.

One more thing of note I often have people argue, is that God wouldn't have let His truth be stamped out some two thousand years ago by Rome like that. I have one particularly Catholic uncle who continuously claims that Christ said "On this rock I will build my church and the gates of Hell will not prevail against it!" and claims this means that the original Way could not have been cast down and lost for a time, because this would be the gates of Hell prevailing against it. I disagree with this assertion for many reasons, but one of which is the gates of hell are very much a real thing, in a very real place, and thankfully, if we are in Christ, we will never have to pass through them in the next life. There is one passage though that directly contradicts this assertion and just may shed light on why Rome was allowed to eclipse the true faith.

Revelation 13:7-10 It was granted to him (the beast) <u>to make war with the saints and to overcome them.</u> And authority was *given him over every tribe, tongue, and nation. 8 All who dwell on the earth will worship him, whose names have not been written in the Book of Life of the Lamb slain from the foundation of the world. 9 If anyone has an ear, let him hear. 10 He who leads into captivity shall go into captivity; he who kills with the sword must be killed with the sword. Here is the patience and the faith of the saints.*

So we see at least one time at the end, the beast is allowed to overcome the saints. It could be this prophecy too has a double fulfillment, one fulfillment being when the beast (Rome) overcame the saints the first time shortly after the gospel began to spread, and will again happen at the end when the beast will once again make war with the saints and overcome them. Remember that the beast was given exactly 1260 years before the mortal head wound. What has been, will be again. I believe God allowed Rome to all but stamp out the gospel of the kingdom, while preserving the gospel of salvation so that even though the gospel of the kingdom was lost for a time, men were still able to be born again. I believe in these last times, God is waking up His people, and calling them back to the old paths, the Gospel of the kingdom, and this gospel of the kingdom will be spread to all four corners of the earth, and then the end will come.

Next, I want to recover another thing that has been lost.

20

Know Him

We have lost our independence from the Catholic Church. We have lost our cleanness from idolatry. We have lost our identity, we have lost our name. We have lost many things, and out of all of these, one of the saddest things we've lost, is the name of our God. As I said earlier, the name of God has been completely taken out of our Bibles and replaced with the generic title of "the lord" hearkening back to Baal. That's one of the prices we pay by taking our translations of the scripture from the beast. I have asked different Christians what the name of God is, and many don't have a clue. They just know Him by the generic title of God, or the term "The Lord". Why would people know His name though? What literature do we have in the body of Christ today that actually speaks the name of God? His name has been taken out of everything, and all we are left with is a generic title. So, there are a few questions we should be asking. What is His name? Also, why have very few Bibles actually translated His name? Why does it even matter?

The first thing I want you to see is this, His name is very important.

> *Exodus 20:7 You shall not take the name of the Lord your God in vain, for the Lord will not hold him guiltless who takes His name in vain.*

Matthew 6:9 In this manner, therefore, pray: Our Father in heaven, hallowed be <u>Your name</u>.

Matthew 28:19 Go therefore and make disciples of all the nations, baptizing them in <u>the name</u> of the Father and of the Son and of the Holy Spirit,

Psalm 20:7 Some trust in chariots, and some in horses; but we will remember <u>the name</u> of the Lord our God.

Psalm 66:1-2 Make a joyful shout to God, all the earth! 2 Sing out the honor of <u>His name</u>;

Now, as I said, it would seem that the majority of Christians have forgotten His name, and worse still, replaced it. We can understand why the King James translation replaced it, as it was made by the Catholic Church and they worship "the lord" Baal. But why have other translations done the same? Here is a direct quote from one of the translators of a popular Bible version, the NIV, when asked why they did not include the actual name of God in their translation.

Edwin H. Palmer, Th.D.,

Executive Secretary for the NIV's committee wrote :

"Here is why we did not: You are right – that Jehovah is a distinctive name for God and ideally we should have used it. But we put 2 1/4 million dollars into this translation and a sure way of throwing that down the drain is to translate, for example, Psalm 23 as, 'Yahweh (Jehovah) is my shepherd.' Immediately, we would have translated for nothing. Nobody would have used it (or purchased it). Oh, maybe you and a handful [of] others. But a Christian has to be also wise and practical. We are the victims of 350 years of the King James tradition. It is far better to get two million to read it - that is how many have bought it to date - and to follow the King James, than to have two

thousand buy it and have the correct translation of Yahweh(Jehovah) . . . It was a hard decision, and many of our translators agree with you." [52]

It would seem that it does not make business sense to include the name of God in the Bible. In a way, people have traded His name for material wealth. What about me? Why have I excluded the actual name of God throughout this book and called Him by the generic title of God or The Lord? Well, because sadly, as they stated, many wouldn't have read any of the book if I had used it, but now that you have been thoroughly prepared by seeing the error and idolatry in modern Christianity, you are likely ready to receive what I have to say on the matter, whereas you may not have been at the outset. We have been conditioned for years by the church to reject anything we are not familiar with, being told the lie that the church collectively already knows all the truth there is, so anything we don't know must not be the truth. This puts us in a position of never looking outside of our little box, and ignorantly hiding in what we've always known. In other words, it's a trap to keep us from finding the truth.

The name of God is very important to Him, and He wants it made known to the nations. His name is beautiful and rich, and full of meaning, but it has been forgotten and left by the way side, sold off for money. God knew this would happen, and it isn't the first time it has happened.

Jeremiah 23:25-27 "I have heard what the prophets have said who prophesy lies in My name, saying, 'I have dreamed, I have dreamed!' 26 How long will this be in the heart of the prophets who prophesy lies? Indeed they are prophets of the deceit of their own heart, 27 who try to make My people forget My name by their dreams which everyone tells his neighbor, as their fathers forgot My name for Baal."

I have one more verse that shows that He knew it was coming, especially at the end times, but the impact of this verse has been lost in translation.

To see what the verse is really saying, we need to go into the interlinear Bible and see what the verse said in the original Hebrew.

> *Hosea 2:16-17 And it shall be in that day says (God), that you will call me "my husband" and no longer call me **Baali**. 17 For I will take from her mouth the names of the Baals, and no longer shall their names be remembered.*

What is this word Baali in verse 16? It means, my Baal. It is Strong's #1180:

> *Definition: "my Baal" a symbolic name for Yah*

Now in the Strong's lexicon, they claim this is a symbolic name for Yah, but this is the only instance of this word being used, and they claim it as a symbolic name for God, because they do not understand the verse. Why would God have "my Baal" as a symbolic name for Himself? That's nonsense. No, God knew that His name would be replaced in the end by the generic term "The Lord", Baal, and the next verse solidifies this, as He says He will take the name of the Baals from her lips. Another note is that while the nations used the term Baal as Lord, the Hebrew language had another term that meant a similar thing, that was put alongside His name quite frequently. This term is Adonai and it means my master. Multiple examples can be seen through the Bible of the phrase "Adonai Yahweh." This solidifies even more that the definition for Baali would not logically be a name for Yah, but a term for Baal. One last note is that the term "my husband" and "my master" are not actually mutually exclusive. After all, Sarah referred to Abraham her husband as her master, and we know even after the ekklesia is married to Christ, He is still our master and our King, adding just a bit more weight to this assertion. So, once more, with these things in mind, here is this passage as translated from the NKJV:

> *Hosea 2:16-17 "And it shall be, in that day," says the Lord, "That you will call Me 'My Husband,' And no longer call Me 'My*

Master,' 17 For I will take from her mouth the names of the Baals, and they shall be remembered by their name no more.

Unless you looked in the interlinear at verse 16, this passage would make little sense, but with the full understanding, we know that God did indeed prophecy that His name would be forgotten at the end of days, and replaced with the name of Baal. We also know this prophecy is about the last days as, if you read Hosea 2, the context clearly places it after Christ returns. This is a prophecy that pertains to the near future, and the prerequisites to fulfill it, the replacing His name with Baal, is happening right now.

Alright, so what is the name of God? We've already seen Him referred to as Jehovah, Yahweh, and Yah. Which is it? Well, we need to understand a few things first. First of all, His name came from the Hebrew language. The original letters in His name were the Hebrew letters Yod, Hey, Waw, Hey, or in it's closest English letter equivalent, YHWH. Now, one thing you may not know about Hebrew is that Hebrew never originally had any way of writing vowels. The letters, such as with the name above, did not have an vowel marks so they did not have any pronunciation guide. It was either a word of mouth type of deal on the pronunciation or there was some kind of guide to the vowels that have been lost. Now because of this, His name has been a bit lost, as to the definitive absolute verifiable name, but you can do some research to get a pretty good idea. Some have done this research and came up with YaHWeH, pronounced Yah-way, and this is a pretty good estimation. The name JeHoVaH, is another translation, but there are a few problems with it.

First of all, believe it or not, the letter J is only about 500 or so years old. In fact, even in the 1611 King James Bible, the name for Jesus was Iesus, spelled with an I instead of a J, which we will look at more in depth in a bit. Therefore it could not have been Jehovah, but if we change that J to a Y, we have YeHoVaH. Which is another strong contender. So with these two, we have two options that might fit. All this detective work seems a bit silly, as we should just be able to ask the Jews who speak the language right? Wrong.

The Jews have a law in the Talmud, that states that Ha'Shem (which simply means "the name") must be hidden from the general populous at all costs, as only Jewish priests are "holy" enough to speak His name. Meanwhile the Bible all over says to make His name known, so there's a prime example of the traditions of men overriding the commandments of God. So, we are left to try to figure this out on our own.

Yehovah, and Yahweh are both very good options. There is still an issue with Yehovah though, and that is this, Hebrew literature while it does conceal the full name of God, it has at times mentioned the name of Yah. This would be the first two letters of the name YH with the vowel a pronounced as "ah" between them, giving us Yah. This is actually consistent with a much older word that you are familiar with but maybe didn't realize. That word is Hallelujah, which is pronounced Hah-lay-loo-Yah. Halelu means praise be to, or be praised, the jah at the end, or the pronounced Yah, is the first part of the name of God, thus HalleluYaH. So it couldn't really be YeHoVaH, it would very likely be closer to YaHoVaH, which is very close to YaHWeH. The main difference between these two, besides the vowel sound, is the middle letter, Waw, which troublesome enough, is also called a Vav, or a Uau.

There are other clues however that help us to sort this discrepancy out, as there are names that contain part of the name of Yah. By the way, I will be, from here on out, referring to God as Yah, being a single syllable shortened form of His ACTUAL name, and not a generic title. See, there are many gods. The Romans had many gods, the Hindus have many gods, the Vikings had many gods, but there is only one Yah, and He is the One True God. So, tangent aside, what are these other names that help us to ascertain the full name of Yah?

The first name I want to look at is Elijah. Now remember, the letter "J" wasn't around back when Elijah was living. The original Hebrew name was actually Eliyah, or Eliyahu, and is in fact still in use by the Jews today. Now this name, has two parts to it. The first part is "Eli". Now Eli is actually a name unto itself, and if you look up the meaning, it means "My God". To further break this down, in Hebrew "el" is the same as our word "god" being an impersonal noun. The "i" attached to the end of "el" means "my" just as Baali means "my Baal". Thus "Eli" means "my God". The second part, Yah or Yahu, as I mentioned earlier, is the first half of the name of Our God. So from this name, we can infer the first and second vowel sounds of the name of God, YaHu being pronounced yah-hoo, which differs from the pronunciation of yah-ho with a long o sound, as it is in Yehovah. I have two more names here to back this up, though there are many, many more examples.

The second name I want to examine is Isaiah. Now Isaiah was originally Yesha'yah or Yesha'yahu in the Hebrew. This name is once again, made up of two parts. The first is Yasha, or Yesha, which meant "to save" or "salvation" and once again, Yahu or Yah, which is the first half of the name of our God. Altogether meaning Salvation is [in] Yah. Pronunciation wise this would've been yesh-ah-yah which when brought into English became Isaiah originally pronounced Ie-sah-yah but eventually for the sake of ease became pronounced eye-zae-yuh.

Lastly, we have Jeremiah. Jeremiah was originally in the Hebrew Yirmeyahu, or Yirmeyah. This name follows the same idea as the other two names. This name was comprised of two parts put together that brought new meaning. The first is the part Yirme, which meant "to lift, or raise" and Yahu or Yah, once again being the first half of the name of Yah. This resulted in Yirmeyahu or Yirmeyah, which translates into Yah will uplift. The pronunciation was yir-may-yah-hoo, but when brought into English became Jeremiah pronounced Jehr-uh-my-yah.

So there are three names that demonstrate clearly that the first half of the name of God is Yahu pronounced yah-hoo. The rest of the name, I'm afraid, is rather up for debate. The closest approximations include Yahuah, adopting the "w" sound as ua "oo-ah" which is a slower version of the w sound, matching the YHWH combined with the soft vowel sound for the letter "a" being "ah". This name could also just as easily be spelled Yahwah. Others still stick to Yahweh, adopting the hard a sound "ay" and becoming pronounced yah-way. These are our closest two approximations. We are essentially one vowel off from cracking the code, but honestly, getting this close is, in my mind, close enough. I know some people who use Yahuah, some who use Yahweh, and some that even use Yehovah. I think the important part is that we've attached a proper name to our God using the four letters of His name that we do have, thus giving ourselves the ability to stop calling Him simply "God" and especially to stop only referring to Him as "The Lord" and forgetting His name.

Why does any of this matter? Well, as we saw above, there are some very strong verses specifically regarding His name. His name is to be praised, and proclaimed, and shared. When we are talking to others, and we use the name "God" we don't specify which god we are talking about. We can say the "God of the Bible" but even with that, there are many who are teaching in the present day that the God in the Old Testament, and the God in the New Testament are different Gods altogether. This is blasphemous.

Further, there have been many falsehoods attributed to "God". Phrases like "God doesn't care what you do, He just loves you." or "We are all God's children, no matter what we believe." These things sound nice, but they are actually very dangerous, and are nothing more than arsenic mixed with honey. It's sweet on the tongue, but when ingested it will cause many to perish. So what God are they attributing these things to? It isn't my God. My God said "I must be regarded as Holy" and "I am a jealous God". My God can only be approached through Christ, and no other way will work. I differentiate my God from all the other gods by using His name, Yahuah, and I will honor Him by proclaiming His name.

Imagine this scenario. I go to a party with my wife, Janet. I run into an old friend I haven't seen for years named John. John has never met Janet, so an introduction is needed. I say, "Friend, this is wife. Wife, this is friend" and then leave it at that. People have names that differentiate them, names that have meaning, and importance. It's not very loving to John or Janet in this example to introduce them by an impersonal noun, and I would think they would likely feel rather unappreciated and probably be a bit upset with me. How much more should we want to use the proper name of the One who created us and has saved us through Christ, and not introduce

Him as the impersonal noun "God"? Even our American dollar bill has the slogan "In God we trust" while having the all seeing eye, and a host of Masonic symbology all over it. Many celebrities claim to be Christians who trust in "God" but which god are people like the Pope trusting in? Not Yahuah.

2 Corinthians 4:4 whose minds the god of this age has blinded (...)

Regarding the god of this age, I want to show you one more thing regarding this differentiation between using "the Lord" and the name of Yahuah.

1 Kings 18:21 And Elijah came to all the people, and said, "How long will you falter between two opinions? If the Lord is God, follow Him; but if Baal, follow him." But the people answered him not a word.

This verse is during Elijah's stand off with the false prophets on mount Carmel. If you look in the interlinear you will find this verse extremely interesting. If you remember, Baal can be translated as The Lord. Now according to the interlinear what Elijah actually says, is basically this, "How long will you falter between two opinions? If Yahuah (a proper name, which they translated as the Lord) is God, follow Him, but if Ba'al (which can be accurately translated as "the lord"), follow him." The way this verse is translated, it almost seems to remove the option of Yahuah being God altogether. Basically it says either the lord (Baal) is god, or Baal is god. I don't like either of these options personally. The Lord, is not God. The lord, Baal, is the god of this age. Yahuah, YHWH, is the One True God. Elijah stood on mount Carmel and declared to the people, "How long will you falter between two opinions? If Yahuah is God, follow Him; but if the lord, follow him." I believe this question and declaration rings as true today as it did back then.

259

Now there is one more thing I will mention in this section regarding the name of Yahuah. To understand this point, we need to understand a bit more about Hebrew. The Hebraic language has actually gone through three alphabets over the years. The oldest form of Hebrew is known as "proto-sinaitic Hebrew" which was actually a pictographic language, in that each letter was an image that represented different meanings within the word. The next iteration was a simplified pictographic alphabet known as "paleo Hebrew" or "Aramaic Hebrew". The final evolution of Hebrew occurred years later, and is the same alphabet in use today, it is known by many names, but "new Hebrew" or "modern Hebrew" are the most common.

Now, as I said, each of the letters in the Hebrew language that comprised a word, also had independent meaning as letters, and sadly, the vast majority of these meanings have been lost to time. Most of what remains is speculative, and can be a bit dangerous, as sometimes people get lost looking into hidden meanings in words instead of just reading the text, and people can easily go astray. Personally, I try to stay away from attempting to interpret these things, but there is one word that I absolutely love in this old Pictographic Hebrew, and that is the name of YHWH. This is an image of the original Pictographic Hebrew language name of Yah, read right to left.

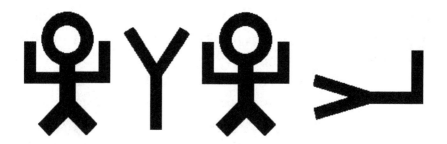

These images make up the original pictographic letters of the name of Yah, YHWH. Now what's very cool about this is the meaning of the pictographs. The first letter, the Y, means "hand" and looks like a bit like an arm bent to the side with a hand on the end. The second letter, H looks like a man with his hands up, and it means "behold". The third letter, the W looks a bit like the letter Y, but also like a stake. This letter means "stake" or "nail". The final is a repeat of the previous H, meaning once again, "behold". Altogether, we have "hand, behold, nail, behold". The name that God gave His people for Himself perfectly points to Christ and His work on the cross! Keep this in mind as you read this next verse. I am going to use the NKJV, but switch out the term "The Lord" with "Yahuah"

> *Exodus 34:6-7 And Yahuah passed before him and proclaimed, "Yahuah, Yahuah God, merciful and gracious, longsuffering, and abounding in goodness and truth, 7 keeping mercy for thousands, forgiving iniquity and transgression and sin, by no means clearing the guilty, visiting the iniquity of the fathers upon the children and the children's children to the third and the fourth generation."*

Our God is incredible, and when I see Him proclaiming His name, I see Him proclaiming all the work of Christ. From the death on the cross embedded in His very name, to the merciful and gracious high priest making intercession for us, to the forgiving perfect sacrifice, to the righteous judge and king over all. This name is incredible, and our God is incredible.

I would like to say "From here on out I will replace all instances of 'The Lord' wherever it appears in scripture", but in an effort to make the rest of the book as easy to follow as possible, I am keeping the verses in the same state you would find them in your average translation, unless I state otherwise. Anyways, let's move on.

21

What's in a Name?

Now, I know I am going to get a lot of people mad at me for this, but if you are actually still reading this book, dear reader, it shows you want to know the truth and have the humility and determination to keep learning in spite of the uncomfortable nature of much of what we've learned. There is one other name that has been lost to the ages, and replaced. That is the name of our Messiah. Now as I said, this is a hotly debated subject, but I want to ask a simple question; why the name Jesus? Is this the name our Messiah was actually called while alive? Is this the name the angel dictated to Mary? Most already realize that it wasn't what He was called. Why then do we stick to it so vehemently? The answer is quite simple, years of conditioning and tradition. Many know it is not His name, but continue to use it anyways out of tradition. This is the same thing many have done celebrating Christmas as His birthday even though they knew it wasn't, and look how that turned out.

We have had the name of Jesus hammered through our heads since we were young. Many of us are given verses such as this one when we were younger:

Acts 4:10-12 let it be known to you all, and to all the people of Israel, that by the name of Jesus Christ of Nazareth, whom you crucified, whom God raised from the dead, by Him this man

> *stands here before you whole. 11 This is the 'stone which was re-*
> *jected by you builders, which has become the chief cornerstone.'*
> *12 Nor is there salvation in any other, for there is no other name*
> *under heaven given among men by which we must be saved."*

For those who didn't grow up in Christianity, this is still one of the first verses we're shown. We are told "See? It's the name of Jesus Christ! No other name!" but is that really the name that was used when the declaration was spoken? Did the Hebrew speaking Jewish man Peter, who was on trial in the Hebrew speaking Jerusalem, who was speaking to the Jewish pharisees who also spoke Hebrew, about the Hebrew speaking Jewish Messiah, use the name "Jesus Christ"? How about this verse?

> *Matthew 1:21 And she will bring forth a Son, and you shall call*
> *His name Jesus, for He will save His people from their sins."*

Did the angel direct the Hebrew speaking Jewish Mary to name the child Jesus? The second part of the verse in essence says, name Him this, because He will do this. This suggests that the name that the angel told Mary to call him had meaning pertaining directly to His task. See, names mean something, and this is almost always derived from etymological pieces of a language fit together to have a meaning. We saw this is the names of Isaiah, Jeremiah, and Elijah in the previous chapter. These are made up of parts that have meaning. Is the name Jesus made up of parts that mean something?

Would it shock you to learn that the name Jesus is only about 300 years old? Remember that I said the letter J is only about 500 years old or so? Before the name Jesus, they used the name Iesus, with an "i" instead of a "j" and pronounced yay-soos. So in the earlier translations in the 1600s, it was "there is no other name besides the name of Iesus Christos (yay-soos) by which men must be saved." If you sat down with one of the reformationists, and tried to suggest the name Jesus pronounced jee-zuhs, would they have been okay with this name change? Would they have angrily shouted back at you, "No! There is no other name under heaven by which men must be saved than the name of Iesus (yay-soos) Christos!"? Would they have been right or wrong to do so? I bring this up because quite often, when people try to show others that the name of Jesus is not actually the name of Messiah, they begin to get angry and defensive. They usually revert to this verse in particular, and act as if by suggesting some other name than Jesus, you are somehow rejecting Messiah. Is any of this at all logical? Is there logical, truthful evidence to suggest the name of Jesus is correct, or is this nothing more than tradition and repetition? I want to explore this name with you, and see if there is any reason we should be using this name other than it being tradition and habit, which have proven to be dangerous reasons.

Now, as I said, the name Jesus is only a few hundred years old. The name we hold today, Jesus (gee-zuhs), was introduced some time after 1611, though we're not sure exactly when the first instance of this name was used. We do however know that this was the name Iesus (yay-soos) brought into modern English from Old English, as mentioned earlier. With this change, the letters and pronunciation changed. Now this name Iesus, was derived from the Latin Iesous (yeh-soos). This change occurred when the Catholic Church took the Greek texts, translated them into Latin. The Latin Iesous was derived from the Greek Iesous with the same general spelling, but pronounced yeh-soo-uhs. Finally, this name Iesous was taken from the Hebrew name commonly pronounced Yeshua.

Now, I have studied, and continue to study the actual details of this name. Honestly, there is so much debate on it, I don't have a definitive answer for you. All I can do is present you with the basics, and let you do the homework yourself. The name I have personally come to after much study and research is the name Yod Heh Waw Shin Ayin, pronounced Yahusha.

One of the reasons this name is so hard to nail down is multiple variations on the name. In the Masoretic text we find Yod Heh Waw Shin Ayin (Yahusha), we find Yod Heh Waw Shin Waw Ayin (Yahushua) and finally Yod Shin Waw Ayin (Y'shua). That being said, we know Messiah shared His name with Joshua in the Old Testament, and we know that the name given to Joshua son of Nun by Moses was Yod Heh Waw Shin Ayin (Numbers 13:16). We also know that the Old Testament is full of prophecies about the coming "Salvation", and according to Matthew 1:21, we know Mary was instructed to call Him a name that had to do with salvation. We also know Messiah came bearing His Father's name (John 5:34), so it would make sense that part of His name would contain at least a part of the name of Yahuah. We also know the name Joshua means Yahuah is Salvation.

The reason Yod Heh Waw Shin Ayin makes sense is because it fulfills all of these things. First of all, the word for salvation is Yasha, or Yesha, spelled Yod Shin Ayin. We also know that the letters that make up the name of Yahuah are Yod Heh Waw Heh. Thus if we take the first half of Yod Heh Waw Heh, and combine it with the second half of Yod Shin Ayin, we end up perfectly with Yod Heh Waw Shin Ayin, or Yahusha, meaning Yah's Salvation, again being the name that Joshua received from Moses. Thus it makes sense that His name would be Yahusha because He would save His people from their sins, and also bear a distinct part of His father's name.

That being said, by far the most common pronunciation of His name is Yeshua. Now some people say this form is correct, others are adamantly against it for different reasons. Personally, I use this variation rather frequently as frankly it's just far easier to pronounce with our western dialect and people are more comfortable with it. I encourage you to do your own research, and come to your own conclusions, but I also admonish you to do so in humility and love. It is very difficult to know for certain the exact details of His name, but we can at least get in the ball park with it. Yahusha, Yahushua, or Yeshua, are all a whole lot closer to His name than Jesus.

Now, what we have with the name of Jesus is a name that was taken from Hebrew, transliterated into Greek, then transliterated into Latin, then transliterated into Old English, then transliterated into modern English. In other words, the name has undergone about four major alterations, thus losing half of the original letters. Now, I want to ask a simple question. If we have verses like Acts 4:10-12 stating "by no other name" why then have we so carelessly changed the name that many times and altered it so far from the original? Ironically, it is the people who are most adamant about the name of Jesus, that should be the most interested in finding His true name. To put it another way, the people who are the most adamant about the name Jesus, are adamant about it because they realize the importance of His name, so why would they want to stick to a name that has been so radically altered from the original by the RCC?

Now, with the transliterations, it is important to note that with the vast majority, if not all of the names, when the Bible was translated into a new language, they transliterated the names directly from the original language. In other words, when the Bible was brought into modern English, translators went back to the Greek and Hebrew manuscripts directly to get the names as close as possible. Examples of this are Aquilla, Sarah, Nebuchadnezzar, Joshua, and many, many others. This is how names should be handled, getting the absolute closest approximation of a name that you can in the language you're bringing it into. It seems every other name in the Bible received this careful treatment, except for the two most important names, the name of Yahuah, and the name of Yahusha.

My wife's name is Janet. Imagine that me and Janet went on a trip around the world. We leave the United States and I am calling her Janet. We land in Mexico, and due to the letter "J" having the "H" sound, and their use of the soft "a" sound (ah) being the prominent vowel sound, I alter her name, and begin calling her Hahnet. Well, after we leave Mexico we head to Japan. In Japan, they don't have a letter "t" by itself in the katakana alphabet, and so we replace the "t" at the end of her name with "to" which they have a letter for. Thus I begin calling her Hahneto. From there, we leave and fly to Hawaii. Now in the Hawaiian language, they have all the letters for Hahneto, but they pronounce the letter "o" differently. I adjust the spelling according to their vowel pronunciations, and out comes the name Hahnaytah. Thus I now introduce my wife as Hahnaytah. When I come back to the States, I just keep pronouncing her name that way, and introducing her to people as Hahnaytah, completely changing her name. Do you think she might be a bit perturbed with me? This name hardly resembles her name at all, but all I did was take her name from language to language, keeping the alterations between, and trying to find a close approximation. This is exactly what they did with the name of our Messiah.

We also saw last chapter that the name of Yahuah was completely taken out of our modern Bibles. What this means is this: every name in the entirety of the Bible was treated with care and respect, except for two names, the name of our God, which was completely taken out and replaced, and the name of His Son, our Messiah which was so carelessly transliterated from language to language, it hardly bears any resemblance to His original name. If this seems backwards to you, it's because it is. These two names should have taken center stage while the rest were secondary, and yet here we are. This is once again thanks to the tireless efforts of the RCC to distort and alter our faith wherever and however it can.

Now, why does any of this matter? Well, for a few reasons. The first one is simply this: His name matters. It's important for us to know His name. Further, it's a matter of love. We should want to know and use His real name out of love for Him. Now I was born again when I gave my life to Him, and when that happened I still called Him Jesus, but now that I know that is not His name, I no longer call Him by a name that has been so changed, out of love and respect for Him.

The second reason is this: although it seems as if the name was just brought from form to form, it is hotly debated that the name of Jesus was dragged through the mud during transliterations. For example, the Greek version of the name, Iesous being pronounced (yay-soos), may or may not have had associations with the name of Zeus, being pronounced pretty much identically. As we learned in prior chapters, Zeus was one of the primary gods in Greek culture, so it is possible that it could have had connections to Zeus, but there's no real way I have found to prove or disprove this assertion. Another assertion is that the Latin form of the name Iesus, contains in the end of it the word "sus" which is the Latin word for pig. You can literally go to the Google Latin to English translator and type in "Iesus" and you will get "Ie pig".

Now again, some vehemently claim that these claims are just paranoid interpretations from people who know nothing of language, but others insist they are very real and at times they have valid points. Personally, I cannot find conclusive evidence one way or the other, and so I remain semi neutral on the subject, but I also avoid using the name Jesus myself because it may or may not have been polluted by the pagan god Zues, as well as the Latin word for pig. On the chance that it has actually been polluted, these are two things I would never want to call my savior, even by accident. If it is all bogus, I would still rather be safe than sorry, and further, there is no real reason to use the name Jesus anyways, as that was not even His name when He walked the earth.

The last reason is to differentiate the identity of my Christ, from that of the RCC's christ. Along with a badly transliterated name, the RCC also provided us with an image of their christ, based upon the face of Cesare Borgia, the homosexual son of Pope Alexander VI, who they depict as a delicate, long haired, pale white, effeminate man who looks like he just stepped off the set of a Revlon commercial. My Savior is, yes, gentle and kind, and loving enough to give His life for mine, and humble enough to wash His disciples feet. He is also the mighty King of Kings and Lord of Lords who is coming dressed in a robe dipped in blood, who will make war, and slay the wicked with a sword that proceeds out of His mouth, and will rule over the nations with a rod of Iron (Revelation 19:11-15).

I don't want my mighty, true Christ to be mixed up with their emasculated effeminate one. The Catholic Jesus doesn't care what road you take, because he says all roads lead to heaven. My Yahusha declares He is the only way to the Father. Their Jesus is spoken for by the Pope. My Yahusha speaks through His perfect Spirit and His Word. Their Jesus is a feminine, Greco-Roman white man. My Yahusha is the Lion of the tribe of Judah. Their Jesus is timid and passive. My Yahusha boldly spoke against sin and is coming to rule the nations with a rod of iron. Their Jesus disregards the law of Yah and replaces it with the law of the Pope. My Yahusha IS the law of Yah as His Word and Judge over all. Their Jesus presides over their "church". My Yahusha is the King of Israel and is coming to rule over the whole world.

Now am I saying everyone who uses the name Jesus is doing evil or that you can't be saved unless you call Him the right name? Not at all. As I said, I myself was born again calling Him by the name Jesus. He hears our cries and sees our hearts when we are seeking for Him. The phonetics are secondary, knowing who He is, His nature, is what's important. Am I suggesting however that it may be wise to begin calling Him by His true name? Yes, for the reasons already listed. As deception sweeps over the world with a ferocity previously unknown, it is important that we are presenting truth and not misrepresenting our Messiah. I want to note as well that I used the name Jesus a few times in this book prior to this point, so as not to scare anyone away at the outset before hearing what I had to say. From here on out though, I will be using the name Yahusha, which means "Yah's Salvation" except when quoting scripture, as I've done with the name of Yah.

One last note, as I did with the name of Yahuah, I have one more little bonus fact for the name Yahusha. When Yahusha was on the cross, there was an inscription hung above His head.

John 19:19 Now Pilate wrote a title and put it on the cross. And the writing was: JESUS OF NAZARETH, THE KING OF THE JEWS.

But interestingly, in the original Hebrew, it would've read as such:

Yahusha Ha'nazaeri W'melech Ha'yahudiym

Did you catch it? The first letter of each word spells out YHWH. Yahusha had the name of His father hanging above His head on the cross. In fact, this could explain why the chief priests were upset about this inscription.

> *John 19:21-22 Therefore the chief priests of the Jews said to Pilate, 'Do not write, 'The King of the Jews,' but, 'He said, 'I am the King of the Jews.'' : 22 Pilate answered, "What I have written, I have written."*

At first glance, it could be that they just didn't like Him being called the King of the Jews, but it could also be that they recognized the name of Yahuah was hidden in plain sight above the head of our Savior. Just a fun little fact.

Ultimately, each one of us have to walk in our convictions, but I cannot think of a single reason why we would want to stick to the name Jesus when we know it wasn't His real name. There is also a lot of baggage hanging over it, from questionable origins, to the RCC giving us this transliteration and their image and false character attached to that name. Personally, I will continue to call Him by His name, full of meaning and prophetically significant, Yahusha.

One more quick note that may be useful to you is that the term HaMashiach, means "The Christ". Ha means the, and Mashiach is where we get the word Messiah. Yahusha Ha'Mashiach means Yahusha the Messiah, or Yahusha the Christ, the anointed, chosen one. So, let's wrap all of this up. The Hebrew speaking Jewish man Peter, spoke to the Hebrew speaking Jewish Pharisees, in the Hebrew speaking Jerusalem, in front of the Hebrew speaking Sanhedrin, and declared:

> *Acts 4:10-12 let it be known to you all, and to all the people of Israel, that by the name of Yahusha HaMashiach of Nazareth, whom you crucified, whom God raised from the dead, by Him this man stands here before you whole. 11 This is the 'stone which was rejected by you builders, which has become the chief cornerstone.' 12 Nor is there salvation in any other, for there*

is no other name under heaven given among men by which we must be saved."

22

Signs and Seasons

Finally, as I stated much earlier, I want to explore the meanings behind the feasts and the Sabbaths.

So, in previous chapters I already used some of the scripture I wanted to use in this chapter regarding the Sabbath, but I don't think it's a bad thing to repeat scripture. We're going to move fast, as there is a lot to cover here. Let's start in Exodus:

> *Exodus 20:8-11 "Remember the Sabbath day, to keep it holy. 9 Six days you shall labor and do all your work, 10 but the seventh day is the Sabbath of the Lord your God. In it you shall do no work: you, nor your son, nor your daughter, nor your male servant, nor your female servant, nor your cattle, nor your stranger who is within your gates. 11 For in six days the Lord made the heavens and the earth, the sea, and all that is in them, and rested the seventh day. Therefore the Lord blessed the Sabbath day and hallowed it.*

The first thing I want to point out, is the context of these verses. This is in Exodus 20, the famous Ten Commandments chapter. If you read the previous chapters of Exodus, Israel has just come out of captivity and have come out into the wilderness. Yah chooses Mount Sinai as the place to meet with the people who came out of Egpyt. Remember once again that those who came out of captivity were a mixed multitude.

> *Exodus 12:38 A mixed multitude went up with them also, and flocks and herds—a great deal of livestock.*

So this mixed multitude came out of Egypt to follow Yah. These were natural born Israelites as well as those grafted into Israel, as we are. They followed Him out into the wilderness, and it was at this place, Mount Sinai, where Yah decided to enter into covenant with these people, making them His people. He commanded the people to purify themselves for three days, at the end of which, there was a mighty thunder and trumpet, and Yah descended upon the mountain. This was the place He personally met with Moses, and gave His laws to him. He began with only ten that He spoke to all the children of Israel before Moses went to meet with Him privately. These ten were kind of like the framework for all the others. Pretty much all the other commandments that were given throughout the rest of the Old Testament can be divided into one of these 10 categories. Interestingly, these 10 commandments can also be divided into two other categories. The first four commandments deal with loving Yah, and the last six deal with loving one another. Sound familiar?

> *Matthew 22:36-40 "Teacher, which is the great commandment in the law" 37 Jesus said to him, "You shall love the Lord your God with all your heart, with all your soul, and with all your mind.' 38 This is the first and great commandment. 39 And the second is like it: 'You shall love your neighbor as yourself.' 40 On these two commandments hang all the Law and the Prophets."*

Yahusha said that all the law and the prophets hung upon these two commandments. This is true. Each of the ten commandments have to do with either one or the other of these commandments, and all the other commandments given thereafter had to do with one of the two as well. Anyways, Yah gives His top ten as it were. Interestingly the two commandments here that He spent the most time expounding upon were not to make any graven images (which the RCC completely removed), and to remember the Sabbath day which they changed. Out of all the commandments He gave, these two had the longest explanations attached to them while the others were mostly short and sweet. So, what did He have to say about the Sabbath?

> *Exodus 20:8-11 "Remember the Sabbath day, to keep it holy. 9 Six days you shall labor and do all your work, 10 but the seventh day is the Sabbath of the Lord your God. In it you shall do no work: you, nor your son, nor your daughter, nor your male servant, nor your female servant, nor your cattle, nor your stranger who is within your gates. 11 For in six days the Lord made the heavens and the earth, the sea, and all that is in them, and rested the seventh day. Therefore the Lord blessed the Sabbath day and hallowed it.*

So He doesn't just say, "Remember the Sabbath". He also says to keep it holy, or set apart. He says this day must be dedicated to Him. He then expounds upon what this means. He says you can't work on it, your sons, your daughters, your servants, your cattle, and not even someone staying with you is allowed to work on this day. You're not allowed to compel someone else to work for you on this day either. It would seem He took this commandment pretty seriously. He then explains why He gave it. To paraphrase, he says, when I made the earth, I made it in six days, and rested on the seventh day, so you need to do the same thing. Then He even goes on to say that He blessed the Sabbath, and hallowed it. To hallow something means to honor it as Holy. So Yah personally blessed, and honored the Sabbath. This day was a very big deal to Yah, and as He does not change, it is a very big deal to Him now.

Now out of all the commandments He gave, this one in particular was special. As we saw earlier, this covenant that Yah made with the children of Israel at mount Sinai was a marriage covenant, where He would be their God, and they would be His people, but out of all the commandments He gave forth, one of them had especially special meaning to Him. Remember that the ten commandments came at the beginning of when Yah began to speak to Israel before He began to give Moses the rest of the law. At the very end of it all, all the way in Exodus 31, Yah finishes setting down all of His ground rules, and then says one more thing:

> *Exodus 31:12-18 And the Lord spoke to Moses, saying, 13 "Speak also to the children of Israel, saying: 'Surely My Sabbaths you shall keep, for it is a sign between Me and you throughout your generations, that you may know that I am the Lord who sanctifies you. 14 You shall keep the Sabbath, therefore, for it is holy to you. Everyone who profanes it shall surely be put to death; for whoever does any work on it, that person shall be cut off from among his people. 15 Work shall be done for six days, but the seventh is the Sabbath of rest, holy to the Lord. Whoever does any work on the Sabbath day, he shall surely be put to death. 16 Therefore the children of Israel shall keep the Sabbath, to observe the Sabbath throughout their generations as a perpetual covenant. 17 It is a sign between Me and the children of Israel forever; for in six days the Lord made the heavens and the earth, and on the seventh day He rested and was refreshed.'" 18 And when He had made an end of speaking with him on Mount Sinai, He gave Moses two tablets of the Testimony, tablets of stone, written with the finger of God.*

So Yah goes through giving the ten commandments, and during the opening, the top ten as it were that He gave to the mixed multitude, He makes special mention of the Sabbath, and expounds upon it longer than any other command in the list. Then, after He's all done mentioning all the other laws, commandments, and statutes, He comes back once more to His Sabbaths (feasts) and the seventh day Sabbath. He says it is a sign between Him and the children of Israel (us). Now this is special, as if you think about it, when you marry your spouse, you give them a sign or mark of the covenant between you and them as well. That sign is usually in the form of a ring. This sign was in the form of the Sabbath. He says this was the sign between Him and His people and the time frame He put on this sign was "throughout your generations" a "perpetual covenant" and also that it is "forever". This was obviously very important to Him, as He gave it special mention, twice, and even gave it the position of the sign between us and Him. Isn't it interesting that the RCC's "The Lord's Day" is also the sign or mark of their authority as well? Satan counterfeits all that he can. Personally, I don't want any sign of covenant between me and the beast.

Anyways, not only did Yah create the world and everything in it in six days, resting on the Sabbath, but we have also gone through about 6000 years of human history according to Biblical account, and we know the end of the age is near. At the very end, Christ returns and sets up His millennial reign for one thousand years. Thus mankind has striven and suffered for 6 sets of 1000 years and rests on the seventh set of 1000 years.

> *Psalm 90:4 For a thousand years in Your sight are like yesterday when it is past, and like a watch in the night.*

> *2 Peter 3:8 But, beloved, do not forget this one thing, that with the Lord one day is as a thousand years, and a thousand years as one day.*

So even human history itself keeps the Sabbath. In fact, this break we see is only temporary, as after the 1000 year Sabbath is up, Satan is released once again to deceive the nations. We have no idea really just how long he has to work in that next release, but we know that Satan himself is forced to observe the millennial Sabbath as well, as he is physically bound and prevented from working for 1000 years but then afterward is freed to work once more before the end. The Sabbath is kind of how Yah set up everything, so no wonder it is His sign. As I stated, for those up in arms for my suggestion that the Sabbath still matters, I promise we will get to that in the next three chapters. Enough about the Sabbath though, we still have a lot of ground to cover so let's move into the feasts.

There are seven feasts that Yah gives in the Old Testament for His people to keep. They are:

1. Passover
2. Feast of Unleavened Bread
3. First Fruits
4. Pentecost
5. Trumpets
6. Day of Atonement
7. Feast of Tabernacles

Now what's really cool about each of these feasts is that all of them directly pertain to Christ and His roles and life. That's why Yah directly calls them His feasts. Because they are all about Him and His Son.

Passover

The first feast in the spring is Passover. Passover was implemented back in the days of Egypt when the children of Israel were in captivity. Moses came as a deliverer, and poured out plagues on Egypt. The final plague to come was that the firstborn male of every family would die, unless they had blood on their door post. They were commanded to slay a lamb, and paint the door post of their house with the blood, so that the angel of death that passed through Egypt would pass over the children of Israel who obeyed Yah. The Passover lamb that would be sacrificed had to be perfect, without spot or blemish. The lamb also had to be drained of all it's blood before being accepted as a sacrifice. All the instructions in Exodus twelve are rather lengthy, so for the sake of conserving space, I will just include this last portion.

Exodus 12:13-14 Now the blood shall be a sign for you on the houses where you are. And when I see the blood, I will pass over you; and the plague shall not be on you to destroy you when I strike the land of Egypt. 14 'So this day shall be to you a memorial; and you shall keep it as a feast to the Lord <u>throughout your generations.</u>

This was all a perfect picture of Christ. Yahusha came into the world, and lived a perfect, sinless life. He then gave His life on the cross, having every drop of blood in His body spilled for us until nothing but water came out. He gave His life as the perfect eternal sacrifice for us, so that death would pass over us and we could have eternal life. In fact, through scripture we know that the day Christ was put to death was actually known as preparation day, the day before Passover, when they would slay the lamb, and drain the blood out of it and get all the other food and places prepared in preparation for the coming Sabbath.

John 19:14-16 Now it was the Preparation Day of the Passover, and about the sixth hour. And he said to the Jews, "Behold your King!" 15 But they cried out, "Away with Him, away with Him! Crucify Him!" Pilate said to them, "Shall I crucify your King?" The chief priests answered, "We have no king but Caesar!" 16 Then he delivered Him to them to be crucified. Then they took Jesus and led Him away.

Christ was even slain and drained of His blood the exact time that the Passover lamb would have been. He provided the perfect sacrifice, becoming our Passover Lamb.

1 Corinthians 5:7-8 Therefore purge out the old leaven, that you may be a new lump, since you truly are unleavened. For indeed Christ, our Passover, was sacrificed for us. 8 Therefore let us keep the feast, not with old leaven, nor with the leaven of malice and wickedness, but with the unleavened bread of sincerity and truth.

This by the way, was what the last supper was, and what the ekklesia in the New Testament kept when they kept "communion" though it wasn't on the night of Passover, as it was the day before preparation day, we know they had a meal of unleavened bread, and wine which were the exact foods eaten on Passover. The only thing that wasn't eaten at that meal was the Passover Lamb, because it had not yet been slain. That's why Christ specifically took unleavened bread and wine and declared these things:

1 Corinthians 11:24-26 and when He had given thanks, He broke it and said, "Take, eat; this is My body which is broken for you; do this in remembrance of Me." 25 In the same manner He also took the cup after supper, saying, "This cup is the new covenant in My blood. This do, as often as you drink it, in remembrance of Me." 26 For as often as you eat this bread and drink this cup, you proclaim the Lord's death till He comes.

Unleavened bread and wine were two of the three things Israel was supposed to eat on Passover. What Christ was saying was, He was the bread of life, completely unleavened with sin thus the unleavened bread was a picture of Christ. This was His body that was broken. The wine represented His blood, poured out to the last drop, bringing salvation as we put His blood over the door post of our hearts and lives so that we might live. This is how we proclaim His death until He comes again. We eat of the Passover meal each year, remembering His sacrifice, and trusting in His blood to cleanse us from sin, so that death might pass over us.

Interestingly, this is confirmed not only by the above portion, but by another one.

1 Corinthians 11:27-30 Therefore whoever eats this bread or drinks this cup of the Lord in an unworthy manner will be guilty of the body and blood of the Lord. 28 But let a man examine himself, and so let him eat of the bread and drink of the cup. 29 For he who eats and drinks in an unworthy manner eats and drinks judgment to himself, not discerning the Lord's body. 30 For this reason many are weak and sick among you, and many sleep.

If you take Passover unworthily, there will be consequences? Do we see a command not to take Passover unworthily elsewhere?

Exodus 12:43-49 And the Lord said to Moses and Aaron, "This is the ordinance of the Passover: No foreigner shall eat it. 44 But every man's servant who is bought for money, when you have circumcised him, then he may eat it. 45 A sojourner and a hired servant shall not eat it. 46 In one house it shall be eaten; you shall not carry any of the flesh outside the house, nor shall you break one of its bones. 47 All the congregation of Israel shall keep it. 48 And when a stranger dwells with you and wants to keep the Passover to the Lord, let all his males be circumcised, and then let him come near and keep it; and he shall be as a native of the land. For no uncircumcised person shall eat it. 49 One law shall be for the native-born and for the stranger who dwells among you."

According to Exodus, a man must first be circumcised before he can partake of Passover, thus when those uncircumcised in heart partook of Passover, there were consequences as they were breaking the commandment of Yah. There is much more to study here, but as I am aiming to give a brief overview of the feasts, I will move on.

Unleavened Bread

Unleavened bread is the next feast that takes place in the year. This feast is a week long. It follows Passover, as the first day of Unleavened Bread is the day after Passover. This feast was also commanded to Moses and Aaron at the same time Yah gave the command for Passover and is found here:

> *Exodus 12:15-17 Seven days you shall eat unleavened bread. On the first day you shall remove leaven from your houses. For whoever eats leavened bread from the first day until the seventh day, that person shall be cut off from Israel. 16 On the first day there shall be a holy convocation, and on the seventh day there shall be a holy convocation for you. No manner of work shall be done on them; but that which everyone must eat—that only may be prepared by you. 17 So you shall observe the Feast of Unleavened Bread, for on this same day I will have brought your armies out of the land of Egypt. <u>Therefore you shall observe this day throughout your generations as an everlasting ordinance.</u>*

So the first day of unleavened bread involved getting all the leaven out of your house. People were to purge all leaven out of their lives, and not eat any leavened bread for 7 days. This was spiritually significant, remember, leaven multiple times throughout scripture is compared to sin. This is also why in the passage above in 1 Corinthians Paul talks about purging out the leaven of wickedness. So Christ gave Himself as the Passover Lamb, and after His sacrifice, He purged us of our leaven, our sin. It also means once our houses, our lives and hearts, are purged from leaven, we are not to return to the leaven of sin. We are to be Holy as He is Holy. This is the significance behind Unleavened Bread. Immediately after we have come under the blood of Christ and death has passed over us, we are to purge our lives of the leaven of sin, and not return to it.

First Fruits

The next feast given was Firstfruits. Firstfruits takes place the first day of the week after the last day of unleavened bread. Now this feast, was given after Israel had been led out of Egypt. Remember that Egypt represents the world in scripture. Thus this is the first feast celebrated after accepting Christ as Passover lamb, and having Him cleanse us from our old leaven of Sin and have come out of the world. This feast was implemented here:

> *Deuteronomy 26:1-4 "And it shall be, when you come into the land which the Lord your God is giving you as an inheritance, and you possess it and dwell in it, 2 that you shall take some of the first of all the produce of the ground, which you shall bring from your land that the Lord your God is giving you, and put it in a basket and go to the place where the Lord your God chooses to make His name abide. 3 And you shall go to the one who is priest in those days, and say to him, 'I declare today to the Lord your God that I have come to the country which the Lord swore to our fathers to give us.' 4 "Then the priest shall take the basket out of your hand and set it down before the altar of the Lord your God.*

There is much more to this passage, but basically, they were to take the first fruits of what they had grown in the land, and offer them to Yah, and declare that He saved them, and brought them into the kingdom. This is what takes place after we accept Christ. We are translated out of the kingdom of darkness and into the kingdom of light becoming first fruits in the spirit.

> *Romans 8:23 Not only that, but <u>we also who have the firstfruits of the Spirit</u>, even we ourselves groan within ourselves, <u>eagerly waiting for the adoption, the redemption of our body.</u>*

This also pertains to the resurrection of the saints. Those who have walked faithfully with Yah will receive a new body that is eternal and incorruptible, and on that day, we will also inherit the kingdom of Christ when He reigns over the earth forevermore.

> *1 Corinthians 15:23 But each one in his own order: <u>Christ the firstfruits</u>, afterward those who are Christ's at His coming.*

Thus we will be like him being firstfruts with Christ.

> *1 John 3:2 Beloved, now we are children of God; and it has not yet been revealed what we shall be, but we know that when He is revealed, we shall be like Him, for we shall see Him as He is.*

Christ is the firstfruits, having obtained the resurrection and eternal life. When He returns, those who follow Him and are found in Him will also receive the same reward, thus we will become like Him. He is the firstborn among many brothers.

> *Romans 8:29 For whom He foreknew, He also predestined to be conformed to the image of His Son, that He might be the firstborn among many brethren.*

The feast of firstfruits is both about Him being the firstfruits, as well as us striving to attain being in the first resurrection and being firstfruits together with Him.

> *Revelation 20:4-6 And I saw thrones, and they sat on them, and judgment was committed to them. Then I saw the souls of those who had been beheaded for their witness to Jesus and for the word of God, who had not worshiped the beast or his image, and had not received his mark on their foreheads or on their hands. And they lived and reigned with Christ for a thousand years. 5*

> *But the rest of the dead did not live again until the thousand years were finished. This is the first resurrection. 6 Blessed and holy is he who has part in the first resurrection. Over such the second death has no power, but they shall be priests of God and of Christ, and shall reign with Him a thousand years.*

The feast of firstfruits has both been fulfilled by Christ, but will also be fulfilled by those in Christ at the end of the age. Further, there is some debate, as to when exactly Christ rose from the dead, whether during the feast of Unleavened bread, or the feast of firstfruits, but in either case, we know that Passover, unleavened bread, and firstfruits are all in quick succession with one another. We also know the fulfillment of the first half of Christ's earthly ministry was fulfilled during this time. Whether it was the day He rose from the grave, or the day he appeared to His apostles I cannot definitively tell you, what I can tell you is there are multiple scriptures that confirm Christ's resurrection is represented by first fruits, thus this cluster of three feasts represents the death (Passover), atonement, justification, and sanctification (unleavened bread), and resurrection (firstfruits) of Christ.

Pentecost

The next feast to take place after this trio of feasts is Pentecost. Pentecost takes place a bit after Passover, and was a celebration instituted after Israel came into covenant with Yah. This was a feast pertaining to the time of harvesting wheat, and was celebrated by baking two loaves and making a grain offering.

> *Leviticus 23:15-17 'And you shall count for yourselves from the day after the Sabbath, from the day that you brought the sheaf of the wave offering: seven Sabbaths shall be completed. 16 Count fifty days to the day after the seventh Sabbath; then you shall offer a new grain offering to the Lord. 17 You shall bring from*

your dwellings two wave loaves of two-tenths of an ephah. They shall be of fine flour; they shall be baked with leaven. They are the firstfruits to the Lord.

Now most Christians know about what took place on Pentecost.

Acts 2:1-4 When the Day of Pentecost had fully come, they were all with one accord in one place. 2 And suddenly there came a sound from heaven, as of a rushing mighty wind, and it filled the whole house where they were sitting. 3 Then there appeared to them divided tongues, as of fire, and one sat upon each of them. 4 And they were all filled with the Holy Spirit and began to speak with other tongues, as the Spirit gave them utterance.

So what transpired at Pentecost was the coming of the Holy Spirit with power from on high. Now what was the purpose of these tongues of fire and the coming of the spirit?

Acts 2:11 Cretans and Arabs—we hear them speaking in our own tongues the wonderful works of God.

This was the beginning of the spread of the gospel. The disciples had already received the Spirit according to John 20:22, but they hadn't received the full power of the Spirit as of yet. Remember Christ commanded them to go forth and preach the gospel to all nations, but He also commanded them to wait in Jerusalem until they received power from on high. This was the power from on high. The Spirit that convicts the world of sin. The spirit that can tear down language barriers and miraculously spread the message of the true gospel. What does this all have to do with wheat? Everything.

Matthew 13:24-30 Another parable He put forth to them, saying: "The kingdom of heaven is like a man who sowed good seed in his field; 25 but while men slept, his enemy came and sowed tares among the wheat and went his way. 26 But when the grain had sprouted and produced a crop, then the tares also appeared. 27 So the servants of the owner came and said to him, 'Sir, did you not sow good seed in your field? How then does it have tares?' 28 He said to them, 'An enemy has done this.' The servants said to him, 'Do you want us then to go and gather them up?' 29 But he said, 'No, lest while you gather up the tares you also uproot the wheat with them. 30 Let both grow together until the harvest, and at the time of harvest I will say to the reapers, "First gather together the tares and bind them in bundles to burn them, but gather the wheat into my barn." ' "

Matthew 13:37-38 He answered and said to them: "He who sows the good seed is the Son of Man. 38 The field is the world, the good seeds are the sons of the kingdom, but the tares are the sons of the wicked one.

Pentecost was the celebration of the wheat coming in with the harvest. Pentecost was the beginning of the harvest of the souls of men coming into the kingdom. This was when men truly began being born again by the Spirit and thus these first believers began to bring in the rest of the harvest. These four feasts have all been fulfilled in the death and resurrection of Christ and the coming of the Spirit to spread the gospel. There are three more feasts, that are the fall feasts, which have not yet been fulfilled.

Trumpets

The first of the fall feasts is the feast of trumpets. The portion regarding this feast is short and sweet.

Leviticus 23:23-25 Then the Lord spoke to Moses, saying, 24 "Speak to the children of Israel, saying: 'In the seventh month, on the first day of the month, you shall have a sabbath-rest, a memorial of blowing of trumpets, a holy convocation. 25 You shall do no customary work on it; and you shall offer an offering made by fire to the Lord.' "

There really isn't much more to this feast than that. I believe this is because of the nature of what this feast means. Well, blowing the trumpet in the Old Testament is often associated with danger.

Joel 2:1 Blow the trumpet in Zion, and sound an alarm in My holy mountain! Let all the inhabitants of the land tremble; for the day of the Lord is coming, for it is at hand:

Ezekiel 33:2-6 "Son of man, speak to the children of your people, and say to them: 'When I bring the sword upon a land, and the people of the land take a man from their territory and make him their watchman, 3 when he sees the sword coming upon the land, if he blows the trumpet and warns the people, 4 then whoever hears the sound of the trumpet and does not take warning, if the sword comes and takes him away, his blood shall be on his own head. 5 He heard the sound of the trumpet, but did not take warning; his blood shall be upon himself. But he who takes warning will save his life. 6 But if the watchman sees the sword coming and does not blow the trumpet, and the people are not warned, and the sword comes and takes any person from among them, he is taken away in his iniquity; but his blood I will require at the watchman's hand.'

It should be rather clear at this point what this feast points to.

Revelation 8:1-6 When He opened the seventh seal, there was silence in heaven for about half an hour. 2 And I saw the seven angels who stand before God, and to them were given seven trumpets. 3 Then another angel, having a golden censer, came and stood at the altar. He was given much incense, that he should offer it with the prayers of all the saints upon the golden altar which was before the throne. 4 And the smoke of the incense, with the prayers of the saints, ascended before God from the angel's hand. 5 Then the angel took the censer, filled it with fire from the altar, and threw it to the earth. And there were noises, thunderings, lightnings, and an earthquake. 6 So the seven angels who had the seven trumpets prepared themselves to sound.

On this day, the judgement of Yah is poured out on the earth and this world will be completely decimated by it. About half of the world population dies, and the earth itself is ravaged by the plagues being poured out. This is the feast noting the day of the wrath of the Lamb, when His wrath is poured out full strength upon a wicked world that hates Him and persecutes his people.

Atonement

Next is the most solemn feast in the entirety of the scripture. The day of atonement.

Leviticus 23:26-32 And the Lord spoke to Moses, saying: 27 "Also the tenth day of this seventh month shall be the Day of Atonement. It shall be a holy convocation for you; you shall afflict your souls, and offer an offering made by fire to the Lord. 28 And you shall do no work on that same day, for it is the Day of Atonement, to make atonement for you before the Lord your God. 29 For any person who is not afflicted in soul on that same day shall be cut off from his people. 30 And any person who does any work on that same day, that person I will destroy from among his people. 31 You shall do no manner of work;

it shall be a statute forever throughout your generations in all your dwellings. 32 It shall be to you a sabbath of solemn rest, and you shall afflict your souls; on the ninth day of the month at evening, from evening to evening, you shall celebrate your sabbath."

This day is what it sounds like, it is the day that the nations will atone for their sins. After pouring out the wrath of Yah, the nations of the world will still gather together against Christ. He will return and separate out the nations, striking down those who have joined with the beast with a sword out of His mouth. Mystery Babylon will fall, and she will have received double according to her transgressions. Beyond that, this feast very likely also pertains to the great white throne judgement some time after the millennium when every man, woman, and child who's ever lived that was not part of the first resurrection will be judged according to their works. This is a very solemn and serious day. On this day we are supposed to reflect upon our lives, and acknowledge and repent of any sin in our lives. It isn't the most enjoyable day, but it is a day that is very necessary in our lives.

Tabernacles

The final Biblically commanded feast is the feast of Tabernacles. Where as Atonement is the most serious and solemn feast, tabernacles is one of the most fun.

Deuteronomy 16:13-15 "You shall observe the Feast of Tabernacles seven days, when you have gathered from your threshing floor and from your winepress. 14 And you shall rejoice in your feast, you and your son and your daughter, your male servant and your female servant and the Levite, the stranger and the fatherless and the widow, who are within your gates. 15 Seven days you shall keep a sacred feast to the Lord your God in the

*place which the Lord chooses, because the Lord your God will
bless you in all your produce and in all the work of your hands,
so that you surely rejoice.*

Now after the trumpets of judgement, and the dividing of the nations,
the Millennial reign begins and peace and prosperity will return to the
earth. There are so many scriptures that talk about this period of time, and
nearly all of them speak of peace, and joy, and blessing being poured out as
the righteous King of Kings rules and reigns on the earth. Tabernacles is
traditionally celebrated by making a tabernacle, or a temporary dwelling,
and covering it in branches and staying in it, as per the instructions in
Leviticus 23. This is a time of celebration. The scripture states that it is
to commemorate the children of Israel being brought out of Egypt, but it
also represents Christ tabernacling with mankind for 1000 years. Another
interesting note is that Yahusha was prophesied about in the Old Testament
as being Immanuel, God with us, as explained earlier in this book. The
idea is that in Christ, Yah tabernacled among us. John reinforces this idea
in his Gospel.

*John 1:14 And the Word became flesh and dwelt among us, and
we beheld His glory, the glory as of the only begotten of the
Father, full of grace and truth.*

The word for dwelt here is Strong's #4637 skenoo, and it means "I dwell
as in a tent, encamp, have my tabernacle". So the Word became flesh, and
tabernacled among us. The spiritual side of this idea is the same, that we
are currently dwelling in tents of flesh as temporary tabernacles that we
will eventually leave when either we die, or put on incorruption. These
tabernacles, these bodies, will indeed pass away because they are only
temporary and corruptible. Another very cool thing, is that it is believed
that Yahusha was born on the feast of tabernacles. This would explain why
Mary and Joseph came to Bethlehem, not only for the census, but because
they were going to be keeping the feast, and dwelling in tents. This would

also explain why there were no rooms available at any inns, because there were so many people in town for the feast. It could very well be that Yah chose the feast of Tabernacles for Christ to be born as it was the day the Word officially came and tabernacled with us.

As you can see, all of these feasts are beautiful in meaning, and are perfect replacements for the pagan holidays that celebrate the antichrist. These are the feasts of Yah that glorify His Son, and bring Him glory. These are the ways that Yah asked His people to celebrate Him, thus making them acceptable offerings of praise, as opposed to trying to offer Him praise through pagan holidays filled with idolatry. In fact, Paul verifies this for us.

> *Colossians 2:16-17 So let no one judge you in food or in drink, or regarding a festival or a new moon or sabbaths, 17 which are a shadow of things to come, but the substance is of Christ.*

People oddly try to use these verses to justify them keeping Christmas and Easter, but as we already learned, the substance of those holidays is antichrist. In fact, Paul worried for the believers who were turning back to their old pagan holidays.

> *Galatians 4:8-11 But then, indeed, when you did not know God, you served those which by nature are not gods. 9 But now after you have known God, or rather are known by God, how is it that you turn again to the weak and beggarly elements, to which you desire again to be in bondage? 10 You observe days and months and seasons and years. 11 I am afraid for you, lest I have labored for you in vain.*

Remember that Paul is writing to the Galatians who are "gentiles" (new converts who do not yet know the law because they didn't grow up with it) in Galatia, surrounded by pagans. He then clearly says that before coming to Yah, they served those who are not gods, i.e. idols. Now after you are known by Yah, why would you return to the weak and beggarly elements of the days and months and seasons and years that are dedicated to idol worship? That's exactly what this verse addresses. Knowing Yah but continuing or reverting to idolatry. We will look at Paul's writings much more in the next chapter.

Bonus: Hanukkah

I want to look at one more feast, that though it was not commanded, is a rather interesting feast. This feast is Hanukkah. Now, if you want to be technical, this feast is in fact a "Jewish" feast. It was not commanded by Yah, therefore it was not one of His feasts, and it was in fact created and instituted by the Jews. For all intents and purposes, this is a Jewish feast. Nevertheless, it is actually a rather cool little feast, and can be a lot of fun, as well as a good way to fill the hole that ditching Christmas leaves. Hanukkah is the feast of dedication. The story behind Hanukkah is recorded in the apocryphal book of Maccabees that though it is not canonical, it is considered historically accurate. The story is basically this: There was a Roman emperor named Antiochus Epiphanes. This emperor was an evil man, and decided to make war with Jerusalem. He believed himself to be Zeus incarnate. He forcibly took over the temple in Jerusalem, sacrificed a pig on the alter to profane it, set up a statue of Zeus, and demanded to be worshiped. This is basically a perfect mirror of the antichrist. Anyways, there was a family at that time known as the Maccabees. This family rallied the Jews together to revolt against Antiochus, eventually defeating him and casting him out of the temple. In order to restore the temple as Holy, they had to rededicate it, purifying the alter, tearing down and destroying the idol, and rededicating it to Yah. Thus it is called the feast of dedication, and Hanukkah is just the Hebrew word for dedication.

Now interestingly, Yahusha Himself actually observed this feast when He walked the earth by going to the temple in Jerusalem on this day.

John 10:22-23 Now it was the Feast of Dedication in Jerusalem, and it was winter. 23 And Jesus walked in the temple, in Solomon's porch.

So that is one interesting note. A more interesting note is that Hanukkah is also commonly known as the festival of lights. They put up a menorah with 9 candles, eight of which are smaller and each represent one of the eight days of Hanukkah, and one ninth candle who is above all the others that is known as the servant candle. This menorah is allegedly to remember a miracle that occurred in the temple where when they dedicated the temple, they needed to have the menorah lit in accordance with Torah, but only one small vial of oil was found. It was only enough oil for one day, and to make more oil would take another 7 days. Nevertheless they lit the menorah with this vial of oil, but miraculously instead of lasting one day, it lasted eight days. Some historians claim this story wasn't actually established until later as a way to explain a military victory, but it is interesting none the less.

What's even more interesting is if you find the feast of Tabernacles, when it is believed that Yahusha was born, and count back the nine months that Mary would've been carrying Christ, it is quite likely He was conceived during Hanukkah. This would be very significant as inception is when life truly begins, and it would've been this day that the light of the world entered into the world. It is also worthy to note that Christ came as a servant, being a light that stood above all the other lights that he lit under Him. Thus bringing light to all mankind. Now again, this holiday isn't commanded, and is technically only a tradition of men, but nevertheless, at least the origins of this holiday are pure, and have nothing to do with idolatry. It also just might have a lot of significance in Christ as well.

This concludes this section about the feasts, and Sabbath. Again, many people claim that these things are strictly Jewish, but outside of Hanukkah, the scriptures do not bear this out. The assertion that these are Jewish feasts and a Jewish sabbath was an assertion made by Rome when it was stamping out the true followers of Christ who walked as He walked.

23

Bewitched

"Foolish Galatians! Who has bewitched you?!" Many people will look at the last chapters and decry that we are somehow turning against our faith by trying to walk in obedience to the laws and statutes of Yah, as if somehow obedience and faith are opposites. Did Paul really teach that trying to be obedient to Yah's laws is somehow evil? Did he teach the law is a terrible bondage? One of the biggest issues in the church today keeping people deceived, are the interpretations of Paul's letters. People claim that according to Paul, trying to keep the law is trampling on your faith, because you're relying on the law for salvation. They claim Paul states that any believer who tries to keep the law is bewitched and being led away from the faith by Satan. Now, I can't possibly address all of Paul's writings in this chapter, or in this book. Paul has 13 letters and to dissect all of them would be a very long and arduous task indeed, so instead, I'm going to address these ideas as a whole. These points will be broken down into 9 subsections for ease of reading.

Dangerous scriptures

Paul's writings are the most complicated in the entire Bible, and people twist his teachings all the time. Whether on purpose, or on accident, there is no other author in the entirety of the Bible who's writings are more debated and misused. People take Paul's writings completely out of context, or without understanding, and use them to found their doctrine claiming they have scriptural basis for their doctrines. The trouble is, out of context and without understanding, Paul in fact has many very dangerous verses, and we can basically make Paul say whatever we want.

Galatians 3:28 (...) there is neither male nor female (...)

1 Corinthians 10:23 All things are lawful for me, (...)

1 Corinthians 13:13 And now abide faith, hope, love, these three; but the greatest of these is love.

Ephesians 2:8-9 For by grace you have been saved through faith, and that not of yourselves; it is the gift of God, 9 not of works, lest anyone should boast.

I have heard Christian proponents of the LGBTQ+ use Galatians 3:28 to "biblically" defend their position of supporting transgenderism. I have heard Christians defend getting fall down drunk with 1 Corinthians 10:23 because "all things are lawful". I have been yelled at by Christians for trying to teach repentance from these things I have mentioned above as well as others, and have been "rebuked" by 1 Corinthians 13:13, because telling people they are living in sin is not very "loving" according to some, even if you do it the most gentle and kind of ways. I have encountered people entrenched in sin leading to death, and had them shrug and say, "I'm saved by faith, not works." and carry on in their sin. People take Paul's writings and use them to stubbornly dig their heels into their positions of error more often than any other author in the entirety of the Bible, hands down. All of that being said, did you know there is actually a warning against Paul's writings in your Bible? This is extremely significant, because in the entire Bible, there is never a warning against any other author anywhere, except for Paul. This warning is found in second Peter.

2 Peter 3:15-17 and consider that the longsuffering of our Lord is salvation—as also our beloved brother Paul, according to the wisdom given to him, has written to you, 16 as also in all his epistles, speaking in them of these things, in which are <u>some things hard to understand</u>, which <u>untaught and unstable people twist</u> to their own destruction, as they do also the rest of the Scriptures. 17 You therefore, beloved, since you know this beforehand, beware lest you also fall from your own steadfastness, being led away with the error of the lawless;

In some translations, that last word there, "lawless" is sometimes translated as "wicked". It is Strong's #113, athesmos, and it means "lawless, unrestrained, and licentious". Anyways, let's break this portion down. Second Peter warns us to be very careful with how we handle Paul's letters. He even gives us the specific reason why we need to be careful of Paul's letters, because they're hard to understand, and it's very easy to be led away with the error of lawlessness. What is lawlessness by definition? Being without the law. Lawfullness would be the opposite, and would be keeping the law, right? So the very thing people use Paul's writings for, to claim the law is done away with, i.e. lawlessness, is the very thing that second Peter warns against. Why have people fallen into this error of lawlessness? Because they are untaught and unstable.

Many Christians and Pastors have the best of intentions, but when they claim that Paul taught the law is done away with so we don't need to follow it anymore, they are proving that they are unlearned in scripture. Why is that? Because as we have seen, and will see more in this chapter and later on, to believe in the law being done away with is completely against the vast majority of scripture and contradicts hundreds of verses. There are dozens of verses in the New Testament, not just the Old, that explicitly say we should be keeping the law. When pressed, more often than not, they resort to dispensational theology which claims different portions of the Bible were given to different people. We already have seen major issues with dispensationalism based upon the scriptures we've already looked at, many of which were written by Paul.

They say that Paul was the apostle to the gentiles, and so we only have to listen to what Paul taught. I have had people tell me that even the teachings of Christ Himself, directly from the famous "sermon on the mount" were only for the Jews, and not for us, all to defend their lawless theology. They are untaught in the scriptures because they have eagerly swallowed a lie that says our conduct is of little importance, while "faith" is the only thing we really need. The truly sad thing is, Paul foretold this, and warned of it, and people have ended up using Paul's writings to move it forward.

> *2 Thessalonians 2:7-12 For the mystery of lawlessness is already at work; only He who now restrains will do so until He is taken out of the way. 8 And then the lawless one will be revealed, whom the Lord will consume with the breath of His mouth and destroy with the brightness of His coming. 9 The coming of the lawless one is according to the working of Satan, with all power, signs, and lying wonders, 10 and with all unrighteous deception among those who perish, because they did not receive the love of the truth, that they might be saved. 11 And for this reason God will send them strong delusion, that they should believe the lie, 12 that they all may be condemned who did not believe the truth but had pleasure in unrighteousness.*

There is so much here to look at. First of all, Paul said even at that time, the mystery of lawlessness was already at work. We saw a prime example of that with Ignacious of Antioch. John echoed this when he said many antichrists were already in the world and the spirit of antichrist was at work even then. We saw Rome, the beast, take this lawlessness, and in fact mandate it via military force. Now if we back up just a few verses, we see exactly what this coming of lawlessness was referred to.

> *2 Thessalonians 2:3 Let no one deceive you by any means; for that Day will not come unless the falling away comes first, and*

the man of sin is revealed, the son of perdition,

This lawless movement in the body of Christ is the falling away. Compare that with this passage.

> *Matthew 24:10-12 And then many will be offended, will betray one another, and will hate one another. 11 Then many false prophets will rise up and deceive many. 12 <u>And because lawlessness will abound, the love of many will grow cold.</u>*

I sat under a pastor a few years ago, who I still respect in many ways. He said one time he was in prayer, and asking Yah when this falling away would take place. He said Yah answered him and said, "There isn't going to be a great falling away, you're already in it." I absolutely believe this was spoken to him. He took that to mean that the body of Christ around him was already in the falling away, but I believe it was more than that. I believe it meant he was already under the influence of it to some extent as well. This falling away, is the mystery of lawlessness. Where does this mystery of lawlessness come from?

> *2 Thessalonians 2:11 For this reason <u>God will send them strong delusion, that they should believe the lie,</u>*

This delusion is sent from God. By what means?

> *Matthew 24:11 Then many false prophets will rise up and deceive many.*

Why are people being allowed to come under this delusion?

> *2 Thessalonians 2:10 ...<u>because they did not receive the love of the truth</u>*

What is the truth?

Psalm 119:142 Your righteousness is an everlasting righteousness,
And <u>Your law is truth</u>.

John 1:14 And <u>the Word</u> became flesh and dwelt among us

1 John 2:4 He who says, "I know <u>Him</u>," and does not keep <u>His</u> <u>commandments</u>, is a liar, and <u>the truth</u> is not in him.

Romans 8:7 Because the carnal mind is <u>enmity against God</u>; for it <u>is not subject to the law of God</u>, nor indeed can be.

So the mystery of lawlessness, the great falling away, came through false prophets near the end of the age, and Yah Himself sent it as a judgment, because people didn't receive the love for His word, a large part of which is His law. If you want a refresher on how false prophets brought the mystery of lawlessness, go reread Chapter 18. This enmity against the law is rampant in Christianity today. People call it a burden, a bondage, and witchcraft. Meanwhile the man after Yah's own heart said things like this:

Psalm 119:16 I will delight myself in <u>Your statutes</u>; I will not forget <u>Your word</u>.

Psalm 119:19-21 I am a stranger in the earth; do not hide Your commandments from me. 20 My soul breaks with longing for Your judgments at all times. 21 You rebuke the proud—the cursed, who stray from Your commandments.

Psalm 119:34-35 Give me understanding, and I shall keep Your law; indeed, I shall observe it with my whole heart. 35 Make me walk in the path of Your commandments, For I delight in it.

James called the law the "perfect law of liberty".

> ***James 1:22-25 But be <u>doers of the word</u>, and <u>not hearers only</u>,
> deceiving yourselves. 23 For if anyone is a hearer of the word
> and not a doer, he is like a man observing his natural face in a
> mirror; 24 for he observes himself, goes away, and immediately
> forgets what kind of man he was. 25 But he who looks into the
> <u>perfect law of liberty</u> and continues in it, and is not a forgetful
> hearer but a doer of the work, this one will be blessed in what
> he does.***

What was the word James was speaking of? The law and the prophets. That was the only word they had at that time. Therefore being a doer of the word, was doing the commandments contained in the word, right? He confirms this by calling it the perfect law of liberty. People claim this law of liberty is liberty from the law, but isn't ignoring the law being a hearer of the word, and not a doer? Logically and in context, this law of liberty is clearly the law given in the word, which we are to be doers of.

Ultimately, we are in this mess because of a lack of knowledge, and a lack of love for the word of Yah. We begin building our theology off of the New Testament first, and then moving back to the Old with our lawlessness fully in mind. There's one glaring problem though; Building your theology starting with the New Testament then moving backwards is like trying to build a house starting with the roof and working your way downward. Second Peter tells us in order to understand Paul's letters, you had better be learned in the scriptures. Which scriptures were considered as such at the time this statement was made? The Old Testament law and the prophets was the only scripture they had as already stated. Why would someone need to understand the OT scriptures before trying to interpret Paul's writings? This brings us to our second point.

Paul The Pharisee

Paul was in fact a pharisee. The scriptures tell us that Paul was the student of Gamaliel.

> *Acts 22:3 'I am indeed a Jew, born in Tarsus of Cilicia, but brought up in this city at the feet of Gamaliel, taught according to the strictness of our fathers' law, and was zealous toward God as you all are today.*

Gamaliel was, according to Jewish records as well as historians such as Josephus, one of the most respected and knowledgeable pharisees alive during that time period. In order to become one of his pupils, sources claim that you had to have memorized the entirety of the Old Testament, and have been able to quote them on command. This meant Paul would have had the word memorized backwards and forwards. After having sat under Gamaliel for a time though, he had his conversion on the road in Acts 9. After this took place, many people think Paul abandoned his role as pharisee and abandoned the law, but this isn't the case at all.

> *Acts 23:6 But when Paul perceived that one part were Sadducees and the other Pharisees, he cried out in the council, "Men and brethren, <u>I am a Pharisee</u>, the son of a Pharisee; concerning the hope and resurrection of the dead I am being judged!"*

Paul didn't declare that he had been a pharisee, he said "I AM a pharisee". This event took place long after Paul had been writing to the churches and traveling around. Many of his letters would have been written before this declaration of being a pharisee which meant the entire time that Paul was supposedly teaching against the law, he was a pharisee. In fact, Paul ended up on trial here, because people claimed that Paul was teaching against the law, and wanted to put him on trial for it. Just 2 chapters earlier we have this portion:

Acts 21:20-24 And when they heard it, they glorified the Lord. And they said to him, "You see, brother, how many myriads of Jews there are who have believed, and they are all zealous for the law; 21 but they have been informed about you that you teach all the Jews who are among the Gentiles to forsake Moses, saying that they ought not to circumcise their children nor to walk according to the customs. 22 What then? The assembly must certainly meet, for they will hear that you have come. 23 Therefore do what we tell you: We have four men who have taken a vow. 24 Take them and be purified with them, and pay their expenses so that they may shave their heads, and that all may know that those things of which they were informed concerning you are nothing, but that you yourself also walk orderly and keep the law.

So in this portion, these brothers meet with Paul and they're like, hey, Paul, the Jews are angry, they heard you've been teaching against the law, and against circumcision. Take these four men who will swear an oath with you, and prove you aren't teaching against the law, and that you still keep the law. Paul sets out to do this very thing, but ultimately is derailed in a series of incidents. So did Paul teach against the law? If so he was prepared to make four men bear false witness with him. The point is though, that Paul still kept the law himself. He says so again in another portion as well.

Philippians 3:4-6 though I also might have confidence in the flesh. If anyone else thinks he may have confidence in the flesh, I more so: 5 circumcised the eighth day, of the stock of Israel, of the tribe of Benjamin, a Hebrew of the Hebrews; concerning the law, a Pharisee; 6 concerning zeal, persecuting the church; concerning the righteousness which is in the law, blameless.

So Paul declared he was a pharisee, and blameless concerning the law. So again, did Paul keep the law, but teach others not do, being a hypocrite, and a liar, or did he teach the law? Did he say there is no longer Jew nor Greek, and then make a distinction between them thus contradicting himself? Did he teach the two becoming one new man, and then teach some to keep the law and some to break it? Were those who were born Jews given different laws than those who were born gentiles? We'll answer that question in the next chapter.

We also know from Chapter 19 that Paul still kept the feasts long after he began to preach the gospel. With this in mind, there are two verses that tell us how to walk out our faith.

> *1 John 2:6 He who says he abides in Him ought himself also to walk just as He walked.*

In this context, John was talking about Christ, and to walk as He walked, which was not in the traditions of men, and not in lawlessness, but perfectly walking in the law. Then there's this verse.

> *1 Corinthians 11:1 Imitate me, just as I also imitate Christ.*

Paul also kept the law and knew it backwards and forwards. So both of the examples in the Bible we are told to follow, both kept the law, the feasts, and the Sabbath. Paul did not abandon the law when he was born again. Paul kept the law himself, and assured people multiple times that he believed and kept the law. He said to imitate him as he imitated Christ. If you want to imitate Paul, obey the law.

Paul's Teachings on Sin and Law

Believe it or not, Paul taught obedience to the law quite often, but people don't even see it, because they've been deceived. Allow me to demonstrate.

> *Galatians 5:19-21 Now the works of the flesh are evident, which are: adultery, fornication, uncleanness, lewdness, 20 idolatry,*

303

sorcery, hatred, contentions, jealousies, outbursts of wrath, self-ish ambitions, dissensions, heresies, 21 envy, murders, drunkenness, revelries, and the like; of which I tell you beforehand, just as I also told you in time past, that those who practice such things will not inherit the kingdom of God.

Paul gives us a list of the works of the flesh. Let's see what the law says about some of this list.

1. **Adultery:** Against the law (Exodus 20:14)
2. **Fornication:** Against the law (If a man committed fornication with a woman, he was forced to take her as his wife, Exodus 22:16)
3. **Idolatry:** Against the law (We've seen tons of these already in the last section)
4. **Sorcery:** Against the law (Deuteronomy 18:10-12)
5. **Hatred & Murder:** Against the law (Christ equated these things to one another, Exodus 20:13)
6. **Jealousy & Envy**: Against the law (Exodus 20:17)
7. **Heresies:** Against the Law (Deuteronomy 13:1-5)
8. **Drunkenness:** Warned against in the law and prophets (Isaiah 5:11, Proverbs 20:1)

Geez Paul, you taught a lot of law here! Don't you know we're under grace? Don't you know gentiles ONLY have to abstain from food sacrificed to idols, things strangled, and sexual immorality? Don't try to weigh me down with that heavy burden! Are you seeing the issues here? Paul taught the law quite frequently, he just didn't always say it was the law. How about these passages?

Romans 8:7 Because the carnal mind is enmity against God; for it is not subject to the law of God, nor indeed can be.

Romans 8:5-6 For those who live according to the flesh set their

*minds on the things of the flesh, but those who live according to
the Spirit, the things of the Spirit. 6 For to be carnally minded
is death, but to be spiritually minded is life and peace.*

Think back to all the times that Paul talks about walking according to the
flesh, and being carnal. He says clearly that a carnal mind is not subject
to the law of Yah. He also presents being carnally minded, and spiritually
minded are opposites. So if being carnally minded is not being subject
to the law of Yah or disobedient to the law, wouldn't that make being
spiritually minded being obedient to the law of Yah?

Romans 7:14 For we know that the law is spiritual ...

What spirit is put inside of us? The Spirit of Christ right? Christ perfectly
kept the law. This lawful Holy Spirit dwells in us, and according to multiple
prophets the job of the Spirit is to write His laws on our hearts. So therefore
if we are walking according to the Spirit, who's job is to write His laws
on our hearts, then we would be keeping the law. This is the only logical
conclusion. So every time Paul talks about walking according to the spirit,
is he talking about walking according to the spiritual law, instead of the
fleshly carnal walk that is not subject to the law? It would seem so. Paul
talks about walking according the the spirit A LOT. The spirit's job is to
write His law on our hearts. If we are interpreting Paul according to his
own teachings and the rest of scripture, we have to logically conclude he
taught keeping the law. How about when Paul teaches against sin?

*Romans 4:7 Blessed are those whose <u>lawless</u> deeds are forgiven,
And whose <u>sins</u> are covered;*

*Romans 6:1-2 What shall we say then? Shall we continue in sin
that grace may abound? 2 Certainly not! How shall we who
died to sin live any longer in it?*

305

So what is sin anyways? We see that he equates sin with lawless deeds. Are there any other verses that back this up? I'm gonna use KJV instead of NKJV for this one, because I think the KJV states it much better.

> *1 John 3:4 Whosoever committeth sin transgresseth also the law: for sin is the transgression of the law.*

So is Paul teaching against transgressing the law every time he teaches against sin? It would seem so, after all, transgressing the law is the definition of sin is it not? We have to interpret Bible according to Bible. The word sin itself can be translated as missing the mark. What then is the mark we aim for? It is Christ, who was the Word, the law, made flesh, who perfectly walked in the law. Walking according to the law inwardly and outwardly just as Christ did is the mark we are aiming for. If we miss the mark, we have sinned. It's very simple.

What about all the times that Paul teaches about righteousness?

> *Romans 6:19 I speak in human terms because of the weakness of your flesh. For just as you presented your members as slaves of uncleanness, and of lawlessness leading to more lawlessness, so now present your members as slaves of righteousness for holiness.*

> *Psalm 119:142 Your righteousness is an everlasting righteousness, and Your law is truth.*

> *Isaiah 51:7 "Listen to Me, you who know righteousness, you people in whose heart is My law:...*

> *2 Corinthians 6:14 Do not be unequally yoked together with unbelievers. For what fellowship has righteousness with lawlessness? And what communion has light with darkness?*

So if uncleanness and lawlessness are the opposite of righteousness, then doesn't that make righteousness keeping the law? If darkness is lawlessness, doesn't that make lawfullness light? What about Christ's imputed righteousness?

> **Romans 5:19 For as by one man's disobedience many were made sinners, so also by one Man's obedience many will be made righteous.**

What was Christ's righteousness? That He was obedient and perfectly kept the law of Yah both outwardly, and inwardly. So we have the righteousness of keeping Yah's law, imputed to us through the blood of Christ. Does that mean we no longer have to keep the law and can walk in sin?

> **Romans 3:31 Do we then make void the law through faith? Certainly not! On the contrary, we establish the law.**

> **Romans 6:1-2 What shall we say then? Shall we continue in sin that grace may abound? 2 Certainly not! How shall we who died to sin live any longer in it?**

In fact, on that note, regarding Christ, why do we even need a high priest, or a sin sacrifice, if the law doesn't matter? Why do we need to accept the Lamb of Yah as the sacrifice for our sin if the law is no longer in effect? Without the law, the entire gospel collapses. Without the law, there is no sin, without sin, there is no need for a Savior, without the Savior, we have no gospel.

We actually see elsewhere too that righteousness and lawlessness appear to be opposites coinciding with Christ's righteousness having been in keeping the law perfectly both inwardly and outwardly.

> **Hebrews 1:9 You have loved righteousness and hated lawlessness**

Thus we can easily conclude that righteousness and lawfulness (keeping the righteous law) coincide and are the same thing. Paul did indeed teach the law as a pharisee. What he did not teach, was the Sanhedrin's traditions of men.

A Curse?

What of the times Paul says keeping the law is a curse? People frequently claim that Paul says walking in the law is a curse. They reference this passage:

> *Galatians 3:10-12 For as many as are of the works of the law are under the curse; for it is written, "Cursed is everyone who does not continue in all things which are written in the book of the law, to do them." 11 But that no one is justified by the law in the sight of God is evident, for "the just shall live by faith." 12 Yet the law is not of faith, but "the man who does them shall live by them."*

They interpret this to mean that if you are doing works according to the law, you are under a curse because when you try to obey the law, you are then obligated to keep all the law. This is actually very comical. The reason it's comical is that Paul in the same breath makes the scripture reference "the man who does them shall live by them." which is a reference to this verse found in Leviticus:

> *Leviticus 18:5 You shall therefore keep My statutes and My judgments, which if a man does, he shall live by them: I am the Lord.*

The comical part is not immediately apparent until you read the rest of the chapter that comes after this statement. This statement in context comes right before the law given pertaining to sexual immorality and Yah states that if anyone commits any of these things, He will be put to death, so the man who lives by these statutes, to obey them, will live by them (and not be put to death). These statutes include prohibitions against adultery, incest, homosexuality, and bestiality. If Paul was saying that trying to keep any of the law means you are cursed to keep all of the law and live by them, why did he reference this chapter of all chapters? If Paul was saying that the law no longer matters and is in fact a curse, why would he pick the chapter dealing with sexual immorality that he frequently taught against? Is it a curse not to commit adultery, not to sleep with your family, not to have sex with animals, and not to sleep with the same sex? Are keeping these things some huge unbearable burden? Dear reader, I sincerely hope keeping these commandments are not a huge burden to you or we have bigger problems to address.

Paul also makes the reference "Cursed is everyone who does not continue in all things which are written in the book of the law, to do them" which is a reference to Deuteronomy.

> *Deuteronomy 27:26 'Cursed is the one who does not confirm all the words of this law by observing them.'*

Once again claiming that Paul is saying that keeping the law is a curse is amusing in light of the context of this reference. This chapter is talking about a specific pronouncement of laws that the priests are to pronounce to the people, that if they break any of these laws, they will be cursed. This list of these laws?

> *Deuteronomy 27: 15-26 'Cursed is the one who makes a carved or molded image, an abomination to the Lord, the work of the hands of the craftsman, and sets it up in secret.'*
> *"And all the people shall answer and say, 'Amen!'*
> *16 'Cursed is the one who treats his father or his mother with contempt.'*

"And all the people shall say, 'Amen!'

17 'Cursed is the one who moves his neighbor's landmark.'

"And all the people shall say, 'Amen!'

18 'Cursed is the one who makes the blind to wander off the road.'

"And all the people shall say, 'Amen!'

19 'Cursed is the one who perverts the justice due the stranger, the fatherless, and widow.'

"And all the people shall say, 'Amen!'

20 'Cursed is the one who lies with his father's wife, because he has uncovered his father's bed.'

"And all the people shall say, 'Amen!'

21 'Cursed is the one who lies with any kind of animal.'

"And all the people shall say, 'Amen!'

22 'Cursed is the one who lies with his sister, the daughter of his father or the daughter of his mother.'

"And all the people shall say, 'Amen!'

23 'Cursed is the one who lies with his mother-in-law.'

"And all the people shall say, 'Amen!'

24 'Cursed is the one who attacks his neighbor secretly.'

"And all the people shall say, 'Amen!'

25 'Cursed is the one who takes a bribe to slay an innocent person.'

"And all the people shall say, 'Amen!'

26 'Cursed is the one who does not confirm all the words of this law by observing them.'

"And all the people shall say, 'Amen!' "

Man, what a curse and a bondage this law is! No making idols?! No sleeping with family members or animals?! No pushing the blind off the road?! No stealing your neighbors land?! No getting paid to murder the innocent?! What a curse! This law is such a curse and burden! Do you see why this might be a comical interpretation of Paul in light of the context of Paul's references? So Paul is writing a letter to the Galatians and thinks back to the law contained within these chapters and thinks to himself; "man what a curse to have to live by these laws"? I surely and sincerely hope that Paul wasn't referencing these chapters and saying that keeping these things are a curse and a burden, or he has some serious explaining to do. Funny that while Paul spends quite a lot of time referencing Old Testament scriptures, people rarely look up the reference and read them in context. Meanwhile the Bereans were commended for looking into the things Paul taught and testing them against scripture, and if Paul's writings are anything like his sermons, they were likely checking through the many references he made to the Old Testament. There aren't many good Bereans these days sadly.

The sad truth is, most people don't know the first thing about the Old Testament law because they've been told it's a curse and a burden, so they don't even bother to look into it. They see the heavy and arbitrary traditions and interpretations of the Jewish people and erroneously think that is what the law looks like. When referring to these traditions of men even Christ called them an unbearable burden that they (the pharisees) lay on proselytes and don't lift a finger to help them, because their traditions certainly are a massive burden. That being said, the law at face value, without the ridiculous interpretations of ungodly men, is not a burden at all, but a blessing. The Old Testament law for the common Israelite who was not a Levite priest are much the same as the laws you've already seen. They are not burdensome at all, but common courtesy and basic morality. Truly all the law can be summed up in two, to love your neighbor as yourself, and to love Yah with all your heart. If one reads the law and comes away thinking that it's some kind of dreadful burden and curse, it is because they have a carnal mind and a wicked heart.

Romans 8:7 Because the carnal mind is enmity against God; for it is not subject to the law of God, nor indeed can be

Lastly, Paul said this:

2 Timothy 3:16 All Scripture is given by inspiration of God, and is profitable for doctrine, for reproof, for correction, for instruction in righteousness,

ALL scripture is profitable for instruction in righteousness. When Paul wrote this, the only scripture they really had was the Old Testament. He is saying the Old testament, i.e. the law and the prophets, are good for instruction in righteousness. We learn how to walk in righteousness from the law. So, Paul actually taught about keeping the law quite a lot, but in veiled terms. This is another reason we need to know the Old Testament before we study Paul. A few more verses from Paul himself.

Romans 2:12-13 For as many as have sinned without law will also perish without law, and as many as have sinned in the law will be judged by the law 13 for not the hearers of the law are just in the sight of God, but the doers of the law will be justified

Romans 2:17-20 Indeed you are called a Jew, and rest on the law, and make your boast in God, 18 and know His will, and approve the things that are excellent, being instructed out of the law, 19 and are confident that you yourself are a guide to the blind, a light to those who are in darkness, 20 an instructor of the foolish, a teacher of babes, having the form of knowledge and truth in the law.

Romans 7:7 What shall we say then? Is the law sin? Certainly not! On the contrary, I would not have known sin except through the law. For I would not have known covetousness unless the law had said, "You shall not covet."

Romans 7:12 Therefore the law is holy, and the commandment holy and just and good.

Romans 7:22 For I delight in the law of God according to the inward man.

Justification and Sanctification

There are times that Paul does indeed appear to teach against the law. Galatians is a prime example of that. The thing is, there is a big difference between Justification, and Sanctification. See, Justification is the thing that we receive the moment we accept Christ. We accept His sacrifice for our sins, and we enter into covenant with Him, accepting Him as Lord and Savior, and submitting to His will. No amount of keeping the law can forgive you for your sins, only Christ can do that. Only faith in Christ can justify us. However, this is not to be confused with sanctification. Sanctification is the lifelong process where we become more and more like Christ, and walk more in step with how He walked. Sanctification is the process of line upon line, precept upon precept, having His laws written on our hearts. Sanctification never stops. Keep this in mind as you look at these verses.

> *Galatians 3:11 But that no one is justified by the law in the sight of God is evident, for "the just shall live by faith."*
>
> *Galatians 3:21 Is the law then against the promises of God? Certainly not! For if there had been a law given which could have given life, truly righteousness would have been by the law.*
>
> *Galatians 5:4 You have become estranged from Christ, you who attempt to be justified by law; you have fallen from grace.*

The issue that was facing the Galatians is that teachers had brought to them the idea that JUSTIFICATION came from keeping the law. This is false, as no amount of keeping the law can justify you before Yah or forgive your sin. Everyone has sinned, and therefore we are all already guilty of having broken the law. Therefore no amount of keeping the law now could ever give us eternal life, only faith in Christ can do that. Only the blood of Christ can JUSTIFY you. However, if we have the faith that justifies us, then we need to walk in the process of SANCTIFICATION. The Galatians were dealing with teachers that were saying that in order to be JUSTIFIED, you needed to be circumcised and keep all the law. That is what Paul taught against. If Paul taught against keeping the law, he was a hypocrite and a liar as explained above. We can easily see that Paul did indeed teach against being JUSTIFIED by the law, but not against walking in it, in the process of SANCTIFICATION. If you are trusting in the law to save you, you are indeed fallen from grace, because faith in Christ is the foundation for all our hope. However, do we then ignore the law and become lawless? Certainly not! Does faith make the law void?

> **Romans 3:31 Do we then make void the law through faith? Certainly not! On the contrary, we establish the law.**

How did Yahusha Himself say that we would be sanctified?

> **John 17:17-19 <u>Sanctify them by Your truth. Your word is truth.</u> 18 As You sent Me into the world, I also have sent them into the world. 19 And for their sakes I sanctify Myself, <u>that they also may be sanctified by the truth.</u>**

Sanctification is through the Word of Yah. At this time, there was no "New Testament". Yahusha prays that Yah would sanctify us by His truth, and then directly says His Word is the truth. Sanctification has always been through the Word of truth.

> **Psalm 119:142 Your righteousness <u>is an everlasting righteousness,</u> <u>And Your law is truth.</u>**

One more note, as this does come up from time to time. Did Paul teach against circumcision as a part of Sanctification in Galatians 5? I sure hope not, otherwise he is directly contradicting Yah.

> *Genesis 17:9-14 And <u>God said to Abraham</u>: "As for you, <u>you</u> <u>shall keep My covenant, you and your descendants after you</u> <u>throughout their generations.</u> 10 This is My covenant which you shall keep, between Me and <u>you and your descendants after</u> <u>you</u>: Every male child among you shall be circumcised; 11 and you shall be <u>circumcised in the flesh</u> of your foreskins, and it shall be a sign of the covenant between Me and you. 12 He who is eight days old among you shall be circumcised, every male child <u>in your generations</u>, he who is born in your house or bought with money from any foreigner who is not your descendant. 13 He who is born in your house and he who is bought with your money must be circumcised, and My covenant shall be <u>in your</u> <u>flesh</u> for <u>an everlasting covenant</u>. 14 And the uncircumcised male child, who is not <u>circumcised in the flesh</u> of his foreskin, that person shall be cut off from his people; he has broken My covenant.*

There's that phrase "throughout your generations" and that word "everlasting" again. Paul himself called us the seed or descendants of Abraham, and Yah said this was a covenant between Him and Abraham and his descendants forever, as an EVERLASTING covenant. Funny that people claim over and over again that these things are "done away with" when Yah specifically says they are eternal, everlasting, and forever. If Yah's definition of forever and eternal are so temporary, we have a lot to worry about in the afterlife folks.

And lest people claim that the circumcision we need is only that of the heart, we have this portion in Ezekiel talking about the millennial reign in context.

Ezekiel 44:6-9 "Now say to the rebellious, to the house of Israel, Thus says the Lord God: "O house of Israel, let Us have no more of all your abominations. 7 When you brought in foreigners, <u>uncircumcised in heart and uncircumcised in flesh</u>, to be in My sanctuary to defile it—My house—and when you offered My food, the fat and the blood, then <u>they broke My covenant</u> because of all your abominations. 8 And you have not kept charge of My holy things, but you have set others to keep charge of My sanctuary for you." 9 Thus says the Lord God: "<u>No foreigner, uncircumcised in heart or uncircumcised in flesh</u>, shall enter My sanctuary, <u>including any foreigner</u> who is among the children of Israel."

And this one in Jeremiah talking about the end times when Yah will punish the whole earth.

Jeremiah 9:25-26 "Behold, the days are coming," says the Lord, "that <u>I will punish all who are circumcised with the uncircumcised</u>— 26 Egypt, Judah, Edom, the people of Ammon, Moab, and <u>all who are in the farthest corners</u>, who dwell in the wilderness. <u>For all these nations are uncircumcised, and all the house of Israel are uncircumcised in the heart.</u>"

He punishes the nations that are uncircumcised in the flesh, and the house of Israel who are so often circumcised in the flesh, but uncircumcised in the heart, thus once again showing it takes both. The outward sign of the covenant in circumcision of the flesh, and the inward sign of the covenant in circumcision of the heart. Walking in His ways inside and out. What begins in the heart will come out in the flesh as Christ taught, therefore circumcision in the heart is the first step, but the outward actions in the flesh matter just as much as what is in the heart. If you don't have a murderous spirit against someone in your heart, but you murder them in the flesh, you've still sinned. Both the inward man and the outward man are to be obedient to Yahusha.

Yah is indeed concerned about circumcision of the heart, as being circumcised in flesh, but not in heart, profits nothing. However, according to Ezekiel, and it seems, even in the millennium, Yah is still concerned about circumcision in the flesh as well, as no one will enter the sanctuary if they are uncircumcised in heart or uncircumcised in flesh. Jeremiah says Yah will punish those uncircumcised in flesh and in heart. If Paul was teaching against circumcision in the flesh, he was directly contradicting Yah Himself.

Testing Prophets

If Paul did indeed teach against the law, as many assert, did you know that He is a false prophet as taught by the Old Testament and should've been dismissed as a heretic and cut off from the ekklesia?

> *Deuteronomy 13:1-5 "If there arises among you a prophet or a dreamer of dreams, and he gives you a sign or a wonder, 2 and the sign or the wonder comes to pass, of which he spoke to you, saying, 'Let us go after other gods'—which you have not known—'and let us serve them,' 3 you shall not listen to the words of that prophet or that dreamer of dreams, for the Lord your God is testing you to know whether you love the Lord your God with all your heart and with all your soul. 4 You shall walk after the Lord your God and fear Him, <u>and keep His commandments</u> and obey His voice; you shall serve Him and hold fast to Him. 5 But that prophet or that dreamer of dreams shall be put to death, because <u>he has spoken in order to turn you away from the Lord your God</u>, who brought you out of the land of Egypt and redeemed you from the house of bondage, <u>to entice you from the way in which the Lord your God commanded you to walk</u>. So you shall put away the evil from your midst.*

This passage clearly says that if a prophet arises, and teaches you not to keep His commandments, that you should not listen to him and cut him off from the Body (put him to death), and instead keep the commandments and obey Yah. So if Paul was teaching against the law, according to Deuteronomy, he was a false prophet and had no business being in the ekklesia in the first place.

Two or Three witnesses

Everyone uses Paul's verses to try to establish their doctrine but they forget a very important rule for establishing doctrine. In the mouth of two or three witnesses, let everything be established. Now, what is a witness? It is a person who agrees with or bears witness, to a specific fact. In a court of law, multiple witnesses are usually enough to close a case, because even the secular courts know that one witness by himself can lie, but in the mouth of two or three separate and unrelated witnesses, there is truth. This same principal is applied to establishing doctrine as well, as taking one verse that appears to say something and building a whole doctrine on it without there being any other witnesses to that idea, often leads to error. Therefore if we see something a bit controversial, we need to establish it from multiple sources. Unfortunately, modern Christianity has completely ignored this method of establishing doctrine. If I asked you to find me two or three witnesses that prove we don't need to keep the law would you be able to do it? Most people will pull verses from Ephesians, Galatians, and Romans, claiming they have three witnesses. The issue here however is this: three letters written by Paul, is still only one witness.

If I sat in a court of law, and claimed I had three witnesses that could clear a friend of mine, and then presented three letters written by myself in defense of my friend, would they count that as three witnesses? No, it's still only one witness. I could stand on the witness stand and state 800 times that my friend was innocent, but that would still only be one witness, not 800. The fact is, outside of Paul's writings you won't find any verses that appear to suggest you shouldn't keep the law. Mainstream Christianity claims we only really need to listen to Paul because he was the apostle to the gentiles but that directly contradicts even our methods of establishing doctrines. So if you still want to claim that Paul taught the law was done away with (thus imputing to him hypocrisy) and ignore all of my above points remember this, you still only have one witness. Meanwhile in the entire rest of the Bible:

Jeremiah 7:23 But this is what I commanded them, saying, 'Obey My voice, and I will be your God, and you shall be My people. And walk in all the ways that I have commanded you, that it may be well with you.'

Malachi 4:4 "Remember the Law of Moses, My servant, which I commanded him in Horeb for all Israel, with the statutes and judgments."

Deuteronomy 13:4 You shall walk after the Lord your God and fear Him, and keep His commandments and obey His voice; you shall serve Him and hold fast to Him.

Exodus 20:5-6 For I, the Lord your God, am a jealous God, visiting the iniquity of the fathers upon the children to the third and fourth generations of those who hate Me, 6 but showing mercy to thousands, to those who love Me and keep My commandments.

Joshua 22:5 But take careful heed to do the commandment and the law which Moses the servant of the Lord commanded you, to love the Lord your God, to walk in all His ways, to keep His commandments, to hold fast to Him, and to serve Him with all your heart and with all your soul.

Nehemiah 1:9 but if you return to Me, and keep My commandments and do them, though some of you were cast out to the farthest part of the heavens, yet I will gather them from there, and bring them to the place which I have chosen as a dwelling for My name.'

Psalm 89:30-32 "If his sons forsake My law and do not walk in My judgments, 31 If they break My statutes and do not keep My commandments, 32 Then I will punish their transgression with the rod, and their iniquity with stripes."

Ecclesiastes 12:13 Let us hear the conclusion of the whole matter: Fear God and keep His commandments, For this is man's all.

Matthew 5:17-18 "Do not think that I came to destroy the Law or the Prophets. I did not come to destroy but to fulfill. 18 For assuredly, I say to you, <u>till heaven and earth pass away,</u> <u>one jot or one tittle will by no means pass from the law</u> till all is fulfilled."

Matthew 19:17 So He said to him, "Why do you call Me good? No one is good but One, that is, God. But if you want to enter into life, keep the commandments."

John 15:10 If you keep My commandments, you will abide in My love, just as I have kept My Father's commandments and abide in His love.

1 John 2:3 Now by this we know that we know Him, if we keep His commandments.

Revelation 22:14 Blessed are those who do His commandments, that they may have the right to the tree of life, and may enter through the gates into the city.

How's that for two or three witnesses?

Just a Tutor?

People will also claim that the law is just a tutor to bring us to Christ as seen here:

> *Galatians 3:24-25 Therefore the law was our tutor to bring us to Christ, that we might be justified by faith. 25 But after faith has come, we are no longer under a tutor.*

Paul talks about this same thing here:

> *Romans 7:7 What shall we say then? Is the law sin? Certainly not! On the contrary, I would not have known sin except through the law. For I would not have known covetousness unless the law had said, "You shall not covet."*

So he would not have known that covetousness was sin, unless the law said don't covet. He would not have known what sin was, unless the law spelled it out for him.

> *1 John 3:4 (KJV) Whosoever committeth sin transgresseth also the law: for sin is the transgression of the law.*

Therefore the law was the tutor that taught him what sin was, and that he was a sinner. The law taught him he needed a sacrifice for His sins, and regeneration from them. Thus the law was the tutor who taught him he needed Christ. But now that we are in Christ, is covetousness now okay because we are under Christ and not under the law? Should we break the law now that we are under grace?

> *Romans 6:1-2 What shall we say then? Shall we continue in sin*

*that grace may abound? 2 Certainly not! How shall we who
died to sin live any longer in it?*

It's very simple. The law gives us a standard of righteousness. We cannot
keep the law perfectly as Christ did. When the law says don't covet, and
we realize we have coveted, we realize we are guilty of breaking the law.
When we realize we are guilty of breaking the law, we realize we need
justification and redemption. Thus we run to Christ, and ask for Him to
rule over us, and He provides the atonement and redemption we need.
Once we are under the grace of Christ, and no longer under the judgement
of the law, we should now strive to live under Christ without sin, but we
still stumble and fall from time to time.

> *1 John 2:1-2 My little children, these things I write to you, so
> that you may not sin. And if anyone sins, we have an Advocate
> with the Father, Jesus Christ the righteous. 2 And He Himself is
> the propitiation for our sins, and not for ours only but also for
> the whole world.*

This is the very simple, very plain Gospel message. We broke Yah's law, we
need forgiveness for it. We come to Christ and submit to Him. He atones
for our sin and forgives us of our transgressions against the law. Now that
we are no longer under the judgement of the law, but under grace, if we
sin, we have an advocate who forgives us. That doesn't mean we should
just sin continuously, it means we should strive ever harder to walk as He
walked, perfectly upholding the law. Now, is being under grace merely
the forgiveness of sins? If so, then it would seem Christ Himself needed
forgiveness which we know is impossible.

> *Luke 2:40 And the Child grew and became strong in spirit, filled
> with wisdom; and the grace of God was upon Him.*

Grace isn't only the forgiveness of sin, it is the divine empowerment according to the Spirit to help keep us from sinning, thus the Spirit is given to write the law of Yah on our hearts. That's what it means to be under grace.

Basic Logic

One last thing I want to point out is just pure simple logic. We see that Satan has infiltrated the ekklesia via Catholicism, Judaism, Freemasonry and theosophy, and in many other ways. Now given that we have been infiltrated, it means that we need to test our theology to be sure it too hasn't been infiltrated by Satan. What then would we look for in testing? I've already shown a myriad of verses that clearly state we are to be keeping His commandments. But what about pure simple logic? Let me break this down. Satan spent the entirety of the Old Testament trying to lead Yah's people away from keeping His commandments and obeying Him. He rose up in Rome and began to kill anyone trying to keep the commandments of Yah and replaced them with a new set of commands. In Revelation 12:17 we see at the end of the age Satan will be enraged by those who have faith in Christ, and keep His commandments. Now, if His agenda throughout the ages has consistently been to keep people away from keeping the commandments of Yah, do you really think that somehow he is tempting people in the current age to keep the commandments of Yah?

I have heard people call this whole concept witchcraft, and evil, and a deception. Logically speaking though, Satan has perpetually had the same agenda. Over six thousand years ago Satan deceived Eve to disobey Yah, causing the fall. Years later Satan deceived the entirety of the earth to corrupt itself and disobey Yah to the point that Yah had to destroy the earth and start over with Noah and his family. Thereafter Satan deceived the house of Israel to disobey Yah until they were divorced. Satan deceived the pharisees into disobedience to the point that they killed Messiah, the only Man who ever walked the earth who perfectly kept the commandments inside and out. Satan deceived many of the early ekklesia into rejecting the law of Yah and falling into Catholicism which Rome picked up and made the official religion of Rome and much of the world. Satan deceived Roman rulers into killing anyone who kept the commandments of Yah. After all that, people believe somehow it is Yah's will that we disobey His commandments, and Satan is tempting us to keep Yah's law? Is there any shred of logic in that thought progression?

Many claim that the spirit keeps telling them that they shouldn't keep the law. There are many verses however that claim the whole purpose of the Spirit is to write the laws of Yah on our hearts. If the spirit is telling you to stay away from obeying the commandments, are you sure you have the right spirit? Let me put it another way. Christ came and perfectly kept the law. He was the lawful one who never broke a single one of the laws of Yah inside or out, thus being perfect. Would His spirit teach you to break the law of Yah? Meanwhile we know that according to multiple verses, that antichrist is known as the lawless one, who will make war with those who keep the commandments of Yah, and exalt himself above Yah. We also know that there is a very real antichrist spirit that has been around for at least the past two thousand years. So what do you suppose the spirit of the lawless one, of antichrist would teach and lead to?

There is no logic whatsoever in claiming that the Holy Spirit, would ever lead you to disregard the law of Yah. There is however strong Biblical and logical evidence to suggest that the spirit of antichrist would indeed lead you away from keeping His commandments. Those who look into the law for themselves and pray about it, then claim that walking in the law of Yah is somehow witchcraft or bondage, are indeed under the influence of a spirit, but it isn't the Spirit of Yah. Those who put faith and obedience into opposite camps and call keeping the law witchcraft, while calling disregarding the law and walking according to how you feel the good and narrow way, are calling good evil, and evil good. These are those who are wise in their own eyes.

Isaiah 5:20-21 Woe to those who call evil good, and good evil; who put darkness for light, and light for darkness; who put bitter for sweet, and sweet for bitter! 21 Woe to those who are wise in their own eyes, and prudent in their own sight!

Remember that Paul said the law is holy and good and his inner man delights in Yah's law. James said the law was perfection and liberty. David said the law is a light and his delight. If people are saying keeping the law is somehow evil, they are very deceived, and I pray that Yah will open their eyes. I will end this chapter with just a few more scriptures for you from the man after Yah's own heart.

Psalm 119:53 Indignation has taken hold of me because of the wicked, who forsake Your law.

Psalm 119:136 Rivers of water run down from my eyes, because men do not keep Your law.

Psalm 119:126-127 It is time for You to act, O Lord, for they have regarded Your law as void. 127 Therefore I love Your commandments more than gold, yes, than fine gold!

24

Lawgiver

Many people at this point will begin to get flustered and begin to say that there are different laws for different people. They will claim the law of Christ is different than the law of Moses, and the law of Yah is different from the other two, and the moral law is different from the ceremonial law, and attempt to justify their lawlessness by bringing confusion in as to which law is which. This is actually very simple to break down. First of all, outside of the little subheadings put in later by men, you will find no hint of a separation or distinction between "ceremonial law" and "moral law" anywhere in the Bible. The law is never broken up in this manner. There are some laws that are given to specific people, such as laws for kings, and laws for priests, but most of the laws people fight against were given to all Israel. Nobody has ever kept all of the laws, not even Yahusha. The reason for this, is because some laws are specifically for males, some specifically for females, some for kings, and some for farmers. The fact is, the law has always been a situation of, if you are able to keep it, you keep it. If you are a farmer, you should let the land rest every seven years. I can't do that, as I do not have crops or land. That doesn't mean I can dismiss other laws at random though. Yahusha didn't keep every law, but He never broke a single one either. We should walk as He walked.

Now where did this notion of "moral laws" and "ceremonial laws" come from? Well, as it turns out, it came from the writings of the Jewish Sages, same place the Talmud came from. In other words, this separation is nothing more than a tradition of men. Traditions of men that come from the pharisees that make of no effect the commandment of Yah? Where have we seen this before? You can read your Bible cover to cover, and you will never find even the slightest hint that the law is separated into these subcategories. This is a quote from gotquestions.com on this very subject:

> The division of the Jewish law into different categories is a human construct designed to better understand the nature of God and define which laws church-age Christians are still required to follow. Many believe the ceremonial law is not applicable, but we are bound by the Ten Commandments. All the law is useful for instruction (2 Timothy 3:16), and nothing in the Bible indicates that God intended a distinction of categories. [53]

I disagree with many of the teachings that come from this website and especially on this page as a whole. They teach even the ten commandments are null thus total lawlessness is acceptable. Nevertheless, at least they accurately state where this categorization of the law came from; It is nothing more and nothing less than the traditions of men, with no Biblical foundation whatsoever. We will also see that there are in fact many verses that contradict this tradition of man.

What then, of the times the Bible refers to the "law of Moses" or when Yah calls it "My law" and when Paul speaks of the "law of Christ" or James' "Law of Liberty"? Are these all different? Not at all. The fact is, Moses, Yah, and Christ all gave the same law in one way or another. Allow me to explain.

If we go back in to the Old Testament to Moses, we actually find some really interesting little nuances that are easy to miss but very interesting.

Exodus 3:1-6 Now Moses was tending the flock of Jethro his

father-in-law, the priest of Midian. And he led the flock to the back of the desert, and came to Horeb, the mountain of God. 2 And the Angel of the Lord appeared to him in a flame of fire from the midst of a bush. So he looked, and behold, the bush was burning with fire, but the bush was not consumed. 3 Then Moses said, "I will now turn aside and see this great sight, why the bush does not burn." 4 So when the Lord saw that he turned aside to look, God called to him from the midst of the bush and said, "Moses, Moses!" and he said, "Here I am." 5 Then He said, "Do not draw near this place. Take your sandals off your feet, for the place where you stand is holy ground." 6 Moreover He said, "I am the God of your father—the God of Abraham, the God of Isaac, and the God of Jacob." And Moses hid his face, for he was afraid to look upon God.

I want to point out three interesting things in this passage. First of all, it specifically says and the Angel of Yah called to Moses and appeared in the bush. Now the word angel here is Strong's #4397 malak, and it simply means messenger. Now this messenger of Yah, introduced Himself to Moses as the God of Abraham, Isaac, and Jacob. So who was this messenger of Yah that also claimed to be Yah? Do we see a part of Yah that is a messenger but also Yah? Do we even see one associated with fire?

Acts 2:1-4 When the Day of Pentecost had fully come, they were all with one accord in one place. 2 And suddenly there came a sound from heaven, as of a rushing mighty wind, and it filled the whole house where they were sitting. 3 Then there appeared to them divided tongues, as of fire, and one sat upon each of them. 4 And they were all filled with the Holy Spirit and began to speak with other tongues, as the Spirit gave them utterance.

A part of Yah that is a messenger of Yah that is represented as a fire? The Holy Spirit, the spirit of Yah perfectly fits this description. So in the first instance, Moses very likely met and spoke with the Holy Spirit. Now much later in Moses' life, after delivering the children of Israel, we know that Moses met Yah on Mount Sinai.

> *Exodus 33:18-23 And he said, "Please, show me Your glory." 19 Then He said, "I will make all My goodness pass before you, and I will proclaim the name of the Lord before you. I will be gracious to whom I will be gracious, and I will have compassion on whom I will have compassion." 20 But He said, "You cannot see My face; for no man shall see Me, and live." 21 And the Lord said, "Here is a place by Me, and you shall stand on the rock. 22 So it shall be, while My glory passes by, that I will put you in the cleft of the rock, and will cover you with My hand while I pass by. 23 Then I will take away My hand, and <u>you shall see My back; but My face shall not be seen.</u>"*

So we know that Moses went up, and Yah passed in front of him, and declared His name. It's a beautiful portion of scripture and the name that Yah proclaims is beautiful. Moses even got to see Yah's back. There is one problem though with this account though. Moses saw Yah.

> *John 1:18 <u>No one has seen God at any time.</u> The only begotten Son, who is in the bosom of the Father, He has declared Him.*

> *1 Timothy 1:17 Now to the King eternal, immortal, <u>invisible</u>, to God who alone is wise, be honor and glory forever and ever. Amen.*

> *John 5:37 And the Father Himself, who sent Me, has testified of Me. You have neither heard His voice at any time, <u>nor seen His form.</u>*

Do you see the problem here? This can't happen. How did Moses see Yah if

Yah is invisible, and no man has ever seen Him? One could claim that Yah became visible just for Moses, but that still contradicts the declarations that no man has seen Him at any time or seen His form. So how do we reconcile these verses?

> **Colossians 1:13-15 He has delivered us from the power of darkness and conveyed us into the kingdom of the <u>Son of His love</u>, 14 in whom we have redemption through His blood, the forgiveness of sins. 15 <u>He is the image of the invisible God</u>, the firstborn over all creation.**

So Moses saw a physical image of Yah. This can only be Christ Himself before He took on the form of a man, but still visible as opposed to the invisible Father. Otherwise scripture contradicts itself. So it would surely seem Moses met with Yahusha, the Word of Yah, on Mount Sinai. What does this mean? Well, very simply, it means Yahusha Himself actually gave the law! Yahusha is a part of Yah, the son of Yah, and yet Yah Himself. Therefore Yah gave the law. However Christ is the part of Yah that it seems actually met with Moses and carved the law on tablets of stone with His finger, therefore Christ also gave the law. Further, we know according to John that Yahusha was The Word made flesh right? So wouldn't it make sense that the Word of Yah would give the word of Yah? In fact, if you begin reading the Old Testament you will see this phrase repeated over and over "and the word of the Lord came to (...). Check these out:

> **1 Samuel 3:21 Then the Lord appeared again in Shiloh. <u>For the Lord revealed Himself to Samuel in Shiloh by the word of the Lord.</u>**

> **Psalm 18:30 As for God, His way is perfect; <u>The word of the Lord is proven;</u> He is a shield to all who trust in Him.**

> **Genesis 15:1 After these things <u>the word of the Lord came to</u>**

Abram in a vision, saying, "Do not be afraid, Abram. <u>I am your</u> <u>shield</u>, your exceedingly great reward."

Psalm 33:4 For <u>the word of the Lord is right,</u> And all His work is done in truth.

Psalm 33:6 <u>By the word of the Lord the heavens were made,</u> And all the host of them by the breath of His mouth.

John 1:1-3 <u>In the beginning was the Word, and the Word was with God, and the Word was God. 2 He was in the beginning with God. 3 All things were made through Him, and without Him nothing was made that was made.</u>

Could it be that Christ was working all throughout the Old Testament before He humbled Himself and took on the form of a man? It sure would seem so.

Anyways, back to the law. So the physical manifestation of the invisible God, Yahusha, met with Moses and let Moses see His back. This was both Yah giving the law, as well as Christ giving the law, as they are one. He inscribed the law on tablets of stone and gave them to Moses. Those first tablets were shattered when Moses threw them to the ground upon finding the children of Israel having turned to the golden calf. Moses then had to climb back up the mountain, and this time write the commandments that Yah dictated to him with his own hand.

Exodus 34:27 Then the Lord said to Moses, "Write these words, for according to the tenor of these words I have made a covenant with you and with Israel."

So did Yah give the law? Yes! Did Christ give the law? Yes! Did Moses give the law? Yes! Yes to all the above. It is the law of Moses, and the law of Yah, and the law of Christ. It is all three. Now people claim that the law of Christ is only to love Yah, and to love one another. This is true. These are the two greatest commandments, but as I explained earlier, every single one of the commandments given are in one category or the other. Don't move the property marker on your neighbors land (Deuteronomy 19:14): love one another. Don't rip people off when weighing things on scales (Leviticus 19:35): love one another. Don't steal the meal offering of a priest (Leviticus 22:10): love one another. Don't covet your neighbors wife (Exodus 20:17): love one another. Leave the corners of your field ungathered for the poor (Leviticus 23:22): love one another. Remember the Sabbath and keep it Holy (Exodus 20:8): love Yah. Wear tzitzit on the four corners of your garments so you remember the law of Yah (Numbers 15:38): love Yah. Keep the feasts (commanded all over): love Yah. Have no other gods and no idols (Exodus 20:3-5): l ove Yah. Every single command given in the Old Testament falls into one category or the other. This is why Yahusha said on these two commandments HANG all the law and the prophets. It means every law hangs on one of these two commandments. The law of Christ IS the Old Testament law. If he meant that these were the only two commandments and somehow did away with the other laws, then logically we also have to conclude this also meant that He was doing away with the prophecies as well, as He said on these two hang all the law AND the prophets. So does that mean all the Old Testament prophecies are done away with too that haven't happened yet? Of course not. Neither are the laws of the Old Testament done away with.

If the law isn't divided as such into the two catagories, what then what does it mean to love one another? Some Christians claim performing abortions for teenagers is showing love to those teenagers. Some Christians claim accepting homosexuality and not warning against it is loving. Some believe picketing funerals and screaming derogatory terms at homosexuals is somehow loving one another. "Live and let live" is a common saying even among Christians these days and trying to call anyone to repentance is not "loving" them according to many. Without the law, there is no basis on knowing how we are to love Yah or love one another, and it devolves into the kind of chaos we see in the ekklesia today. Everyone has their own perspective of love, their own perspective of right and wrong, and without a common foundation, there is strife, division, evil and idolatry in the midst. This is the same thing Israel was judged for all throughout the book of Judges.

> *Judges 17:6 In those days there was no king in Israel; <u>everyone did what was right in his own eyes.</u>*

> *Judges 21:25 In those days there was no king in Israel; <u>everyone did what was right in his own eyes.</u>*

This is exactly what we see today. This was when Israel was backslidden and fallen, but you know what, they did what was right in their own eyes. It doesn't say they purposely did evil, or that they attempted to become polluted and sought to turn against Yah, no, they were just doing what THEY thought was right, rather than what Yah knows is right, because they threw out the standard of what is right and wrong, Yah's law. This was primarily due to them not having a king over them. We do have a King in the midst of Israel at the moment, but the issue is, nobody is listening to Him because dispensationalism says not to. What impact does a King have on His subjects if nobody obeys Him? When loving Yah and loving one another is left up to the individual, it's basically just a free for all with everyone doing what is right in their own eyes, rather than doing what is right in the eyes of Yah. They call this self driven morality "walking according the Spirit" but they don't even understand what this means. The proper phrase for what they are doing is being rebellious.

Further, everyone keeps saying that Yahusha did away with or abolished the law, this is exactly what He commanded people NOT to think:

> *Matthew 5:17-18 "<u>Do not think that I came to destroy the Law or the Prophets.</u> I did not come to destroy but to fulfill. 18 For assuredly, I say to you, till heaven and earth pass away, one jot or one tittle will by no means pass from the law till all is*

fulfilled.

He explicitly told us not to think He destroyed the law, and everyone says, "The law was nailed to the cross with Christ!" People also claim that word there, fulfill, means to bring an end to, but this is a direct contradiction with the next verse. In case there was any doubt, He said heaven and earth will pass away before even one jot or tittle will pass from the law. I don't know about you, but I don't recall a historical event where the heavens and earth passed away and were recreated. Last time I looked outside, the heavens and the earth are still very much there, and look the same as they always have. Christ declares He didn't come to destroy the law, He came to perfect it, He came to make it full, to finish it, not in the sense that it is no longer valid, but in the sense that it was lacking before, but now it is perfected, or completed. The law would change the outward actions of man, but did not affect the heart thus it was lacking. What He came to do was to finish the law, making it so the law was not only something to be kept in the flesh, but also in the heart. He then goes on a long discourse explaining exactly what this means.

> *Matthew 5:21-22 "You have heard that it was said to those of old, You shall not murder, and whoever murders will be in danger of the judgment.' 22 But I say to you that whoever is angry with his brother without a cause shall be in danger of the judgment.*

> *Matthew 5:27-28 "You have heard that it was said to those of old, 'You shall not commit adultery.' 28 But I say to you that whoever looks at a woman to lust for her has already committed adultery with her in his heart.*

> *Matthew 5:31-32 "Furthermore it has been said, 'Whoever divorces his wife, let him give her a certificate of divorce.' 32 But I say to you that whoever divorces his wife for any reason except sexual immorality causes her to commit adultery; and whoever*

marries a woman who is divorced commits adultery.

Matthew 5:33-37 "Again you have heard that it was said to those of old, 'You shall not swear falsely, but shall perform your oaths to the Lord.' 34 But I say to you, do not swear at all: neither by heaven, for it is God's throne; 35 nor by the earth, for it is His footstool; nor by Jerusalem, for it is the city of the great King. 36 Nor shall you swear by your head, because you cannot make one hair white or black. 37 But let your 'Yes' be 'Yes,' and your 'No,' 'No.' For whatever is more than these is from the evil one.

So what Christ brings out here, is that under the law, the Old Covenant, to be guilty of breaking a commandment, you had to physically perform an action. Christ says under the New Covenant, (under grace if you will), if you even want to do it, or fantasize about doing it, basically if you entertain that desire in your heart, you're guilty of it. The law was weak, in that though it cleansed the actions of a person outwardly, they could still be full of wickedness in their heart. Prime examples of this were the pharisees.

Matthew 23:25-28 "Woe to you, scribes and Pharisees, hypocrites! For you cleanse the outside of the cup and dish, but inside they are full of extortion and self-indulgence. 26 Blind Pharisee, first cleanse the inside of the cup and dish, that the outside of them may be clean also. 27 "Woe to you, scribes and Pharisees, hypocrites! For you are like whitewashed tombs which indeed appear beautiful outwardly, but inside are full of dead men's bones and all uncleanness. 28 Even so you also outwardly appear righteous to men, but inside you are full of hypocrisy and lawlessness.

What was Christ saying here? Outwardly, in the flesh, they were keeping most of the law and so they looked clean, but inwardly, in their thoughts, motives, and desires, they were full of lawlessness. They were not keeping the law in their hearts. They weren't committing adultery in the flesh, but they were lusting after other men's wives, having carnal imaginations of having relations with them. They weren't outright murdering people, (though ultimately they did), but they very much wanted to. This was what Christ meant when He said that they were clean outwardly, but inwardly were filthy.

This perfecting of the law by the Messiah was foretold in the Old Testament by the prophet Isaiah.

> *Isaiah 42:1 "Behold! My Servant whom I uphold, my Elect One in whom My soul delights! I have put My Spirit upon Him; He will bring forth justice to the Gentiles.*

> *Isaiah 42:4 He will not fail nor be discouraged, till He has established justice in the earth; and the coastlands shall wait for His law."*

> *Isaiah 42:21 The Lord is well pleased for His righteousness' sake; He will exalt the law and make it honorable.*

Isaiah says He will establish justice in the earth and that the coastlands (the coastlands being the gentiles that are mentioned that He will being justice to a few verses prior), will wait for His law. The KJV says that He will magnify the law, this is exactly what Yahusha said He did. This is exactly what He explained during the sermon on the mount. He did not do away with the law, He perfected and magnified it as foretold by the prophet Isaiah. He brought His law to the gentiles and to the coastlands. He did NOT do away with or diminish the law. He did not lessen it or weaken it for the sake of the gentiles. Everything Yahusha did was foretold, from where He was born, the healings He performed, speaking in parables, and even Him walking on the water. Everything was foretold, but you will not find a single shred of a hint of any prophecy that suggests that Messiah would remove, or diminish, or abolish the law, but on the contrary that He would magnify it. This is because He brought the law not only to the flesh in outward ordinances, but also to the spirit of the inward man. We have another witness of this very thing in Isaiah.

> *Isaiah 51:3-7 For the Lord will comfort Zion, He will comfort all her waste places; He will make her wilderness like Eden, and her desert like the garden of the Lord; Joy and gladness will be found in it, thanksgiving and the voice of melody.*
>
> *4 "Listen to Me, My people; And give ear to Me, O My nation: For law will proceed from Me, and I will make My justice rest as a light of the peoples. 5 My righteousness is near, My salvation has gone forth, and My arms will judge the peoples; The coastlands will wait upon Me, and on My arm they will trust. 6 Lift up your eyes to the heavens, and look on the earth beneath. For the heavens will vanish away like smoke, the earth will grow old like a garment, and those who dwell in it will die in like manner; but My salvation will be forever, and My righteousness will not be abolished.*
>
> *7 "Listen to Me, you who know righteousness, you people in whose heart is My law: Do not fear the reproach of men, nor be afraid of their insults.*

So in this passage it specifically says the same thing Christ said. It says heaven and earth and the people on the earth will pass away, but His salvation will be forever. That word there, Salvation, is speaking of the Salvation that came through Yahusha. We certainly believe that right? But in the very same sentence it says His righteousness will NOT be abolished. Understand that in the original scriptures there were no chapter and verse markers, so right after it says His righteousness will not be abolished, it specifically explains what that righteousness is. It says "Listen to me, you who know righteousness, you people in whose heart is My law." His law is the standard of righteousness, and when Isaiah penned these original words, there was only one law, and that is the only one law that there is today. The law of Yah. Once again, no hint of the law being abolished anywhere in the entire Old Testament, but we find witnesses to the contrary all over the place, that it will never be abolished, and that Yahusha will magnify the law and write it on our hearts.

This all goes back to the New Covenant.

> *Jeremiah 31:33 But this is the covenant that I will make <u>with</u> <u>the house of Israel</u> after those days, says the Lord: <u>I will put My</u> <u>law in their minds, and write it on their hearts</u>; and I will be their God, and they shall be My people.*

The purpose of the Spirit within us is to write His laws on our hearts so we begin to naturally do the things in the law, both inwardly and outwardly, after all, the things in the heart eventually come out into actions.

> *Matthew 15:19 For out of the heart proceed evil thoughts, murders, adulteries, fornications, thefts, false witness, blasphemies.*

Thus He needed to purify our hearts and our inward man by putting a new spirit within us, so that we would walk in His standard of righteousness, His law, by nature as we are changed from the image of sinful man into the perfection of Christ. This is also why He told the pharisees to first cleanse the inside of the cup that the outside might be cleaned.

There are other verses that back up this idea of the spirit under the New Covenant regenerating our hearts to keep His law.

> *Ezekiel 11:19-20 Then I will give them one heart, and <u>I will put</u> <u>a new spirit within them</u>, and take the stony heart out of their flesh, and give them a heart of flesh, 20 <u>that they may walk in</u> <u>My statutes and keep My judgments and do them</u>; and they shall be My people, and I will be their God.*

Nearly everyone agrees Ezekiel 11:19 and Jeremiah 31:33 are the same event, but what they ignore is the purpose of this New Covenant, or the function the spirit performs in us. It is to write His law on our hearts, circumcising our hearts, so that we keep His law in our hearts, but also keeping His law in our flesh. Remember that statutes means laws and directives. The purpose of the new spirit is to cause us to walk according to His statutes, not to give us this kind of self determining morality in order to abandon His laws. His standard of righteousness has not changed because our God does not change.

If Yahusha had come to abolish the law or "nail it to the cross" as people assert, there would have had to be prophecies about it, as Yah does nothing without first revealing it through His prophets.

Amos 3:7 Surely the Lord God does nothing, unless He reveals His secret to His servants the prophets.

Again, you can search throughout all the writings of the prophets and you will never once find even a hint that Messiah would abolish the law, but on the contrary, that He would magnify it and bring it to the gentiles. Any suggestion to the contrary contradicts the Word of Yah.

In spite of all these evidences, people will still try to rebel against the law and begin to mock. They claim things like; "You should be killing adulterers and idolaters then if you want to keep the law!" That's correct in a way, but thankfully, the law of sin and death, that is, if you sin, that you will be put to death by men, has been nailed to the cross.

Romans 8:2 For the law of the Spirit of life in Christ Jesus has made me free from the law of sin and death.

After all, that is one of the cornerstones of our faith, that Christ has paid the debt for the whole world, and thus he died the death we deserved, taking away our need to die for our sins if we trust in Him. He was the perfect sacrifice fulfilling the law. He now holds the keys of life and death, and He will avenge and put to death those who He deems fit to, so I no longer have to worry about putting idolaters to death, because Christ does that for us, thus upholding the law. I only have to worry about trying to lead people to accept His sacrifice so they don't need to die in their sin. The only putting to death I'm personally responsible for when it comes to other people, is cutting off people who claim to be brothers in Christ who willfully continue to disobey the commandments. Paul confirms this.

> *1 Corinthians 5:9-13 I wrote to you in my epistle not to keep company with sexually immoral people. 10 Yet I certainly did not mean with the sexually immoral people of this world, or with the covetous, or extortioners, or idolaters, since then you would need to go out of the world. 11 But now I have written to you not to keep company with anyone named a brother, who is sexually immoral, or covetous, or an idolater, or a reviler, or a drunkard, or an extortioner—not even to eat with such a person. 12 For what have I to do with judging those also who are outside? Do you not judge those who are inside? 13 But those who are outside God judges. Therefore "put away from yourselves the evil person."*

By the way, being covetous, an extortioner, an idolater, a reviler, and being sexually immoral, these are all against the Law of Yah. In fact, particularly regarding sexual immorality, the reason there is so much of it in the church today is because we don't even know what it is. Did you know not one place in the New Testament has a prohibition against bestiality? Since that was only according to the "Old Testament law" and the law no longer applies, it's okay to do now right? Wrong. Sexual immorality means sexual lawlessness, and therefore in order to understand what is sexually lawful we need to know the law. Get rid of the law, and you have no standard for what is acceptable, and people fall into sexual immorality not understanding it is sin. I personally know a few open practicing homosexuals who claim they are good Christians walking with Christ. When you try to gently mention according to the Bible, that behavior is sin, they fall back into the same arguments most Christians do: "That was the law, I'm not under the law, I'm under grace!" If they only knew what that meant. Side tangent aside, even these verses above in 1 Corinthians 5 are given for the purpose that through being cut off, and the things those who are will suffer, that they will return eventually to Christ. 1 Corinthians 5:5 is a prime example of that.

I also want to mention that people claim we don't have to keep the law because Christ keeps it for us. In fact, I even said as much above saying that Christ is judge and executioner of who needs to be put to death so I no longer have to do that. Understand that there were once again laws given for high priests, some for priests, some for farmers, some for men, and some for women. The commandment to put to death those who transgress different laws was a responsibility of kings, judges, and courts. It had to be verified through an authority structure before it could be enacted. The ultimate authority structure is Christ, who is also the Judge over all mankind, thus the job of passing down judgments, such as putting a man to death for his sin falls to Christ and not to us, as we are not in that position of authority.

What then of the idea that Christ keeps the law for us so we don't have to? Well, let's look at that assertion for a moment. I have heard it said we no longer have to keep the Sabbath because Christ kept that law for us so we don't have to. I have heard the same said about the food laws, the wearing of tzitzit, and pretty much every other law. If Christ keeps the law for us, does that mean that we no longer have to abstain from adultery? Does that mean we can now steal, because Christ kept the law that prohibits it for us? Does that mean that because Christ upheld the law and did not murder anyone, that we can now go out and murder because He kept that law for us? This is lunacy. The truth is, people use this argument as a weak defense against being obedient. Much of the time the same people who say it's important not to commit adultery, or steal, or murder, are the same people who say "I don't have to keep the law because Christ kept it for me!" Okay so if Christ kept the law for you, then according to that logic, we can completely ignore all the law and go out living out our days as homosexuals and drunkards and extortioners and revilers and idolaters. This is hypocrisy, and the very things I listed are the things Paul said not even to eat with such a one who claims to be in Christ and is doing these things. Just because Christ kept the righteous requirements of the law, does not mean that it makes void the law for us.

Think of it this way, Christ lives in us right? This is the first and simplest truth we teach to our children right? "You need to ask Jesus to come live in your heart." If Christ lives within us, and He is in control, then we should begin to do the things He did right? If Christ is ruling and reigning from the throne in our hearts, then we will walk in the commands and decrees that He gives. This is logical. How then can we claim that the perfect Savior who perfectly upheld the law who now lives and reigns in us is fine with the vessel He lives in disobeying and disregarding the law? How does that make any sense? Further we know from Micah, Isaiah, and many other places that when Christ returns, He will reign over the earth and the people in the earth will be required to keep the law and the law will be in effect. Here are two mirror passages with only subtle differences.

Micah 4:1-2 Now it shall come to pass in the latter days that the mountain of the Lord's house shall be established on the top of the mountains, and shall be exalted above the hills; And peoples shall flow to it. 2 Many nations shall come and say, "Come, and let us go up to the mountain of the Lord, to the house of the God of Jacob; He will teach us His ways, and we shall walk in His paths." For out of Zion the law shall go forth, and the word of the Lord from Jerusalem.

Isaiah 2:2-3 Now it shall come to pass in the latter days that the mountain of the Lord's house shall be established on the top of the mountains, and shall be exalted above the hills; And all nations shall flow to it. 3 Many people shall come and say, "Come, and let us go up to the mountain of the Lord, to the house

of the God of Jacob; He will teach us His ways, and we shall walk
in His paths. 'For out of Zion shall go forth the law, and the
word of the Lord from Jerusalem.

So when Christ rules and reigns from the New Jerusalem, He will be commanding the nations to keep the feasts, to keep the law, and to walk according to it. Why then if Christ rules and reigns in our hearts in the current time would He want us to disregard the law? Why would He want the nations to keep His law, but not want His people to keep His law? This is completely inconsistent and illogical. Yahusha does not change just as Yah does not change, and to say He wants the nations that He will rule over in the millennium to keep the law, but doesn't want us who He rules over today to keep the law, is completely illogical.

People will also claim, "You can't really keep the feasts anyways, because there is no temple!" That is correct. There is no physical temple right now. Thankfully we have a high priest who does these things for us in the eternal temple, the New Jerusalem, and all I have to do is the things I can do, such as abstaining from work, putting leaven out of my house, or spending a week camping out in a tent. Yahusha makes it so easy for us. Just because I can't perfectly keep the feasts, doesn't mean I should disregard or ignore them. How many Christmas movies have you seen where people who are far from home and unable to "keep Christmas" properly still end up doing something special for the day by themselves or with strangers? And that's regarding a pagan antichrist holiday, how much more should we want to observe the feasts of Christ even if we can't do so perfectly? I find it very sad that Christians will fight to keep the traditional pagan holidays of the world while simultaneously fighting against keeping the commanded feasts of Yah that He gave for His people that glorify Him.

The last thing people will claim, even though I've already covered it, is that there are different laws for Jews and gentiles. I'll let the Bible take it from here.

Exodus 12:49 <u>One law</u> shall be <u>for the native-born</u> <u>and for the</u> <u>stranger</u> who dwells among you.

Leviticus 24:22 You shall have <u>the same law for the stranger and</u> <u>for one from your own country;</u> for I am the Lord your God.

Numbers 15:16 <u>One law and one custom</u> shall be <u>for you and for</u> <u>the stranger</u> who dwells with you.

Numbers 15:29 You shall have <u>one law</u> <u>for him who sins</u> <u>unintentionally, for him who is native-born among the children</u> <u>of Israel and for the stranger who dwells among them.</u>

Ecclesiastes 12:13 (NIV) Now all has been heard; here is the conclusion of the matter: Fear God and keep his commandments, for this is the duty of all mankind.

Keep His commandments is not the duty of all "Jew" kind, no, all mankind. If you are a member of mankind, it is your duty to keep His commandments. One law for all. Not different laws for different dispensations. Not different laws for different ethnicities, no, one law for the native born, and the stranger, and the one who sins unintentionally. One law. There is also only one lawgiver. While Moses may have been a lawbringer, he was not the lawgiver. Yahuah and Yahusha, He is the lawgiver as they are one. This is also why there is not a "law of Christ" and a "law of God" that are different laws, because they are one.

James 4:11-12 Do not speak evil of one another, brethren. He who speaks evil of a brother and judges his brother, speaks evil of the law and judges the law. But if you judge the law, you are not a doer of the law but a judge. 12 There is one Lawgiver, who is able to save and to destroy. Who are you to judge another?

James says to be a doer of the law, not a judge of it. Did the New Testament "church" have a different law?

> *1 John 2:3-7 Now by this we know that we know Him, if we <u>keep</u> <u>His commandments</u>. 4 He who says, "I know Him," and does not keep His commandments, is a liar, and the truth is not in him. 5 But whoever keeps <u>His word</u>, truly the love of God is perfected in him. By this we know that we are in Him. 6 He who says he abides in Him ought himself also to <u>walk just as He walked</u>. 7 Brethren, <u>I write no new commandment to you, but an old</u> <u>commandment which you have had from the beginning. The old</u> <u>commandment is the word which you heard from the beginning.</u>*

The same word from the beginning. The scriptures, the Old Testament, the law and the prophets, the Word. Christ was literally the Word made flesh. He was the perfect embodiment of the Word they had at that time, the law and the prophets. He was perfectly lawful, inside and out, and perfectly fulfilled the prophecies surrounding Him. A huge portion of what Yahusha said were direct quotes or references to the Word that was already written including the Old Testament. When you reject the law, you are literally rejecting the Word, and thus rejecting Christ. It's no wonder that He will say I never knew you to the lawless, because they never did know Him, they never knew the Word of Yah.

Remember the parable of the wheat and the tares? Who are the tares that are bundled up to be burned?

> *Matthew 13:37-43 He answered and said to them: "He who sows the good seed is the Son of Man. 38 The field is the world, the good seeds are the sons of the kingdom, but the tares are the sons of the wicked one. 39 The enemy who sowed them is the devil, the harvest is the end of the age, and the reapers are the angels. 40 Therefore as the tares are gathered and burned in the fire, so it will be at the end of this age. 41 The Son of Man will*

> *send out His angels, and they will gather out of His kingdom all*
> *things that offend, and <u>those who practice lawlessness</u>, 42 and*
> *will cast them into the furnace of fire. There will be wailing and*
> *gnashing of teeth. 43 Then the righteous will shine forth as the*
> *sun in the kingdom of their Father. He who has ears to hear, let*
> *him hear!"*

Christ will send out His angels at the end of the age to weed out the tares who practice lawlessness. I didn't write it, I'm just passing the information on to you, dear reader.

Now, I want to make a quick statement regarding all of these things. Many Christians, though they are not walking in all of the law, follow a large portion of it by nature. The weightier matters of the law, justice, mercy, and faith, are often followed by Christians. A few of these commandments include not committing adultery, not murdering, and not stealing. Most Christians keep these laws without even noticing it. This is evidence of their regeneration as the laws have begun to be written on their hearts. How about this law?

> *Deuteronomy 15:7-8 "If there is among you a poor man of your*
> *brethren, within any of the gates in your land which the Lord*
> *your God is giving you, you shall not harden your heart nor*
> *shut your hand from your poor brother, 8 but you shall open*
> *your hand wide to him and willingly lend him sufficient for his*
> *need, whatever he needs."*

Don't most Christians keep this law by nature? But this isn't in the ten commandments, and technically, it says it's only in the land Israel was given, so does that mean we shouldn't keep this law anymore? Of course not, it's written on our hearts. We do it because it is part of our nature now. Christians keep many such laws. Do you cheat your neighbor? If not, you are keeping the law by nature. Would you trip a blind man just for fun? If not, you are keeping the law by nature. What about cursing a deaf man? Is that something you would want to do? These are all laws. Most Christians keep the weightier matters of the law without even realizing it because they are written on their hearts.

The laws they continue to disobey are the laws they are continually told that they should disobey, such as keeping the feasts, eating only clean animals, and wearing tzitzit. Remember there will be those who did not keep the least of the commandments but are still in the kingdom of heaven. However we're also told your righteousness must exceed that of the scribes and pharisees to enter the kingdom of heaven. This isn't really that hard to do though, as the pharisees were arrogant, hateful, murderers who exploited widows and led people astray for the purpose of gaining the praise of men. They kept the little things, but not the weightier matters. Those who are truly born again however, often do the opposite, keeping the weightier matters, but neglecting the little things. We should be perfect, as He is perfect, keeping both the small and great to the best of our abilities.

I also feel I should touch on the food laws in particular as people believe these laws have been done away with and I mentioned them just a minute ago. First of all, if these laws had been done away with, Christ's declaration that one jot or tittle would not pass from the law until heaven and earth pass away would be directly challenged. But beyond this, did Christ teach these laws were done away with? Did Peter receive a vision that said they were? let's quickly look at these allegations.

The first allegation is that Christ taught that all food was declared to be clean.

Mark 7:19 (NIV) For it doesn't go into their heart but into their stomach, and then out of the body." (In saying this, Jesus declared all foods clean.)

Mark 7:19 (NAS) because it does not go into his heart, but into his stomach, and is eliminated?" (Thus He declared all foods _clean.)_

Mark 7:19 (KJV) Because it entereth not into his heart, but into the belly, and goeth out into the draught, purging all meats?

Notice something missing in the KJV translation? Yeah, that sentence where it says Yahusha declared all food clean was never actually in any of the Greek manuscripts, but was actually added by a translation done in the early 1900s by Wescott and Hort, who were a touch blasphemous and more interested in Catholicism and Darwinism than in scripture. There's a youtube video on these guys called "The Great Bible Heist: How the West was lost" by Christian Truthers, check it out if you want to know more about how these new translations altered the Word of Yah. This statement that Christ declared all foods clean is once again, a tradition of men, and in fact this one is particularly distasteful as this is directly putting words in the mouth of Messiah Himself. Check the interlinear for yourself. Never did Christ declare all foods clean. What He was dealing with in this verse becomes very clear in proper context.

Mark 7:5 Then the Pharisees and scribes asked Him, "Why do Your disciples not walk according to the tradition of the elders, but eat bread with unwashed hands?"

So Christ was asked why His disciples weren't keeping the traditions of men, and Christ basically explains that unwashed hands won't defile them, because the body purges out impurities. He did not declare all foods to be clean, He declared that the traditions of the elders were unnecessary.

The other portion of scripture that people try to claim allows us to eat anything is in Acts.

Acts 10:10-16 Then he became very hungry and wanted to eat; but while they made ready, he fell into a trance 11 and saw heaven opened and an object like a great sheet bound at the four

corners, descending to him and let down to the earth. 12 In it were all kinds of four-footed animals of the earth, wild beasts, creeping things, and birds of the air. 13 And a voice came to him, "Rise, Peter; kill and eat." 14 But Peter said, "Not so, Lord! For I have never eaten anything common or unclean." 15 And a voice spoke to him again the second time, "What God has cleansed you must not call common." 16 This was done three times. And the object was taken up into heaven again.

So did Peter receive a vision that told Peter to break the commandments regarding unclean foods and tell him it was okay to eat them now? Before I answer that, I want to note that if Yahusha did indeed declare all food clean, why would Peter still not have eaten anything common or unclean? In fact, why would he be calling any food unclean if Yahusha had already declared all food to be clean? Lying pens of the scribes. Now to answer the matter at hand. First of all, we need to see Peter's reaction. Peter knew better than to think he would ever be commanded to break the law of Yah, and so his reply was "Not so Lord! For I have never eaten anything common or unclean." That should by the way, be our reaction whenever someone teaches us to transgress Yah's law, "Not so!" Anyways, Peter understood that Christ would not be sending him a vision that told him to violate His laws. We know this because of Peter's reaction to this vision.

Acts 10:17 Now while Peter wondered within himself what this vision which he had seen meant, (...)

Again, Peter understood the meaning of the vision could not have been teaching disobedience, as that would contradict the entirety of the scripture and the words of Yahusha Himself, so he wondered what the vision could have meant. He was baffled. Then he explains exactly what the vision meant a few verses later in the same chapter.

Acts 10:28 Then he said to them, "You know how unlawful it is

for a Jewish man to keep company with or go to one of another nation. But God has shown me that I should not call any man common or unclean.

So Peter explains straight up, that the vision was not about unclean foods at all, but about Yah calling Peter to go the gentiles, which according to Jewish Rabbinical tradition, were unclean and a Jewish man was forbidden to enter the house of a gentile. We know that when Yahusha died, He redeemed the house of Israel to Himself, thus tearing down the wall of separation between the house of Israel and the house of Judah, bringing the two into one New Covenant.

Ephesians 2:14-16 For He Himself is our peace, who has made both one, and has broken down the middle wall of separation, 15 having abolished in His flesh the enmity, that is, the law of commandments contained in ordinances, so as to create in Himself one new man from the two, thus making peace, 16 and that He might reconcile them both to God in one body through the cross, thereby putting to death the enmity.

So Peter's vision had nothing to do with declaring food clean at all. It was about breaking down the wall of separation between Jew and gentile. Pork is still an abomination according to the scriptures. In fact, there are verses talking about the end of the age, that mentions this exact issue.

Isaiah 65:1-5 'I was sought by those who did not ask for Me; I was found by those who did not seek Me. I said, 'Here I am, here I am,' to a nation that was not called by My name. 2 I have stretched out My hands all day long to a rebellious people, who walk in a way that is not good, according to their own thoughts; 3 a people who provoke Me to anger continually to My face; who sacrifice in gardens, and burn incense on altars of brick; 4 who sit among the graves, and spend the night in the tombs; who eat swine's flesh, and the broth of abominable things is in their *vessels; 5 who say, 'Keep to yourself, do not come near me, for I* *am holier than you!' these are smoke in My nostrils, a fire that* *burns all the day.*

Isaiah 66:15-17 For behold, the Lord will come with fire, and *with His chariots, like a whirlwind, to render His anger with* *fury, and His rebuke with flames of fire. 16 For by fire and* *by His sword the Lord will judge all flesh; and the slain of the* *Lord shall be many. 17 "Those who sanctify themselves and* *purify themselves, to go to the gardens after an idol in the midst,* *eating swine's flesh and the abomination and the mouse, shall* *be consumed together," says the Lord.*

So contrary to popular belief, even at the end of the age when Christ comes with fire like a whirlwind to execute judgement, He still views eating pork and unclean animals as an abomination. In fact He says those who are going after idols and eating these things will be consumed. I've been mocked for bringing these portions of scripture up to some, but I didn't write it, you'll have to take it up with Yah. If you can't even change your eating habits for Yah, then you don't really love Him.

1 John 5:3 For this is the love of God, that we keep His command- *ments. And His commandments are not burdensome.*

John 14:15 "If you love Me, keep My commandments."

This information may upset a lot of people, but just keep in mind it was always the back-slidden, fallen Israel that put to death the prophets for telling them to repent from their wicked ways. I would admonish you not to be among the hard hearted who stop up their ears from hearing the truth, who hate those who speak the truth, because judgement is coming, and Christ will avenge.

Do you know why Yah declared some foods clean and some unclean? Because the unclean ones are filthy, and full of bacteria and parasites. Most people wouldn't be upset if you told them they couldn't eat rat anymore, but the second you try to take their bacon, they're up in arms. Do me a favor, jump on google, and google "is pork bad for you?" The medical field is finding more and more examples of tumors and infections being attributed to parasites and worms. This is a quote from mayoclinic.org:

Trichinosis (trik-ih-NO-sis), sometimes called trichinellosis (trik-ih-nuh-LOW-sis), is a type of roundworm infection. Roundworm parasites use a host body to live and reproduce. Infection occurs primarily among meat-eating animals (carnivores) such as bears and foxes, or meat- and plant-eating animals (omnivores) such as domestic pigs and wild boar. [54]

This website goes on to say that these parasites are only found in undercooked meat, but there are hundreds of studies that state there is no safe temperature for consumption in which all the worms are definitively dead. Further, whether dead or alive in the meat, you are still consuming worm larva, which is pretty disgusting if you ask me. Notice that it mentions bears, foxes, and pigs in particular, all of which are unclean. Pork was never intended to be food. God created pigs, and made them for a specific purpose. That purpose was to act as a vacuum cleaner for the earth. It sucks up all manner of filth into it's body, and gets trapped there. When you eat it, your body takes those filth ridden nutrients, and tries to repair your body with them, thus you become compromised on a cellular level. In fact, there is evidence that suggests that once your body has been compromised internally by impurities, it damages your bodies defense against other dangers such as harmful bacteria and even cancer cells. I know a shocking amount of Christians that have cancer, and it is extremely sad. Many of them I have spent lots of time praying for. Sometimes Yah in His wisdom allows a person to suffer or pass away from an illness and only He really knows the reason why. In spite of all of that, I cannot help but feel that maybe the Body of Christ would be just a little bit healthier overall if we obeyed Yah and abstained from eating the foods He called an abomination, foods that are filled with impurities and worms and parasites.

It's not just pork either. Shrimp is unclean, and literally has a muck vein full of filth running through it because they vacuum up the feces and filth from other creatures. Shellfish are unclean because they are literally living water filters, and people get sick and even die from shellfish all the time. Again, nobody gets mad if you try to take their roast dog away, but you suggest they shouldn't be eating lobster and they're ready to throw you out the window. Yah gave the food laws for a reason, and to say "Jesus declared all food clean" or "Peter got a vision saying we can eat anything now" is to both rebel against Yah's commandments, as well as to purposefully compromise and destroy your body. If your body is the temple, how do you think Yah feels about you putting things He calls an abomination into it? Yah gave us His food laws because He loves us and wants us to be healthy, not because He's some tyrant who wants to take away your yummy bacon. Your bacon will make you sick, He wants to protect you from that. Enough about the food laws though, you get it or you don't.

To sum it all up, in the entirety of the Bible, there is one message, one God, one Savior, one people, one law, one Lawgiver, and one path that leads to life; faith in Christ, and obedience to His commandments. This is the narrow way.

25

Faith

Let me tie this all in together before we move on from here. The story of the Bible is the story of Yah, His Messiah, and His people throughout the ages and in the ages to come. Genesis to Revelation this is what it has all been about. Let me give you an extremely simplified overlook of the Bible.

All the way at the beginning, Yah made Adam. He said to Adam, I have made you a paradise, I have put you in charge of it, you have peace, you have dominion, you have joy, you have good things to eat, and you get to walk with me and talk with me face to face. I even gave you a beautiful helper to be your companion. All you have to do, is keep my commandment. Don't eat the fruit that will give you knowledge of good and of evil. You can eat fruit from anywhere, the whole garden of Eden is your kingdom, just don't eat from that one single tree. Adam and Eve ate of the tree anyways and disobeyed Yah. He lays a curse on them, casts them out of the garden, and into a dark and difficult world they went.

Some time passes, Yah once more tells people like Cain for example, hey, if you keep my commandments and do what is right, I'll bless you, but if not, you'll be destroyed. They turn to evil anyways and the world overwhelmingly chooses sin, to the point that the entire earth and everything in it becomes corrupted. Yah decides to wipe the slate clean.

He destroys everyone except for Noah and his family. He tells them, walk in my ways, and I'll bless you, otherwise, you'll perish just like the people I just wiped out for their sins. Once again people almost immediately begin to turn against the commandment of Yah and against doing good.

Eventually, we find Abraham, who in spite of all the wickedness going on around him wants to do what's right and serve Yah. Yah meets with him, and enters into covenant with him. He says, believe my words, obey my voice, and I will make you a great nation. Abraham believes Yah, obeys His word, and walks with Him. Abraham begets Isaac, and Isaac begets Jacob, and Jacob begets the children of Israel. The children of Israel sin, and sell off their brother into slavery, and Yah uses it to save them, however, a few generations later, they've become the captives in the very land they sold their brother into. They cry out to Yah, and He says, okay, I'll send Moses, he feared me enough to leave Egypt behind. So Yah meets with and sends Moses who leads the people out of Egypt.

Right out of Egypt, Yah says, okay, since you people obviously don't know how to behave, let me break it down for you. I'll give you my law, the standard of righteousness, my ways, so you'll know exactly what is expected of you. I will enter into covenant with you, if you walk in my ways, and are obedient to my commandments, you'll be blessed, and I'll bring you into a bounteous land flowing with milk and honey and give you an eternal inheritance. If you disobey my law, and do not believe my voice, you'll be cursed, and heap judgement on your heads and be destroyed. They eventually find their way into the land after having to wander in the wilderness for disobedience and murmuring and complaining. Yah says, here's the land I promised you. Don't serve other gods, don't do evil in my sight, look, I've laid it all out for you. All you have to do is keep my commandments and follow the law I've laid out for you. If you do these things, I'll dwell with you, I'll bless you, and I'll give you abundantly more than anything you could hope for. All you have to do, is keep my laws and commandments, and serve me only. If you disobey, I'll bring judgement on you. Israel agrees, enters into covenant and begins to prosper. In their prosperity, Israel forgets about Yah, turning to other gods and breaking His commandments.

He sends prophets to plead with them, and instead of listening, they put the prophets to death, hardening their hearts. Yah sends judgement on them for their stubbornness and rebellion. Israel cries out to Yah, and He says, okay, I'll fix the problem and take away the judgement, I'll bless you again and protect you, all you have to do, is serve me only, do not serve other gods, and keep my commandments and follow my laws. They say, okay, we'll do it. Before too long they once again turn to other gods and break his commandments. This process repeats itself a few times. Finally Yah says, enough, I'll send prophets to tell them that if they do not obey me, and keep my commandments, and forsake their false gods, I'll drive them out of their land, and give them into captivity and hard servitude. Once again instead of listening, they kill the prophets and do even more evil than they did before.

Yah takes ten of the twelve tribes of Israel, and divorces them, and scatters them out to the other nations. This would show the other two tribes, the house of Judah, that He was serious right? This would scare them into obeying Him right? He says, if you don't keep my commandments, and serve me only, I'll scatter you just like I did with the rest of the tribes. I'll send you into captivity, and you'll be desolate, stuck in servitude to cruel masters. In spite of this warning, they turn even harder to evil, and as promised, Yah sends them into captivity. Eventually the time of their punishment is up, and Yah returns them to their land. He says, okay, guys, you've watched as your sister tribes have been destroyed and carried away for not keeping my commandments and serving other gods, and you yourselves have just undergone fierce judgement for a few hundred years for disobeying me, and breaking my commandments, and turning to other gods. Now, I'm telling you again, keep my commandments, and walk in my ways, or else. Things go okay for a while, but Israel once again rebels against Yah, ignoring His commandments and His warnings.

Finally, Yah sends His Son, His Word, to physically come in the flesh. His Son comes and says, guys, you need to repent, you need to turn. You need to keep my commandments. You've replaced my commandments with the commandments of men, and have warped my law into a heavy burden. Repent of your sins and walk in my ways. Look, I've come to bring back the house of Israel who were scattered and restore Israel, and I've come to pay for your sins so that you no longer have to bear them. I've come to redeem you. Believe in me, follow me, enter into covenant with me, and keep my commandments. In spite of this, the house of Judah is so backslidden, instead of hearing Him, they want to kill Him. He says, you know what, I wanted to gather you, and heal you, but you were unwilling, your house is left to you desolate, and I'm going to take your kingdom, your inheritance, and give it to the gentiles, so that anyone who joins themselves to me, to enter into covenant with me, will be saved. The covenant you and I had is done, it is erased, and I am putting forth a new covenant with myself at the center. I am the door to the kingdom now.

He then lays down His life, His own people putting Him to death, and He rises again from the dead. He tells His disciples, go out into the world, tell everyone you find they can enter into covenant with me. Tell everyone the message, believe in me, believe my word, enter into covenant with me, keep my commandments, I will be your God, and you will be my people, and I will give you eternal life, and peace and joy. Look, I'll even send my Spirit to you, so that you can have my Spirit in you, writing my laws on your heart, so that you can walk in my ways, and keep my commandments. With this message in hand, the apostles go out and begin to preach the message. The enemy goes into overtime to stamp out the truth, and replaces the gospel of the kingdom with a new gospel that proposes the law of Yah is done away with, and any obedience to the "Jewish" law, is contrary to the will of Yah. With military force and persecution Satan pushes forward this false gospel and a false church until it becomes a tradition handed down throughout the generations.

In the modern day, Yah has given us His law so we would know what sin is. He has given us the prophets to warn us what happens if we turn from His laws and commandments, and serve other gods. He has given us the history of Israel so we could see what happens when we disobey. He has given us His Son as the pattern of how to walk in His commandments and walk in His ways. He has given us atonement through the blood of His Son, to wipe away our sins. He's given us the writings of His disciples, to teach us and help us in our walk. He's given us His Spirit to write His laws on our hearts, and change us from the inside out so that we will walk in His ways by nature. Christ Himself has personally taken over the duties of high priest, and is Himself the final sin sacrifice needed for all mankind, making keeping the law and walking in His ways easier than ever. We have promises of blessing if we do keep His commandments, we have promises of judgments if we disobey His commandments, we have everything going for us to keep His law that we possibly could.

In spite of all of this, we say "His law is a burden", "You're bewitched if you follow the law", "It's sin to follow the law", "That's only for the Jews", "That wasn't written for us", "Only some of the law matters", "Christ abolished the law", "I'm not under the law", "I'm under grace so the law doesn't matter", and many other things. What more could Yah have possibly done for us? He gave everything. He spelled out the law, He rewarded His people for keeping His law, He punished them for disobeying the law, He gave good promises for those that keep it, He gave curses for those who break it, He gave us His son to forgive us and show us exactly how to keep His laws, He gave us His Spirit to write His laws on our hearts. He even gave us an example in the Old Testament to show us what a man after His own heart looks like. Psalm 119 was written by David, the man after Yah's own heart, and is the longest chapter in the entire Bible, and is all about how much David loves the law of Yah. He even gave time frames for some of His commandments such as "forever", "throughout your generations", and "eternal". Others He said, "until heaven and earth pass away" making sure we know absolutely that His law is in effect in this current age. Still, after all that, we disregard His laws and trample on His commandments.

What more could He have given? What more could He have possibly done? Did He withhold anything from us? Still we disobey Him and trample on His ways calling them a curse, a burden, an evil, and something to throw away and discard and mock. No wonder the worst punishment that has ever fallen on the earth is about to come. No wonder the trumpets and bowls of wrath are to be poured out on the earth. Meanwhile the Christian church who has thrown away His laws and trampled on His commandments and called them a burden and bondage and have fallen into idolatry really think they are just going to escape all of these things and be free from any chastisement. The Bible says judgment begins in the house of Yah, not skips over it. They speak soft and sweet lies to one another saying, "Our actions don't matter, all that matters is that you believe." And "We'll never see judgment, that's for those who reject Him." This was all foretold. We have itching ears that cannot abide sound doctrine. We eagerly swallow sweet lies, while we utterly reject bitter truths. How many lies have we swallowed? How hard have we made our hearts? Truly we honor Him with our lips, but our hearts are far from Him. Yah gave us every possible advantage to walk according to His ways, and still in spite of everything, we are still walking in rebellion.

Matthew 21:33-43 "Hear another parable: There was a certain landowner who planted a vineyard and set a hedge around it, dug a winepress in it and built a tower. And he leased it to vinedressers and went into a far country. 34 Now when vintage-time drew near, he sent his servants to the vinedressers, that they might receive its fruit. 35 And the vinedressers took his servants, beat one, killed one, and stoned another. 36 Again he sent other servants, more than the first, and they did likewise to them. 37 Then last of all he sent his son to them, saying, 'They will respect my son.' 38 But when the vinedressers saw the son, they said among themselves, 'This is the heir. Come, let us kill him and seize his inheritance.' 39 So they took him and cast him out of the vineyard and killed him.

40 "Therefore, when the owner of the vineyard comes, what will he do to those vinedressers?"

41 They said to Him, "He will destroy those wicked men miserably, and lease his vineyard to other vinedressers who will render to him the fruits in their seasons."

42 Jesus said to them, "Have you never read in the Scriptures: The stone which the builders rejected has become the chief cornerstone. This was the Lord's doing, and it is marvelous in our eyes'?

43 "Therefore I say to you, the kingdom of God will be taken from you and given to a nation bearing the fruits of it. 44 And whoever falls on this stone will be broken; but on whomever it falls, it will grind him to powder."

And now the parallel.

Isaiah 5:1-30 Now let me sing to my Well-beloved, a song of my Beloved regarding His vineyard: My Well-beloved has a vineyard on a very fruitful hill. 2 He dug it up and cleared out its stones, and planted it with the choicest vine. He built a tower in its midst, and also made a winepress in it; So He expected it to bring forth good grapes, but it brought forth wild grapes.

3 "And now, O inhabitants of Jerusalem and men of Judah, judge, please, between Me and My vineyard. 4 What more could have been done to My vineyard that I have not done in it? Why then, when I expected it to bring forth good grapes, did it bring forth wild grapes?

5 And now, please let Me tell you what I will do to My vineyard: I will take away its hedge, and it shall be burned; and break down its wall, and it shall be trampled down. 6 I will lay it waste; It shall not be pruned or dug, but there shall come up briers and thorns. I will also command the clouds that they rain no rain on it."

7 For the vineyard of the Lord of hosts is the house of Israel, and the men of Judah are His pleasant plant. He looked for justice, but behold, oppression; for righteousness, but behold, a cry for help.

8 Woe to those who join house to house; they add field to field, till there is no place where they may dwell alone in the midst of the land! 9 In my hearing the Lord of hosts said, "Truly, many houses shall be desolate, great and beautiful ones, without inhabitant. 10 For ten acres of vineyard shall yield one bath, and a homer of seed shall yield one ephah."

11 Woe to those who rise early in the morning, that they may follow intoxicating drink; Who continue until night, till wine inflames them! 12 The harp and the strings, the tambourine and flute, and wine are in their feasts; but they do not regard the work of the Lord, nor consider the operation of His hands.

13 Therefore my people have gone into captivity, because they have no knowledge; their honorable men are famished, and their multitude dried up with thirst. 14 Therefore Sheol has enlarged itself and opened its mouth beyond measure; Their glory and their multitude and their pomp, and he who is jubilant, shall descend into it. 15 People shall be brought down, each man shall be humbled, and the eyes of the lofty shall be humbled.

16 But the Lord of hosts shall be exalted in judgment, and God who is holy shall be hallowed in righteousness. 17 Then the lambs shall feed in their pasture, and in the waste places of the fat ones strangers shall eat.

18 Woe to those who draw iniquity with cords of vanity, and sin as if with a cart rope; 19 That say, "Let Him make speed and hasten His work, that we may see it; And let the counsel of the Holy One of Israel draw near and come, that we may know it."

20 Woe to those who call evil good, and good evil; who put darkness for light, and light for darkness; who put bitter for sweet, and sweet for bitter! 21 Woe to those who are wise in their own eyes, and prudent in their own sight! 22 Woe to men mighty at drinking wine, woe to men valiant for mixing intoxicating drink, 23 who justify the wicked for a bribe, and take away justice from the righteous man!

24 Therefore, as the fire devours the stubble, and the flame consumes the chaff, so their root will be as rottenness, and their blossom will ascend like dust; <u>because they have rejected the law of the Lord of hosts, and despised the word of the Holy One of Israel. 25 Therefore the anger of the Lord is aroused against His people</u>; He has stretched out His hand against them and stricken them, and the hills trembled. Their carcasses were as refuse in the midst of the streets. For all this His anger is not turned away, but His hand is stretched out still.

26 He will lift up a banner to the nations from afar, and will whistle to them from the end of the earth; surely they shall come with speed, swiftly. 27 No one will be weary or stumble among them, no one will slumber or sleep; Nor will the belt on their loins be loosed, nor the strap of their sandals be broken; 28

Whose arrows are sharp, and all their bows bent; Their horses'
hooves will seem like flint, and their wheels like a whirlwind.
29 Their roaring will be like a lion, they will roar like young
lions; Yes, they will roar and lay hold of the prey; They will
carry it away safely, and no one will deliver. 30 In that day
they will roar against them like the roaring of the sea. and if
one looks to the land, behold, darkness and sorrow; And the light
is darkened by the clouds.

You can try to hide behind the doctrines of men. You can try to reason your way around things. You can point to your theology degree, or look at all the people around you who hold the same theology. You can claim these things were written for others. You can say belief is the only thing that matters. You can keep telling yourself you're rapture ready and no wrath will come against you. You can tell yourself that no matter how backslidden you get, you'll never face judgement. You can do all of these, but you cannot change the Word of Yah, and you cannot stand against Him. Truly, many will say to Yahusha, "Lord look at all the things I did for you! I witnessed to people! I was in your house every Sunday faithfully! I saw people healed, and demons cast out! You know me!" but He will say "depart from me you who practice lawlessness, I never knew you." You can claim faith all day long, but do you know what faith looks like?

James 1:1 James, a bondservant of God and of the Lord Jesus
Christ, to the twelve tribes which are scattered abroad:

James 1:22-25 But be doers of the word, and not hearers only,
deceiving yourselves. 23 For if anyone is a hearer of the word
and not a doer, he is like a man observing his natural face in a
mirror; 24 for he observes himself, goes away, and immediately
forgets what kind of man he was. 25 But he who looks into the
perfect law of liberty and continues in it, and is not a forgetful
hearer but a doer of the work, this one will be blessed in what

he does.

James 2:18-26 But someone will say, "You have faith, and I have works." Show me your faith without your works, and I will show you my faith by my works. 19 You believe that there is one God. You do well. Even the demons believe—and tremble! 20 But do you want to know, O foolish man, that faith without works is dead? 21 Was not Abraham our father justified by works when he offered Isaac his son on the altar? 22 Do you see that faith was working together with his works, and by works faith was made perfect? 23 And the Scripture was fulfilled which says, "Abraham believed God, and it was accounted to him for righteousness." And he was called the friend of God. 24 You see then that a man is justified by works, and not by faith only. 25 Likewise, was not Rahab the harlot also justified by works when she received the messengers and sent them out another way? 26 For as the body without the spirit is dead, so faith without works is dead also.

Faith without works is dead because works are the evidence of faith. Works do not save you, but faith without works is not faith at all. Not everything that swims is a fish, but every fish swims. No amount of works can give you salvation. Salvation comes only through trusting Christ. It is a free gift that none of us deserve. But the proof that you have been born again, that you have salvation, is that you walk in His ways and forsake your sins.

What if Abraham had heard Yah command him to offer Isaac and disobeyed? What if he had decided offering Isaac didn't make sense to him, or was too big of a burden for him and decided not to do it? Would he have still had faith? That he offered Isaac willingly in obedience is the evidence that he did have faith. What of Rahab? Rahab said the reason she didn't want trouble to come on the spies was because she feared the God they served and had heard Jericho would be destroyed. She heard what Yah spoke, and decided to believe what had been spoken, and respond accordingly. She sent a scarlet thread out her window as a sign, she took her whole family and hid them in her house during the siege. Yes she believed in Yah, but that was only the first step, and that alone would not have saved her and her family. She heard the warnings that Yah gave and the judgement He promised. She acted accordingly and changed her actions to align with His Word, thus she was saved.

This is faith. It is not merely belief, it is adjusting your life according to His word. It is not merely a hope that you won't come under judgement, it is taking actions to ensure that you don't according to His word, because you believe what He says. He makes it abundantly clear what is expected of us, and very clear we will face judgment if we do not obey Him. Thus if we have faith, we will obey Him because we believe that He will punish those who disobey and reward those who obey, as He has said that He will. That is true faith. Believing you can act however you want, and trample on His commandments, and because you said a little prayer you're exempt from all judgement is faith in the false teachings and doctrines of men, and not in the Word of Yah. The gospel that all you have to do is believe that God has a son who died for you and you're headed to heaven is not good news but a sweet lie. The true gospel requires obedience and submission. Salvation is a free gift, but we have to walk in that gift, as a new creation, not as in the former lusts. The true gospel declares that Yahusha is Lord and Master, not just a ride along buddy who keeps you out of the fire. He is King of Kings, and His Word and His commandments stand. He and His Father are one, and whoever has seen Him has seen the Father. His law is His Father's law, and that law is for the native born among the kingdom, and the stranger and foreigner who sojourns with Him. One law for all men.

Too many have disobeyed the gospel.

Romans 10:16-17 <u>But they have not all obeyed the gospel.</u> For

Isaiah says, "Lord, who has believed our report?" 17 So then faith comes by hearing, and hearing by the word of God.

Most don't even know that you can disobey the gospel. This is because the gospel so often preached doesn't even mention obedience. It is true that if you seek to be justified by keeping the law that you will find no salvation for your soul. There is no other way into the kingdom but through Christ. However, once we enter into covenant and become part of the kingdom, we are responsible to obey the laws of the kingdom. If an immigrant comes to the United States and wants to become a part of the US, they are expected to keep the United States laws. They do not get to steal and murder and run red lights just because they were not born here. If they want to be a citizen of the nation, they follow the laws of the nation.

In this passage above Paul also directly references Isaiah here so maybe we should see what Isaiah has to say. Faith comes by hearing and hearing by the Word of Yah. Isaiah is a part of the Word of Yah. Who has believed Isaiah's report?

Isaiah 5:24 Therefore, as the fire devours the stubble, and the flame consumes the chaff, so their root will be as rottenness, and their blossom will ascend like dust; because they have rejected the law of the Lord of hosts, and despised the word of the Holy One of Israel.

Isaiah 24:5 The earth is also defiled under it's inhabitants, because they have transgressed the laws, changed the ordinance, broken the everlasting covenant.

Isaiah 30:8-9 Now go, write it before them on a tablet, and note it on a scroll, that it may be for time to come, forever and ever: 9 That this is a rebellious people, lying children, children who will not hear the law of the Lord;

Isaiah 42:23-24 Who among you will give ear to this? <u>Who will listen and hear for the time to come?</u> 24 Who gave Jacob for plunder, and Israel to the robbers? Was it not the Lord, He against whom we have sinned? <u>For they would not walk in His ways, nor were they obedient to His law.</u>

Isaiah 48:17-18 <u>Thus says the Lord, your Redeemer, the Holy One of Israel:</u>
"I am the Lord your God, who teaches you to profit, who leads you by the way you should go. 18 <u>Oh, that you had heeded My commandments!</u> Then your peace would have been like a river, and your righteousness like the waves of the sea.

Isaiah 51:6-8 Lift up your eyes to the heavens, and look on the earth beneath. For the heavens will vanish away like smoke, the earth will grow old like a garment, and those who dwell in it will die in like manner; <u>But My salvation will be forever, and My righteousness will not be abolished.</u> 7 <u>"Listen to Me, you who know righteousness, you people in whose heart is My law:</u> Do not fear the reproach of men, nor be afraid of their insults. 8 For the moth will eat them up like a garment, and the worm will eat them like wool; but My righteousness will be forever, and My salvation from generation to generation."

Isaiah 56:1-8 Thus says the Lord:
"Keep justice, and do righteousness, for My salvation is about to come, and My righteousness to be revealed. 2 Blessed is the man who does this, and the son of man who lays hold on it; who keeps from defiling the Sabbath, and keeps his hand from doing any evil."
3 Do not let the son of the foreigner who has joined himself to the Lord
speak, saying, "The Lord has utterly separated me from His

people"; Nor let the eunuch say, "Here I am, a dry tree." 4 For thus says the Lord: "To the eunuchs who keep My Sabbaths, and choose what pleases Me, and hold fast My covenant, 5 Even to them I will give in My house and within My walls a place and a name better than that of sons and daughters; I will give them an everlasting name that shall not be cut off.

6 "Also the sons of the foreigner who join themselves to the Lord, to serve Him, and to love the name of the Lord, to be His servants— everyone who keeps from defiling the Sabbath, and holds fast My covenant— 7 Even them I will bring to My holy mountain,
and make them joyful in My house of prayer. Their burnt offerings and their sacrifices
Will be accepted on My altar; For My house shall be called a house of prayer for all nations." 8 The Lord God, who gathers the outcasts of Israel, says, "Yet I will gather to him others besides those who are gathered to him."

By the way, in Isaiah 56:1 when it says "My Salvation is about to come", the word for salvation there is literally Yeshua. So the verse reads, "Keep justice and do righteousness, for My ~~Salvation~~ Yeshua is about to come." What time do you think this is speaking of? Clearly it is talking about the time right before Yahusha returns. It also talks about His house being a house of prayer for all nations and Him bringing men to His holy mountain which will all be after Yahusha returns adding weight to this assertion. He says those who keep His Sabbaths and hold fast to the covenant and do righteousness will be rewarded. The Sabbath is done away with and the feasts are only for the Jews? Do you believe the Word of Yah? Because it specifically mentions the stranger, and the foreigner who joins himself to Yah that they should keep these things up until the time that Yahusha comes. These things are not for the Jew only, but for everyone who accepts the gospel of the kingdom.

Again, there are many who are born again who do not know these things. They are walking in what they have been given, but they are not walking fully in truth. I believe there is indeed salvation for them. I do not believe you have to perfectly keep the law to have salvation, as salvation comes from repenting from our sins, and trusting in Christ as the only atonement for our sin, but we need to be striving to walk as He walked. We need to follow Him. We need to take up our cross. We need to abide in Him.

> *John 15:1-8 "I am the true vine, and My Father is the vinedresser. 2 Every branch in Me that does not bear fruit He takes away; and every* branch *that bears fruit He prunes, that it may bear more fruit. 3 You are already clean because of the word which I have spoken to you. 4 Abide in Me, and I in you. As the branch cannot bear fruit of itself, unless it abides in the vine, neither can you, unless you abide in Me. 5 "I am the vine, you* are *the branches. He who abides in Me, and I in him, bears much fruit; for without Me you can do nothing. 6 If anyone does not abide in Me, he is cast out as a branch and is withered; and they gather them and throw* them *into the fire, and they are burned. 7 If you abide in Me, and My words abide in you, you will ask what you desire, and it shall be done for you. 8 By this My Father is glorified, that you bear much fruit; so you will be My disciples.*

Faith is not merely understanding or knowledge. It is trust that what Yah says will come to pass. It is trust that when He says His commandments are forever and will not be abolished, that they will not be abolished. It is trusting in His word when He says those who disobey His law will not go unpunished. It is changing your ways to align with His. It is being willing to change because you fear Him, love Him, and want to please Him. It is walking with Him and abiding in Him and obeying His Word. It is not a works based salvation, but a faith based justification followed by a sanctification process through taking up our cross and following Him and abiding in Him and bearing fruit.

Do you have faith? Do you believe the Word of Yah? Have you believed the report of Isaiah and the other prophets? Will you walk in His ways, or will you disobey the gospel? I beg you, dear reader, do not turn your ear against hearing the law of Yah, lest your prayers be ignored.

> *Proverbs 28:9 One who turns away his ear from hearing the law, even his prayer is an abomination.*

Listen and obey His word, serve Him only, and walk with Him, or else.

> *Jeremiah 11:9-11 And the Lord said to me, "A conspiracy has been found among the men of Judah and among the inhabitants of Jerusalem. 10 They have turned back to the iniquities of their forefathers who refused to hear My words, and they have gone after other gods to serve them; the house of Israel and the house of Judah have broken My covenant which I made with their fathers." 11 Therefore thus says the Lord: "Behold, I will surely bring calamity on them which they will not be able to escape; and though they cry out to Me, I will not listen to them.*

> *Zechariah 7:12-13 Yes, they made their hearts like flint, refusing to hear the law and the words which the Lord of hosts had sent by His Spirit through the former prophets. Thus great wrath came from the Lord of hosts. 13 Therefore it happened, that just as He proclaimed and they would not hear, so they called out and I would not listen," says the Lord of hosts.*

If you do not believe the words I have spoken to you in the past few chapters, I ask that you believe the prophets that Yah has sent to proclaim His words to His people. If you are among His people, these words are for you. Repent from your lawlessness, and turn to Him. Believe His Word, keep His commandments, submit to His son, and have faith. This is the gospel of the kingdom.

26

Digging Our Own Graves

So, as I mentioned much earlier, dual covenant theology and dispensationalism has helped to set up the deception of the end times, and has led to complete lawlessness. We also saw that it was the wealthy elite that pushed forward this theology through Scofield and Darby, and is heading towards a very definitive goal. What is this goal? It's very simple, the kingdom of the antichrist. What does dual covenant theology have to do with the reign of the antichrist? Well, as stated multiple times, dual covenant theology suggests that there are different laws for the Jews and gentiles, and this ideology isn't just present in Christianity. It is in fact heavily present in the world of Judaism as well. There is a movement being pushed forward by the wealthy elite and the Zionist powers in Jerusalem for a universal law to be enforced in the earth. These laws are known as the seven Noahide laws. Like many Christians, they claim the Old Testament law is only and exclusively for the Jews, and the gentiles have a different law altogether. They claim that these seven laws were given by Yah, to Noah, and are the foundation for all "gentile" morality. They are as follows:

1. Do not commit idolatry
2. Do not blaspheme God
3. Do not murder
4. Do not engage in illicit sexual relations

5. Do not steal
6. Do not eat from a live animal
7. Create a legal system of justice

Now these don't appear bad on the surface, in fact, many of them mirror those found in the ten commandments. This is what Christians often refer to when they're talking about the "moral laws" without knowing it. The issue isn't in the actual commandments, but the ones who will be enforcing them, and how they are interpreted.

Before we go any further in this chapter, I want to remind you, dear reader, that the information contained in this chapter does not encompass all of those of Jewish descent, or even all the adherents to Judaism. Much of this information is concealed until you have been in Judaism for a while, and even then these things aren't always eagerly published. I have no desire to create animosity towards anyone, but nevertheless have to expose the darkness so you see what's really going on in the world.

Alright, back to the Noahide laws, Before we delve into the issues the laws present, we need to understand just how significant the move for these laws is. The seven Noahide laws are being accelerated into acceptance at an alarming rate and in fact have been quietly moving into place for quite some time. In 2007, there was a meeting that took place between a Vatican official and a member of the Bilateral Commission. Here is an excerpt from the official document on that meeting, quoted from the official Vatican website, Vatican.va

> 3. God has created the human person as a social being which by definition places limits on individual human freedom. Moreover freedom of choice is derived from God and therefore is not absolute, but must reflect Divine will and law. Accordingly human beings are called to freely obey the Divine will as manifested in the Creation and in His revealed word.
>
> Jewish tradition emphasizes the Noachide Covenant (cf. Gn 9: 9-12) as containing. the universal moral code which is incumbent

on all humanity. This idea is reflected in Christian Scripture in the Book of Acts 15: 28-29. [55]

So the Vatican officially recognizes that the "Noachide Covenant" or the Noahide laws, "contain the universal moral code which is incumbent on all humanity" and even claim that Acts supports this. In other words, the Vatican agrees with the Noahide laws as being the standard for morality and claims the Bible does as well. We will dissect that more in a moment. The United States echoed this assertion in 1991 under the leadership of George H.W. Bush. This record is found in the official congress.gov website.

—H.J.Res.104—
H.J.Res.104
One Hundred Second Congress of the United States of America
AT THE FIRST SESSION
Begun and held at the City of Washington on Thursday, the third day of January, one thousand nine hundred and ninety-one
Joint Resolution
To designate March 26, 1991, as 'Education Day, U.S.A.'.
Whereas Congress recognizes the historical tradition of ethical values and principles which are the basis of civilized society and upon which our great Nation was founded;
Whereas these ethical values and principles have been the bedrock of society from the dawn of civilization, when they were known as the Seven Noahide Laws;
Whereas without these ethical values and principles the edifice of civilization stands in serious peril of returning to chaos;
Whereas society is profoundly concerned with the recent weakening of these principles that has resulted in crises that beleaguer and threaten the fabric of civilized society;
Whereas the justified preoccupation with these crises must not let the citizens of this Nation lose sight of their responsibility to transmit these historical ethical values from our distinguished past to the generations

of the future;

Whereas the <u>Lubavitch movement has fostered and promoted these</u> <u>ethical values and principles throughout the world;</u>

Whereas <u>Rabbi Menachem Mendel Schneerson, leader of the</u> <u>Lubavitch movement,</u> is universally respected and revered and his eighty-ninth birthday falls on March 26, 1991;

Whereas in tribute to this great spiritual leader, 'the rebbe', this, his ninetieth year will be seen as one of 'education and giving', the year in which we turn to education and charity <u>to return the world to the</u> <u>moral and ethical values contained in the Seven Noahide Laws;</u> and

Whereas this will be reflected in <u>an international scroll of honor</u> <u>signed by the President of the United States and other heads of state:</u> Now, therefore, be it

Resolved by the Senate and House of Representatives of the United States of America in Congress assembled, That March 26, 1991, the start of the ninetieth year of Rabbi Menachem Schneerson, leader of the worldwide Lubavitch movement, is designated as 'Education Day, U.S.A.'. The President is requested to issue a proclamation calling upon the people of the United States to observe such day with appropriate ceremonies and activities.

Speaker of the House of Representatives.
Vice President of the United States and
President of the Senate. [56]

I apologize for the long quote, but it was important for you to see all of it. The Vatican and the United States both have official documentation that they affirm the Noahide laws are the standard of ethics and the building blocks of society, and the United States speaks of helping to "return the world to the moral and ethical values contained in the Seven Noahide Laws". They also mention Rabbi Menachim Schneerson, who was really not the greatest guy and we have a quote from him a bit further on. Beyond the Vatican and the United States, the UN has even picked up this torch and is moving this agenda forward as well. This is an excerpt from the official UN website, UN.org

> *UNITED NATIONS, New York(June 10, 2013)–On the heels of the Lubavitcher Rebbe's 19th Yahrtzeit, members of the UN Diplomatic corps, UN Press Officers, and other officials gathered at the UN headquarters in New York to learn how the Seven Noahide Laws must play a key role in international efforts for world peace. "On this day, people from all over the world gathered on behalf of the Laws of Noah," said Rabbi Yakov D. Cohen, head of the Institute of Noahide Code, which sponsored the conference. "Their observance is required, so that the vision of the United Nations—to have a settled and civilized world, filled with economic justice and righteousness—will prevail." [57]*

So these laws are even approved by the UN and fit in with their vision of a unified world and "play a key role in international efforts for world peace". There are groups such as the "Noahide in Moscow" in Russia, who are actively working to promote these laws as well. All over the world nations are being brought together to accept and declare these Noahide Laws. Now, again, this doesn't sound dangerous until you realize some of the details.

First of all, one of the Noahide Laws is to establish a judicial system. The UN, America, the Vatican, and others are completely on board with this. This judicial system will have to be represented in one system with a council over it, making judgments based upon these Noahide laws. Where might this system be instituted and who will be presiding over it? Why Jerusalem of course. After all, the Rabbinical Jews are the ones who have put forward these Noahide laws. These laws are according to their traditions and interpretations, so it would make sense they would oversee the enforcement of these laws right? Thus we have the "High Council of B'nei Noach". This is an excerpt from the Wikipedia page regarding this council.

> *The High Council of B'nei Noah is a group of Noahides who, at*

the request of the nascent Sanhedrin, gathered in Israel on Monday January 10, 2006/10 Tevet 5766 to be recognized as an international Noahide organization for the purpose of serving as a bridge between the Sanhedrin and Noahides worldwide. There were ten initial members who flew to Israel and pledged to uphold the Seven Laws of Noah and to conduct themselves under the authority of the Noahide beit din (religious court) of the Sanhedrin. [58]

So in Israel, in Jerusalem, there is a group of ten members of this council, who will act as the bridge to help enforce and oversee the Noahide laws throughout the world. In other words, Jerusalem will be, in a way, ruling over the world.

> **Revelation 17:18 And the woman whom you saw is that great city which reigns over the kings of the earth."**

It also just so happens that there are exactly 10 members of this High Council that essentially dictate to the nations the interpretations and methods of enforcement of the Noahide laws.

> **Revelation 17:12-13 "The ten horns which you saw are ten kings who have received no kingdom as yet, but they receive authority for one hour as kings with the beast. 13 These are of one mind, and they will give their power and authority to the beast.**

Now, what is so wrong with enforcing laws against murder and adultery and other "moral" laws? Very simple, the interpretations and the space between the lines.

First of all, understand that according to Judaism, Yahusha was just some upstart Jew who claimed to be God, and sparked a cult following. In fact, technically the reason they had Yahusha put to death was for "blasphemy".

> **Matthew 26:63-66 But Jesus kept silent. And the high priest**

answered and said to Him, 'I put You under oath by the living God: Tell us if You are the Christ, the Son of God!"

64 Jesus said to him, 'It is as you said. Nevertheless, I say to you, hereafter you will see the Son of Man sitting at the right hand of the Power, and coming on the clouds of heaven."

65 Then the high priest tore his clothes, saying, "He has spoken blasphemy! What further need do we have of witnesses? Look, now you have heard His blasphemy! 66 What do you think?" They answered and said, "He is deserving of death."

The Jews at that time denied that Yahusha was the Christ, the Son of Yah, and they deny it to this day. That means anyone who claims that Yahusha is the son of Yah is a blasphemer. Anyone who serves Christ or bows to Him is an idolater according to the Rabbinical Jews. A quote from the Encyclopedia Judaica:

G-d alone is to be worshipped, directly and with-out any conjoining or intermediary, and He alone desires and hears prayer out of His love for all mankind.

1 Timothy 2:5 For there is one God and one Mediator between God and men, the Man Christ Jesus,

What's the penalty for breaking this or any other Noahide laws? From Sanhedrin 57a:

The Gemara asks: And is a descendant of Noah executed for idol worship? But isn't it taught in a baraita: With regard to idol worship, matters for which a Jewish court executes the transgressor are prohibited to a descendant of Noah. The Gemara infers: Yes, there is a prohibition for a descendant of Noah, but there is no death penalty. Rav Naḥman bar Yitzḥak says: Their prohibition is their death penalty. Since the only punishment mentioned in the Torah

for transgressing a Noahide mitzva is execution, any descendant of
Noah who transgresses is liable to be executed. [59]

Any "descendant of Noah" (which we all are, since everyone except Noah
and his descendants were wiped out during the great flood) who breaks any
of the Noahide laws (mitzva means laws) is executed. The short hand for all
of this is, anyone who proclaims Christ as the Son of Yah, or worships Him,
will be executed. What is the method of execution according to multiple
sources including the Encyclopedia Judaica?

In the elaboration of these seven Noachian laws, and in assigning
punishments for their transgression, the Rabbis are sometimes more
lenient and sometimes more rigorous with Noachidæ than with
Israelites. With but a few exceptions, the punishment meted out to a
Noachid for the transgression of any of the seven laws is decapitation,
60

Yep, the penalty for breaking any of the Noahide laws, including "idolatry"
i.e. worshiping our Messiah, is decapitation.

Revelation 20:4 Then I saw the souls of those who had been
beheaded for their witness to Jesus and for the word of God, who
had not worshiped the beast or his image, and had not received
his mark on their foreheads or on their hands.

If this wasn't already bad enough, it gets worse. You see, this council
won't only have presence in Jerusalem. Oh no, they want their presence
everywhere. The high council will sit in Jerusalem, but the arms of the
council will be everywhere. From the Encyclopidia Judaica once again:

The Noachidæ are required to establish courts of justice in every city
and province; and these courts are to judge the people with regard to
the six laws and to warn them against the transgression of any of

them (ib.; "Yad," l.c. ix. 14, x. 11; comp. Naḥmanides on Gen. xxxiv. <u>*13, where the opinion is expressed that these courts should judge also*</u> <u>*cases other than those coming under the head of the six laws, as, for*</u> *example, larceny, assault and battery, etc.).*

They want to set up these courts in every city. These courts also aren't limited to only cases dealing with the Noahide laws either. They can be called into place for any number of offenses at all. So we will be decapitated for worshiping Christ under the term "idolatry". Further, remember a few chapters ago I said one of the traditions of the Jews is that speaking the name of Yahuah is forbidden? Anyone (except priests) and particularly any gentile speaking the proper name of Yah will be under Jewish tradition, guilty of a form of blasphemy. So if you even speak the name of Yahuah, the penalty is decapitation.

> *Psalm 105:1-6 Oh, give thanks to the Lord!* <u>*Call upon His*</u> <u>*name; Make known His deeds among the peoples!*</u> *2 Sing to Him, sing psalms to Him; Talk of all His wondrous works! 3* <u>*Glory in His holy name; Let the hearts of those rejoice who*</u> <u>*seek the Lord!*</u> *4 Seek the Lord and His strength; Seek His face evermore! 5 Remember His marvelous works which He has done, His wonders, and the judgments of His mouth, 6* <u>*O seed*</u> <u>*of Abraham His servant, You children of Jacob, His chosen ones!*</u>

Outside of those two laws, the other ones are easy enough to avoid, but those two in particular will spell the end for anyone who is professing Christ or making known the name of Yah. It gets worse.

In keeping with the "Christian" tradition of dual covenant theology, the gentile law and Jewish law are kept separate. So separate in fact, that if any gentile even attempts to keep the law, such as the Sabbath, or the feasts, or even read the Torah (the law) for themselves, they will be severely beaten or killed. Melachim uMichamot (Mishnah Torah) 9:

A gentile who studies the Torah is obligated to die. They should only
be involved in the study of their seven mitzvot.

Similarly, a gentile who rests, even on a weekday, observing that
day as a Sabbath, is obligated to die. Needless to say, he is obligated
for that punishment if he creates a festival for himself. [61]

From Sanhedrin 58b:

A heathen who keeps a day of rest, deserves death, for it is written,
And a day and a night they shall not rest, and a master has said: Their
prohibition is their death sentence. Rabina said: Even if he rested on
a Monday. Now why is this not included in the seven Noachian laws?
— Only negative injunctions are enumerated, not positive ones. [62]

By the way, did you catch that little bit at the bottom? It asks why these
prohibitions are not included or listed, in the Noahide laws. It answers that
only negative injunctions are enumerated, or listed, and not positive ones.
In other words, the Noahide laws not only contain a list of seven actions
that will result in punishment, it also has unspoken, unlisted laws of things
that if you do them, there will be punishment. If anyone even attempts
to keep the commandments of Yah, such as His eternal sign between Him
and His people, they will be put to death. This is the same exact thing that
happened at the hands of Rome way back when.

Oh and by the way, I've already personally experienced Christians
bearing this exact spirit and opinion, as they go on the attack whenever
they find out I walk according to the law to the best of my ability. They
accuse those who are obedient as being heretics who have turned from
the faith. Christianity Today, the major publication published an article
on April 6th, 2017 entitled "Jesus Didn't Eat a Seder Meal Why Christians
shouldn't either." What a lie. He ate that meal every year until His death in
accordance to the law of Yah. Anyways, it outlines how Passover is a strictly
Jewish observance, and it shouldn't be done unless you are overseen by a
Jewish Rabbi. Many Christians will be duped into these Noahide laws and

indeed, all the theology of dual covenant theology and dispensationalism is already in place in their minds. They teach we have "freedom" in Christ from those "burdensome laws" and Christians shouldn't be in bondage under them. They yell at and attack any Christian who keeps the law, or claims others should. Why would they fight against a system of law that upholds the same values?

> *John 16:2-3 (...) yes, the time is coming that whoever kills you will think that he offers God service. 3 And these things they will do to you because they have not known the Father nor Me.*

> *Matthew 7:23 And then I will declare to them, 'I never knew you; depart from Me, you who practice lawlessness!'*

Remember who the beast is enraged with?

> *Revelation 12:17 And the dragon was enraged with the woman, and he went to make war with the rest of her offspring, who keep the commandments of God and have the testimony of Jesus Christ.*

> *Revelation 14:12 Here is the patience of the saints; here are those who keep the commandments of God and the faith of Jesus.*

The followers of The Way. Keeping faith in Christ and keeping His commandments.

Beyond all of these things, Jews and "noahides" are given different priority. The Jews see themselves as being "God's chosen people" and Christianity nods along. What many don't realize is that because of this deceptive dichotomy between Jews and gentiles, Jews have rights far above that of a gentile according to Rabbinical Judaism. Remember Rabbi Schneerson I mentioned earlier that the US venerated? There was semi-recently a bus company known as Egged (ee-gehd) that bore a quote from Schneerson written in Hebrew that was put on buses all over Israel. The advertisement read:

> *"Statement of the kingdom. From the instructions of the [Lubavitcher] rabbi:*
>
> *The Gentile does not want anything. He waits to be told what the Jew wants!"*

This embodies their view of gentiles. Once again from Encyclopedia Judaica:

> *A Noachid who slays another Noachid, or worships idols, or blasphemes, or has illicit connection with the wife of another Noachid, and then becomes a proselyte, is free from punishment. If, however, he has killed an Israelite, or has had illicit connection with the wife of an Israelite, and then becomes a proselyte, he must submit to the punishment that is inflicted upon an Israelite found guilty of such a transgression (Sanh. 71b; "Yad," l.c. x. 4).*

Allow me to translate, if a noachid (gentile) commits a crime, and then becomes "Jewish" via a series of rituals and instructions out of Rabbinical teachings (including the talmud, Kabbalah, and Mishnah Torah), that gentile convert pays no penalty for his crimes. If a gentile kills a man, rapes his wife, and then while being pursued converts to Judaism, he pays no penalty for his crime. If however a gentile does any of these things to an "Israelite" (Jew), and converts, he pays the full penalty of his crimes. Further, if a gentile does these things to a Jew and does not convert, he is still guilty and must pay for his crimes. So if a gentile wrongs a gentile, he is guilty, if a gentile wrongs a Jew, he is guilty, but if a jew harms a gentile, there is no penalty. This is rather buried in the text, but is that not what is being said here? A Jewish man is not punished for things done to a gentile, but a gentile is punished for things done to a Jew. This is the attitude of the Rabbinical authorities. From the Encyclopedia Judaica once again:

In the case of murder, if the Noachid slay a child in its mother's womb, or kill a person whose life is despaired of ("ṭerefah"), or if he cause the death of a person by starving him or by putting him before a lion so that he can not escape, or if he slay a man in self-defense, the Noachid is guilty of murder and must pay the death-penalty, although under the same circumstances an Israelite would not be executed (ib. *57b*; *"Yad," l.c. ix. 4; comp. "Kesef Mishneh," ad loc.).*

A different law for the Jew and for the gentile. This is where dual covenant theology and dispensationalism is leading Christianity today. This is the true face of Zionism, and those who have not received a love for the truth, who are promoting this agenda, are helping to set up the kingdom that will ultimately be their undoing. This is the abominable truth hidden from the general public, being pushed forward by the unending love, support, and financial efforts of Zionist Christians who want to bless and help "God's holy people" in any way they can, as taught by the Masonic fueled teachings of Darby and Scofield. These once again, so often have the best of intentions, and I myself have been in this camp in the past, but once you really begin to see these things, you realize just how large and dangerous a deception this really is.

Dispensationalism says that the Old Testament was written exclusively for the Jews. The Gospels were written to the Jews as that's who Christ was speaking to most of the time. A dispensational teacher recently told me that regarding the books of first, second, and third John, they are written for those who are left on earth during the tribulation. He believes the Jews to be the only ones here at that time, thus first, second, and third John are only for the Jews. Regarding the Pauline letters, anything Paul teaches that is according to the law is apparently "for the Jews" the working of the Spirit is "only for the early church" and we also don't have to walk as Paul walked because he was a Jew, nor do we have to walk as Christ walked because He was a Jew. So we are left with no "gentile" pattern, and the leftovers after you remove all of these other authors are what we have to pick through. So, if we lose pretty much our entire Bibles, except for certain portions of Paul's letters, and we lose any semblance of a Biblical pattern, why even bother having our Bibles at all? If the vast majority of the writings are "not for us" why should we even bother reading it? By that logic, it would be dangerous for a person to read the other books, especially the Old Testament lest they be confused, as that's all exclusively for the "Jews" anyways. The Noahide laws willingly agree.

Read the following statements and ask yourself if these statements are more in line with Rabbinical Judaism, or with dual covenant dispensational theology.

You should be careful how you read your Bible, lest you confuse the "gentile" law, with the "Jewish" law. You should make a distinction between the "Jew" and "gentile". You should treat the "Jew" as superior because they are the flesh and blood descendants of Abraham. If you bless the Jews, you will be blessed, if you curse them, you will be cursed, if you harm them, you will be harmed. We need to give our love and support to the Jews in Israel in any way we can. If we turn against Israel, God will turn against us, because we have poked the apple of His eye. You shouldn't try to do "Jewish" things like the feasts or Sabbath, because those are exclusively for the Jews. The Jews are God's Holy people and we need to treat them as such.

So where are these statements more likely to be spoken, among the Sanhedrin, or in Christian churches? The answer is, I have heard both of each of these assertions from both Orthodox Judaism and dispensational Christianity multiple times. They both speak the same lies.

The Jews are indeed the flesh and blood descendants of Abraham, but what did John the baptist have to say?

Matthew 3:7-10 But when he saw many of the Pharisees and Sadducees coming to his baptism, he said to them, 'Brood of vipers! Who warned you to flee from the wrath to come? 8 Therefore bear fruits worthy of repentance, 9 and do not think to say to yourselves, 'We have Abraham as our father.' For I say to you that God is able to raise up children to Abraham from these stones. 10 And even now the ax is laid to the root of the trees. Therefore every tree which does not bear good fruit is cut down and thrown into the fire.

What did Paul say?

Galatians 3:28-29 There is neither Jew nor Greek, there is neither slave nor free, there is neither male nor female; for you are all one in Christ Jesus. 29 And if you are Christ's, then you are Abraham's seed, and heirs according to the promise.

Romans 9:6-8 But it is not that the word of God has taken no effect. For they are not all Israel who are of Israel, 7 nor are they all children because they are the seed of Abraham; but, "In Isaac your seed shall be called." 8 That is, those who are the children of the flesh, these are not the children of God; but the children of the promise are counted as the seed.

So what do we do with this? How should we then treat the Jews? The answer is, we should treat them the way we should treat everyone else; with love. We should warn them of the judgement coming upon them. We should pray for their eyes to be opened. We should seek their salvation. With gentiles however, we should be doing the exact same thing. Treating people with love, warning them of coming judgement in love, praying for their eyes to be opened, seek their salvation. These are the things we should do for all of mankind, not showing partiality, but speaking the truth in love to all who will hear it.

If you speak the truth regarding Israel, and Judaism, and dual covenant theology, you will indeed be labeled as antisemitic. You will have Christians angry enough at you that they will want to stone you. These things have not changed.

Matthew 23:29-34 "Woe to you, scribes and Pharisees, hyp-

ocrites! Because you build the tombs of the prophets and adorn the monuments of the righteous, 30 and say, 'If we had lived in the days of our fathers, we would not have been partakers with them in the blood of the prophets.' 31 "Therefore you are witnesses against yourselves that you are sons of those who murdered the prophets. 32 Fill up, then, the measure of your fathers' guilt. 33 Serpents, brood of vipers! How can you escape the condemnation of hell? 34 Therefore, indeed, I send you prophets, wise men, and scribes: some of them you will kill and crucify, and some of them you will scourge in your synagogues and persecute from city to city,

John 16:2-4 They will put you out of the synagogues; yes, the time is coming that whoever kills you will think that he offers God service. 3 And these things they will do to you because they have not known the Father nor Me. 4 But these things I have told you, that when the time comes, you may remember that I told you of them.

Instead of pharisees who are the religious leaders, who hold the traditions of men above the laws of Yah, we have pastors who are the religious leaders who hold the traditions of men (dispensationalism and dual covenant theology) above the commandments of Yah. Instead of getting thrown out of synagogues, you will be thrown out of churches. Instead of being physically stoned, many are having their reputations stoned, though the day is indeed coming when all who speak the truth will be put to death. Remember the beast is enraged with those who keep the commandments of Yah and have faith in Christ and speak the truth. As said, many pastors and teachers simply do not know the truth because they have not heard it yet, but many, when brought these things, will begin to become very angry, very quickly. They will begin to shout things like "heretic" "false prophet" "wolf in sheep's clothing". They will stop up their ears, or put you out of their church or house, or will try to silence you however they can. They did the same to Stephen.

> *Acts 7:51-54 "You stiff-necked and uncircumcised in heart and ears! You always resist the Holy Spirit; as your fathers did, so do you. 52 Which of the prophets did your fathers not persecute? And they killed those who foretold the coming of the Just One, of whom you now have become the betrayers and murderers, 53 who have received the law by the direction of angels and have not kept it."*
>
> *54 When they heard these things they were cut to the heart, and they gnashed at him with their teeth.*

> *Acts 7:57-58 Then they cried out with a loud voice, stopped their ears, and ran at him with one accord; 58 and they cast him out of the city and stoned him.*

History repeats itself, and nothing changes. There are still many who offer Yah praise and worship day after day, but their hearts are far from Him. They claim to know Him but they hate His commandments.

> *1 John 2:3-7 Now by this we know that we know Him, if we keep His commandments. 4 He who says, "I know Him," and does not keep His commandments, is a liar, and the truth is not in him. 5 But whoever keeps His word, truly the love of God is perfected in him. By this we know that we are in Him. 6 He who says he abides in Him ought himself also to walk just as He walked. 7 Brethren, I write no new commandment to you, but an old commandment which you have had from the beginning. The old commandment is the word which you heard from the beginning.*

We know that we know Him by keeping His commandments. What does it look like to have a heart far from Yah?

Matthew 15:6-9 <u>*Thus you have made the commandment of God*</u> <u>*of no effect by your tradition.*</u> *7 Hypocrites! Well did Isaiah prophesy about you, saying:*

8 'These people draw near to Me with their mouth, and honor Me with their lips, but their heart is far from Me. 9 And in vain they worship Me, teaching as doctrines the commandments of men.' "

What does a heart after Yah's own heart look like?

Psalm 119:33-35 Teach me, O Lord, the way of Your statutes, and I shall keep it to the end. 34 Give me understanding, and I shall keep Your law; indeed, I shall observe it with my whole heart. 35 Make me walk in the path of Your commandments, for I delight in it.

There are many uncircumcised in heart in the world today who claim to know Him, and love Him, but they do not know Him, and instead work lawlessness. They worship Him with their lips, but their hearts are far from Him. They teach traditions of men that make null the commandments of Yah. They stop up their ears and gnash their teeth against the truth. You've seen both of these passages of scripture in separate places at separate times, but I want you to see once more, the full context of both of these passages. This is without the normal section breaks that were later added into Bibles, this is all according to how it was actually written.

Matthew 7:15-23 "Beware of false prophets, who come to you in sheep's clothing, but inwardly they are ravenous wolves. 16 You will know them by their fruits. Do men gather grapes from thornbushes or figs from thistles? 17 Even so, every good tree bears good fruit, but a bad tree bears bad fruit. 18 A good tree cannot bear bad fruit, nor can a bad tree bear good fruit. 19 Every tree that does not bear good fruit is cut down and thrown into the fire. 20 Therefore by their fruits you will know them. 21 Not everyone who says to Me, 'Lord, Lord,' shall enter the kingdom of heaven, but he who does the will of My Father in heaven. 22 Many will say to Me in that day, 'Lord, Lord, have we not prophesied in Your name, cast out demons in Your name, and done many wonders in Your name?' 23 And then I will declare to them, 'I never knew you; depart from Me, you who practice lawlessness!'

Within context, these false prophets who are wolves in sheep's clothing are directly linked with those who claim they prophesied, cast out demons, and did many wonders in His name, but He will say to them, "I never knew you; depart from Me, you who practice lawlessness!" Further, Matthew 7 is still a part of the sermon Yahusha began preaching back in Matthew 5, where He specifically says "Do not think that I came to destroy the Law or the Prophets. I did not come to destroy but to fulfill" and then goes on to explain exactly what this means with several examples. All of these things taken in context of one another give us a clear picture. The law did not die with Christ on the cross, the penalty for breaking it died with Him if we accept Him. The law was magnified, was exalted, was made perfect through Him. The prophet Isaiah plainly spells out Christ would perfect the law and exalt it, not do away with it. It says His law would be brought to the gentiles, not destroyed for the sake of the gentiles. You will not find one hint anywhere in the Old Testament that suggests that Christ would do away with the law, on the contrary you find verses that say the opposite. To say that Christ did away with the law is to contradict what He Himself said, what the prophets said, and to push forward an idea you will find no hint of anywhere in the Old Testament.

Be prepared, dear reader, if you speak the truth, they will come after you. But don't worry, our Beloved Savior already gave us instruction regarding this.

Matthew 10:16-28 "Behold, I send you out as sheep in the midst of wolves. Therefore be wise as serpents and harmless as doves. 17 But beware of men, for they will deliver you up to councils and scourge you in their synagogues. 18 You will be brought before governors and kings for My sake, as a testimony to them and to the Gentiles. 19 But when they deliver you up, do not worry about how or what you should speak. For it will be given to you in that hour what you should speak; 20 for it is not you who speak, but the Spirit of your Father who speaks in you.

21 "Now brother will deliver up brother to death, and a father his child; and children will rise up against parents and cause them to be put to death. 22 And you will be hated by all for My name's sake. But he who endures to the end will be saved. 23 When they persecute you in this city, flee to another. For assuredly, I say to you, you will not have gone through the cities of Israel before the Son of Man comes.

24 "A disciple is not above his teacher, nor a servant above his master. 25 It is enough for a disciple that he be like his teacher, and a servant like his master. If they have called the master of the house Beelzebub, how much more will they call those of his household! 26 Therefore do not fear them. For there is nothing covered that will not be revealed, and hidden that will not be known.

27 "Whatever I tell you in the dark, speak in the light; and what you hear in the ear, preach on the housetops. 28 And do not fear those who kill the body but cannot kill the soul. But rather fear Him who is able to destroy both soul and body in hell.

But, if you faithfully keep His word, His name, and persevere, there is blessing to come. The Old Testament is full of some of the most beautiful promises of restoration, redemption, and mercy in the whole Bible. These promises were made to His people, and specifically to those who obey

Him. Persecution comes, but those who hold fast to His Word will see Salvation. Let us be those who walk in His ways, have faith in His Word, and persevere.

IV

The End of the Matter

27

Return of the Ancients

We're almost through, dear reader. Two more chapters after this one. This one won't be too long, and the next ones shouldn't be either. This chapter is called Return of the Ancients. It deals with exposing many of the ways idolatry has made significant returns in modern society without most ever realizing it. This will be another challenging chapter depending on who you are, but walking in The Way isn't always easy. So in recent years, there has been a massive return to idolatry especially in forms of entertainment. Things that the body of Christ used to stay far away from are now accepted with wild abandon as innocent fun or entertainment. Some of things are more obvious, such as the movement "Christian Wicca" which is gaining popularity that is literally a fusing of witchcraft and faith in Christ, but others are far more subtle. This will by no means be an exhaustive list, but more a short chapter to make you aware of some things, and help you to look for more things on your own.

I want to start with one of the most innocent seeming, and that is a string of movies from Disney/Pixar. These movies have gained a lot of popularity in recent times, and for all intents and purposes, they are fun movies. They are visually stunning, exciting, they have fun songs, but ultimately are completely based on idolatry. Two that come to mind immediately are Coco, which is a film all about the Mexican Dia de Muertos, and Moana, a movie all about the island mythologies. On the surface they seem pretty innocent, no swearing, no suggestive themes, nothing too violent, and as I said, they are actually quite enjoyable. However, the entire movie premise for both of these movies is based almost entirely on idolatry.

Coco follows a young boys journey through the afterlife to meet with his dead relatives and solve the mystery of why his grandma hates music. This movie contains things such as offrendas, which are alters to honor the dead that have direct affects on the afterlife, complete with offerings such as food and drinks for the dead. It also contains a dog that becomes a guide in the spirit world hearkening back to spirit guides and familiars, and overall, is chalk full of idolatry. It seems fun and innocent, and from a worldly perspective, it is, but from Yah's perspective, I don't think He is pleased with us letting our children learn about the ways the pagans serve their gods.

Moana is another movie, and before finding all of these things, was one of my favorite kid's movies. I've always loved islands, and the ocean, and this movie was a no brainer. However, after learning Yah's feelings on idolatry, I had to let this one go. The movie premise follows Moana, who goes on a journey to save her island via finding Maui, the magical shape-shifting demigod, and returning the heart of Tefiti, a giant island nature goddess. The adventures are entertaining, but the entire time they are indoctrinating kids with island mythology that teaches that it was Maui that created islands of dry lands, and gave them food, and controls the sun to give longer days, and many other things. It is indeed presented as a story, and understood to be such, but beyond teaching the customs, nature, and personalities of these pagan gods, it is also presenting idolatry as being a fun little cultural thing. These two movies are mere examples, and there are many others that are chalk full of idolatry. Disney's Hercules is another example.

We wouldn't let our children watch cartoons that trivialize adultery or homosexuality or murder because we don't want our children to be exposed to these things, and be drawn into them. We don't want our children growing up thinking these things are acceptable behavior. Yet we often completely overlook idolatry as something we shouldn't let our children be exposed to. We let our children see these things and perceive idolatry as being a fun cultural thing, rather than adultery against the Most High, and a very serious sin. These cultural stories are not innocent in the eyes of Yah. They give glory to false gods that have received prayer, praise and sacrifices for ages from the people who trusted in them and perished. We should view movies teaching idolatry as being every bit as harmful to our children, as a show teaching adultery or homosexuality or murder.

Beyond children's movies and shows, we also have more adult centered movies that are also chalk full of idolatry. In particular, the Marvel and DC movies are at the top of the list. Movies like the Thor movies are literally non stop idolatry. They show you Asgard, the realm of the gods, they show you Odin, Loki, Hel, and Thor as well as others. They depict this pagan antichrist as being attractive with a good sense of humor and a strong sense of justice. They depict Thor as being the hero who saves the day. They're entertaining movies, no doubt, but they are full of idolatry. DC does the same thing. Aquaman is all about the demigod son of the sea goddess. Wonder woman is a based off of the various Roman goddesses of war. Beyond teaching idolatry, these movies are also subtly teaching a one world religion. The Avengers movies in particular are a prime example of this. When you see the neopagan psychic, Scarlett Witch, fighting alongside the god of thunder Thor, with the assistance of the Christian Captain America, with Black Panther, who gets his strength from the African panther god Bast, you begin to see what I'm talking about. These movies are absolutely full of the antichrist agenda.

Other trends are popping up all over, such as astrology making a major return. I have overheard Christians talking about their horoscope with one another. These things are very old, very pagan, and have their roots in nothing but idolatry. This is pretty much direct worship of the sun, moon, and stars, as they act as if these things are controlling their lives and causing things to happen to them. Star signs, zodiac signs, all of these things are of pagan origin. Things like Yoga are becoming increasingly prominent. Now, regarding Yoga, I do not believe stretching and breathing exercises to be wrong. They have been proven to be very beneficial for the body, however, there is a whole world of eastern mysticism that goes along with yoga. The meditation practices where you "empty yourself out and let the universe in" all have their root in idolatry and open you up to demonic influence. Things like mantras and chants are just as dangerous. The "fun" yoga greeting "Namaste" originates from eastern mysticism and in Hinduism literally means "I bow to the divine in you". It goes back to beliefs in universalism, and apotheosis.

Other doctrines have begun popping up such as the power of "I am" that a certain prominent teacher is teaching. He says "what follows the 'I am' will come looking for you." This is nothing more than the occult law of attraction or manifestation, that essentially teaches what you set your heart to desire will manifest itself before you. If you desire and declare "I am" wealthy, "I am" healthy, and want it, it'll come to you. This is literally doctrine straight out of the grimoires of witches. Other prominent organizations are teaching things like "Christian spirit animals" that will help you to follow Yah. Christian Alchemy is on the rise. Basically, Christianity has become like a brand name slapped on different products. Kirkland's Best is the Costco brand that has water, clothing, food, furniture, and pretty much anything you can think of. Christianity has begun to do the same thing, Christian Wicca, Christian Alchemy, Christian astral projection, Christian ouija boards, basically, any occultic practice you want to participate in, there's a vein of Christianity for it. Slap the Christian sticker on it, and people think it's just fine to be participating in.

I have seen Christians tattooed with Ankhs and the eye of Horus. I know Christians who have sworn oaths to pagan gods through organizations like the Free Masons. The hippocratic oath is an oath all doctors must swear. Do you know where this oath came from? This is the original first few lines of the hippocratic oath:

I swear by <u>Apollo</u> Physician and <u>Asclepius</u> and <u>Hygieia</u> and <u>Panaceia</u> and <u>all the gods and goddesses</u>, making them my witnesses, that I will fulfil according to my ability and judgment this oath and this *covenant:*

There is a modern version of the oath that takes out this first part about who you're swearing the oath to, but the oath has changed very little, you still swear an oath to someone. Meanwhile in Matthew:

> *Matthew 5:33-37 "Again you have heard that it was said to those of old, 'You shall not swear falsely, but shall perform your oaths to the Lord.' 34 But I say to you, do not swear at all: neither by heaven, for it is God's throne; 35 nor by the earth, for it is His footstool; nor by Jerusalem, for it is the city of the great King. 36 Nor shall you swear by your head, because you cannot make one hair white or black. 37 But let your 'Yes' be 'Yes,' and your 'No,' 'No.' For whatever is more than these is from the evil one.*

People swear oaths all day long to pagan gods and goddesses, making covenants with demons, and think nothing of it. With the medical industry in particular by the way, I would be extremely cautious. The amount of outright disturbing things you will learn if you begin to look into the medical industry are astounding. Take a moment to look up Strong's #5331, pharmakeia. Look up new treatments such as CAR-T therapy where they take your white blood cells, genetically splice them with white blood cells from mice or other animals, and re-inject them into your body. As in the days of Noah indeed. I know it's a hotly debated subject, but take some time to look through the ingredients found in your average modern day vaccination. Look up some of the chemicals used, and then look up how much of said chemical is considered harmful. Explain why there are pieces of animal DNA mixed in the vaccination soup and look up how foreign injected DNA can mess with your body. No wonder they swear oaths to pagan gods, truly they work witchcraft.

We need to be on guard. We need to test everything, and make sure the things we are walking in are grounded in scripture. We need to make sure we are testing our traditions, practices, entertainment, and every other thing in our lives. We are called to be pure, and to remove the leaven of sin from our lives. Satan has subtly added leaven into everything he possibly can, and if we don't guard ourselves, we will become infected.

All of this idolatry is by design by the way. The glorification of false gods, the combining of religions and the flood of idolatry. The enemy is gearing up for his kingdom to rule over the earth, but before he can have a people to rule over, he needs to fully indoctrinate and familiarize these people with his ways and beliefs. He needs to teach the people that the pagan gods are heroes. He needs to teach people that trans-humanism is a good and helpful thing we should pursue. He needs to teach people that inclusivity and acceptance is the most important thing, and that the only enemy are those who won't go along with the crowd. By the way, Holiness is the exact opposite of going along with everything and accepting everything. It is being set apart. All of these agendas are moving the people of the world ever closer to accepting the reign of the antichrist. I could go on and on, but the best thing i can tell you, dear reader, is be on guard. Test everything, bring anything you're not sure about to Yah and ask Him to show you the truth. Be humble and willing to learn, but be careful as to what you allow yourself to take on. Be harmless as doves, but wise as serpents (Matthew 10:16).

Ultimately, no form of entertainment in this current age is perfect, and honestly, I think without some entertainment from time to time, we might all go completely mad in this dark and twisted world we live in. The idea though is to try to make sure that the things we are letting into our eyes and ears are as close to clean as they can reasonably get. It is not my job to tell you what you should and should not be watching, but I would encourage you to just begin asking Yah if there is anything in your life He doesn't want you participating in any longer, and when He convicts you of different things, obey Him. That's really the key to all of this, seek Him, ask Him to show you His ways, and when He does, be obedient.

28

The Greatest of These

We have learned many, many things in this book. Many of these things are very controversial. You may agree or disagree with any number of the things I have presented in this book. You may get on Facebook to warn people against reading this book. You may get on Facebook to recommend this book to others. You may throw it in the back of your closet and forget about it completely. No matter what you do, dear reader, do everything you do in love.

As I have searched and studied, and listened to different teachers and watched different communities and congregations, and scrolled through social media, I am saddened. Everywhere I look, there are contentions, striving, arguments, malice, harshness, and a pronounced lack of love. This isn't to say that I don't see love too in these places at times, but I see far too much strife. If you have heard nothing else in this entire book, hear this: without love, nothing you do will be pleasing to Him. Paul stated it rather well I think.

1 Corinthians 13:1-3 Though I speak with the tongues of men and of angels, but have not love, I have become sounding brass or a clanging cymbal. 2 And though I have the gift of prophecy, and understand all mysteries and all knowledge, and though I have all faith, so that I could remove mountains, but have not love, I am nothing. 3 And though I bestow all my goods to feed the poor, and though I give my body to be burned, but have not love, it profits me nothing.

It doesn't matter how much knowledge you have, it doesn't matter how much you give to the poor, it doesn't matter how much scripture you understand, if you don't have love for one another, it avails nothing. It's pointless. Without love, you cannot please Yah. In fact, if you have not love, you don't know Yah, because He is love.

1 John 4:7-11 Beloved, let us love one another, for love is of God; and everyone who loves is born of God and knows God. 8 He who does not love does not know God, for God is love. 9 In this the love of God was manifested toward us, that God has sent His only begotten Son into the world, that we might live through Him. 10 In this is love, not that we loved God, but that He loved us and sent His Son to be the propitiation for our sins. 11 Beloved, if God so loved us, we also ought to love one another.

As stated in this book, I believe we should be keeping the feasts and Sabbath and walking in the law of Yah, but if we don't have love, none of it matters one bit.

Isaiah 1:13-17 Bring no more futile sacrifices; incense is an abomination to Me. The New Moons, the Sabbaths, and the calling of assemblies—I cannot endure iniquity and the sacred meeting. 14 Your New Moons and your appointed feasts My soul hates; they are a trouble to Me, I am weary of bearing them. 15 When you spread out your hands, I will hide My eyes from you; even though you make many prayers, I will not hear. Your hands are full of blood. 16 "Wash yourselves, make yourselves clean; put away the evil of your doings from before My eyes. Cease to do evil, 17 Learn to do good; Seek justice, Rebuke the oppressor; Defend the fatherless, Plead for the widow.

Does this verse mean that Yah hates His feasts and Sabbaths that He commanded Israel to observe? Of course not. It means if people are keeping these feasts, and offerings and other things, but are also busy murdering and oppressing and acting without love, none of these things matter.

> *Matthew 23:23-24 "Woe to you, scribes and Pharisees, hypocrites! For you pay tithe of mint and anise and cummin, and have neglected the weightier matters of the law: justice and mercy and faith. These you ought to have done, without leaving the others undone. 24 Blind guides, who strain out a gnat and swallow a camel!*

The scribes and pharisees were complete hypocrites because though they kept some of the commandments, they neglected the weightier matters of the law, justice and mercy and faith. Every commandment, every statute revolves around loving Yah, or loving one another. You cannot love Yah and not love others. Yah goes as far as to say if you aren't showing love to one another, He doesn't even hear your prayers no matter how much you pray. This is a matter of the utmost importance. Christ Himself says that the watermark for a believer is loving one another.

> *John 13:34-35 A new commandment I give to you, that you love one another; as I have loved you, that you also love one another. 35 By this all will know that you are My disciples, if you have love for one another."*

There are times that you will be attacked for standing for truth. You may have theology that differs with another and you may be attacked or slandered. Is this license to attack and slander back?

Matthew 5:43-44 "You have heard that it was said, 'You shall love your neighbor and hate your enemy.' 44 But I say to you, love your enemies, bless those who curse you, do good to those who hate you, and pray for those who spitefully use you and persecute you,

This is how our King commanded us to walk. Christ, our example, among the last words he spoke as He died were "Father, forgive them, for they know not what they do." When people whipped, and mocked, and beat, and spit on, and cursed, the King of Kings, He answered with asking Yah to pardon their sin. What an incredible love and humility. This is how we should act. In Acts we see this same behavior from another.

Acts 7:59-60 And they stoned Stephen as he was calling on God and saying, "Lord Jesus, receive my spirit." 60 Then he knelt down and cried out with a loud voice, "Lord, do not charge them with this sin." And when he had said this, he fell asleep.

Again, the final words Stephen spoke on this earth were asking Yah not to impute this sin to them. This is what love looks like. This is how we should act. We should return cursing with blessing, hatred with love, anger and pride with gentleness and humility. Dear reader, I am preaching to myself as much as anyone. It is very difficult, to act with love towards someone who is attacking and persecuting you. It is very difficult to bless someone who is slandering you and your loved ones. Nevertheless, this is what we are called to do. Once again, Paul summed up what love looks like rather nicely.

1 Corinthians 13:4-6 Love suffers long and is kind; love does not envy; love does not parade itself, is not puffed up; 5 does not behave rudely, does not seek its own, is not provoked, thinks no evil; 6 does not rejoice in iniquity, but rejoices in the truth;

James echoes much of this.

> *James 3:13-18 Who is wise and understanding among you?*
> *Let him show by good conduct that his works are done in the*
> *meekness of wisdom. 14 But if you have bitter envy and self-*
> *seeking in your hearts, do not boast and lie against the truth.*
> *15 This wisdom does not descend from above, but is earthly,*
> *sensual, demonic. 16 For where envy and self-seeking exist,*
> *confusion and every evil thing are there. 17 But the wisdom*
> *that is from above is first pure, then peaceable, gentle, willing*
> *to yield, full of mercy and good fruits, without partiality and*
> *without hypocrisy. 18 Now the fruit of righteousness is sown*
> *in peace by those who make peace.*

We as followers of Christ do have a responsibility to speak truth and to shine light in the darkness, but we must do this in love. You can warn a person of error without biting their head off. You can correct someone in humility and love. Remember that not every fellow servant is going to see things the same way you do. That does not give you a right to beat your fellow servants.

> *Matthew 24:45-51 "Who then is a faithful and wise servant,*
> *whom his master made ruler over his household, to give them*
> *food in due season? 46 Blessed is that servant whom his master,*
> *when he comes, will find so doing. 47 Assuredly, I say to you*
> *that he will make him ruler over all his goods. 48 But if that*
> *evil servant says in his heart, 'My master is delaying his coming,'*
> *49 and begins to beat his fellow servants, and to eat and drink*
> *with the drunkards, 50 the master of that servant will come on*
> *a day when he is not looking for him and at an hour that he*
> *is not aware of, 51 and will cut him in two and appoint him*
> *his portion with the hypocrites. There shall be weeping and*
> *gnashing of teeth.*

Note that the faithful and wise servant is continuing in what he was given to do. Meanwhile the wicked servants are careless, and are busy beating one another, and attacking one another. Compare that portion to this portion.

Revelation 3:7-12 "And to the angel of the church in Philadel-phia write,

These things says He who is holy, He who is true, "He who has the key of David, He who opens and no one shuts, and shuts and no one opens": 8 "I know your works. See, I have set before you an open door, and no one can shut it; for you have a little strength, have kept My word, and have not denied My name. 9 Indeed I will make those of the synagogue of Satan, who say they are Jews and are not, but lie—indeed I will make them come and worship before your feet, and to know that I have loved you. 10 Because you have kept My command to persevere, I also will keep you from the hour of trial which shall come upon the whole world, to test those who dwell on the earth. 11 Behold, I am coming quickly! Hold fast what you have, that no one may take your crown. 12 He who overcomes, I will make him a pillar in the temple of My God, and he shall go out no more. I will write on him the name of My God and the name of the city of My God, the New Jerusalem, which comes down out of heaven from My God. And I will write on him My new name.

The congregation of Philadelphia is one of the only two congregations that were not corrected for anything. Note that they are kept from the trial that comes upon the whole world. Also note that these will become pillars in the temple and bear the new name of Yahusha. The reason I brought this portion up is not immediately apparent, but this was written to the congregation in "Philadelphia". This word is made up of two Greek words; phileo, which means love, and adelphos which means brother. Out of two congregations, this is the only congregation that was not rebuked out of the seven and gets to escape the trial coming on the whole world. This is the congregation of brotherly love who are walking faithfully in the commandments of Christ.

This also goes for showing love to the "Jews" and "gentiles". I have shown many things throughout this book that paint the Jews in a pretty poor light, but they are just people who need Christ as well. They have been given lies just as we have, and they are loved as much as the next person. There is a remnant of the Jewish who will be saved just as there will be a remnant of the gentiles who will be saved. I know one guy in particular who I care for, but he is so wrapped up in racial tensions, and the "them versus us" mentality that he is blinded and cannot see the truth in spite of him being one who desires truth more than most I know. Many of the things I said in this book will be taken as antisemitic, but this isn't the case at all. I have just as much love for the Jew as I do for anyone else, because Yah created them too.

> *2 Peter 3:9 The Lord is not slack concerning His promise, as some count slackness, but is longsuffering toward us, <u>not willing that any should perish but that all should come to repentance.</u>*

We should be praying for Israel, we should be praying for the Jews. Just as much as we should be praying for our neighbor down the street, and for the United States. We should desire to see all come to repentance, not condemning anyone based upon something they have no control over, such as bloodline. We all came from Adam, whether white, black, or any other color, and we are all made in the image of Yah. Every man has the ability to accept Christ and be grafted into His people, and that should be among our chief desires, to see the body of Christ grow. God's people are those who submit to Christ and become born again of the spirit. Not a specific race, and not excluding any race, but only those in Christ.

> *Revelation 7:9 After these things I looked, and behold, a great multitude which no one could number, <u>of all nations, tribes,</u>*

peoples, and tongues, standing before the throne and before the Lamb, clothed with white robes, with palm branches in their hands,

Now, regarding love, ignoring sin is not love. Pretending that a person's sin won't bring destruction upon them is not love. Accepting every wickedness is not love. We must blow the trumpet to warn people of their sin, lest their blood be upon our heads.

> *Ezekiel 33:6 But if the watchman sees the sword coming and does not blow the trumpet, and the people are not warned, and the sword comes and takes any person from among them, he is taken away in his iniquity; but his blood I will require at the watchman's hand.'*

We should be correcting each other, and helping each other, and admonishing each other, and calling men to repentance, but we had better be careful how we do so. Correcting someone is the biggest service you can do for them, if it is done in the right way, and if the correction is really based in truth. I have watched many become bitter towards those of the faith because they were treated spitefully and hurtfully. We need to be very careful in how we correct each other, and we need to be very careful to make sure we remove the plank from our own eye, before we remove the speck from our neighbors. We need to be more ready to receive correction than to give it. There is indeed much wickedness in this world that we need to be speaking against, but remember that our true enemy is not found in flesh and blood, but in the kingdom of darkness that is manipulating men to carry out the agendas of Satan. It is good to be zealous against the darkness, but it is important that we do so in the right way.

The biggest way we can guard against strife and unkindness is humility. Humility is absolutely one of the biggest keys to our walk and I cannot overstate it's importance.

Proverbs 16:18-19 Pride goes before destruction, and a haughty spirit before a fall. 19 Better to be of a humble spirit with the lowly, than to divide the spoil with the proud.

James 4:6 But He gives more grace. Therefore He says: "God resists the proud, but gives grace to the humble."

Pride is the quickest way to find yourself in spiritual danger. The scripture is clear, if you are walking arrogantly, Yah Himself is against you and there is no greater force that can come against you than Him. Pride is the quick ticket to destruction.

Pride is arrogant, short tempered, easily provoked, self seeking, wants to be right, wants to look good, wants to be in prominent positions, wants to be heard and acknowledged and honored, and demands respect and servitude. It cannot admit it is wrong, it is quick to speak and slow to listen, it deflects guilt, and is quick to point the finger, and wants to be in control. Pride creates arguments, divisions, bitterness, enemies, cruelty, and many other abominations. Humility is patient, willing to listen, willing to help, eager to serve even if it is not seen, it is patient, it is kind, it is gentle and it is loving. Humility turns heated arguments into fruitful discussions, it turns strife into peace, it turns enemies into brothers, it turns oppressors into servants, it turns hearts of stone into hearts of flesh. The humble heart is the heart of a servant. In all that you do, in all that you say, let it be in humility and in love.

Once you begin digging into truth and learning about the true state of the world around you, it is easy to become arrogant. Knowledge puffs up. We must remember that knowledge is never a substitute for wisdom.

Philippians 2:3 Let nothing be done through selfish ambition or conceit, but in lowliness of mind let each esteem others better than himself.

Lastly, be teachable, dear reader. Be wise, and not foolish.

Proverbs 9:8 Do not correct a scoffer, lest he hate you;
Rebuke a wise man, and he will love you.

Be humble, be loving, be faithful to warn others, be teachable, and keep His commandments.

Micah 6:8 He has shown you, O man, what is good;
And what does the Lord require of you
But to do justly,
To love mercy,
And to walk humbly with your God?

29

Finale

You made it, dear reader. Thank you for staying all the way through this journey. I know I threw a lot of information at you, and I know much of it has been very uncomfortable, and very challenging. For all intents and purposes, the things we have learned should radically change the form and function of our faith and in many ways polarize us from what we once knew. When one begins really searching out the truth, and learning and walking in it, it becomes a very lonely and at times frightening road. When the vast majority is saying something is white, but you're looking at it and it looks black, often times, you feel as if you're the one who's crazy, but as you study these things out you will come to the place where you realize that you have scripture, logic, and history on your side, while the vast majority have a blind confidence that becomes agitated when you try to pull the scales from their eyes.

If you are on the fence about the information, or opposed to, or in agreement with what I have presented, I encourage you to do your own research. Begin to search for truth. Humble yourself before Yah, ask the God of Abraham, Isaac, and Jacob, to guide you and teach you, and show you the truth. Get hungry for the truth. We fill our lives with so many things, jobs, hobbies, entertainment, social engagements, and dozens of other things. None of these things are necessarily bad, but when they begin to take over your life and shift your focus off of eternity, they become dangerous. This life is a vapor, a drop in the ocean of time, here for a moment and gone the next. How much money you made, how many movies you watched, how many dishes you brought to the potluck, how many books you've read, how good you are at playing an instrument, how many degrees you have, none of these things matter in view of eternity, and though these things can be used by Yah, in and of themselves, they are empty.

Our top priority needs to be serving Yah, and making sure we are found in Christ, and not fooling ourselves. We need to be seeking wisdom.

> *Proverbs 2:1-5 My son, if you receive my words, and treasure my commands within you, 2 So that you incline your ear to wisdom, and apply your heart to understanding; 3 Yes, if you cry out for discernment, and lift up your voice for understanding, 4 If you seek her as silver, and search for her as for hidden treasures; 5 Then you will understand the fear of the Lord, and find the knowledge of God.*

Be diligent, dear reader, to seek out and find the truth for yourself. Even if you disagree with every word I've written in this book, go search out the truth. Do so with an honest and humble heart, not seeking to find information and scripture that fits your view, but seeking to find information and scripture to form your view. Be willing to re-evaluate your doctrines, to challenge your theologies. Hunger for truth, search the scriptures.

Many will call this book a part of the "Hebrew Roots" movement. I disagree with many of the things coming out of this umbrella term called Hebrew Roots, and there are many dangerous doctrines arising therein. That being said, there is a truth there: One always has roots, dear reader. Everything we do that has been handed down has been handed down from somewhere. Our "roots" ought to be in Christ, but lest we forget, we have a Hebrew God, a Hebrew Savior, a mostly Hebrew Bible, and a Hebrew destiny, hopefully living alongside Yahusha in the New Jerusalem as His people, keeping His feasts. The Roman roots of Sunday Sabbath, of idolatry, of lawlessness, of contempt for the ways of Yah, these are all rotten roots, and come from the false christ who will deceive the nations. There is a very real spirit behind much of this, and as I have spoken to people about these subjects, I have encountered people enraged when I begin to show them truth. There is a very real spirit that is present in the earth today. Even as there is the spirit of Christ, there is also the spirit of antichrist who is at work even now. This spirit tries to imitate the true Spirit, and remember, can produce lying signs and wonders, but it is not of Christ.

More and more as time goes on, there is a line being drawn in the sand. People are being separated out. There are those who love Yah, and want to walk in His ways, and there are those who love themselves, and want to walk in their own ways. There are now, and have always been, the wheat and the tares, the sheep and the goats, the Holy and the profane, and they are being sifted out right now, as the end of this age draws to a close. The difference between these two groups, is faith and obedience to Yah. There are many who honor God with their lips, but their hearts are far from Him. There are many who are unknowingly calling good evil, and evil good, and acting as if grace and faith are the opposite of obedience. The truth is that obedience is the true fruit of faith and grace, and without works, your faith is dead. These works are obedience to the Word of Yah, and choosing to walk in His ways rather than our own. To act in a way that recognizes that one day we will have to stand before the throne of the mighty creator of the heavens and the earth, and give an account for our actions.

Many will say "Lord, Lord" and will swear that they followed Christ their whole lives. They will have works that seem by all appearances to be from the Holy Spirit. They will seem to cast out demons, they will appear to prophecy, they will do many wonders, but they do not know Him. They will deceive others, even deceiving themselves, genuinely believing that they are on their way to spend eternity with Christ, and professing to others the same. They will swear up and down that they belong to Christ, but they will be in for a rude awakening on the day that they go to meet

Him.

> *Matthew 7:22-23 Many will say to Me in that day, 'Lord, Lord, have we not prophesied in Your name, cast out demons in Your name, and done many wonders in Your name?' 23 And then I will declare to them, 'I never knew you; depart from Me, you who practice lawlessness!'*

So, how can we know that we are not one of the deceived who truly think they know Him, but don't? We can't trust our pastors to tell us, as only Christ knows our hearts. We can't trust what our heart tells us, as it is deceitful and wicked (Jeremiah 17:9). We can't trust in spiritual experiences, as those who were told to depart had those. In fact, I would suggest that spiritual experiences, if that's all we are seeking, can be very dangerous. I once was talking to a few old coworkers. I brought up that there is not one verse in the entirety of the scripture that support praying to or worshiping Mary. I showed them from scripture that Yahusha was the only mediator between God and man. I showed them that we are to make our requests known to Yah through Yahusha, not through Mary. They got angry with me, and they began to recount spiritual experiences that they and their relatives had. They said Mary had given them prophetic dreams, and they had seen Mary heal people. They said Mary had done all these amazing experiences, never knowing that the "Mary Queen of Heaven" they were worshiping was Semiramis, Venus, Diana, Asherah, and known by many other names. They said nobody could ever dissuade them from trusting in Mary, because of the things they had experienced. This is the danger in trusting in signs and wonders. So if we can't trust in these things, How can we be sure we are in Him? How we must test our faith? We have tests given us in the scripture that make it very simple.

> *1 John 2:3-7 Now by this we know that we know Him, if we keep His commandments. 4 He who says, "I know Him," and does not keep His commandments, is a liar, and the truth is not*

in him. 5 But whoever keeps His word, truly the love of God is perfected in him. By this we know that we are in Him. 6 He who says he abides in Him ought himself also to walk just as He walked. 7 Brethren, I write no new commandment to you, but an old commandment which you have had from the beginning. The old commandment is the word which you heard from the beginning.

1 John 5:1-3 Whoever believes that Jesus is the Christ is born of God, and everyone who loves Him who begot also loves him who is begotten of Him. 2 By this we know that we love the children of God, when we love God and keep His commandments. 3 For this is the love of God, that we keep His commandments. And His commandments are not burdensome.

1 John 3:4-6 Whoever commits sin also commits lawlessness, and sin is lawlessness. 5 And you know that He was manifested to take away our sins, and in Him there is no sin. 6 Whoever abides in Him does not sin. Whoever sins has neither seen Him nor known Him.

This last verse does not mean that we never fall or stumble, otherwise it would contradict this verse.

1 John 1:8-10 If we say that we have no sin, we deceive ourselves, and the truth is not in us. 9 If we confess our sins, He is faithful and just to forgive us our sins and to cleanse us from all unrighteousness. 10 If we say that we have not sinned, we make Him a liar, and His word is not in us.

What John is saying is that we no longer choose to walk in lawlessness, in sin. We are striving for perfection, and we are not there yet. Often times our imperfections manifest themselves, and we stumble and fall. The important thing is that we strive for Holiness, and choose His way, rather than our own way.

> *Proverbs 24:16 For a righteous man may fall seven times and rise again, but the wicked shall fall by calamity.*

We have all fallen into idolatry and lawlessness in some areas and ways. The important thing is to get up, and try again. The danger is not in the sin we have accidentally fallen into, or the sin we strive against but stumble in, no, we all fall, we all fail. The danger lies in the sin we accept into our lives. The sin that we get comfortable with and embrace, the sin we justify and explain away, the sin we pretend isn't a big deal and willfully continue in, is where true danger lies. There have always been two choices. Obedience, and disobedience, humility and pride, submission and rebellion, ultimately, life and death. The ways of idolatry and rebellion are the ways of death. There is a broad, easy, all embracing road, but it leads to destruction. The narrow road is just that, narrow, and often times lonely, and it's difficult, and a bit scary at times, but the end thereof is life. Sadly, few find this road, though everyone seems to think themselves walking the narrow road.

> *Matthew 7:13-14 "Enter by the narrow gate; for wide is the gate and broad is the way that leads to destruction, and there are many who go in by it. 14 Because narrow is the gate and difficult is the way which leads to life, and there are few who find it.*

In order to find this road, you must look for it.

> *Matthew 7:7-8 "Ask, and it will be given to you; seek, and you will find; knock, and it will be opened to you. 8 For everyone who asks receives, and he who seeks finds, and to him who knocks it will be opened.*

We need to get on our knees before Yah, and truly humble ourselves. We need to repent of our idolatry, our adultery against Him. We need to decide to walk in His ways, and not our own, and we need to decide to be obedient to Him. If you take this path, there will be opposition, you will be hated, and some will turn against you. You will be called a heretic, a false teacher, a danger, and a nuisance, but we have already been warned that this would happen if we walked in truth.

> *Matthew 10:22-26 And you will be hated by all for My name's sake. But he who endures to the end will be saved. 23 When they persecute you in this city, flee to another. For assuredly, I say to you, you will not have gone through the cities of Israel before the Son of Man comes. 24 "A disciple is not above his teacher, nor a servant above his master. 25 It is enough for a disciple that he be like his teacher, and a servant like his master. If they have called the master of the house Beelzebub, how much more will they call those of his household! 26 Therefore do not fear them. For there is nothing covered that will not be revealed, and hidden that will not be known.*

Yahusha told us plainly that we would be hated. In fact, He even said many people will claim we are somehow of the household of the devil. The sad truth is, the people who will fight against obedience the fiercest, are often times those in the church. They claim that by trying to be obedient, you are somehow turning to witchcraft. They quote books like Galatians, not understanding the rest of the Bible and being untaught, twisting Paul's writings in particular to their own destruction, being led away with the error of the lawless (2 Peter 3:15-17). When Yahusha walked the earth, the greatest opposition he faced was from the religious pharisees, who hated Him the most. He spoke the truth, and they could not abide Him. They slandered Him, mocked Him, forbid others to speak to Him, attacked Him, and had Him put to death. Things have not changed, dear reader. Many in the church today are far more interested in the doctrines of men, than the commandments of Yah, and they slander and attack and mock anyone who suggests they actually walk as He walked. These modern day pharisees hold the doctrines of men over the Word of Yah and will claim that by walking in obedience you are somehow trampling on your grace, or forfeiting your faith. This is the doctrine of antichrist who says rebel when Yah says obey, who says grace when Yahusha says repent. Beware of these false teachers lest they lead you to hear "depart from me you who practice lawlessness, I never knew you."

Everything I have said in this entire chapter and much of the book can be summed up in this passage:

> *Deuteronomy 30:15-20 "See, I have set before you today life and good, death and evil, 16 in that I command you today to love the Lord your God, to walk in His ways, and to keep His commandments, His statutes, and His judgments, that you may live and multiply; and the Lord your God will bless you in the land which you go to possess. 17 But if your heart turns away so that you do not hear, and are drawn away, and worship other gods and serve them, 18 I announce to you today that you shall surely perish; you shall not prolong your days in the land which you cross over the Jordan to go in and possess. 19 I call heaven and earth as witnesses today against you, that I have set before you life and death, blessing and cursing; therefore choose life, that both you and your descendants may live; 20 that you may love the Lord your God, that you may obey His voice, and that you may cling to Him, for He is your life and the length of your days; and that you may dwell in the land which the Lord swore to your fathers, to Abraham, Isaac, and Jacob, to give them."*

There is one choice to make.

> *Joshua 24:14-15 "Now therefore, fear the Lord, serve Him in sincerity and in truth, and put away the gods which your*

fathers served on the other side of the River and in Egypt. Serve the Lord! 15 And if it seems evil to you to serve the Lord, choose for yourselves this day whom you will serve, whether the gods which your fathers served that were on the other side of the River, or the gods of the Amorites, in whose land you dwell. But as for me and my house, we will serve the Lord."

Will you walk in the doctrines of men, forsaking the law of Yah, continuing in the idolatry that you have walked in, thus choosing death? Or will you humble yourself, repent, and choose to obey Him, walking in His ways, and choose life? The choice is yours, dear reader. But as for me and my house, we will serve Yahuah.

A Note From The Editor

The internet is an amazing thing that puts endless information at our fingertips, but it is also ever changing and transient. You never know when a webpage won't be available anymore. For that reason we tried to save every link to the internet archive wayback machine at web.archive.org. You can search any web address and it will show snapshots that people saved at different times.

We've also created a Youtube playlist with helpful resources if you are interested in learning more about these subjects. Some of these videos provide a deeper look at much of the information found throughout this book. This playlist can be found here: https://tinyurl.com/IdolatryPlaylist

Keep in mind that drastic changes are coming to Youtube as of this year. If videos in the playlist are missing, this is likely to be why.

One final note, when writing this book it was our desire to make the information in this book available to the masses. Many people do not have the financial means to purchase a book like this. We did not want anyone to be unable to access this information because of their financial situation. Because of this, we have a website up that has this book available in multiple file types available for free. If you want to share this book with others, feel free to give them the link so they can download a copy of it for themselves. If you are reading this as a digital version, and want a physical copy for yourself, or if you'd like to get physical copies for others, there is a link on the following website to allow you to order physical copies. Due to printing costs these will be available for purchase. The files and links can be found at joshuamug.wixsite.com/books/idolatry

Also on the webpage we have included a donation link. If you have found this book helpful to your walk, donations of any size would be appreciated as this was a labor of love and a lot of time and effort went into the writing of this book.

Thank you very much, dear reader, for taking the time to read this book. May Yah bless you and lead you into all truth for His name's sake.

Notes

THE GRAND MYTHOS

1   http://www.mc.maricopa.edu/~thoqh49081/StudentPapers/canaanite.html

R.C.C.

2   http://catholicstraightanswers.com/what-are-the-origins-of-all-saints-day-and-all-souls-day-are-these-linked-with-paganism-and-halloween/

3   http://www.newmanreader.org/works/development/chapter8.html

4   http://stpetersbasilica.info/Exterior/Obelisk/Obelisk.htm

5   https://www.bbc.com/news/magazine-33682878

TIMES AND SEASONS

6   http://www.vatican.va/archive/ccc_css/archive/catechism/p2s1c2a1.htm

OSTARA

7   https://journeyingtothegoddess.wordpress.com/2012/03/17/goddess-ostara/

8   https://www.joyofsatan.org/www.angelfire.com/empire/serpentis666/HOLIDAYS.html

9   https://www.learnreligions.com/egg-magic-and-folklore-2562457

10   https://www.learnreligions.com/spring-equinox-celebrations-around-the-world-2562486

11   https://www.huffpost.com/entry/ostara-2014_n_4999306

SAMHAIN

12   https://en.wikipedia.org/wiki/Samhain

13   https://www.churchofsatan.com/faq-holidays/

14   https://www.thesun.co.uk/fabulous/4711600/samhain-is-the-pagan-origin-of-halloween-and-its-terrifying-rituals-include-human-sacrifices-and-pumpkins-filled-with-burning-human-fat/

15   http://www.av1611.org/halloween.html

16   https://www.britannica.com/topic/All-Saints-Day

17   https://www.elizabethclareblog.com/16-ways-to-celebrate-all-saints-day/

18 https://en.m.wikipedia.org/wiki/Day_of_the_Dead

YULE

19 https://www.history.com/news/when-massachusetts-banned-christmas

20 https://en.wikipedia.org/wiki/Yule

21 https://www.churchofsatan.com/faq-holidays/

22 https://www.norwegianamerican.com/featured/dont-take-odin-out-of-yule/

23 https://www.history.com/news/dont-forget-santas-cookies-and-milk-the-history-of-a-popular-christmas-tradition

24 https://www.catholic.com/magazine/online-edition/the-truth-about-santa-claus

25 https://www.syracuse.com/entertainment/2015/12/reindeer_names_origins.html

26 https://oldweirdalbion.wordpress.com/2009/12/25/santa-last-of-the-wild-men/

27 http://forum.schoolofdragons.com/content/mythology-robin-goodfellow-aka-puck

28 https://www.nationalgeographic.com/news/2018/12/131217-krampus-christmas-santa-devil/

29 https://www.joyofsatan.org/www.angelfire.com/empire/serpentis666/HOLIDAYS.html

30 http://carnaval.com/saturnalia/

31 https://www.joyofsatan.org/www.angelfire.com/empire/serpentis666/Baal-Berith.html

DOMINUS

32 https://amazingdiscoveries.org/S-deception-Sabbath_Sunday_Catholic_Church

33 http://www.vatican.va/archive/ccc_css/archive/catechism/p2s1c2a1.htm

34 https://www.biblestudytools.com/dictionary/baal/

35 https://www.etymonline.com/word/church

36 http://grahamhancock.com/phorum/read.php?4,762067,762067

37 https://amazingdiscoveries.org/S-deception-Sabbath_Sunday_Catholic_Church

REVELATIONS

38 http://www.michaeltsarion.com/history-of-the-medes.html

39 https://www.khanacademy.org/humanities/world-history/ancient-medieval/roman-empire/a/roman-republic

OUT OF THE FRYING PAN

40 https://en.wikipedia.org/wiki/Talmud

41 https://carm.org/interesting-quotes-kabbalah-sources

42   https://en.wikipedia.org/wiki/Kabbalah

43   http://kce.kabbalah.com/content/astrology

PAGAN PARAMOUR

44   https://en.wikipedia.org/wiki/Balfour_Declaration

NATION STATE

45   http://theremnants.info/with-approval-from-vatican-canaanite-idol-moloch-put-on-display-in-rome/

IDENTITY THEFT

46   http://www.lloydthomas.org/7-EndTimeIssues/Darby.htm

47   https://en.wikipedia.org/wiki/C._I._Scofield

48   https://www.wrmea.org/015-october/the-scofield-bible-the-book-that-made-zionists-of-americas-evangelical-christians.html

BRANCHES

49   http://nazarenespace.ning.com/page/panarion-29-the-nazarenes

50   https://www.nazareneisrael.org/books/nazarene-israel-v4-1/what-was-the-original-faith-3/

     https://runtoourhebrewroots.wordpress.com/tag/catholicism/

51   https://www.jewishvirtuallibrary.org/justinian-i-x00b0

KNOW HIM

52   https://researchsupportsthetruth.wordpress.com/2013/07/08/why-is-gods-name-missing-from-many-bibles/

LAWGIVER

53   https://www.gotquestions.org/ceremonial-law.html

54   https://www.mayoclinic.org/diseases-conditions/trichinosis/symptoms-causes/syc-20378583

DIGGING OUR OWN GRAVES

55   http://www.vatican.va/roman_curia/pontifical_councils/chrstuni/relations-jews-docs/rc_pc_chrstuni_doc_20070313_commissione-bilaterale_en.html

56   https://www.congress.gov/bill/102nd-congress/house-joint-resolution/104/text

57   https://www.un.org/ecosoc/sites/www.un.org.ecosoc/files/files/en/2016doc/list-oral-statment-institute-of-noahide-code.pdf

58   https://en.wikipedia.org/wiki/High_Council_of_B%27nei_Noah

59   https://www.sefaria.org/Sanhedrin.57a.12?lang=bi&with=all&lang2=bi

60   http://jewishencyclopedia.com/articles/9679-laws-noachian

61   https://www.chabad.org/library/article_cdo/aid/1188355/jewish/Melachim-uMilchamot-Chapter-10.htm

62   http://come-and-hear.com/sanhedrin/sanhedrin_58.html

CPSIA information can be obtained
at www.ICGtesting.com
Printed in the USA
BVHW050542150921
616752BV00011B/702

9 780578 626819